Smart Cards, Tokens, Security and Applications

T0189481

Smart Cards, Tokens, Security and Applications

by

Keith E. Mayes and Konstantinos Markantonakis
Information Security Group Smart Card Centre
Royal Holloway, University of London
UK

 Springer

Keith E. Mayes
Information Security Group
Smart Card Centre
Royal Holloway
University of London
Egham Surrey
TW20 0EX
United Kingdom

Konstantinos Markantonakis
Information Security Group
Smart Card Centre
Royal Holloway
University of London
Egham Surrey
TW20 0EX
United Kingdom

Smart Cards, Tokens, Security and Applications
by Keith E. Mayes and Konstantinos Markantonakis

ISBN-13: 978-1-4419-4426-9   e-ISBN-13: 978-0-387-72198-9

Printed on acid-free paper.

9 8 7 6 5 4 3 2 1

springer.com

I would like to dedicate this book to Susan, George and Amelia, to my mother and to the memory of my late father.
Keith Mayes

I would like to dedicate this book to Maria and my parents Maria and Georgios Markantonakis, a constant source of inspiration and kindness.
Konstantinos Markantonakis

Founders Message

The ISG Smart Card Centre was officially established in 2002 as a result of the Founders' shared and long held vision for a specialist Centre of Excellence, to complement the world leading work of the Information Security Group (ISG). A Centre that would work in close co-operation with a cross section of industry and government, addressing a broad field of endeavour, including smart cards, tokens, RFIDs, security and applications. From its humble beginnings the Centre has grown rapidly and is now a thriving, well established and properly equipped unit. In parallel with this, the interest and demand for smart card training and research has been ever increasing, as evident from the many post-graduate students who have chosen the Smart Card Centre teaching module and projects. To find reference texts to cover the full breadth of this teaching has so far proved impossible and so this textbook should make a valuable addition to the published work. The Founders are proud to be associated with this book and hope it serves to educate and inspire readers around the world.

The Founders:
Prof. Michael Walker
FREng Group Research and Development Director
Vodafone.

Dr. Klaus Vedder
Head of Telecommunications
Giesecke & Devrient

Prof. Fred Piper
Founder Director of the Information Security Group
Royal Holloway University of London.

Foreword

The idea of inserting a chip into a plastic card is nearly as old as public-key cryptography. The first patents are now thirty years old, but practical, massive application deployment started only fifteen years ago due to limitations in storage and processing capacities of past circuit technology. Today, new silicon geometries and cryptographic processing refinements lead the industry to new generations of cards and more ambitious applications.

Over the last decade there has been an increasing demand for smart cards from national administrations and large companies such as telephone operators, banks and insurance corporations. More recently, other markets have opened up with the increasing popularity of home networking and Internet and the advent of ICAO passport standards.

The traditional carrier for a conventional smart card is a plastic rectangle on which can be printed information concerning the application or the Issuer (even advertising) as well as readable information about the card-holder (as for instance, a validity date or a photograph). This carrier can also include a magnetic stripe or a bar code label. An array of eight contacts is located on the micromodule in accordance with the ISO 7816 standard, but only six of these contacts are normally connected to the chip, which is (usually) not visible. The contacts are assigned to power supplies, ground, clock, reset and a serial data communication link (commonly called I/O). However, over the last years, mainstream protocols and technologies such as USB, http and SOAP were adopted by the card industry and the card's form factor has evolved. In the same time, contactless cards have become increasingly popular.

Current smart card CPUs range from simple 8 bit microcontrollers to sophisticated 32 bit architectures. RAM capacities, historically limited to a few hundreds of bytes are steadily increasing. ROM and EEPROM are being progressively replaced by Flash, while native execution is commonly substituted by Java applets.

Cutting one's way through such a technology-rich environment requires several years of industrial experience or a very thorough reference, such as this book.

Throughout the years of research in Royal Holloway's Smart-Card Centre, Kostas and Keith, have invented, implemented and benchmarked an incredible number of card technologies. Their industrial background and academic approach are, to my knowledge, unique in the field.

I hope that you will enjoy reading and learning from this book as much as I did.

Université Paris II, Panthéon-Assas   *Professor David Naccache*
Laboratoire d'informatique de l'Ecole normale supérieure
October, 2007

Preface

This book is all about smart cards and security tokens in the widest sense. The aim was to provide a complete story, looking at a cross section of technologies, processes, applications and real-world usage. The original motivation for the book was to provide a suitable reference text for the aptly titled MSc module, "Smart Cards Tokens, Security and Applications" which is part of the Masters course in Information Security, run by the Information Security Group at Royal Holloway University of London. However as the planning for the book advanced we realised that various industries and government departments can become quite narrow in their understanding of smart cards/RFIDs and that looking across industry and across roles (such as technical, business and logistics) could be beneficial for a wide range of readers. To deliver such a breadth of information requires input from many experts and so we are very pleased and proud of the calibre of the authors and reviewers that have made this book possible. We hope that you will enjoy this book and find it a useful guide and reference.

Structure of the book

This book consists of fifteen chapters. Each chapter is a completely autonomous contribution in a chained discussion which aims to bring researchers, practitioners and students up to speed with the recent developments within the smart card arena. In order to enhance the reader experience each book chapter contains its own abstract, introduction, main body and conclusion sections. Furthermore, bibliography resources can be found at the very end of each chapter. The following list provides a more detailed overview of the topics that are discussed in the different chapters of this book.

Chapter 1 provides an introduction to a very wide range of smart card related issues. It surveys the different types of cards, tokens and it also considers the main types and capabilities of popular applications utilising smart card technology. The chapter is considered as a good starting point for newcomers to the field and perhaps those that have perhaps focussed on one business or technical area.

Chapter 2 discusses the different steps in the smart card production chain. The analysis covers all the main steps during the smart card manufacturing phase starting with the production of the card body, chip moulding and smart card personalisation and delivery. Finally, it concludes with current and future trends and challenges.

Chapter 3 provides an overview of the most widely utilised smart card operating systems and platforms that enable multiple applications to be securely managed and reside in the same smart card.

Chapter 4 discusses the role of the SIM and USIM in the mobile telecommunications industry and describes the associated standards. It presents the authentication and ciphering processes in some depth and provides a practical comparison between the two technologies prior to exploring further value added service and toolkit features. Finally, it provides some insight into the future evolution of technology.

Chapter 5 examines the role of smart card technology within the financial payments industry. It examines how the credit card industry has evolved over the decades and explains some of the issues with magnetic stripe card technology. Subsequently, it presents the main features of smart card technology in the light of the EMV card specifications. The discussion continues with 3D secure and token authentication.

Chapter 6 deals with the issues around content protection in the satellite TV industry. In particular it examines the commercial motivation as the driving force behind content protection, how smart card security is utilised in order to provide the necessary functionality and finally highlights how a typical pay-TV system operates.

Chapter 7 provides and overview the Trusted Platform Module (TPM) and highlights commonalties and differences with smart cards. It provides an introduction to the security mechanisms provided by the TPM and provides a guide to the associated standards and literature.

Chapter 8 explains how Common Criteria evolved, how it is defined and how it is used in practice. More importantly it examines how Common Criteria is applied to the complex and demanding field of smart card security evaluations.

Chapter 9 focuses on the various attacks and countermeasures that apply to smart cards. As many applications rely on cryptographic algorithms for sensitive operations this chapter focuses on the attacks that could affect smart cards performing cryptographic operations. Furthermore, it provides references to the corresponding countermeasures and emphasises the need for rigorous design, implementation and test of cryptographic algorithms and their underlying host platforms.

Chapter 10 provides a brief overview of the wide range of issues associated with the smart card application development processes. In particular it examines the development of an application for the popular Java Card platform. It also highlights practical issues around application development and monitoring tools. Finally it looks into development of the mobile phone applications that can exploit SIM and USIM card capabilities by using it as a trusted security element.

Chapter 11 analyses the use of the smart card within the telecommunications industry as a managed platform. It examines how the mobile phone operators are using the necessary tools and technology in order to remotely update and enhance, Over-The-Air, the functionality of SIM and USIM cards.

Chapter 12 provides a valuable introduction to the main standards used to manage and access smart card readers connected to personal computers. Their main functionality is analysed and attached code samples aim to provide a detailed overview, but also to enable the reader to reuse them in order to quickly develop sample host applications that will communicate with smart cards.

Chapter 13 provides an introduction to the RFID concepts and also summarises the aspects most relevant to contactless smart card systems. Several different systems along with operating principles are described. The chapter also provides an overview of the main Radio Frequency (RF) interface and communication theory along with the various RF standards.

Chapter 14 explains how national requirements for eID cards and e-Passports can be realised by utilising physical, logical and hardware functionality. Furthermore, it highlights the importance and requirements of the relevant standards.

Chapter 15 first examines the historical use of technology in smart cards before highlighting the future trends. It looks into the different options and choices which can be made within a smart card scheme along with the issues which affect the design of the card and its applications. Finally it discusses issues around consumer demand and the drivers that will define the smart card technology of the future.

In order to make reading of this more convenient, we also provide a subject index at the very end of the book. Furthermore, there is also a website for this book:

http://www.scc.rhul.ac.uk/book

The website will allow readers to obtain additional and up-to-date information about the topics covered in the book.

The ISG Smart Card Centre,   *Keith Mayes*
Royal Holloway, University of London   *Konstantinos Markantonakis*
October, 2007

Acknowledgements

We would like to thank Vodafone and Giesecke & Devrient for their fantastic support of the Smart Card Centre, without which this book would never have been written. Individually we would like to thank Mike Walker, Klaus Vedder, Fred Piper (of course) and Peter Wild. We also owe an enormous debt of gratitude to all chapter authors and reviewers who were forced to work in outrageously short timescales. We would like to give a special thank you to David Naccache for writing the foreword of this book and last but not least we would like to thank Xuefei Leng, Lishoy Francis, Weidar Chen and Gerhard Hancke for their tremendous efforts in helping to bring this book to print.

Contents

9   Smart Card Security   195

Michael Tunstall

List of Figures

List of Tables

List of Contributors

Keith E Mayes
is the Director of the ISG Smart Card Centre (www.scc.rhul.ac.uk) at Royal Holloway University of London. He is also the founder and managing Director of the consulting company Crisp Telecom Limited (www.crisptele.com). He is currently a non-executive independent Director of AIMs listed GMO ltd., a provider of mobile services in China and a Director of IWICS Europe Limited, a 4G mesh radio network company. Dr Mayes has a Bachelor of Science degree in Electronic Engineering and a PhD in Digital Image Processing from the University of Bath. He is a Chartered Engineer and Member of the Institute of Engineering and Technology. He is also a Member of the Licensing Executives Society and a Founder Associate Member of the Institute of Information Security Professionals. During a long and varied industry career he has worked for Philips, Honeywell Aerospace & Defence, Racal Research and finally for the Vodafone Group as the Global SIM Manager responsible for SIM card strategy and harmonisation. Aside from his current research and teaching focus on smart cards, RFIDs and security, he has maintained an active interest in mobile communications, hardware and software development, Intellectual Property and radio relay trials.

Claus Ebner, born 1962 in Krumbach, Germany, studied mechanical engineering at the Technical University of Munich. Afterwards he did his doctorate at the Institute for Machine Tools and Industrial Management of the same university. In 1995 he joined Giesecke & Devrient in Munich as head of IT and development in the card service centre. After his involvement in the introduction of an ERP system for the card business he took over responsibility for the international production software development of G&D. This centre provides software for smart card production to the worldwide subsidiaries of G&D and supports the setup of card production or personalization sites in G&D's solution business as well.

Konstantinos Markantonakis
received his BSc. in Computer Science from Lancaster University in 1995, his M.Sc. in Information Security in 1996, his Ph.D. in Information Security in 1999, and his

MBA in International Management in 2005 from Royal Holloway, University of London. His main areas of interest are smart card security and smart card applications, security protocol design, mobile devices, tokens and information security. Since completing his PhD, he has worked as an independent consultant in a number of information security and smart card related projects. He has worked as a smart card manager in Visa International EU, responsible for multi-application smart card technology for southern Europe. More recently, he was working as a Senior Consultant in Steer-Davies-Gleave responsible for advising transport operators and financial institutions on the use of smart card technology. He is also a member of the IFIP Working Group 8.8 on Smart Cards. He is currently a member of the Information Security Group, as a Lecturer in the Smart card Centre. He continues to act as a consultant in a variety of topics including information security protocols, mobile devices, smart card security, smart card migration program planning/project management for financial institutions and transport operators.

Tim Evans
is the SIM/USIM authority for Vodafone UK and a pivotal figure in the technical specification of the SIM/USIMs used throughout the Vodafone Group. Prior to joining Vodafone, Tim was a SIM expert at NEC in the UK. He is an active figure in the international standardisation of telecommunications smart cards and has been elected as the chair of the influential ETSI SCP Requirements group.

Allan Tomlinson
received a BSc in Applied Physics from the University of Strathclyde in 1981; MSc in Microelectronics in 1987, and doctorate in 1991; both from the University Edinburgh. His thesis was on "VLSI architectures for cryptography". He then joined the Institute of Microelectronics at the National University of Singapore, working on secure NICAM broadcasting and video compression. In 1994 he moved to General Instrument in California to work on the Digicipher II Conditional Access system for digital video broadcasting. Before joining the Information Security Group at Royal Holloway, he was Principal Engineer at Barco Communications Systems where he was responsible for the development of the "Krypton" DVB Video Scrambler. He also served for a number of years on the DVB Simulcrypt committee. His current research interests are distributed systems security, trusted computing, and mobile network security.

John Tierney
after gaining his degrees in Pure Mathematics and Computing from Sheffield (B.Sc.) and Numerical Analysis from Liverpool (Ph.D.) Universities, Dr. John Tierney initially worked in communications security, including early ITSEC work in the early nineties. Following a stint developing auto-layout algorithms for FPGAs, he has worked with smart cards for the last 15 years. Initially this was to develop a secure operating system and applications for a security module system for prepaid payphone smart cards. Joining the Mondex security team in 1999, he worked on a series of Common Criteria evaluations on smart card products ranging from EAL1+

to EAL4+. He also successfully led an ITSEC E6 evaluation on a multi-application operating system. Since 2002 he has worked for MasterCard as a project manager, assisting banks who are implementing new products using multi-application chip cards. His current projects concentrate on the introduction of contactless technology by banks. Married with two children, his hobbies include long-distance running, reading and music. He lives in Wirral and supports Liverpool FC.

Michael Tunstall

has been involved in the research and development on the implementation of cryptographic algorithms on embedded platforms for close to nine years. He was originally employed by Gemplus (now called Gemalto after a merger with Axalto) to develop authentication algorithms for GSM SIM cards. After several years working for Gemplus Michael changed roles within the team to focus on research into attacks and countermeasures that could be applied to smart cards. He was involved in evaluating Gempluss products to determine whether a suitable level of security had been achieved. The research conducted while Michael was at Gemplus enabled him to start a PhD. At Royal Holloway, University of London resulting in his thesis entitled Secure Cryptographic Algorithm Implementation on Embedded Platforms. Michael is currently employed at University College Cork as a post-doctorate researcher, and is currently funded by an Enterprise Ireland grant to develop side-channel countermeasures for FPGA implementations of AES and elliptic curve cryptographic algorithms.

Gary Waite

began his career in the semiconductor industry in the mid eighties as a software engineer, developing a number of applications that were used by the entire DRAM memory industry and also most of the CPU manufacturers, for testing and diagnosing faults with their emerging chip products. In 1992, moving into the GSM sector, Gary developed what became the de facto standard SIM/Mobile Test & Diagnostic tool, and headed up a company called Aspects that sold this product into all of the main players globally. Thus success enabled the business to attract nearly $20m venture capital funding allowing further product developments. At the same time Gary became a key player in the standardisation activities of the GSM SIM card, and continues that role today in a number of standards groups. For the last 5 years Gary has been with O2 and advises the business technically in a number of areas, including SIM, DRM, data cards, location technologies, messaging, and now Machine-to-Machine.

Joos Cadonau

received his BSc in Electronic Engineering in 1994 from the university of applied sciences in Burgdorf, Switzerland. After his degree he worked for the Swiss Telecom Company designing applications for managing the subscriber access to the network. In 1999 he joined Ascom AG, a Swiss technology and telecommunication provider, leading projects for Private Branch Exchange PBX switches. In 2001 he started at Sicap AG managing Over-the-Air projects in Europe and Japan. In 2004 he took over the Product Management of Over-the-Air solutions at Sicap.

Damien Sauveron
is assistant Professor at the XLIM (UMR 6172 University of Limoges / CNRS –
France) laboratory since 09/2004. Damien Sauveron worked during three years for
the ITSEF of SERMA Technologies on the Java Card security. During his thesis that
he carried out in the Distributed Systems and Objects team of the LaBRI he was one
of the main developers of a Java Card emulator, he introduced the concept of pre-
persistance in Java Card and he highlighted a new category of attacks on the open
multiapplication smart cards. From 01/02/2006 to 10/08/2006, he was an invited researcher at the ISG-SCC (Information Security Group - Smart Card Centre) of the
Royal Holloway, University of London (RHUL). He is member of the IFIP WG 8.8
Smart Cards, member of the IFIP WG 11.2 Small System Security and member of
IEEE.

Gerhard Hancke
received a Bachelor of Engineering degree in Computer Engineering from the University of Pretoria (South Africa) in 2002 and a Masters of Engineering degree from
the same institution in 2003. At the end of 2003 he started reading towards a PhD in
Computer Science with the Security group at the University of Cambridge's Computer Laboratory. In August 2007 he was appointed as a research assistant in the
Smart Card Centre at Royal Holloway University of London. His main interest is
proximity identification and the security of RFID/contactless systems.

Ingo Liersch
joined Giesecke & Devrient in 2001. Until 2003 he was Product Manager for Smart
Card Operating Systems and Card Applications. 2004 - 2005 he was in charge of
international ID and Health Card projects. Since 2006 he is Head of Segment Marketing in the newly established Division "Government Solutions", which devises
security-related solutions for passport and visa systems as well as ID and health
care cards for national governments and their agencies. Ingo Liersch holds a degree
in Electrical Engineering and in Industrial Engineering.

Chris Shire
joined Infineon Technologies (then Siemens Semiconductors) in 1998 as the Business Development Manager for Security & Chipcard IC's, with 20 years experience
in the semiconductor industry. His focus is on the financial, telecoms and government markets for smart cards. He has been active on several government advisory
committees and working on contactless card standards in the UK, and support new
security solutions. He has spent considerable time working with biometrics integration with cards. He is involved in the project management of solutions as diverse
as ID cards to transport. Prior to Infineon Technologies, Mr Shire was employed
by Philips Semiconductors for over 15 years in a number of roles. He has been
responsible for the managing of resources across the globe, including business development of organizations in both South Africa and Israel. Mr Shire received his

degree in Electronics & Electrical engineering from Kingston in 1977. Mr Shire is an avid member of the IET and Intellect and also has been a speaker at many seminars

List of Reviewers

Patrick Baier

Shane Balfe

Weidar Chen

Tim Evans

Klaus Finkenzeller

Lishoy Francis

Eimear Gallery

Gerhard Hancke

Peter Howard

Xuefei Leng

Konstantinos Markantonakis

Keith Mayes

Geraint Price

Wolfgang Rankl

Damien Sauveron

Chris Shire

William Sirett

Dave Taylor

Michael Tunstall

Erez Waisbard

Garry Waite

Chapter 1
An Introduction to Smart Cards

Keith Mayes

Abstract The concept of a smart card is not particularly new, however the practical use of smart cards in a range of diverse applications has never been more popular. This chapter provides a first introduction to a wide range of smart cards and tokens, considering the various types, capabilities, popular applications and the practicality of their development and deployment.

Key words: Smart Cards, Tokens, Security, Applications, Java, Multos, RFID, SIM, ID Contact-Less, Microprocessor Cards, Chip Card, Magnetic Stripe Card, Memory Card, Development, Lifecycle

1.1 Introduction

Smart cards are perhaps some of the most widely used, but underestimated electronic devices in use today. In many cases these devices are in the front-line, defending citizens and systems alike against attacks on information security. Because they have tended to be small and often concealed, smart cards have carried on their important work, largely unnoticed, but this is changing. High profile use of smart cards for IDs [29], passports [14], credit cards [9] and e-tickets [28] means that the smart card is now a regular topic for the popular press. Furthermore some recent and startling advances in technology and associated standards means that the influence and use of new generation smart cards could have a dramatically expanded role in some industries. With all this activity and positive momentum, one would expect that the term smart card has a clear definition and the physical devices would be easy to identify. Unfortunately this is not the case and ambiguity abounds, so the

Keith Mayes, Director of the ISG Smart Card Centre,
Royal Holloway University of London,
e-mail: keith.mayes@rhul.ac.uk

1

first priority in this book is to provide some clarity and definitions to be used within the chapters

1.2 What is a Smart Card?

It is perhaps a little surprising to start a smart card text book with such a trivial sounding question as "What is a smart card?". However judging by some press articles and even technical reports, the answer seems to elude even the great and the good.

Normally at this point, a text book would dive into the ancient history of card evolution, which basically says we have such wonders because some rich guy forgot his wallet one day. However this can add to the confusion regarding what is, or is not a modern-day smart card, so the history trip will come later once we have a few definitions to work with.

Part of the problem stems from the use of "smart". If a system is much more convenient because a particular card is being used then that is a pretty smart thing to do, even if by technical standards the card is quite stupid. The next problem comes from "card" which to most people would imply say a credit card sized piece of plastic, whereas various sizes are possible and indeed the innards of the device could be embedded in something completely different like a passport or phone.

The candidates that could be described as smart cards are therefore numerous and so the definition will be refined a little to weed out some of the least relevant.

A smart card;

1. can participate in an automated electronic transaction
2. is used primarily to add security and
3. is not easily forged or copied.
   In support of (2) and (3), two more definitions will be added i.e.
4. can store data securely
5. can host/run a range of security algorithms and functions.

This definition will now be applied to a few well known card types to see if they are truly "smart".

1.2.1 Magnetic Stripe Cards

Magnetic stripe cards are widely used in a range of applications. They are characterized by being low cost and relatively easy to read/write. An example is shown in Fig. 1.1. For many years this type of card was been used for credit and debit card financial applications, although in Europe it is being phased out by EMV cards described in chapter 5. The cards are still widely used throughput the world and indeed for a

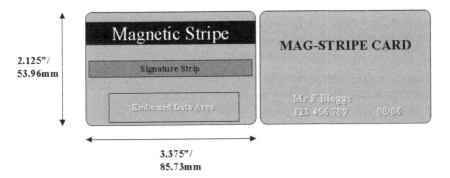

Fig. 1.1 A Typical Magnetic Stripe Card

diverse range of applications including entitlement cards, tickets and access control systems.

In terms of our smart card definitions, the magnetic stripe card can be regarded as follows;

- It is clearly involved in electronic transactions and
- in many cases it is meant to be provide some security element, unfortunately it is very poor when tested against the third definition, i.e. it can be copied or forged.

Considering Fig. 1.1 in closer detail, we have a piece of plastic which is used as a carrier for a stripe of magnetic tape. The plastic card may also carry some text or images designed more for human interpretation and checking rather than the electronic transaction that is of primary interest. Invisible to the human eye is the information stored within the magnetic stripe. The stripe is not dissimilar to that used in a cassette recorder i.e. a strong magnetic field controls the alignment of magnetic dipoles into various orientations along the length of the tape. The alignment is preserved even when the polarizing field is removed and so information is stored by the dipoles. The alignment can be simply tested and the information recovered by a tape reader head. Because the tape and the equipment used is relatively crude, the information storage capacity is quite limited. To maximise this in a practical manner multiple tracks are stored along the stripe - again similar to an audio tape-recorder. On each track one can store a few bits of identity related information and the method of storage is known as Wiegend [13] format. A fairly exhaustive description of these cards is beyond the scope of this book and the curious reader can consult other references [25].

The important thing to say about magnetic stripe cards is that they are not smart cards because they fail the third smart card definition and quite disastrously too. It is therefore quite astonishing to see how long they have survived in financial applications. The root of the problem is quite easy to find. The magnetic stripe is not much more than a piece of audio tape and so it can be easily read and indeed rewritten with relatively simple equipment. This means that it is quite trivial to forge/clone magnetic stripe cards. A lot of effort has gone into making the plastic carrier harder to duplicate (although with limited success), but there is not much that can be done about the magnetic stripe used in the automated transactions. Two types of magnetic stripe fraud [5] have become legendary;

- Skimming - Here the information from a valid card's magnetic stripe is copied to another card for use in fraudulent automated transactions.
- Counterfeiting - here the plastic carrier/card is very carefully copied, but the magnetic stripe may be blank or invalid

How a skimmed card may be exploited is fairly obvious, but counterfeiting deserves a few word of explanation. Although there are various countermeasures on cards to discourage counterfeiting, such as special graphics, embossed printing and holograms, they really just represent more inconvenience and time for an attacker, rather than serious obstacles. The counterfeit is to fool a human operator rather than an automated process, so how can this be useful when most physical transactions tend to be automated? The reason is that it is a very common occurrence for the magnetic stripe on a valid card to be unreadable due to wear and tear. This has lead to an acceptance for the manual fall-back mechanism. For example, a man goes into a petrol station to buy fuel. The assistant swipes the card once, twice, rubs the stripe on his sleeve and tries once more but in vain. He then simply reads the numbers printed on the card plastic and types them into the point of sale terminal to complete the transaction. For internet purchases it is even easier as there is no attempt at an automated process and the attacker only needs to have read the required information from the source card, rather than create the counterfeit.

Because of the prevalence of skimming and counterfeiting, magnetic stripe cards can no longer be recommended to safeguard significant financial transactions. Far better is the electronic chip based solution standardized by EMV and described in detail within chapter 5. The EMV solution is now the standard in some countries such as the United Kingdom where it has drastically reduced fraud for card-holder-present transactions [2] (e.g. physical transactions in a store). However EMV has not yet delivered similar safeguards for the increasing volume of internet transactions which are now the most worrying form of fraud and hence the industry focus for countermeasure development.

There can be a future for magnetic stripe cards where the solutions are very cost sensitive and the cards are not protecting anything of significant value, for example a loyalty card or a library access card etc. The lack of reliability of the stripe is perhaps not a problem when the cards are only required to have a limited lifetime and usage. For all other applications the trend is towards the use of electronic chips embedded within the card, in order to improve, functionality, reliability and security.

1.2.2 Chip Cards

As the name suggests a chip-card is basically a plastic card, rather like the magnetic stripe card that has an electronic chip embedded in it. Historically these cards were easy to identify by virtual of the contacts that where usually gold colored (sometimes silver). The use of these contacts is described within standards [16] and an example is shown in Fig. 1.2. Essentially the contacts provide power to the chip via

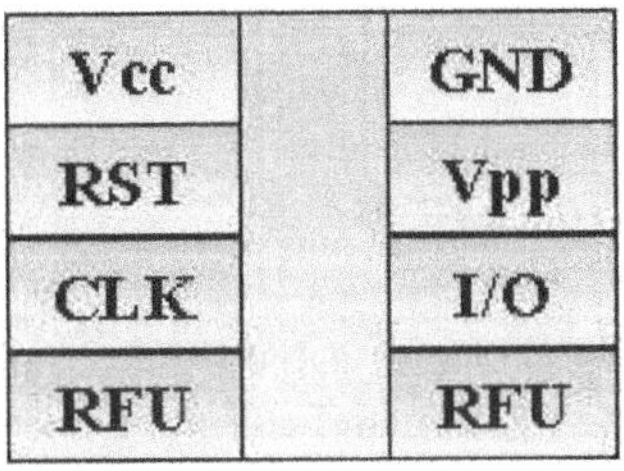

Vcc	GND
RST	Vpp
CLK	I/O
RFU	RFU

Fig. 1.2   Contacts of a Chip Card

Vcc/GND, a communications I/O line, a clock and a reset line. The VPP PIN was once used for re-programming old-style EEPROM memories but is now obsolete. Because the two lower pins were historically unused some cards and readers only make use of the six upper contacts. However some industries have already planned to use the RFU and VPP contacts for new services. Mobile communications for example is planning to use the spare pins for a high speed USB interface and for a Near Field Communication interface [8] - as described in Chapter 4.

A chip card is accessed by placing it within a card reader which simply makes physical contact with the gold pads, allowing the chip to be powered and clocked and for communication to take place. The low level electrical interface is described in ISO standards [16]. Communications is half-duplex with the reader/host taking the role of master and the card the slave. There are in fact two low level protocols that can be used to exchange information, known as T=0 and T=1 and both are defines in ISO standard [16]. The T=0 protocol is favored by the mobile communications industry and is simply a byte interface where information is sent a byte at a time, rather like communicating with a modem over a serial link. By contrast T=1 is a block protocol favored by financial institutions.

One could fall into the trap of assuming that all chip cards are more secure than magnetic stripe cards and that the presence of the gold contacts implies that this is a smart card. These assumptions are incorrect and dangerous.

The simplest chip card could contain a single fixed value. The application protocol would simply be to read this fixed value for comparison. It would be trivial for an attacker to read the value from a valid card and produce a copy and so this type of card fails our third smart card definition in the same way as the magnetic stripe card.

Another type of card is the memory card that may be used to perhaps keep a count of purchased telephone call minutes or accumulated loyalty points. Such cards need have no added security and so are easily read and copied. Moreover the memory may be re-written to undermine the application or change IDs etc. The simple memory card also fails our third requirement for a smart card as it can be easily copied or modified. Note that there are memory cards that incorporate fixed functionality security (e.g. MIFARE) that are used in popular systems, however as we are interested in more general purpose security devices the focus moves towards microprocessor chip cards.

1.2.3 Microprocessor Chip Cards

Microprocessor cards have the scope to satisfy the requirements for a smart card because they are not only able to store and communicate stored values, but can do so within the context of security protocol programs. The protocol interface to the device can be defined such that it is logically impossible to extract information or reprogram the contents without appropriate permissions which are checked and enforced by cryptographic functionality. At first glance one would think that the search is over and that the presence of a microprocessor chip card is synonymous with a smart card, but this is not necessarily the case. A conventional non-specialized microprocessor card can give you logical security, but that is insufficient for a smart card. Attackers are not put off by logical security, but would employ a range of techniques that attack the chip directly or exploit information leakage from an operating device. These attacks are described in detail within chapter 9 but suffice to say that a microprocessor used in a smart card is designed in a very specialized way to be "tamper-resistant" [1]. This is perhaps the most important property to remember about a smart card. When considering conventional smart cards our definition could now be;

- A smart card contains a tamper-resistant microprocessor chip (incorporating countermeasures against known attacks) that is difficult to forge or copy. It can participate in automated electronic transactions, can store data securely and run/host a range of security protocols and algorithms.
- The consideration so far has focused on conventional smart cards i.e. those that make use of electrical contacts to the chip. However there is growing interest and usage for cards that do not have physical contacts but exploit radio techniques instead.

1.2.4 Contact-less Smart Cards and RFIDs

The smart card industry tends to talk about cards with contacts or contact-less smart cards, however industries that have been concerned with tagging product coding and tracking tend to talk about RFIDs. If the definition of a smart card has been much abused then so too has RFID. Because of this someone may refer to a contact-less smart card as a RFID or vice versa. This section will try and remove some of the ambiguity, but there will still be a grey area of overlap.

In principle RFID is very simple to define. It is a device that presents an ID to a reader device via radio frequency (RF) means. It does not imply any protocol security, clone prevention or tamper-resistance, however some real-world devices may incorporate such measures. It might even be argued that a magnetic stripe card should be regarded as a RFID, as it is makes use of an electromagnetic field to communicate, although its probably best to ignore this possibility as there is enough confusion already.

A chip card that presents an ID (perhaps for door access) could therefore be considered as a special case of a RFID.

Generally RFIDs tend to be less sophisticated than contact-less smart cards (although there is no fundamental technical reason for this) and do not make use of the physical card format. Whilst lower layer protocols tend to be standardized [17] the application layer is often proprietary and the design information is held secret. From a security perspective the reliance on secret proprietary protocols and algorithms is always treated with much skepticism

A very popular proprietary system is the MiFare [20] solution from NXP. Its security solution is not publicly known, although it is believed to sit somewhere between the capabilities of a general purpose contactless smart card and RFID/Memory i.e. it has a fixed function symmetric key algorithm that provides a level of security and protection. MiFare is usually provided in a card form although the chips can be housed in a range of devices such as watches, phones etc.

1.2.5 Smart Tokens

In the title of this book it mentions smart tokens. A smart token can be considered as a personal device that has all the useful security, functional and tamper-resistant properties of the smart card, but is not provided in a normal plastic card format. Interestingly the smart card that is most prevalent in the world (the GSM SIM card) might be regarded as a smart token instead. Whilst it started life in the full-card format and is still produced by a card manufacturing process, it is usually only used in the plug-in format see Fig. 1.3. In the future, mobile communications may make increasing use of the third form factor that is even smaller than the plug-in and not much bigger than the contact module. Just about any format is possible and a range of communication and powering methods could be considered.

One thing that is clear from looking at the types of device and their names is that there is a lot of overlap. The literal explanation of the device name and or acronyms might once have been simple and accurate, however the names have evolved in the public perception e.g. no one thinks of a card that is smart in some way, but rather of a smart card. Similarly it is doubtful that anyone will remember that RFID is strictly

Fig. 1.3 A Plug-in Format SIM Card

an ID presented via Radio Frequency means, because RFID has simply become a modern word. Most often we are concerned with passive contact-less cards/RFIDs that extract their power from the readers electromagnetic field and then modulate the field to communicate. However there are also active RFIDs that incorporate their own power sources. A common example is the keyfob for remote central locking of a car. Active RFIDs/tags also tend to be used where passive devices would struggle, for example, situations requiring a long read range or where there is a lot of metal that can adversely affect the electromagnetic fields used by passive devices.

Just in case we do not have enough names and confusion we must also be aware of Near Field Communications (NFC) [8]. The simplest way to describe this is as a contactless/RFID interface for a mobile phone. Essentially this now standardised functionality allows the phone to act as a contactless smart card/RFID or indeed as the reader to communicate with an external card.

For the remainder of this book, unless there is a particular need to differentiate devices, the name smart card will be used to represent all types of device incorporating a tamper-resistant microprocessor chip supporting secure data storage and security functions/algorithms. In most cases the actual physical format and low-level communications interfaces will be ignored. This serves to illustrate that what is of real interest and value is the chip at the heart of the device. The term RFID will be used for simpler radio frequency tags.

1.3 Smart Card Chips

The microprocessor found in a smart card bears little resemblance to the processor you will find in a modern PC although the core of the smart card chip is not dissimilar to some of the PC's early ancestors. Smart card chips tend to be very small and so there is always a limit to what functionality and resources can be crammed in. There are several historical reasons for the size limitation. Firstly the cost of a chip is proportional to the area of silicon used and although individually, this may not be a lot, smart cards may be ordered in their millions and so are always very cost sensitive. Secondly, because smart cards are often delivered via the normal post they must withstand bending and twisting stresses. If the chip is too large then these stresses will break the chip or the wires connecting the chip to contact pads or antennas. Lastly as the chip gets larger and more complex, its power requirement would normally increase. Host devices tend to be quite miserly when supplying power and even if they were not there could be heat dissipation problems within the module. In the future, some of these restrictions may ease, especially for mobile communication smart cards, which are set to evolve into high capacity devices with faster interfaces and processors [19]. This requires commitment to standardisation and the SIM (smart card) becoming a more rigid security and memory token. For now we will stick to conventional chips and an old-style layout is shown in Fig. 1.4. As men-

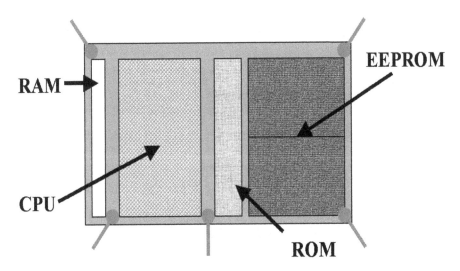

Fig. 1.4 A Smart Card Chip (old)

tioned previously, the device has no clock or in-built power supply, but it does have a CPU and 3-types of memory as well as the interconnecting circuitry. Understanding the types of memory is important as what is stored where, is usually a trad-off decision for the designer.

The Read Only Memory (ROM) is some times referred to as the chip mask. It is characterized by the fact that its contents (which are identical for all cards in the batch) can only be set/written to during card production and then only read during normal card operation.

The Random Access Memory (RAM) is used for dynamic storage of program run-time variables and the stack. In this respect it is similar to the RAM in a PC although there is much less of it. When power is removed the RAM loses its contents.

Electrically Erasable Programmable Read Only Memory (EEPROM) is very useful as it can be programmed after manufacture and does not lose its contents when the power is removed i.e. it is non-volatile.

Looking at Fig. 1.4 one could easily get the wrong idea about the likely proportions of RAM, ROM and EEPROM. This arises because the memories have different packing densities i.e. how many bits fit into a given silicon area. ROM packs best of all so is an area and cost efficient method of storage, however the fact that it cannot be rewritten is a serious drawback making it useless for user data and function storage. For well tested common functionality and constant data it is fine. Next best for efficiency is the EEPROM, which can be used for all kinds of data and application storage. RAM packs poorly and is very restricted and is a current challenge for program developers, which is only likely to get worse as application sophistication increases.

A typical relationship between the memory types is shown in Fig. 1.5

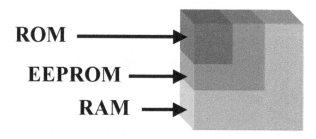

Fig. 1.5 Comparison of Chip Area Needed for Various Memory Types

It is worth mentioning another type of storage known as flash memory. This is well known for memory sticks, but has been less commonly used for smart cards. It seems that this situation is changing and that flash could become the dominant memory type in smart cards. It has a number of advantages that make it attractive when compared to EEPROM. Firstly an EEPROM memory ages i.e. it can only be written to a certain number of times (few hundred thousands), which can limit the lifetime of certain card applications. A flash memory does not have this problem and is also much faster to write. The designer does not have the same ROM/EEPROM dilemma as the split can be adjusted during the design phase, although it must lock down the flash equivalent to ROM space after production, for security reasons. RAM is still at a premium as for the conventional card case. For the manufacturer there are also advantages as it is not necessary to create many different customer masks as the different configurations can be soft loaded. One potential drawback is that any soft loading may take extra time in production and whereas chip area is proportional to chip cost, production time is proportional to the cost of the final smart card. Lastly, some card Issuers still have concerns about the security of flash memory technology and may simply forbid its use in their product specifications.

For now we will stick with the concept of real RAM, ROM and EEPROM within our smart card device. The use of RAM is quite evident and so the first question to consider is what can be put in the ROM for maximum benefit. Typically the ROM would contain the operating system, well tested common functions and constant data. The EEPROM can be used for user data, user programs as well as general application data and functions that require modification during operational life. Sometimes the EEPROM is simply used for functionality that would just not fit in the ROM and/or patches to compensate for the bugs and extensions of the ROM programs.

EEPROM is a very useful resource, especially as there are techniques to update its contents whilst in the field. Therefore to create a future proof device one would try and issue a larger smart card with plenty of spare EEPROM to accommodate fixes and new functionality. However this increases the chip area and hence cost, which means it will be strongly resisted by whoever is signing the cheque for the next million devices. The battle between the alien mindsets of designers/strategists and purchasers is quite a common occurrence. On the one hand you have the purchasers arguing for savings today, whereas the designers/strategists push to spend more now to avoid future problems from built in obsolescence. Unfortunately modern business has a very short-term focus and so the head-in-the-sand savings argument wins far too often.

1.4 Tamper Resistance

One of the key strengths of the smart card (which really means the chip) is its tamper-resistance i.e. the ability to resist known and anticipated attacks. Looking at the picture in Fig. 1.4 one might think that the attackers job is not so hard as its very easy to identify the attack targets such as memories and busses that might yield valuable secrets and permit card cloning. However this is not the case and the chip layout shown is very old and presented for clarity of explanation. In reality the first thing that an attacker may encounter is a physical layer of silicon that prevents probing of the circuit (see Fig. 1.6).

If this can be overcome then there may be an active current-carrying layer, so that any break renders the chip useless to the attacker. Get beyond this layer and you may find that the circuitry has been scrambled making it difficult to find the attack target. If a bus or memory is eventually found then it may well be encrypted. Clearly if an attacker has expensive equipment, expertise and is prepared to destroy many cards, he may eventually extract some information, but unless this is a global secret arising from a bad design it is difficult for much advantage to be gained. Smart card attacks and countermeasures are covered in detail within chapter 9 but for now it suffices to say that the smart card chip mounts a very robust defence, even when faced with sophisticated attacks from well equipped experts.

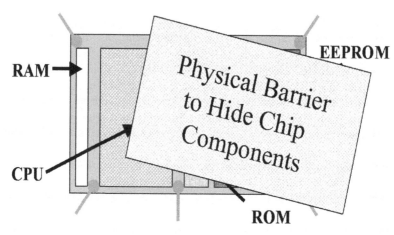

Fig. 1.6 Smart Card Chip Anti-Probing Layer

1.5 Smart Card Characteristics

So far a fairly glowing report has been given of smart cards, however like any device they have both strengths and weaknesses. In order to exploit smart cards appropriately it is just as important to appreciate the weaknesses as well as the strengths. Table 5.3 presents this is a summary form.

Table 1.1 Summary of Smart Card Strengths and Weaknesses

Features	Limitations
CPU (>32bit)	**Helpless Alone**
RAM (>8kb)	-No internal power supply
ROM(>200kb)	-Externally restrictions on power consumption
EEROM(>64kb)	-No user interface
Crypto-processor option	-No clock
Very Small	**Limited (by PC comparison)**
Low power	-Memory
Low cost	-CPU speeds
Secure	**Issued device**
Standardised	-Legacy cards may be inflexible
Operating Systems	-New cards require deployment
Development Tools	
Multiple Suppliers	
Consistent & Controllable	

Bearing in mind that the smart chip might only be $9mm^2$ then the processor and memory capabilities are surprisingly good, however compared to a PC processor the card is rather feeble and would not be a good choice for handling large amounts of data or time critical processing. However cards with co-processors are no slouches when it comes to specialised cryptographic processing. The main positive features include the tamper-resistant security, the precise standardisation and the resulting consistency and control. Obvious weaknesses include the fact that the card is helpless on its own and thus is always reliant on other system elements. For example, a conventional smart card has no internal power-source, no direct user-interface and not even a clock. From a system management perspective another significant feature is the ability to personalise the smart card to a particular customer or account. Smart cards tend to be issued in very large numbers and so one of the ever present problems is dealing with legacy devices. A great new service that only works on newly issued cards may take years to reach a large proportion of the customer base. Legacy problems can be minimised by forward looking design and lifecycle management systems, however legacy problems are often "designed-in" to satisfy short term cost savings.

One of the features that could be described as an advantage or limitation, depending on your viewpoint is the Issuer control of the smart card platform.

1.6 Issuer Control

Most smart cards are given to customers by Issuers such as banks, mobile network operators, government, transport companies etc. Usually in the fine print of an agreement it will say that these cards still belong to the Issuer, even if the customer has parted with some money to obtain it. The reason for this is that the cards are important to the Issuers both from a business and security point of view and so the Issuers want to retain management rights e.g. decide what data and functionality is offered. In that respect the smart card is very different to a PC on which the customer can download any data and applications that he choses. As an example, consider the case of putting a value added application onto a smart card. Historically the Issuer would give a specification to the various smart card providers who would then implement the functionality in a proprietary manner and deliver this only in new batches of cards. These days card implementations need not be so proprietary (e.g. Java Card [27]) and there is the capability to load new data and functionality after manufacture (e.g. via GlobalPlatform [12]) so the situation is more flexible. The Issuer or its sub-contractor could personalise the cards and load appropriate data and applications not only prior to issue but could also load/manage the card contents after issue to the customer. It is therefore technically feasible for third parties to develop applications and offer them direct to customers, however in practice this is extremely rare. Basically all the functionality that permits the card to be managed must also be secure to prevent abuse from attackers. The secure protection is provided in the form of cryptographic functions that rely on secret keys. Card management is therefore only possible for the Issuer who holds onto these secret keys. The management functionality is quite flexible and supports the idea of multiple security domains on a smart card with delegated management, although it is unlikely to be used in practice. Issuers would likely argue that Issuer control is a positive thing as it ensures tight control of the card contents and behaviours and thereby maintains security, however there is a risk that frustrated application developers will implement on alternative and more open devices, in order to give customers the services that they desire.

1.7 Current Applications for Smart Cards

Smart cards are used in many current and real-world systems and are proposed for many future applications. In fact the capability and numbers of cards are growing rapidly in just about all areas of use. Some of the most notable applications include;
- Mobile Telephony
- Banking
- Transport
- Identity Cards/Passports
- Entitlement cards/Health cards
- Physical Access control
- IT access control
- Satellite TV

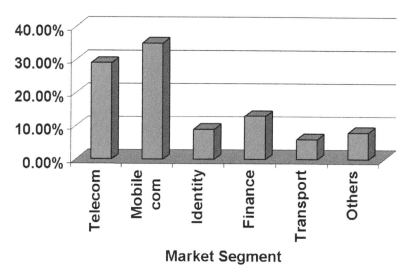

Fig. 1.7   Snapshot of Smart Card Applications by Sector

A rough breakdown of usage by major sector is shown in Fig. 1.7. Of these Mobile Telephony consumes by far the largest numbers of smart cards in the form of the GSM [21] Subscriber Identity Module (SIM) or 3G/UMTS [11] equivalent

USIM. At the time of writing there are over 2 billion mobile phone subscribers and so there must be at least that many smart cards. Given customer churn/growth one would expect to need an extra 25 percent each year and so it is not surprising that it is such an important business application. Furthermore these cards tend to be amongst the most technically advanced cards in use, which is in contrast to the very simple telecom phone cards. After communications, banking is still in second place and its volumes may grow as the EMV chip and PIN standard gains momentum around the world. Coming up fast are transport cards which have only achieved a fraction of their potential. Identity cards and passports with chips still have a huge roll out to come. There is also a lot of interest in entitlement cards and health cards and such systems may entail a roll out to every citizen within the service area. Physical and IT access systems exist in patches and one might argue that with all the other cards and IDs it might not be necessary to have separate cards for access control, but time will tell. There are many people watching satellite TV and quite a lot trying to hack the security. The smart cards are doing a reasonable job at defending the TV systems, but the future is not very clear as it seems there are all sorts of ways of delivering TV and other valued content to consumers. Note the list of applications has so far excluded tagging, which if predictions prove valid will be an enormous consumer of RFID devices. Although these devices will need to be very low cost the sheer volumes needed may well make the RFID/tagging business of comparable size to the current smart card market.

1.7.1 Mobile Telephony

Chapter 4 will provide an in-depth study of the ubiquitous SIM/USIM devices found in modern mobile phones, however no introduction would be complete without taking a quick look at the most widespread and successful smart card application of all time. It is particularly useful to understand why there are smart cards in mobile phones, especially when they are not really used like physical cards at all. To find the answer requires a little trip back into history and before the GSM digital phone standard was introduced. In the UK for example there was an analog mobile phone system in use, known as Total Access Communications System (TACS for short). Being an early pioneering system, the design emphasis was on simply making the radio/communications systems work. The fact that this was achieved with the technology of the time was an astonishing achievement, but it meant that other issues such as privacy and security were rather primitive. Essentially a mobile phone held two identifiers used to authenticate the phone/user to the network. One was the normal telephone number (MSISDN) and the other was a unique electronic serial number for the handset (ESN). When a user wanted to make a call there was a signalling exchange involving the two identifiers and if the network judged the parameters to be correct and appropriately paired then this was a valid (authenticated) user. Unfortunately that is where the security stopped and so far "confidentiality" has not been mentioned. In fact with a radio receiver an eavesdropper could listen

in to any call as there was no encryption. It was also possible to identify calling
parties as the MSISDN was transmitted. Clearly this was very bad from a confidentiality and privacy perspective and it lead to some embarrassing incidents that were
bad for the industry. However the worst was yet to come as the eavesdropper was
also able to receive the ESN. In theory this should have offered no advantage as the
handsets were supposedly designed to prevent unauthorised re-programming of the
ESN/MISIDN pairs. Unfortunately the handset security proved weak and so it was
possible to create "clones" i.e. phones with the MSISDN and ESN from legitimate
accounts. The first sign of cloning was when a user received a huge monthly bill for
call usage. In summary, there was a huge problem coupled with a lack of confidence
in handset security and so the mobile operators decided that in the next generation
of phones (GSM) they would embed a security module in the form of the SIM card.

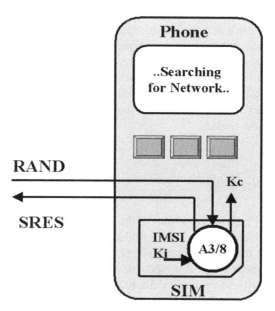

Fig. 1.8 Phone and Its SIM

Fig. 1.8 shows the phone with its embedded SIM. The SIM incorporates a number of
features that were meant to overcome the problems of the earlier analog systems,(see
chapter 4 for a more detailed description). Firstly it holds a customer (really card)
ID called an International Mobile Subscriber Identity (IMSI). The IMSI is mapped
to the real telephone number back in the network, making it harder to identify who
is making a call - in fact there is also a Temporary IMSI (TMSI) that helps to further
disguise the users identity. The SIM also hosts 2 algorithms and a secret key used
for symmetric key cryptography. The naming of the algorithms is not very inspiring
but related to the candidate algorithms considered by the standards committees. A3
is used for authentication and A8 is used to support ciphering. The mobile network

operator has a server (called an Authentication Centre AuC) that has copies of all the card keys as well as the algorithms. Note that an Operator is free to design and use their own proprietary A3/A8 algorithms. The operation is quite simple. The AuC generates a challenge in the form of a random number. It feeds this into its copy of A3 and works out the correct result for the particular card that is being authenticated. The challenge is sent to the SIM via the phone and the subsequent result is then returned and compared with the expected result to decide if the SIM is authenticated. In parallel with this the A8 algorithm calculates a cipher key which is then used by the phone (A5 algorithm) and the network to cipher subsequent communications. Whilst there have been a few avoidable problems (COMP128-1 algorithm [7]) the approach taken with GSM has been remarkably successful and the 3G USIM has now taken this even further by eliminating some potential weaknesses in the 2G solution, (see chapter 4).

1.7.2 Banking

In the last section we discussed how a major security and business problem justified the use of a smart card in mobile communications and now we see it is a similar story for credit and debit cards. In fact with bank cards you can not only improve security, but add new functionality in the form of off-line transactions supported by public key cryptography. The rationale for introducing the smart card and in particular the EMV smart card was the widespread fraud from using magnetic stripe cards. The reader is referred to chapter 5 that explores banking cards and transactions in great detail.

1.7.3 Transport

The use of smart cards in Transport is becoming a growth area because it offers flexibility, fraud reduction, speed and simply because users like them. The Transport for London Oyster card [28] is a prime example allowing customers to use public transport within London without the need to carry cash, queue for tickets or worry about getting the cheapest fare. There are similar systems around the World (e.g. Hong Kong [24]) and there is a lot of interest in the use of multi-functional smart cards (e.g. credit card plus e-ticket [3]) and mobile phones with contact-less card interfaces (NFC) to make these systems even more convenient and popular.

It is worth noting that the challenges for a transport card system are a little different to say a mobile communications or financial transaction. Transport card transactions need to be fast because you can't afford huge bottlenecks of customers at train stations or when entering a bus. This normally means that you can't use an extra PIN code as you might with an EMV card and so we are restricted to single factor authentication (something you have). This is an operational rather than technical limitation, but it probably means you would wish to restrict the maximum value transacted in this manner. There are technical challenges in how to get enough power through the contactless interface to work rapidly. In fact there is always a very sensitive trade-off between the transaction speed, security and cost of the card. Perhaps the biggest challenge to transport systems comes from standardisation of the e-ticket. Customers would like to have one ticket that they can use for all travel nationally and ideally internationally. In the UK the ITSO [18] organisation has been arguing this point and has proposed some supporting standards and requirements, however at the time of writing the most successful UK system (Oyster [28]) is not an ITSO system.

1.7.4 Identity and Passports

As more and more government and regional systems move to electronic processes and transactions, it becomes necessary for citizens to have some kind of compatible electronic identity. For example the modern passport includes a smart chip which can be accessed as part of normal travel processes and many countries have national ID cards, some of which are based on smart card chips, however the introduction of new cards can be emotive. The planned scheme for the UK has sparked controversy, partly because of the biometric information to be stored on the card, but primarily because of the large amount of personal information that will sit on central databases that seem to be accessible by numerous organisations. The proposed cost of the passports or ID cards is at least an order of magnitude greater than the best smart cards used in banking and mobile communications and so there is more than enough scope to include a technically advanced and secured chip. Perhaps the biggest problem is if the card is regarded as some magic element that will make the system secure, whereas the real challenges will be in the rest of the system and the associated processes.

1.7.5 Entitlement and Health

Entitlement and Health cards are perhaps good examples of smart cards that prove an identity and associate with it some private data and rights, but then so too are SIMs, EMV cards, IDs and passports. Clearly there are many reasons for a citizen to be able to identify themselves electronically and whilst smart card chips have the technical capabilities to satisfy the requirements of multiple systems and services, it appears that we will be burdened with more and more smart cards for the foreseeable future. Considering the entitlement card, how might it differ from say a passport? Well entitlement cards are likely to be issued regionally perhaps for low value privileges such as library access or discounted transportation. As they are part of public service delivery and often aimed at disadvantaged citizens, the cards are likely to free issued or at low cost. These factors taken together suggest that the smart card chips might be low cost with limited security and that systems from different national and international regions may not be standardised and/or compatible. Health cards by comparison are likely to have similar cost pressures, but are more likely to be standardised at least nationally. Data privacy is the major factor for any system that is used to secure health records, as misuse of this information could lead to discrimination and could damage an individuals relationships and reputation. It is therefore vital that a health smart card is not only very secure (despite the cost pressures) but that it underpins a complete system that has been rigorously evaluated for the protection of citizen's private health information.

1.7.6 Physical and IT Access Control

It is quite common for employees to be given an ID card to gain access to their place of work. Unfortunately the cards are often not very smart e.g. either the simplest of contact-less smart cards or perhaps magnetic stripe cards. Where a magnetic stripe card has been replaced by a contact-less card it may have had more to do with a desire to improve reliability than security. In fact the very simplest contact-less cards are the classic RFIDs i.e. they present an ID by radio means with no attempt at adding security or disguising the transmitted ID. As an RFID may be remotely eavesdropped (sniffed) you might even argue that the simplest cards are less secure than magnetic stripe as you at least need possession of the latter to read it! The real reason that these cards are used is that the companies consider that a sophisticated attack will not be used to gain access, basically because there are much easier ways. Cards often get left at home, lost or destroyed by various means and its an operational challenge to know if every card in the company database exists (or not) and whether they are all still in the hands of authorised employees. Stealing a card is the easiest way to gain access but you can raise the security bar a little by requiring employees to also enter a PIN code, although this impacts on the convenience and the flow through access points as well as the operational management of PIN codes for forgetful humans. It is interesting to note that IT Access control can be more sophisticated than physical access control especially as physical access might allow a criminal to steal all the company assets including the IT systems! Smart cards for IT access are issued for good security reasons and normally with the support of the IT department who are well used to managing user accounts, passwords and PINs. IT hardware and software is generally expensive and so the cost of the smart cards readers, whilst not negligible, is not a huge cost impact and so it should be possible to buy cards with reasonable capabilities. Normally these would be compatible with IT defacto standards e.g. for access to Microsoft Windows.

1.7.7 Satellite TV

Whilst commerce usually centred around the exchange of physical items, todays customers are keen to buy less tangible goods that have no less perceived value. In the digital multi-media domain we may want to watch something or listen to something for our entertainment and therefore have to pay for the right. This is generally called digital rights management [6] and a good example is satellite TV where a customer can decode a transmitted programme such as a football game if he is in possession of a set-top-box receiver with appropriate security functionality and rights. Satellite TV is very desirable and not particularly cheap and so is a prime target for hackers. Defending the rights is not trivial as this is a broadcast media and so there has to be some global secret elements. Various security solutions exist [4, 15, 23] (see chapter 6 for a detailed discussion) that can be crudely grouped into smart card based and non-smart card based systems. The defenders of satellite TV systems have a realistic outlook on life i.e. they expect to get attacked, to resist for a while, to update a few times to fix weaknesses and finally to roll out a new solution. This outlook is why the card based solutions exist because it is much cheaper to issue a new smart card to improve security than a whole set-top box. It is also a convenient way to adapt and configure a general set-top-box to different security/content providers. Not a great deal is published about the cards used in satellite TV systems (aside from hacker forums) and the arguments against security by obscurity cut little ice with the security system providers. Everything is done to make the hackers task as difficult as possible and so cards can be completely non-standard and armed with a few hidden tricks and surprises.

1.8 Smart Card Application Development

From the foregoing text it can be seen that the smart card is a secure microcontroller that has been successfully used in a wide variety of applications. There are in fact many more applications including, e-purses, lottery, voting, loyalty, user menus, games etc, but all of them had to be developed at some stage. An important consideration is therefore how to implement a smart card application and whilst this should not be beyond the capabilities of most programmers there are quite a number of ways to go about this - especially in the case of SIM/USIM cards. The obvious starting point is that a microcontroller can be programmed in a form of assembly code or perhaps via a C- compiler. You can easily buy smart cards for this, but they tend not to be secure i.e. they are not designed for attack resistance. Of course the secure chip manufacturers and smart card vendors have developed secure devices but you would normally be prevented from accessing the very low level code and have to content yourself with developing above the operating system and via some API or toolkit/interpreter. There are good security reasons for this and the API interfaces offer a lot of convenience to the programmer at the expense of speed. In the SIM world one of the earliest programming facilities was know as a SIM Toolkit Scripting. The

SIM Toolkit functionality was originally described in GSM 11.14 [10] and was implemented in the form of a primitive scripting language which could be understood by a script interpreter on the SIM card. The most common and successful use of this was for custom service menus that appeared (to the user) to be stored in the handset, but where actually managed by the SIM. Earlier implementations were not flexible and so it was difficult to correct or change the menu services although this improved over time. The biggest problem was that the scripting languages were vendor proprietary and so a network operator would have to implement/test the "same" functionality multiple times. Bearing in mind that the vendors used different development tools and that testing with many handsets requires a huge effort, the problem should not be underestimated.

As a solution, another development route was created which in principle offered many advantages over the SIM Toolkit scripting. The idea was to implement a very simple menu browser on the SIM so that it provided simple menu options and handled the user or network responses. There were a variety of browsers including the WIB (Wireless Internet Browser [26] - from SmartTrust) and the S@T Browser (SIMAlliance Browser). The clever part was that the SIM services sat on a network server rather than in the SIM itself, so providing you did a good job of testing the browser implementations from the various card suppliers, you could implement new SIM controlled services without changing its stored functionality or necessarily retesting the SIM. In practice some re-testing was advisable, but all the changes were really in the network. This all held great promised until you realise that an SMS bearer was used, so when you selected a menu option an SMS had to be sent to the server and a response message returned also via SMS. At the height of the browser development, the SMS service was quite unreliable and transmission might take a few seconds but could also take a minute. Measures to get a faster turnaround of SMS helped the situation and some operators went for a menu caching approach, but that really made it a conveniently managed set of SIM hosted services rather than the true browser approach. Another problem was that although the browser approach removed some of the problems from card vendor proprietary systems it risked bringing in a proprietary and single vendor system component. The popular WIB needed a Wireless Internet Gateway (WIG) in order to be useful and whilst the WIB was free the WIG represented a considerable investment and potential dependency on a single supplier. This is one of the reasons why the Alliance of SIM vendors produced the S@T browser. Although the SIM browser seems to be rather side-lined as a development method, the idea was pretty good and faster communications plus a more open-source approach to the gateway might see a resurgence. The odds may not be great as in the meantime developers have found their favourite platform in the form of the Java Card [27].

Java is popular as it abstracts the programming environment from the underlying chip platform, which means that applications should in theory run unmodified on Java Cards supplied by different card vendors and using different chips. For a long time this was far from reality and even today it is wise to repeat testing for all card types. Of course someone still has to develop the low level code to provide an operating system plus the Java virtual machine/run-time environment, but that is just done once and usually by the chip or card vendor. Flexibility and card management is provided by the GlobalPlatform [12] functionality which helps to support secure application and data loading, modification and quite sophisticated security domains and channels for isolating multiple applications. Java Card still suffers from the fact that the functionality has to be developed and loaded on the card itself (rather than a remote server), which in some applications creates testing and card management issues. Java Card and GlobalPlatform are described in detail within Chapter 3 along with another multiapplication card that was in use whilst Java Card was in its earlier stages and that some would claim is more secure than Java Card. Given that smart cards are usually used for their security attributes, it might therefore seem a little odd that MULTOS [22] was not the developers favourite in place of Java Card, especially as Java is one of the languages that can be used for MULTOS development. The reason is partly due to the fact that MULTOS was designed with the highest standards of security in mind and that meant the whole development and application processes were very controlled, requiring various approvals/certifications and accompanying paperwork before a developer could get his application approved and loaded onto a card. This seemed to deter developers and as the vast majority of smart card were (and still are) for mobile networks that did not exist on formal security evaluations a lot of the activity headed into the Java camp, which also meant that more freely available tools became available to ease development. MULTOS has not disappeared however and should still be given consideration particularly for very high security applications.

1.9 Development, Roll-Out and Lifecycle Management Issues

Developing software for smart cards is in many respects like any other software development, but if you make a mistake it can be a very big one that can haunt you for a long time. When you design the data content and functionality of a smart card you should capture all current and foreseeable future requirements which is really an impossible task as no one can accurately predict the future. If you are smart, you design in some flexibility to make changes and add more data and functionality in future although this will be resisted by the purchasing department who believe in saving pennies today rather than the promise of rich yet unspecified new services in the future. Whatever the final agreed compromise, it is translated to a smart card profile that is a definition of how the chosen smart card should be configured. Depending on the application there may be a great many profiles and reader combinations in use. For example you could have a 100 SIM profiles and 1000s of phones in your network. Testing is really important and to really understand this, consider how much money you could lose your company. Lets say we have a new mass-market commercial card that we think is properly tested and a big order of 1 million cards is needed which for simplicity we will says costs £1 million. If you missed a serious bug you may need to recall and replace the cards, a process that is known to cost an order of magnitude more than the cards i.e. £10 millions. This is one of the reasons you build in remote management - but changing 1 million cards would still be a major undertaking.

You might decide to live with a minor bug and so then the interest will be on the normal card lifecycle. For bank cards this is defined as a few years, but for other cards e.g. SIM there are no expiry dates and it is not uncommon to find cards in use that are over 10 years old. This comes to another important point regarding new service roll-out. A company will want a great new service to reach all its customers instantly, however card based applications can rarely offer this. If the service requires a new form of card then on the launch date you will have zero customers. If you wait for the cards to expire or wear-out then you may wait many years and if you swap customer cards you know it will be expensive. This sounds like some unfortunate bad-luck situation but often this legacy problem was actually designed in because of the catch-22 (conflicting logic) of smart card deployment. That is, you need spare capacity and perhaps the most advanced capabilities of the smart card for important services that are not identified when the card is designed, whereas the cost of the card is only justified by the applications that are known to be essential at design time. The situation is not helped by the fact that a marketing strategy or service plan is usually much shorter duration than the life of the card. Another way to get things wrong is to succeed in providing all the necessary and forward thinking card capabilities only to find that the envisaged local/remote management platform is deficient or has simply became a budget cut. One must always remember that a smart card is a sophisticated, personalised and managed computer platform that is vital to a users secure use of a system or service. With proper design and supporting management systems it can be used for many years. Over-specifying a smart card from the bare minimum has a very tangible cost and although it may only be a few pennies or cents per card this starts to become significant for large deployments. However the true cost of issuing minimum specification devices is less simple to determine as it may be the denial of a new service to a customer, a reduced card lifetime (and earlier replacement cost), a poor service or perhaps the loss of the customer to a competitor.

1.10 In Conclusion

This chapter has attempted to provide an introduction to a very wide range of smart card related issues which has hopefully been a good starting point for newcomers to the field and those that have perhaps previously focussed on one business or technical area. Of course only an overview has been possible here, but much more detail can be found in the following chapters. A few words of wisdom might be useful to finally conclude this introduction;

- smart cards are primarily used because they are tamper (attack) resistant security tokens
- They are often personalised and managed computer platforms that can be in operation for many years

- They are not magic devices that make a system secure when it has bad implementation, algorithms and or short keys
- They are always part of a system
- and they tend to be the simplest part of that system.

Acknowledgement

The author wishes to thank Vodafone, Giesecke and Devrient plus all the SCC industry supporters for their encouragement and support.

References

1. Anderson, R. and Kuhn, M., *Tamper Resistance - a Cautionary Note*, In the Second USENIX Workshop on Electronic Commerce Proceedings (pp. 1-11), 1996.
2. APACS report "The definitive overview of payment industry fraud and measures to prevent it", 2007. More Information Available via
   http://www.cardwatch.org.uk/publications, Cited 03 Oct 2007.
3. Barclays, Barclaycard and TranSys sign agreement to put Oyster on credit cards, 2007. More Information Available via
   http://www.newsroom.barclays.co.uk, Cited 03 Oct 2007.
4. Canal+ website. More Information Available via
   http://www.canalplusgroup.com, Cited 03 Oct 2007.
5. Card Watch "Types of Card Fraud". More Information Available via
   http://www.cardwatch.org.uk/, Cited 03 Oct 2007.
6. CEN ISSS *Digital Rights Management Final report*, 2003. More Information Available via
   http://ec.europa.eu/enterprise/ict/policy/doc/drm.pdf, Cited 03 Oct 2007.
7. COMP128-1 attack. More Information Available via
   http://www.isaac.cs.berkeley.edu/isaac/gsm-faq.html, Cited 03 Oct 2007.
8. ECMA (Standard ECMA-340) Near Field Communication Interface and Protocol NFCIP-1, 2nd Edition, 2004. More Information Available via
   http://www.ecma-international.org/publications/standards/Ecma-340.htm, Cited 03 Oct 2007.
9. EMV Books 1-4, Version 4.1, 2004. More Information Available via
   http://www.emvco.com/specifications, Cited 03 Oct 2007.
10. ETSI, *GSM 11.14 Specification of the SIM Application Toolkit for the Subscriber Identity Module- Mobile Equipment Interface*, version 8.3.0, 1999. http://www.3gpp.org/, Cited 03 Oct 2007.
11. Friedhelm Hillebrand, *GSM & UMTS - The Creation of Global Mobile Communication -* Wiley, 2002.ISBN: 978-0-470-84322-2.
12. GlobalPlatform, 2006, Global Platform Card Specification. More Information Available via
    http://www.globalplatform.org/, Cited 14 Aug 2007.
13. HID Corp Technology Basics Whitepaper Understanding Card Data Formats, 2005. More Information Available via
    http://www.hidcorp.com/documents/understandCardDataFormats_wp_en.pdf, Cited 03 Oct 2007.

14. International Civil Aviation Organisation (ICA0) Doc 9303 Part 1. More Information Available via
    `http://www.icao.int/icao/en/m_publications.html`
15. Irdeto website. More Information Available via
    `www.irdeto.com`, Cited 03 Oct 2007.
16. International Organization for Standardization, ISO/IEC 7816-1-4, 1999.
17. International Organization for Standardization, ISO/IEC 14443 Identification cards - Contactless integrated circuit(s) cards - Proximity cards, 2000.
18. ITSO, Specification v2.1.2, 2007. More Information Available via
    `http://www.itso.org.uk`, Cited 03 Oct 2007.
19. Mayes K and Markantonakis K On the potential of high density smart cards, Elseivier Information Security Technical Report Vol11 No3, 2006.
20. MIFARE. More Information Available via
    `http://www.mifare.net`, Cited 14 Aug 2007.
21. M. Mouly, M-B Pautet, The GSM System for Mobile Communications, Cell & Sys. Correspondence, 1992.
22. MULTOS website. More Information Available via
    `http://www.multos.com/`, Cited 03 Oct 2007.
23. NDS website. More Information Available via
    `www.nds.com`, Cited 03 Oct 2007.
24. Octopus. More Information Available via
    `http://www.hong-kong-travel.org/Octopus.asp`, Cited 24 Aug 2006.
25. W. Rankl and W. Effing - Smart card handbook, 3rd edition, John Wiley ,2000.
26. Smart Trust WIB, 2007. More Information Available via
    `http://www.smarttrust.com/mobile_solutions`, Cited 03 Oct 2007.
27. Sun microsystems, 2006, Java Card 2.2.2 Specifications. More Information Available via
    `http://java.sun.com/products/javacard/`, Cited 14 Aug 2007.
28. Transport for London Oyster Card. More Information Available via
    `http://www.tfl.gov.uk/tickets/oysteronline`, Cited 03 Oct 2007.
29. UK Home Office Identity and Passport Service Website. More Information Available via
    `http://www.identitycards.gov.uk/index.asp`, Cited 03 Oct 2007.

Chapter 2
Smart Card Production Environment

Claus Ebner

Abstract This chapter gives an introduction to the production steps in the lifecycle of a (smart) card. After a short introduction the manufacturing of the card body will be described. The next paragraphs give information on the personalization process chain from data processing and on to card personalization and additional services such as packaging and shipment. A separate paragraph focuses on quality and security issues. At the end there are a few thoughts on current trends and challenges for the smart card industry.

Key words: Data Preparation, Services, Card Body Production, Smart Card Personalization, Personalization, Security

2.1 Introduction

There are two main ways to distinguish card types. On the one hand it is based on the related application/Issuer type, on the other it is the technical features and/or physical characteristics. As there is a close relation between the two - e.g. an ID card for government bearing security features in the card body - this chapter will focus on the "application view":

In banking there are the standard debit and credit cards in ID-1 format (see Table. 2.1) - both with similar characteristics: A multi-layer (usually 4 to 5 layers of individual plastic foils) card body with printed design, some optional printed security features, a magnetic stripe, a signature panel, a hologram and (more and more) with a chip. The optical personalization of the card is either done by embossing or by laser engraving.

New variations include non-standard ISO/IEC7810 cards in smaller sizes (e.g. VISA mini) or different shapes (e.g. MasterCard MC^2) [2]. With the evolving trend

Claus Ebner, Giesecke & Devrient, Germany,
e-mail: claus.ebner@gi-de.com

to contactless payment even other form factors have shown up like key fobs or modules embedded in the shell of a mobile phone.

In telecoms there are prepaid telephone memory cards and microprocessor cards for mobile telephones. The card body may be either multilayer or injection moulded - with a decreasing trend for multilayer. For cards either with a short life cycle, or only serving as carrier for the plug-in module until mounted in the mobile, usually the cheaper variant is chosen.

For a card body which has no security elements, optical personalization is either done by inkjet and thermal transfer printing or by laser engraving.

Mobile phones which take a complete ID-1 card are long gone, but even the ISO/IEC 7810 ID-000 plug-in size has already a smaller successor: The Mini-UICC or 3rd FormFactor (3FF) (see Fig. 2.1).

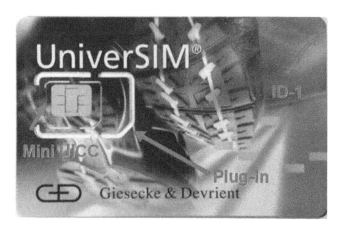

Fig. 2.1 A G&D UniverSIM Card

Table 2.1 Smart Card Sizes

Card Type	Explanation	Size
ID-1	Usual smart card	54,0 x 85,6 mm
Plug-In	for GSM	15,0 x 25,0 mm
Mini-UICC	for GSM (3FF)	12,0 x 15,0 mm
Visa Mini	for Credit/Debit	40,0 x 65,6 mm

The highest requirements for the card body can be found for government cards and here of course especially for ID cards. The card body is usually of multilayer type (up to 9), containing security features such as mentioned for payment cards plus even more sophisticated ones, e.g. a multiple laser image, micro line print, guilloches, invisible fluorescent ink print. Health care cards usually have a contact based chip and most new ID cards use contactless technology.

For optical personalization all techniques can be used - preferably laser engraving due to security reasons. For photos also colour dye sublimation or retransfer technology is used.

2.2 Smart Card Production Steps

2.2.1 Overview

On the way to the final product for the customer there are several steps in card production. First there is the manufacturing of the card body - which includes making of the plastic, printing, and adding additional elements, such as the magnetic stripe. This is followed by embedding the smart card module, which itself went through the steps of test and probably completion and initialization.

An optical and electrical personalization transforms the smart card to an individual one. This often is accompanied by related services, such as card carrier personalization, mail fulfilment and packaging. The following paragraphs describe these steps in more detail.

2.2.2 Card Body Manufacturing

The card body production itself may be divided into several steps again - depending on the technologies used and the features of the card (see Fig. 2.2).

2.2.2.1 Materials

The basic material used for cards is either supplied as foil for laminating or as granulate in case of injection moulding. The classical material used is PVC, but due to environmental discussions and higher lifetime requirements as well, other materials gain importance. Table. 2.2 gives a short overview, summarized from [1].

2.2.2.2 Printing Technologies

The offset printing technique is the most common one used today in industry. It starts with the making of offset printing plates for each printing colour, usually directly from a digital source made with the computer ("Computer to plate" - CTP).

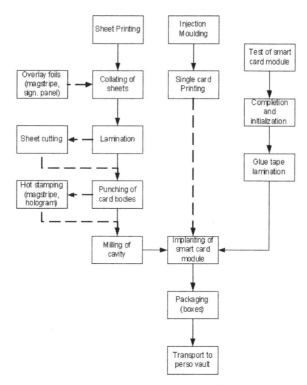

Fig. 2.2 Card Body Manufacturing Flowchart.

The image is exposed to the light sensitive plates with a laser beam. After development of the plate and chemical treatment there are zones which attract ink and others which attract water.

The plates are mounted to printing cylinders which during their rotation run against water rollers and ink rollers. The water rollers dampen the non-image parts of the plate, the ink rollers dampen the image area of the plate with ink.

The plate then transfers the ink to the rubber blanket of a second cylinder, which in turn offsets the image onto the foil running between it and an impression cylinder.

There is also a waterless variant of offset printing using special inks and UV technology. This technique is used in machines for single card printing, where the design is applied to white cards - mostly coming from an injection moulding process.

Screen Printing

The other technique used for card printing works with a porous woven fabric which is stretched over an aluminium frame. A stencil is created on the screen by filling its mesh for the negative parts of an image.

Table 2.2 Card Materials

Material	Advantages (+) / Disadvantages (-)
PVC	(+) Low price, many years of experience, recycling possible (-) Environmental compatibility, limited thermal stability
PC	(+) high temperature stability and mechanical strength, recycling possible (-) high price, low scratch resistance
ABS	(+) injection moulding suitable, temperature stability, recycling possible (-) does not comply with ISO standard, not classified as environmentally friendly
PETG	(+) best material regarding environmental compatibility, middle price, recycling possible (-) process not as easy and well-known as for PVC

The common method to do this is the photo emulsion technique. A positive film of the image is made and placed over the screen, which is coated with a light sensitive emulsion. Exposed to ultraviolet light, the emulsion will harden in the parts of the screen, where the UV light passes through the transparent areas of the film. The non-hardened emulsion will be washed away afterwards from the screen and a negative stencil of the image will be left.

In the press the screen is placed over the foil to be printed and filled with ink. A rubber blade (called squeegee) then is pulled across the screen which fills the holes of the mesh with ink. In a second step a squeegee will press the ink through the mesh onto the foil which is pressed against it.

The printed foil must now dry before the next colour can be applied.

Digital Printing

For high volume printing today there is no alternative to the techniques described above. But as there is a trend to address card Issuers more and more individual, small editions (even "lot size 1") are topics for the card industry.

Digital printers working with thermal sublimation dye or retransfer printing are used to print individual designs onto white cards. Though the quality of this technique has so far not reached the level of Offset or Screen Printing, the results are already very well accepted by card Issuers.

2.2.2.3 Lamination

Card bodies manufactured with the lamination technique consist of two or more foils, which are pressed together under high temperatures. As the foils are of thermoplastic material they will establish a connection under heat when their softening temperature is reached.

The most common compositions are four- and five-layer cards, for contactless and ID cards even up to nine layers are put together. No matter how many layers are used, as the physical parameters of a card are defined in ISO, the sum of the foil thicknesses has to be less than 840 microns.

To protect the design printing there are two ways: If there is external printing on the outer layers of a card the surface will be covered by a transparent varnish. In the most common case of internal printing, transparent overlay foils will be laminated over the design which provides a better resistance against scratching and abrasion.

Besides design and overlay foils there are other components which can be applied in the lamination process. Magnetic stripes and signature panels brought onto a foil before are often added in this process step already. For contactless cards a "pre-lam" inlay containing the chip module and antenna is one of the layers in the lamination process.

Before entering the lamination press the layers have to be collated in such a way that the images for front and back side match exactly and the location of additional elements, such as magnetic stripes or contactless inlays, is within given tolerances. This may either be done by hand or using a sheet collating machine. The simplest way is to align the sheets using their ledges or using adjustment holes in the sheets. If more precision is needed, printed crosses on the foils are brought together using a special table with two cameras - one for the front and one for the back design. In any case the foils will be stapled together by a heated spot stamp in the rim.

These pre-mounted sheets are stacked together with thin, highly polished metal plates. This stack is put between one of the several heating plate pairs in the laminator. Depending on the necessary process parameters - which are specific for each product (regarding the type of materials etc.) - the layers are heated for a certain time and under certain pressures. After cooling down under pressure of the laminated sheet, the card bodies will be punched out in the next process step. If necessary, the sheets will be cut to fit the punching machine.

2.2.2.4 Injection Moulding

For GSM cards which mainly serve as carrier for the plug-in module, the trend is to choose the cheaper process of injection moulding. The cavity needed for the chip module is already created in this process, so that no milling is necessary afterwards.

The preferred material for injection moulding is ABS. The plastic granulate is pressed under high pressures into the pre-heated mould form. The material melted by heat and shearing forces fills the shape of the mould and solidifies. The form is opened and the work piece ejected.

The two main challenges for injection moulded cards are to find the right process parameters to cope with the shrinkage of the material and to ensure the quality of the relatively thin part under the module cavity.

Another important attribute of injection moulded cards is their printability, as the card design will be applied afterwards in a single card printing process before the chip module is implanted.

2.2.2.5 Adding other Card Elements

Signature Panel

Everybody who has a payment card in his wallet, knows that he has to sign his card before he may use it. In order to do so with a customary ballpoint pen, a special signature panel is necessary.

Signature panels are applied with two different techniques: Laminating or hot-stamping.

Paper signature panels are mounted to the outside overlay foil of a card and will connect to the card surface during the lamination process. Another option is to create overlay foils with a printed signature panel by the use of special colours in a screen printing process. Again, this overlay will be applied in a lamination process.

The hot-stamping technique works with prefabricated elements which are transferred from a carrier tape to the card body by the usage of a heated stamp. The elements - such as signature panels - are covered with an adhesive which activates under heat and pressure. Under the hot stamp the element will bond to the card surface and in turn lose its connection to the carrier tape.

Magnetic Stripe

The magnetic stripe which is a main element for all payment cards, needs to be put onto the card at a certain position. The techniques used to apply it are the same as for signature panels. Either the magnetic stripe comes on an overlay foil and is laminated or a hot-stamping process is used.

Hologram

Another security element - for example known from some payment cards - is the hologram. It also is applied to the card body using a hot-stamping process.

Components for contactless Cards

While for smart cards with contacts the chip module will be embedded after card body production, for contactless cards this happens by lamination of inlays which contain antenna and contactless chip module.

There are three main ways to manufacture the antenna for such an inlay:

- In the wire embedding technique the wire is laid directly onto a plastic foil and melted into it by using ultrasonics.
- Etched antennas are created using photolithography with copper covered plastic foils. The surplus copper will be etched away by acids only leaving the antenna shape on the plastic foil.
- The printed antenna can be produced using a special silver ink in a silk screen printing process.

The technology to connect the smart card module to the antenna depends on the antenna type. For embedded antennas it is micro welding while for etched antennas it is soldering.

No matter what technologies are used to create a contactless card, it is essential that the unevenness caused by antenna and module is equalized to achieve a good card surface.

2.2.2.6 Preparation of the Chip Module

In most cases chip modules are shipped on reels to the smart card manufacturer. In a first step an incoming inspection will be made on a test handling machine to ensure the quality of the modules before embedding. Usually the ATR of the chip is checked and read/write tests on the EEPROM are performed.

As machine costs for test handlers are lower than for card personalization machines, they are often used to already load data to the chip which are common for a range of products.

For ROM masks this is the completion of the ROM OS in the EEPROM, e.g. for extensions and patches. For Flash controllers the complete OS has to be loaded in this step.

Depending on the contents of the initialization file loaded afterwards, file structures and also partly their contents will be created, applications and keys will be available on the chip.

The criteria which parts to load in which step will not only be dependant on cost calculations but also on the product and related security requirements. So for some products it is necessary to have a clear separation between the initialization and the personalization. For other products it may be better to perform the initialization as late as possible. This avoids logistic problems, as not too much variants have to be kept in stock for the subsequent processes.

As the modules have to be glued into the card body another step is necessary before embedding which applies an adhesive tape to the modules.

2.2.2.7 Milling, Implanting and Punching

Before the smart card module can be embedded, a cavity needs to be milled into the card body (of course this step does not apply for injection moulded cards which already have it).

Now the "marriage" of card body and the module can happen. The module will be applied and glued to the card body in an implanting machine. To verify that the module is still alive after this process step, usually an ATR test is performed in the implanting machine. For some products it is also necessary to write some information onto the card body. This is possible via an inkjet printer within the machine.

For mobile phone cards (Subscriber Identity Module - SIM) finally a punching of the Plug-In is needed. Depending on the type of the punch (ID-000, UICC) different tools are used in the machine.

2.2.3 Personalization and related Services

In personalization an individual product will be created for the end customer. The data necessary to do this is usually provided by the card Issuer - sometimes enhanced by data generated in the process at personalization (see Fig. 2.3).

2.2.3.1 Data Transfer

Customer data usually enters the smart card via ISDN dial-up data connections or encrypted channels over the internet. For big volumes sometimes also tapes or other media are still used.

The data has to be encrypted and will be decrypted only after being transferred to the production network. Depending on the card Issuer's system and the number of products, several files will be provided. Quite often similar products are within one file, e.g. VISA and MasterCard credit cards.

2.2.3.2 Data Capturing

In most cases the card Issuer will supply the data of his customer, but there are also data capturing services performed by personalization bureaus. In a typical scenario the customer apply form for a card has a special part for the photo, which is teared off and sent directly to the personalization bureau. The photo will be scanned and stored under a reference number, so it can be linked with the other personalization data sent by the card Issuer to create a photo card.

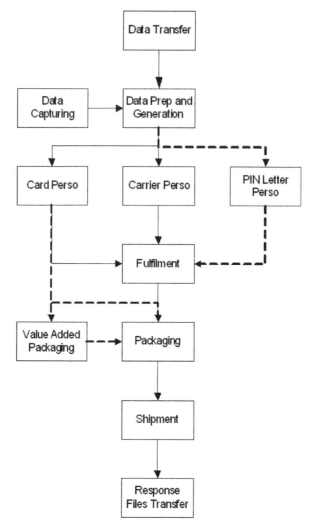

Fig. 2.3 Personalization and Related Services Flowchart.

2.2.3.3 Data Preparation and Generation

Due to security requirements the production network is logically separated from the data transfer network. So before the data can be processed a transfer of the data via the separating firewall has to be initiated.

After decryption of the files a validation of the data takes place. Sometimes also a conversion has to be done, e.g. for banking card Issuers with mainframe systems it is quite common to convert their EBCDIC data to ASCII before further processing.

For validation first the file structure and integrity will be checked, and then also whether the data fields contain allowed values. This may be simple checks like whether a field is numeric or checks whether there is a defined product and process available as requested by control fields of the customer data.

In many cases a grouping and sorting of the data will be the next task. So there may be different service levels and certain records have to be processed and produced on the same day while for others there is a bigger time frame. Other criteria may be different shipment methods (by mail, by courier, etc.), different enclosures to go with the card mailing or different addresses of the card Issuer's locations where the cards should be sent to.

A merge of data from different sources is another task of data processing. This may be photos or logos for optical personalization as well as data for different applications on the chip.

For many products it is also necessary to generate additional data which will go into the chip. This is very common for SIMs, where the network operator often only provides the basic numbers (ICCID and IMSI). .The values for keys (e.g. the Ki) and secret values (e.g. PIN, PUK) have to be generated with a random generator or are derived by using certain card Issuer keys and/or calculation methods. In that case the card Issuer needs to receive a response file which contains all the values generated, so he can store it in his systems.

Another task for products being sent out by direct mail is to create the postage information - depending on mail type, weight and destination. Due to the requirements of the local mail service this information needs to be printed on the carrier, probably leads to the usage of different envelopes in fulfilment and must be provided in a billing report.

Also for credit cards with chip (EMV) there is a process which takes the magnetic stripe data and some card Issuer keys to generate data for the chip.

As the secure storage and generation of keys and the encryption of production data is a basic requirement today, a key management system and the usage of Hardware Security Modules (HSMs) is a must.

At the end of the data preparation process there are several outputs: Data validation reports, production files for the different card personalization machines, printing files for carriers and labels, information on the products (bill of material, process steps) for production and sales (what to bill to the card Issuer?), log files and audit trails and also response files for the card Issuer [3].

2.2.3.4 Card Personalization

Depending on the product machines have to offer a wide range of personalization technologies. Most machines can be set up individually by combining different machine modules and can also be adjusted for further requirements later (see Fig. 2.4).

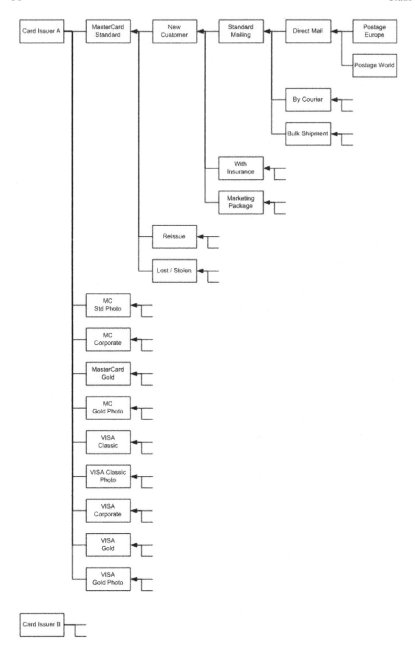

Fig. 2.4 Variants in Personalization (Example).

Laser Engraving

Laser engraving is the most secure way of optical personalization. Its result can be seen in the different layers of a card and be felt on the surface of the card. The laser can either personalize vector fonts or raster images. The latter one takes more time, so for bigger images (photos, logos, barcodes) it is necessary to have more laser modules in one machine for a high output.

Another advantage for laser personalization is reduced cost, as no ink or transfer film is needed.

Embossing and Indent Printing

Embossing and Indent printing are the classical methods for personalizing credit cards. Still in many countries credit cards are not processed online, so the embossed characters are needed to create the receipt. Embossing is done with typewriter wheels with standardized font types (OCR-A, OCR-B). In modern high speed machines two or more modules are used to enable high throughputs. Printing on the rear side of the card is called indent printing, characters are not embossed in that case.

Inkjet

Inkjet printing is often used in conjunction with simple products such as voucher cards. There are machines available which have a very high throughput (40000 cards per hour). On the other hand inkjet also can be used for colour images.

Thermal Transfer, Colour Dye Sublimation and Retransfer Printing

These techniques work with ink ribbons and thermal print heads.

Thermal transfer printing is used for monochrome images, such as logos or barcodes. It delivers high optical quality, but less security than laser engraving, as the ink is applied to the surface only and does not go into the deeper layers.

For colour dye sublimation a three-pass process is necessary, using ribbons for Yellow, Magenta and Cyan. Usually an overlay ribbon is applied on top of the images to protect them against abrasion and fading. Again, the images are only on the surface and therefore not as secure against copying as laser images.

The retransfer method is similar to colour dye sublimation, but instead of printing directly to the card a reverse image is printed to a transfer film which is then applied to the card body. The main advantages are better quality, as an unevenness of the card does not affect the printing result and that the image can be printed over the full surface area of the card and no white borders can be seen. This technique is used for "picture cards" where the end customer may choose his personal design from a given choice of pictures or even by sending his own photo taken with a digital camera.

Magnetic Stripe Encoding

To encode the magnetic stripe with its three tracks (e.g. for credit cards track 1 and 2 are used) magnetic stripe readers are used. Usually there's at least two of them in a machine: The first one encodes the magnetic stripe, the second one reads back the information from the magnetic stripe to ensure that it is written correctly. It is also possible to pre-encode a card's magnetic stripe to use that information in personalization - e.g. to check whether the right plastic is used.

Chip Encoding

Chip personalization has become quite a complex process in the last few years, as the capabilities of the chips (e.g. Java Card), the memory sizes (Megabytes!) and also the security requirements have increased.

The basic process is that the card reader has to establish a connection to the smart card, perform an authentication by presenting a key and then select files on the smart card and update them with personalized contents provided by the data preparation and generation process.

Depending on the complexity of the product, these steps may involve a mutual authentication between card and reader, the use of an external HSM (Hardware Security Module) to handle/create keys and en-/decrypt the communication channel. Additional data may be loaded from different sources (configuration files, databases) or also be generated during the personalization process and passed back to data preparation. So the smart card itself may perform asymmetric key generation and export the public part for a certificate request.

To cope with the amount of data and the throughput needed, a number of high performance card readers are needed in personalization machines. It must be possible to change parameters like voltage, frequency or divider in a wide range for optimization. With local memory available on the readers, also certain parts of the personalization data can be stored there to improve performance. New and future products also offer new smart card protocols, like USB or SWP (Single Wire Protocol).

There are also high requirements to the hard- and software handling the personalization data and process - regarding quality, performance and stability. A typical scenario today is to handle 60 smart cards in parallel and load each one individually with some hundred kilobytes with other components involved (HSMs, databases etc.).

Typical Personalization Machines

As mentioned before most machine vendors offer a modular design of their machines to fit a wide range of requirements. The input and output modules either handle a loose stack of cards or work with magazines. Some machines may have more than one input module, so different plastics can be mixed in personalization. If the same plastic has to be separated for different card Issuers or sorted for later shipment more output stacks are an option as well.

A typical machine for credit card personalization will have a magstripe reader module, followed by a chip encoding module for EMV cards. With a thermo transfer module (for front and/or rear side) an additional logo can be placed on the design - e.g. a company's logo for company credit cards. A colour dye sublimation module may follow to personalize a photo of the cardholder - again this may be for the front or rear side. The last stations in the machine will be the embossing units, one with types to emboss the credit card number, one or more (for high throughput) other units to emboss the remaining lines, e.g. the cardholder name.

The performance range starts with 200 cards per hour (cph) for small desktop systems and ends at 3000 cph for high volume systems.

A typical machine for SIM card personalization may have a vision system after the input module, which serves two purposes: Verify that the right card body is used and calculate offsets for the origin for optical personalisation to equalize punching tolerances. As the data volume for the chip can be quite high for SIM cards, there will be multiple chip encoding heads working parallel to ensure the machine throughput does not go down for longer loading times. High volume machines which run at more than 3000 card-per-hour may have 40, 60 or even more chip encoding heads. Many SIM cards will only receive an optical personalization with a number (the ICCID), some may also have a barcode. So the typical number of laser stations is one or two. To be flexible for either front or rear personalization often a flip over station is used. To verify the quality of the optical personalization, a vision system can be the last module before the cards go to the output stacker.

If cards can't be processed (e.g. if the chip does not work) the machines will treat them as rejects and put them on a separate reject output stack.

Additional modules are available for printing the card carrier, affixing the card to the carrier and also to put this in an envelope, probably together with some additional enclosures. Higher volumes are often handled on separate machines instead of this "inline process". This will be described in the next two paragraphs.

2.2.3.5 Carrier and PIN Letter Personalization

The letter to the end user which carries the card is in most cases personalized using a laser printer. For small volumes this may be simple office printers, for high volumes there are high speed machines printing up to 250 pages per minute (ppm) for cutsheet printers or even over 1000 ppm for continuous feed printers.

Most card Issuers today provide a blank paper which only has their pre-printed logo and probably some fixed text on the rear side. All the rest will be printed variable, which gives the card Issuer a maximum of flexibility and enables him to address his customers very personally. For smaller volumes colour printers are an option as well, which will print all information including logos etc. on a white sheet of paper.

To enable an automatic matching of the card and the carrier in the fulfilment step, a machine readable card identification number needs to be printed onto the carrier - either as barcode or using an OCR (Optical Character Recognition) font type.

PIN (Personal Identification Number) letter personalization today most often also works with laser printers. One method is to cover the PIN with a sealed label after printing, another one works with a special paper which already incorporates a sealed label.

Another method still used works with needle printers and carbon coated multilayer paper. There is no carbon ribbon in the printer, so the PIN cannot be seen during printing - but will be found in the PIN letter after tearing off the seals.

2.2.3.6 Fulfilment

The most common way to hand out a card product to the end customer is to attach it to a personalized letter (carrier), optionally add some information leaflets (enclosures) and put it all into an envelope.

Depending on the card Issuer requirements this leads to a high variety of products, e.g. by sending out the same card product with different enclosures.

The process may either be handled manually for small batch sizes or by dedicated mail processing systems for higher volumes, with a throughput of up to 8000 mailings per hour. These machines are set up from different modules; a typical configuration looks like as follows:

The paper feed module will take the pre-printed carriers, in case of continuous paper a cutter will then cut it into single sheets. In the next module an adhesive label will be placed onto the carrier. The card attaching station reads information from the card (usually from the magnetic stripe or chip) and the corresponding information from the carrier (usually OCR or barcode). If the information matches, the card will be affixed to the carrier. It is also possible to attach more than one card to the carrier - so a bank may send out a MasterCard and a VISA card on the same carrier to its customers or a family receives all their health cards within one mailing.

Afterwards the carrier with the attached card is folded (e.g. z-fold, wrap fold) and inserted into the envelope. An inserter module consists of a number enclosure stations from which for each mailing additional enclosures can be individually pulled and inserted. Most often these are non-personalized information leaflets or booklets, but also personalized items are possible, e.g. by matching them via a barcode.

After all components are in the envelope, it is sealed and a weighing scale behind it checks the weight of each mailing. This may be used to check whether the mailing is correct (e.g. the card didn't get lost in the machine) and to calculate postage or to sort out different mailing types as well. From the output stacker module the operator can the take the mailings and put them into boxes, which will then be handed over to the shipment area..

2.2.3.7 Packaging

For products which are not sent directly to the end customer, packages have to be made according to the logistical needs of the card Issuer. These packages may either contain only cards or cards in mailings which are distributed in other ways after they leave the personalization bureau. Related to packaging there is the printing of shipment lists and identification labels to the cardboard boxes. As these lists and labels apart from some overall product information also contain some personalization data (e.g. first and last card number in a box, on a pallet) the data has to be provided by the personalization data processing systems.

2.2.3.8 Value Added Packaging (VAP)

To address customers even more individually, there are many variants to packaging of cards. In nearly all cases this is a manual process, as the individual items cannot be handled by a machine and the volumes usually are not high enough for the investment in an automated solution.

Typical products for VAP are gift or SIM cards. There's a wide range of boxing available, e.g. CD boxes, sophisticated cardboard boxes, blister packages and even wooden boxes or leather cases. With the cards may go user guides, mobile phone handsets and manuals or different marketing items.

2.2.3.9 Response Files

Last but not least there are also non-physical products which have their origin in personalization. During data generation and processing some data is created which the card Issuer may need in his systems for either logistical or technical reasons.

Some card Issuers need the information which card number has when left the personalization site. On the one hand so they are able to answer requests from their customers "(When will I receive my card?) ", on the other hand this information may be necessary for them to start a related process, e.g. printing and sending out a PIN letter.

Whenever a card contains individual values created or allocated in personalization, the card Issuer will need these values in his system. This may be individual card keys like the Ki for GSM cards which is needed in the provider's authentication system or a chip hardware identification number to be stored in a CAMS (Card Application Management System) for later purpose.

For some processes it is even necessary to send a response file to the card Issuer or another related party and wait for an answer to this response file to continue production. For example this applies to load certificates for keys generated on the smart card: During personalization the smart card generates an asymmetric key pair, the public key is sent in a certification request to an external certification authority (a trust center) and the certificate received gets personalized to the smart card in a second personalization step.

2.2.3.10 Logistics

One of the challenges in personalization is to handle logistics most effectively. Due to the many variants which are generated by different card bodies, carrier papers, enclosures and shipment methods production breaks down into small lot sizes.

On the other hand there are very restrictive rules how cards have to be treated in a secure production environment. The cards are stored in a vault and any movement and withdrawal has to be recorded. A counting of cards takes place between the significant process steps. When a card is spoiled in a process, this of course has to be recorded as well. At any time a "four-eyes-principle" has to ensure the integrity of the process.

There are two main ways to provide the cards to personalization: Either the amount of cards given by the card Issuer order is moved to personalization and rejects produced on the machines have to be pulled in an additional run - or a higher amount is moved to production and the rest needs to be balanced at the end when returned to the vault.

In order to reduce machine setup times, similar orders can be processed together - this can also be supported by intelligent data preparation. Example: There are four different card designs which are applied to the same type of carrier paper. The data preparation will create one carrier printing file and four card embossing files. So there is only one order at the printer instead of four. The same then applies to fulfilment where the card stacks are combined and the machine can produce with one carrier stack in one run.

2.2.4 Security and Quality

Security is one of the main issues in smart card production. A card manufacturing plant or personalization bureau has to fulfil high requirements on physical security. This starts with the fences around the building, which must constructed in a way that no car or lorry simply can break through it. Additional electronic systems detect any other trials to break through this first barrier. Video cameras need to survey the whole plant area as well. The building itself has to fulfil certain standards (wall thickness, stability of doors, etc.) and of course especially in the production area.

The security areas may only be entered via man-traps and there are clear policies for any access necessary by non-registered staff (e.g. for service of production machines). Only people who are able to prove their integrity may work in those areas and all their comings and goings are recorded. No single person is allowed in the security area, a four-eyes-principle needs to be guaranteed in any case, supported by video cameras all over.

Security is also part of all processes - there is a continuous counting of security relevant materials, such as cards, holograms etc. during an order workflow. Another very important task to ensure logical security in personalization is the protection of data. Networks for smart card production are strictly separated from other networks and of course from the internet. Access to data is limited to the persons who need to deal with it and encryption of data is applied wherever possible. It is also essential to delete the personalization data after production in a safe way. On the other hand certain data has to be kept on behalf of the card Issuer or to ensure traceability.

Organizations such as MasterCard, VISA or the GSM Association will perform regular audits to prove the physical and logical security in card production sites. If severe problems were detected by them, this could lead to a decertification and such to the loss of the business. Therefore an ongoing process has to be established, which always ensures the compliance with the actual security regulations.

Quality is the other very important issue. Well defined quality management procedures and a quality assurance during the whole product lifecycle are a matter of course. This starts with the definition of a product, continues with development, test and the production release process following it. During the production various sample tests and in some cases 100% tests are performed to finally prove the quality of the products before they get shipped. Examples are:

- Visual and electronical control is performed after printing processes
- An incoming inspection on modules checks the physical dimensions and the EEPROM as well
- A depth control is performed on the milled cavity before embedding the module
- Cards are tested in bending and torsion cycles to ensure they and the smart card module are fit for use
- Personalized cards are checked against the personalization data to ensure that the right data got onto the card
- Sample mailings will be opened to ensure that the end customer gets the product in the right configuration
- Response data is checked against personalized cards to ensure it matches to the product delivered to the end customer

Everyone can imagine that all these investments in security and quality lead to very high initial and ongoing financial efforts. This means high hurdles for newcomers in the market and a challenge for the existing companies to remain competitive.

2.2.5 Current Trends

2.2.5.1 More individual Products and Services

In the last years there has been an emerging trend to supply even more individual products and services to the card Issuer.

It starts with a high variety of card body designs. So a typical bank portfolio comprises MasterCard and VISA credit cards - standard/gold, private/business, in cooperation with other companies (Co-Branding), special editions for an event (e.g. World Cup, Olympics), with and without photo, etc. On top of that there are debit cards, customer cards, savings account cards - again with different characteristics. Up to fifty different designs per card Issuer is not unusual, some even have hundreds.

This leads to small batches in card body production and to even smaller lot sizes in personalization. With the "picture card " this reduces to lot size of one: The individual card design is made from a digital photo provided by the cardholder.

Variants which can be handled quite easily in production are different texts which are printed on the card carrier. Many card Issuers have dozens of text variants to send out the same card on the same carrier to address their customers individually. The print programs will print the different variants in one run, but there is considerable effort to create and maintain the related templates. If the carrier papers also shall be in many different designs, colour printing on demand is a possible solution.

The next level of variety comes with packaging. Much of it can be handled with mail processing systems, which are able to pick different enclosures to create the mailing. But for special formats, enclosures that are not capable of machine handling and VAP, manual work is often necessary.

Finally there are different shipment methods which expand the number of variants. There is bulk shipment using different carriers, there is direct mail with the established post or alternative service providers and there is shipment by different couriers. A related service requested from card personalization bureaus is to pull certain cards during production and switch their shipment type, e.g. from direct mail to courier.

The card Issuer today expects narrow service levels. For the introduction of new card body designs this are still weeks, smaller changes of a product configuration may be already requested on a day-to-day basis. Card personalization and shipment for many products (in the daily low-volume business) are handled within one or two days, but for some products the time-frame is even limited to hours (e.g. emergency credit cards).

2.2.5.2 Extended Data Services

The main business for personalization bureaus today still is "data in - card out - delete data ". But more and more card Issuers ask for also management of their data and request more detailed information on their orders during the production process.

Managing data starts with such simple solutions like the storage of scanned photos or a secure storage of the keysets on a card, which may be recalled for later customer applications. Another more complex example is an internet gateway for the cardholder which enables him to select an individual card design or to provide his digital photo for his personal credit card.

When it comes to completely manage the lifecycle of a card, enable post issuance personalization (e.g. adding a new application to a smart card after the cardholder already received his card) and store and manage all related information, a Card Application Management Systems (CAMS) is required.

As personalization bureaus handle material on behalf of the card Issuers (cards, carrier paper, leaflets, envelopes etc.), the card Issuer either needs continual information to control his stock levels or can ask his supplier to do so for him. Monthly stock reports often are still state of the art, but card Issuers more and more ask for an online and actual access to this data.

Similar requirements are showing up for a more detailed and actual view on the production process. Card Issuers want to view the progress of their order - even down to the cardholder level. As on the other hand requirements on data security are very high, this is not easy to implement.

2.2.5.3 Memory Encoding

One of the challenges of the smart card industry is to cope with the increase in memory sizes now available in chip modules. While for years there were only a few kilobytes to handle in the initialization and personalization, with the propagation of flash technology today a typical SIM card will be loaded with a few hundred kilobytes. And the first SIM products with 512 megabytes or more additional memory are available.

As the encoding times are limited by the standard protocols (T=0, T=1) and in the end physically by the memory write times, personalization machines have to be equipped with a number of card readers to achieve a reasonable throughput. Let us illustrate that with an example: For a throughput of 3600 cards per hour the machine cycle time is only one second for each card. If the chip encoding time is 40 seconds, we need 40 card readers working in the machine in parallel to keep this throughput.

2.2.5.4 Increasing Security Requirements

While the card industry formerly was mainly concentrated on the physical security of the production sites - including walls, doors, vaults, man traps, video systems etc. - today the focus is more on the logical security.

As personalization bureaus handle such sensitive data as credit card numbers, their processes and related IT systems have to be on a very high security level. This involves the secure handling and storage of keys and data, a reliable firewall concept, an effective data access restriction and a gapless monitoring of all activities in the network - right up to the operation of Intrusion Detection Systems (IDS).

The encryption of cardholder data throughout the whole process is one basic requirement, even though the data is already kept in separated network and most of the data can be seen on the card and the carrier during the production process.

Even higher security levels can be achieved by the separation of different fire-walled segments within a production network. This may also be necessary to segregate data from different card Issuers.

The access to data has to be based on a "need-to-know" basis. The requirements here often exceed the capabilities of the on-board functionality of operating systems. So the applications need to establish an additional layer, e.g. by implementing four-eyes-principle, the use of smart cards for access etc.

There is considerable effort to implement such a consistent data security and as it also leads to more complex processes, there are additional ongoing costs as well.

2.3 In Conclusion

Smart card production entails a broad selection of activities and technologies. It begins with printing, laminating or injection moulding of the card body and the application of several card related items - such as magnetic stripes and holograms. It is followed by the test and initialization of the smart card modules which are then embedded into the card body.

In the personalization process of the card there is a physical part performed by laser, embossing and thermo transfer modules. And an electrical part whereby the magnetic stripe and the smart card module (with contacts or contactless) is encoded. Personalization also happens for card carriers, followed by related services such as mail processing, packaging and shipment. All these steps are strongly linked with a data preparation process.

One of the current trends and challenges is the demand for even more individualized products and services, including an extended data management process. Others trends are the increasing memory size of smart cards with its related impact on personalization times and the increasing security requirements, which need to be supported by appropriately improved IT architectures.

Quality and security are the most important aspects in smart card production and mature audited processes need to be implemented at all times.

"This article is the result of the experience of the author and colleagues at G&D, who I would like to thank for their kind support. It represents the author's personal views only and not necessarily those of G&D or any of its affiliates."

Useful Websites

The reader may find the following websites useful:

```
http://www.icma.com
```
- Website of the International Card Manufacturers Association.


```
http://www.gi-de.com
```
- Website of Giesecke & Devrient.

Glossary

3FF	3rd Form Factor.
ABS	Acryl Butadiene Styrene
ASCII	American Standard Code for Information Interchange
ATR	Answer To Request
CAMS	Card Application Management System
Cph	Card per hour
CTP	Computer to plate
EBCDIC	Extended Binary Coded Decimals Interchange Code
EEPROM	Electrically Erasable Programmable Read-Only Memory
EMV	Europay, MasterCard, Visa
GSM	Global System for Mobile Communications
HSM	Hardware Security Module
ICCID	Integrated CirCuit IDentification
IDS	Intrusion Detection System
IMSI	International Mobile Subscriber Identification
ISDN	Integrated Services Digital Network
Ki	Individual Subscriber Authentication Key
OCR	Optical Character Recognition
OS	Operating System
PIN	Personal Identification Number
PC	Poly Carbonate
ppm	Pages per minute
PVC	Poly Vinyl Chloride
PET	Poly Ethylen Terephtalate
PETG	PET Glycol-modified
PIN	Personal Identification Number
PUK	PIN Unblocking Key
ROM	Read Only Memory
SIM	Subscriber Identity Module
SWP	Single Wire Protocol
UICC	UMTS Integrated Circuit Card
USB	Universal Serial Bus
VAP	Value Added Packaging

References

1. Yahya Haghiri, Thomas Tarantino: *Smart Card Manufacturing: A practical guide*, John Wiley & Sons Ltd, 2002.
2. ISO/IEC 7810. More Information Available via
   `http://www.iso.org/iso/iso_catalogue/catalogue_tc/catalogue_detail.htm?csnumber=31432`, Cited 3 Oct 2007.
3. ETSI, *Smart Cards;UICC-Terminal interface;Physical and logical characteristics* (Release 7) TS 102 221 V7.9.0 (2007-07). More Information Available via
   `http://www.etsi.org/`, Cited 3 Oct 2007.

Chapter 3
Multi Application Smart Card Platforms and Operating Systems

Konstantinos Markantonakis

Abstract Although smart card technology has been available for many decades, it is only in the last few years that they have become widely considered as one of the most common secure computing devices. They are encountered in a number of applications (e.g. secure wireless access in mobile networks, banking, identification) satisfying a diverse range of uses. One of the fundamental factor contributing towards the success of smart card technology is tamper resistance. As the underlying smart card processing power increases at a constant pace, more and more functionality becomes available. It was soon realised that in order to grasp the full benefits of the underlying hardware, parallel advances in the corresponding smart card operating systems would be necessary. This chapter provides an overview of the most widely utilised smart card operating systems or platforms that enable multiple applications to be securely managed and reside in the same smart card.

Key words: Java Card, MULTOS, GlobalPlatform, Smart Card Operating System (SCOS), Multi-Application Smart Cards

3.1 Introduction

Smart cards are already playing a very important role in the area of information technology. Smart card microprocessors are encountered as authentication tokens in mobile phones, in bank cards, in passports and identification cards. Since their invention [26], during the 60s and 70s, they were considered as a portable medium for secure data storage. Further key features of smart card technology that can be con-

Konstantinos Markantonakis, Lecturer,
Information Security Group Smart Card Centre,
Royal Holloway University of London,
e-mail: k.markantonakis@rhul.ac.uk

sidered to contribute towards their wider deployment are security, programmability and upgradeability [30].

It is obvious that the smart card hardware and software are very closely coupled together and they both contribute, along with other factors, towards the success of smart card technology. It is only in the last few years that the concept of issuing smart cards and adding code later-on (or further functionality), even when the card is in the cardholders hands, came into existence. This concept is now known as post-issuance capability.

In order to offer such functionality it is essential that both the hardware of the underlying smart card microprocessor and the software are sophisticated enough to address all the additional requirements. In this chapter we will examine several of these platforms (mainly multi-application), classify them and at the same time identify their advantages and disadvantages.

3.1.1 Smart card Platform Evolution

Early in the 1990's the available smart card technology was offering 1-3kilobytes of ROM (Read Only Memory), less than 128 bytes of RAM (Random Access Memory), and approximately 1-2 kilobytes of EEPROM (Electrically Erasable Programmable Read Only Memory). The underlying software platform comprised a number of program routines, often masked in ROM, that allowed the outside world to communicate with the card in a controlled manner. The way in which an entity could communicate with a smart card was specified by the ISO 7816-4 [17] series of standards. This included amongst other things support for simple file management operations(e.g. write/read a block of data) and certain cryptographic operations.

The main reason behind placing most of the smart card functionality in the ROM of the card was that ROM was (and still is) using very little chip area per bit [52] within the overall size of the smart card microprocessor. Additionally, smart cards where mainly utilised for a dedicated function, i.e. they were single application oriented. Economies of scale were also an important influencing factor. If the number of cards was large then it was justifiable for smart card manufacturers to invest in the development of a dedicated ROM mask that offered the necessary functionality. The structures of these cards were often referred to as monolithic as it was impossible to change them after they were embedded in the card. The smart card manufacturers provided certain solutions around this problem [52], mainly by allowing transfer of execution from ROM to certain jump tables within the EEPROM containing the necessary code improvements. However, programming ROM involves a long and expensive development cycle that requires a lot of skills. Thus, the need to be able to quickly develop and securely execute a smart card application became evident.

The next generation of smart cards that claimed to bypass some of the aforementioned problems, introduced the concept of a smart card operating system. A smart card operating system is often defined as "the software that manages the sharing of the resources of a computer [54]" or "a software platform on top of which other programs, called *application programs*, can run. The application programs must be written to run on top of a particular operating system [1]".

The development of smart card operating system followed a similar path to the development of operating systems in traditional computing devices. The main aim was to offer a stable platform that would allow smart card application execution without suffering from the aforementioned problems. Although during the mid 1990's a number of companies claimed that they offered smart cards with a powerful smart card operating systems, the reality was different. As mentioned above, the smart cards were mostly considered as secure storage devices. Furthermore, the smart card application developers had very limited flexibility as the smart card applications were still mainly developed in ROM and in pre-agreed application structures. Smart card applications had to be developed for specific smart card microprocessors. Additionally, most of the card functionality was embedded with the smart card operating system (SCOS). A direct consequence of "security through obscurity" (under which smart card manufacturers attempted to keep confidential any information regarding their products) was that there were very few smart card programmers. Moreover, it was almost impossible to find information on how to program cards and more importantly to obtain tools that would allow you to develop smart card applications.

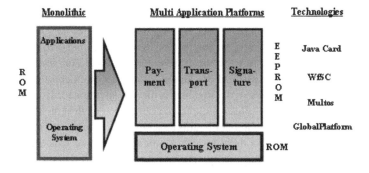

Fig. 3.1 Monolithic and Multi-application Smart Card Platforms [29]

Portability was an issue as a smart card application developed for a smart card utilising a specific smart card microprocessor could not run on a different smart card with a different microprocessor. Platform independence was a real problem that required applications to be rewritten from scratch in order to become portable within different platforms. However, around this period a number of smart card operating systems came into existence e.g. MPCOS from Gemplus, STARCOS from Giesecke & Devrient (G&D), CardOS from Siemens, OSCAR from GIS. Still these smart card applications were very closely coupled together with the underlying smart card operating system and often everything was stored in ROM.

The requirements for adequate memory management, support for state machines, portability and interoperability and advances in microprocessor technology led to new initiatives. The main goals were the complete independence from the underlying operating system, the ability to securely handle multiple applications and also being able to securely modify the content of the card after it was issued. It is evident that security was already playing a very important role in smart card technology, but it was brought further forward in an attempt to provide the necessary reassurance that more openness would not introduce any vulnerability.

This was further realised between 1995-1999 with the introduction of more powerful microprocessors offering approximately 6-8kilobytes of ROM, 128 bytes of RAM and 5-12kilobytes of EEPROM. It is very easy for anyone to realise that the above hardware platform does not offer great flexibility for the design of an operating system within the traditional meaning of the word. However, someone might claim that due to the limited underlying hardware resources, the design of a SCOS should not be a difficult task. Evidently, the underlying hardware has considerable influence in the design of smart card operating systems. Improving the overall performance of the smart card microprocessors was among the main topics of discussion within the smart card communities. In particular, the performance of cryptographic operations was drawing a lot of attention from the academic community. It was however miss-understood that cryptography was among the main delaying factors within a smart card. The communication buffer (usually between 128-250 bytes) that allowed the card to communicate with the outside world, was often overlooked [28].

Its was approximately around this time (last part of the 1990s to early 2000) that the improvements in smart card hardware made it possible for further ideas to evolve and become more realistic. For example, the idea of extending the SCOS functionality, but using patch/extension tables is already mentioned. However, what was needed was the ability to offer a secure and constrained environment that would provide guarantees for controlled application execution. The concept was not new, especially in the traditional computing environments. This was exactly what was offered by a number of source code interpreters (e.g. Microsoft Basic [53]) in early home computers.

The main efforts for the provision of multi-application smart card platforms took place between 1997 and 2001, mainly through the introduction of the following distinct smart card platforms, namely Java Card [31,48,49,55], Multos [35,36], GlobalPlatform [9,12,30], Windows for Smart cards (WfSC) [26,37], Smart-card.NET [16,40], and BasicCard [56]. All these initiatives are supported by a number of companies or consortia, claiming that they fulfilled most of the aforementioned requirements.

There are significant differences, and sometimes misconceptions, on how each of the above technologies is perceived. For example, Multos and WfSC are smart card operating systems. Whereas Java Card, GlobalPlatform, BasicCard, and Smart-card.NET are considered as platforms that should be located on top of a smart card operating system. Java Card and GlobalPlatform are closely coupled together in terms of how they are deployed, especially in the banking and telecommunications sectors. It is becoming evident that Multos, Java Card and GlobalPlatform are the most widely utilised smart card platforms. For the purpose of this analysis, whenever possible the above distinction will be made. However, in general terms we will be referring to the both smart card operating systems and platforms.

3.2 Java Card

This section covers issues around one of the most widely utilised multi-application smart card platforms. We begin our analysis by a brief description of the driving force behind Java Card and we then move onto the details of the underlying technology.

3.2.1 Java Card Forum

Soon after the realization of the Java Card concept (around 1995), a forum was created that will be responsible for promoting and maintaining the Java Card specifications. The Java Card Forum objectives are described in the Java Card Forum web site [24]. In summary the Java Card Forum aims to promote the Java Card standards and exchange technical information among the participating members by fostering a dialogue that will ensure the "write-once-run-anywhere" concept.

Table 3.1 Java card Forum Members

Company Names	
• Gemalto	• Renesas
• Giesecke & Devrient	• Sagem Orga
• Incard	• Sermepa
• Infineon Technologies	• STMicroelectronics
• NXP Semiconductor	• Trusted Logic
• Obertur Card Systems	• Visa

There are different membership levels and depending and each participating organization should be committed in promoting the Java Card concept. Current members[1] of the Java Card Forum are presented in Table. 3.1. We believe that among the driving forces behind the creation of the Java Card Forum was the fact that initially each smart card manufacturer was developing its own implementation of a Java Card. Although these implementations had a common denominator, the Java Card language, they were pretty different and more importantly, non interoperable. Therefore, it was evident that interoperability had to be resolved as efficiently as possible.

---

[1] As of August 2007

3.2.2 Java Card Technology

In this section we highlight the main characteristics of Java Card technology.

3.2.2.1 Why Java?

It was around 1990 that Sun began to lay the foundations for a new programming language that would be "hardware independent" and "secure". Although the new programming language was initially called "Oak" [25], it was later renamed to Java [50]. Java's development coincided with the growth and wider spread of the worldwide web and due to its fundamental characteristics, it became the preferred programming language for a number applications (mainly in the Internet).

Java is an object oriented language which is closely related to C and C++. However, it does not support pointers and it enforces strict type checking. The actual application can be "sandboxed" (i.e. being executed in a restricted environment) as Java is an interpreted programming language, and therefore any side effects of bad programming are confined within boundaries.

Java programs are written in Java source code. A Java compiler will transform the Java source code into a class file, containing Java bytecodes [2]. The bytecode is processor independent code. These bytecodes are interpreted by a Java Virtual Machine (JVM) [7] which is responsible for executing the program via the native program code of the underlying computing platform. The Java Virtual Machine is the actual interpreting environment that enforces all the necessary security checks and at the same time offers the "write-once", "run-anywhere" concept through the hardware abstraction layer.

One of the greatest advantages of Java can also be characterised as one of its main disadvantages. The fact that Java is interpreted means that it comes at a performance price. This becomes more evident when it is compared with other non interpreted programming languages. However, Java enjoyed wide support from a number of programmers, and as a result a number of development tools and extensive documentation became widely available.

A few of the smart card manufacturers, in their attempt to enhance smart card technology, they realised that they needed to overcome the main limitations of existing smart card architectures. This led to the conclusion that: "the problem faced is similar to that of loading code into the World Wide Web browsers, a problem that Java attempted to solve [39]".

It was soon realised that using the Java programming language the development of smart card applications is simplified and improved. The main reason was that Java card applications could be written much more quickly since the details of smart card complexities are hidden. The Java programming language paradigm offered a secure model that prevented programs from gaining unauthorised access to sensitive information. This further implied that Java Card applications adhering to the general Java programming model will be naturally confined within their own operational environment. Furthermore, as Java is based on a runtime bytecode interpreter the portability issue is successfully addressed. This implies that Java Card applications would be portable (at least in theory) between different smart card microprocessors. Upgrading the smart card's functionality could take place with new improved applications that could be installed at any time during the life cycle of the smart card. Therefore, the major problem that had to be solved was the migration of the general Java scheme into a smart card environment (taking into account the smart card hardware and memory constraints).

3.2.2.2 What is Java Card?

Java Card, as it's name imply, should be a smart card capable of executing Java applications. However, the reality is different, mainly due to smart card hardware restrictions. The Java Card language is a subset of the normal Java language. The Java Card Virtual Machine (JCVM) is a subset of the Java virtual machine. Finally, the Java Card API is a subset of the normal Java API. An overview of the architecture of Java Card is presented in Fig 3.2.

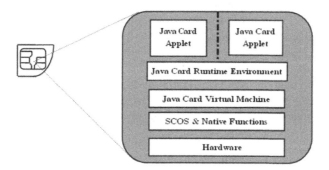

Fig. 3.2 Overview of the Java Card Architecture

The Java Card architecture holds limited resemblance to the normal Java specifications. In the next subsection we will investigate how Java Card technology evolved from the very early stages of its conception, up to the most recent proposals. The Java Card specifications can be obtained from the Sun website www.javasoft. com/javacard free of charge [42].

3.2.2.3 Java Card Evolution

Integrity Arts, a spin-off from Gemplus, was among the first companies that started (around 1995) to openly discuss issues around multi-application smart card technology and code interpretation. They had developed the Clasp interpreter for the

TOSCA programming language [26]. Almost a year later Integrity Arts was bought by Javasoft.

Schlumberger was among the very first companies which announced (late 1996) that it was working on a Java based smart card. This smart card would support a subset of the Java programming language and as a result a subset of the normal Java byte codes. Schlumberger transferred ownership of the Java card specification to Sun Microsystems and at the same time it released (in October 1996) the Java Card Application Programming Interface (API) version 1.0.

3.2.2.4 Java Card API Ver 1.0

The Java Card API Ver 1.0 was the first attempt to bring the benefits of Java to the smart card world. The underlying smart card environment needed to run the Java Card API Ver 1.0 was a 300 KIP (kilo instructions per second) CPU, 12kilobytes of ROM, 4kilobytes of EEPROM and 512 bytes of RAM. The Java Card API supported the following types: boolean, byte and short data, all object oriented scope and binding rules, all flow control statements, all operators and modifiers, plus unidimensional arrays. The API consisted mainly of the *java.iso7816* package which defined the basic commands and error codes, for providing a file system and ability to receive and handle Application Protocol Data Unit (APDU) commands [17], as defined in ISO 7816-4.

Following on from that, Schlumberger and other major companies (e.g. Gemplus, Javasoft, etc.) formed the Java Card Forum in an attempt to foster a dialogue between the industry bodies and more importantly to define additional general purpose APIs for those industries (e.g. the financial and telecommunications industries).

3.2.2.5 Java Card API Ver 2.0

Approximately one year later (October 1997), the Java Card API Ver 2.0 was released by Javasoft. This Java Card API offered significantly more advanced features and extended functionality, which was summarised in three different documents:

- The Java Card Virtual Machine Specification [42] that defined the behaviour of the virtual machine, e.g. Java Card supported and unsupported features, how exceptions are caught, etc.
- The Java Card 2.0 Programming Concepts [43] contained information about the Java Card 2.0 classes and how they can be used in smart card applets. Some of the concepts covered were, transaction atomicity, ISO 7816-4 file system, applet life time, etc.
- Finally, the Java Card API 2.0 Specification [44], which described all the Java Card packages, classes and methods. Among the most notable supported features of the API 2.0 were the following:

    - Packages are used exactly the way they are defined in standard Java.

- Dynamic Object Creation of both class instances and arrays was supported.
- Virtual Methods and Interfaces, could be defined as in standard Java.
- Exceptions were generally supported.

The requirements for additional ROM (16kilobytes) and EEPROM (8 kilobytes) originate from the additional offered functionality. However, due to more adequate optimisation during runtime the requirement for RAM was reduced from 512 bytes to 256 bytes. Furthermore, it was stated that, the Java Card API Ver 2.0 was compliant with the ISO 7816 standard, parts 6, 7 and 8 [18–20].

3.2.2.6 Java Card API Ver 2.1

The next milestone in terms Java Card application development was met in February 1999 when Sun released the latest version of the Java Card API 2.1 [45]. Among the major enhancements and changes from Java Card API 2.0 were the following:

- The applet firewall was more robust and more restrictive. Applets were allowed to communicate with each other through a very well defined shareable interface for object sharing.
- The Applet install method was interoperable. This implied that it was represented in a more portable form by a byte array instead of an APDU object.
- A new Exception class hierarchy was defined.
- The Application Identification (AID) was given a more general scope. For example it became possible to compare AIDs.
- The ISO7816-4 file system extension package *javacardx.framework* was deleted. Files were represented as objects.
- The *java.lang* package, was re-defined as a strict subset of Java.
- The cryptography extension package has been reconstructed. This implied that the *javacard.security* and *javacard.crypto* (subject to export restrictions) packages provide extended functionality for security primitives.
- Particular attention was placed in order to improve application interoperability.
- The supported and unsupported features were defined as shown in Table. 3.2.

Table 3.2 Java Card API 2.1 Major Supported and Unsupported Features

Supported	Not Supported
• Packages,	• Integer, Float, Double, Long, Char,
• Interfaces,	• String, Multi-Dimensional Arrays
• Dynamic object creation,	• Multiple "Threads"
• Virtual Methods,	• Dynamic class loading
• Exceptions,	• Security Manager
• Boolean, byte, short,	• Cloning
• Objects,	• Garbage Collection
• Single dimensional arrays,	
• Flow control statements	

Some smart card manufacturers released Java Card products adhering to the above API, that supported Integer data types and on demand garbage collection.

3.2.2.7 Java Card API Ver 2.2.1

The major improvements within the Java Card API Ver 2.2.1 include the following:

- Support for additional Platforms, e.g. proximity contact-less cards.
- Cryptography is expanded, by including AES and Elliptic Curve cryptographic algorithms.
- Object Deletion mechanism, e.g. being able to delete applets and packages.
- The API offers the ability to open up to 4 logical channels.
- More functionality, in terms of the Java Card Remote Method Invocation (RMI), a long standing Gemplus proposal.

Among the most notable functionality was the JCRMI initiative that was suggested by Gemplus around 1997 [47]. It is a very interesting idea that aims to simplify the way PC/terminal applications interface with smart card resident applications. The terminal application must run in a terminal that supports Java J2SE or J2ME platforms. On the smart card the Java Card Remote Method Invocation (JCRMI) server functionality is been executed. From the PC/terminal application, smart card application functionality can be invoked without utilising APDUs, but simply by referencing the necessary object, as if it was an object directly linked with the terminal functionality, see chapter 10 for more details.

3.2.2.8 Java Card API Ver 2.2.2 Overview

Version 2.2.2 [47] of the Java Card specification introduces several optional and incremental additions to the Java Card Platform. Among the most notable additions are new features for supporting contact-less cards. There are also further attempts to include the necessary enhancements to ensure that the Java Card can be as compliant as possible with the USIM card standards.

This version of the Java Card standard is fully backward compatible with previous versions. Furthermore, it contains additional cryptographic algorithms (e.g. HMAC-SHA1, SHA-256, etc.), support for logical channels, contact-less card support, etc. Key benefits of Java Card 2.2.2 include improved interoperability for cards with multiple communication interfaces, richer cryptography and security features, and standardised biometric support. It also provides a series of new APIs for a more memory efficient application development.

3.2.2.9 Java Card Application Development Cycle

The steps for creating and downloading a Java Card application are the following: first of all, the application programmer must take into account the Java Card APIs and write the Java source code for an application. The application can be developed in any standard Java development environment. The compilation process (with a standard Java compiler) will take as input the Java source file and deliver [32] a class file (the application) and an export file. The class file contains the Java bytecode and the export file contains further supplementary information. The Java bytecodes is "nearly as compact as machine code " [52].

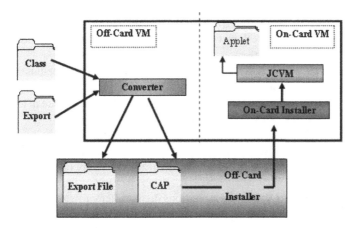

Fig. 3.3 The Architecture of the Java Card Virtual Machine.

Subsequently, the Java Card converter/verifier will have to be invoked and take as input the export and class files and deliver another export file and the CAP file (the inter-operable format for the Java Card platform). The converter is an off-card application and it is considered as part of the "off-card" virtual machine entity. The converter performs a number of static verifications in order to make sure that the application conforms to the Java Card API, and adheres to the Java Card framework security requirements. This process is relatively sensitive as its output will be eventually downloaded in the card. Therefore, it is often recommended that the CAP file is cryptographically protected by a digital signature.

In order for an application to be installed, the "off-card" installer takes as input the export file and the CAP file. In cooperation with the "on-card" installer, they perform all the necessary actions, defined by the Java Card framework in order for the application to be downloaded and/or installed. It is often the case that the loading process is often independent of the Java Card specification and it is offered as part of other technologies (e.g. GlobalPlatform[2]).

---

[2] See also in section 10.3 GlobalPlatform [9]

In the above procedure the smart card can be replaced by a software Java Card simulator. In that case the application is downloaded into the simulator and the overall process of smart card application development is simplified and more importantly has reduced development times. This is achieved since the application developer can very easily monitor certain application variables, debug the application and perform the necessary corrections.

3.2.2.10 Java Card Programming Model

The Java Card concept removes the reliance on the underlying smart card operating system and can reside virtually on top any smart card operating system that offers a Hardware Abstraction Layer (HAL). Among the main reasons behind the perceived security that is offered by the Java Card, is the openness and public scrutiny of the Java and Java Card specifications.

In contrast with traditional Java, the lifetime of the Java Card begins when the smart card operating system and Java Card Virtual Machine are burned into the ROM of the card. The lifetime of the Java Card Virtual Machine, unlike in traditional Java environments, is supposed to run forever.

The lifetime of a Java Card application begins when it is properly installed and registered within the card registry. For this reason the Java Card framework offer a number of routines (e.g. *install, select* that control how an application is installed and selected.

Most of the Java Card VM implementations do not offer garbage collection functionality. This means that application programmers must manually reallocate any memory space which is not used by their application. This forces the Java Card application programmers to think very carefully about how their programs will behave, especially within the limited memory resources of a smart card microprocessor.

The Java Card specification does not define the notion of a security manager as in the traditional Java environment. The VM is indirectly responsible for enforcing a security policy and making sure that applications remain within the predefined boundaries.

Transaction atomicity was among the very early concepts that were defined within the Java Card APIs. Transaction atomicity implies that any updates to persistent objects will be atomic i.e. "a transaction should be done or undone completely".

Among the main security features of the Java Card model is the firewall. The Java Card firewall is responsible of providing the necessary isolation mechanism between the applications, i.e. avoid any unauthoried communication between applications. Through the object sharing mechanisms and the firewall, applications are allowed to communicate with each other. The mechanism that allows inter application communication is very strictly defined with the Java Card APIs. Within this concept, objects are owned by the applet that created them.

The notion of the smart card file system, in the traditional ISO 7816-4 form, has been removed from the recent versions of the Java Card API. However, it is perfectly possible to create file objects with user specific classes.

Optional Java Card packages are denoted by "x" which is often referred to extensions. The *java.lang* package contains all the basic Java Card classes (e.g. exceptions). The *javacard.framework* includes all the main classes for applet management. The *javacard.security* contains provides access to cryptographic primitives. Finally, the cryptography is often provided by the *javacardx.crypto* class which provides an interface to the support cryptographic operations.

The existence of native methods is not allowed by the Java Card specification. "The existence of native methods will completely violate the language based encapsulation model [7] and this one of the main reasons that smart card vendors decided not to offer such functionality. The existence of native methods would also compromise portability. [33]".

Interoperability between the different Java Card implementation was a major issue. Every Java Card developer was implementing the Java Card standard in his own preferred way. This resulted in a lot bad publicity for the Java Card. The existence of the Java Card Protection Profile [46] not only aims to provide the necessary security assurance, but it also attempts to provide the necessary cornerstones for making sure that Java Card implementations can be verified under robust evaluation criteria.

It looks like Java is the most widely utilised programming language for smart card application development. This is particularly true taking into account the vast number of issued Java Cards within the telecommunications and banking sector. However, although it appears that Java Card has been promoted effectively, and seems that it will dominate the smart card market, only time will tell whether it will survive in the long run.

3.2.2.11 Java Card 3

At the time of writing[3], Java Card 3.0 is under development. Some of the most notable suggestions for the next major enhancement of the Java Card standard include:

- HTTP/HTTPs support, so that the card can be integrated into http/web services environments.
- TCP/IP and HTTP client connections.
- Support for jar files.
- Multi threading.
- Support for string variables.
- On-card verification of byte code.

Java Card 3.0 aims to bring smart card programming closer to Java mainstream programming. This a great step forward but on the other hand it increases the Java Card complexity and at the same time it may create (as in desktop Java) new vulnerabilities. Therefore, it remains to be seen how soon the current discussions will be finalised and how Java Cards will behave in widely inter-connected world of mobile phones, PDAs and desktop PCs.

---

[3] August 2007

3.3 GlobalPlatform

This chapter covers the GlobalPlatform card specification as a secure and interoperable multi-application smart card management platform.

3.3.1 The GlobalPlatform Association

During the late 1990s, Visa International, as one of the largest card Issuers in the world, began to explore the issues around multi-application smart card technology.

Table 3.3 GlobalPlatform Members

Full Members	Participating Members	Observer Members	Public Entity Members
• ActivIdentity	• ACI Worldwide	• Bell ID	• Department
• Datacard	Inc.	• BÖWE	of Defense
• France Telecom	• American	• CARDTEC Cassis	• NMDA
• Gemalto	Banknote	• International Pte Ltd.	• Queensland
• Giesecke	Corporation	• Collis	Transport
& Devrient	• Blue Bamboo	• CRYPTOMATHIC	
• Hitachi, Ltd.	• Calton Hill Ltd.	• Datang	
• IBM	• Dai Nippon	• Microelectronics	
• JCB Co. Ltd.	Printing Co., Ltd	• Technology Co.	
• MasterCard	• Fargo	• Financial	
• Worldwide	• Inside Contactless	• Services Co., Ltd.,	
• NTT Corporation	• Smart Trust AB	• Fujitsu	
• NXP	• Sprint Nextel	• Infineon	
Semiconductors	• Texas Instruments	Technologies	
• Oberthur Card	• Trusted Logic	• KEB Technology	
• Systems		• Sagem Orga	
• Renesas		• Toppan Printing	
• SERMEPA		Co., Ltd.	
• StepNexus		• Toshiba Corporation	
• STMicroelectronics		• Watchdata System	
• Sun Microsystems,		• Wuhan Tianyu	
Inc		Information	
• Thales		Industry, Co., Ltd.	
• Visa International			

A couple of years later it created the Visa OpenPlatform (VOP) set of standards. These standards defined how multiple applications could be handled at the card, terminal and smart card management system level. Soon afterwards Visa realised that in order to ensure wider adoption for these standards they had to be as open as possible and publicly available. This along with other business decisions, led Visa to donate the Visa OpenPlatform to the OpenPlatform consortium. The consortium was composed from a number of organisations that possessed an interest in the technology. At that point, the specifications were renamed as the OpenPlatform specifications. Around 1999, as the OpenPlatform consortium was renamed to GlobalPlatform and as a result the specifications were also renamed.

The GlobalPlatform is an independent, non-profit association that is responsible for promoting the GlobalPlatform standards and smart card technology in general. There are different membership levels, see Table. 3.3, leading to different participation preferences and rights. As previously mentioned the GlobalPlatform standards define best practices and architecture for cards and operating systems, terminals, and back-office systems. There are also different committees that oversee the development of the different technologies. The main idea behind the GlobalPlatform standards is to standardise certain aspects of the technology so that interoperability, availability and security of multi-application smart card technology is enhanced. The GlobalPlatform specifications can be obtained from the GlobalPlatform web site www.globalplatform.org free of charge [9].

It is claimed that "There are already in excess of 100 million GlobalPlatform smart cards in circulation across the world and an additional 1 Billion GSM cards that deploy GlobalPlatform technology for over-the-air (OTA) application downloading" [13]. Therefore GlobalPlatform is considered as one of the most widely deployed multi-application smart card platforms. For the purpose of our analysis we will only concentrate on the GlobalPlatform card specification.

3.3.2 The GlobalPlatform Card Specification

In the section we highlight the main components of the GlobalPlatform card specification.

3.3.2.1 GlobalPlatform Architecture

The GlobalPlatform card specification (GPCS) defines a set of logical components that aim to enhance multi-application smart card security, portability and interoperability.

The GlobalPlatform card specification is agnostic of the underlying smart card platform. At the bottom of the suggested GlobalPlatform card architecture we encounter the smart card micro-processor. Usually on top of the smart card hardware we have the Run-Time-Environment (RTE). The RTE is considered as an abstraction layer between the GPCS and the underlying hardware. Typically a RTE is composed of the Smart card operating system (SCOS), a Virtual Machine (VM), and an Application Programming Interface (API). For example, in the context of our analysis, the underlying RTE could be a smart card supporting the Java Card specification. In principle, it could be any other smart card supporting any smart card operating system or underlying VM (e.g. WfSC as it will be explained in the next sections).

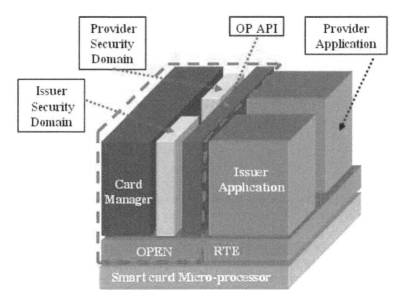

Fig. 3.4 GlobalPlatform Card Architecture.

3.3.2.2 GlobalPlatform Card and Application Lifecycles

The GlobalPlatform card specification defines very rigid stages for the smart card lifecycle. Therefore, a GlobalPlatform smart card can be in one of the following stages:

- OP_READY, defines that the Issuer Security domain is installed and fully operational in handling (as the default selected application) all communication (APDUs) to the outside world. Initial keys are also stored in the card in order to allow the Issuer to securely communicate with the card.
- INITIALIZED, defines an irreversible state transition from OP_READY to INITIALIZED. Its functionality is beyond the scope of the GlobalPlatform card specification. It indicates that the card is not yet ready to be issued to the cardholder.
- SECURED, at this state, the security domain keys and security functionality is in place and the card is ready for post-issuance operations. Getting to this stage is an irreversible operation.
- CARD_LOCKED, at this state, the Issuer has blocked access to third party security domains and applications. The card should not be able to function except via the Issuer security domain. The state transition from SECURED to CARD_LOCKED is reversible.
- TERMINATED, the state transition from any other state to TERMINATED (e.g. under a severe security threat or if the card is expired) is irreversible. Most of

the card's functionality is disabled and the card should only respond to the GET DATA [9] command.

Transition form one state to the other is only done through the appropriate security domains or applications.

An application can be installed only when the card is not in a LOCKED or TERMINATED state. Following on from the installation a GlobalPlatform application can be in one of the following states:

- *INSTALLED*, indicates that an application is properly installed and linked with all in card components. Keep in mind that such an application cannot be selected yet as it may not be personalised.
- *SELECTABLE*, applications are capable or receiving commands from off-card entities. It is up to the individual applications to define their behaviour when they are at this state.
- *LOCKED*, only an application or security domain with the appropriate privileges can bring an application to this state. Applications cannot be selected and only the card Issuer security domain can unlock the card.

3.3.2.3 GlobalPlatform Application Installation

An application can be introduced into a GlobalPlatform card as an Executable Module (executable code) contained in an Executable Load File (on card containers of executable modules). These Executable Modules are processed by the GlobalPlatform and underlying RTE in order to obtain a fully functional and installed application. Executable Load Files can be installed either in ROM/EEPROM during the card's manufacturing phase or in the EEPROM at any later stage during the card's lifecycle. The format of the executable load files are stored in the card are beyond the scope of the specification.

3.3.2.4 GlobalPlatform API

The GlobalPlatform API offers application programmers the ability to access the basic functionality defined within the GlobalPlatform card specification. This functionality varies from initiating a secure channel or locking the card as defined above. It also includes some of the functionality (although it has been extended) which was originally defined within ISO 7816-4.

3.3.2.5 GlobalPlatform Security Domains

Security domains are privileged applications. They are the on-card representative of off-card entities. They have the capability to initiate secure channels (by holding their own keys) but also to handle content management functions. GlobalPlatform applications may be associated with and use the services of a security domain. On the other hand a security domain can also receive information from an application. Therefore, an application provider may communicate with its on-card application via its security domain. There are three main types of security domains in a GlobalPlatform card:

1. Issuer Security Domain. All cards have a mandatory Issuer Security Domain. It is the representative of Issuer.
2. Supplementary Security Domains. They are allocated to individual on-card representatives of application providers
3. Controlling Authority Security Domains are the representative of a controlling authority. Such an entity is responsible for enforcing the security policy on all application code loaded to the card.

3.3.2.6 The GlobalPlatform Card Manager

The GlobalPlatform Card Manager (GPCM) is the central controlling entity in the smart card. It is the ultimate representative of the Issuer. In the current version of the GlobalPlatform card specification the Card Manager can be viewed as three distinct entities:

- The GlobalPlatform Environment (OPEN),
- The Issuer Security Domain,
- The Cardholder Verification Method Services.

3.3.2.7 The GlobalPlatform Environment (OPEN)

The OPEN has extensive responsibilities e.g. to provide an API to applications, perform command dispatching, application selection, (optional) logical channel management, and Card Content management, handling APDUs. Some of this functionality is analysed below. It is stated that these functions shall be implemented by the OPEN, only if they are not provided by the underlying runtime environment.

For example, all communication to the outside world (i.e. through APDUs) are received by the OPEN and redirected to the appropriate on card entities (e.g. application or security domain). Furthermore, the OPEN enforces various card content management operations (e.g. application code verification or application installation certificates). Additionally, OPEN is responsible for performing various security management operations (e.g. locking, blocking and enabling access to the three main entities in the cards i.e. the card, security domains and applications).

In order for OPEN to successfully accomplish all the aforementioned tasks it must have access to all the relevant card information. All this information is stored in the Card Registry. Exactly how this information (e.g. card entity life cycles, entity privileges, memory allocation, etc.) is managed or stored is not defined within the GlobalPlatform card specification. The contents of the Registry can be modified only by an authenticated card Issuer invoked action, an internal OPEN action, or by an operation invoked by an authorised application.

3.3.2.8 The Issuer Security Domain

The Issuer Security Domain is mainly used for card content management and for secure communication during application personalisation and application runtime, as described above.

3.3.2.9 The Cardholder Verification Methods (CVM)

The cardholder verification methods, refer to CVM management services (e.g. Global PIN), that are only accessible to privileged applications. The most obvious supported CVM is a Global Personal Identification Number (PIN). The CVM has different states (e.g. validated, blocked, etc.) and has strict control management on how it should be used.

3.3.2.10 Card Content Management

This is among the main concepts of GlobalPlatform. It is a very critical operation as in case something goes wrong it may put the card under risk.

The content loading process allows an off-card entity (with on card representation, e.g. through a security domain) to add content into the card. The following points will have to taken into account in order to better realise what is involved:

- Card content downloading is not allowed when the card is in the blocked state.
- An Executable Load File contains an application's executable code (i.e. Executable Module).
- A Load File (the actual file transferred to the card) contains the Load File Data Block.
- The Load File Data Block contains all the information (applications or libraries) required for the construction of an Executable Load File (i.e. a smart card application) as specified by the underlying platform. Examples of Load File Data Blocks are the Java Card CAP file format and the Windows for Smart cards OPL file format.
- The Load File Data Block Hash is a redundancy check (i.e. a Hash Function) across the whole Load File Data Block.
- The Load File Data Block Signature (DAP-Data Authentication Pattern) is a digital signature on the Load File Data Block.

Upon the successful completion of the content loading process, an Executable Load File becomes present in the non-volatile memory ready for installation, and an entry is created in the GlobalPlatform registry. Following from that the content downloading procedure can continue into two distinct phases i.e. the content Loading Phase and the Content Installation Phase.

Content Loading is performed by two commands, which are both processed by the Issuer Security Domain before they are forwarded to the OPEN for further processing:

- INSTALL [for load] command, which serves as a load request towards the card and it defines the requirements of the file to be downloaded.
- LOAD command which is used in order to transport the Load File to the card's non-volatile memory.

Upon the successful completion of the loading process, the Content Installation phase can take place at any later stage during the card's lifecycle. For example, a Load File Data Block can be downloaded in the ROM of the card (during the manufacturing phase) and installed after the card has been issued. Card loading in a GlobalPlatform card can be initiated only by authorised (e.g. Issuers or authorised third parties) entities.

3.3.2.11 Issuer Content Loading

Issuers should be in complete control of the card. That means that they should be able to download an application at any stage during the cards lifecycle. When an *INSTALL [for load]* request is received, the OPEN examines whether the same Load File has already been downloaded in the card (this is done by checking the Load File AIDs). If the *INSTALL [for load]* command specifies a security domain (which is to be linked with the application) the OPEN will verify that the security domain exists in the card. Then it will also check whether the security domain has the right privileges and whether it is in a valid state to complete the operations. Finally a Load File Data Block Hash (on the complete Load File Data Block) is send to the security domain.

Suppose that a smart card application, of approximate size 2kilobytes, is about to be downloaded into a GlobalPlatform card. The whole process will be initiated with the *Install [for load]* command. At this point we must take into account that most current smart cards have a communication (APDU) buffer of anything between 98-250 bytes. Therefore, a number of LOAD Commands will have to be issued in order to transmit the complete application to the smart card. For each LOAD command the OPEN will have to verify that there is enough available space in the card.

After the last LOAD command is received, the OPEN will check whether there are any additional checks (Data Authentication Pattern verification privileges). The Mandated DAP means that a security domain, usually the Issuer security domain, should always verify a digital signature on the Load File Data Block. This provides the Issuer with the capability to require (through a Mandated DAP in his Issuer Security Domain) that all LOAD requests are pre-authorised (with digital signature).

3.3.2.12 Delegated Management Content Loading

The concept of Delegated Management allows card Issuers to pre-authorise certain content management operations (e.g. content loading). These pre-authorisations leverage, from card Issuers, the responsibility of managing third party applications. At the same time application providers are empowered with the responsibility or managing their own applications.

This is actually achieved by using *Load Tokens*. A Load token contains a digital signature (from the card Issuer) on the INSTALL [for load] command. The Load Token is included along with the INSTALL [for load] command.

3.3.2.13 Card Content Installation

Up to now we examined how an application can be downloaded in the GlobalPlatform card. However, an application may also have to be installed. Similarly, to content downloading, all *INSTALL [for install]* commands are processed by the Issuer security before they forwarded to the OPEN for further processing. The OPEN will perform some checks (e.g. available memory, no interdependencies, etc.) and if everything appears to be right, it will install the application and perform the necessary linking with the corresponding security domains, and entries in the GlobalPlatform registry. In case of problems, the OPEN will have to terminate the installation process, return both and an error message and the card to a safe state.

3.3.2.14 GlobalPlatform Secure Channel Protocols

The GlobalPlatform card specification defines a number of secure channels protocols. The notion of a secure channel protocol is used for authentication and subsequent cryptographic protection of the communication between the card and the outside world. Secure channels can be used for all GlobalPlatform sensitive commands (e.g. content loading and installation, CVM management, etc.).

3.3.2.15 GlobalPlatform Summary

GlobalPlatform is a multi-application smart card platform that can work with any underlying SCOS. In fact, there are already discussions (in the GlobalPlatform Card Specification 2.2.2 [9]) on how GlobalPlatform can be used with the Multos operating system. The GlobalPlatform card specification is accompanied by the GlobalPlatform Common Criteria Security Target Guidelines [11] (providing information on how a Java Card and GlobalPlatform security target can be developed. Additionally, the GlobalPlatform Card Security Requirements Specification [10] (detailed security requirements) has been made available in an attempt to provide additional evidence on the platforms security.

It appears that GlobalPlatform is taking security very seriously. Great efforts have been utilised to make sure that GlobalPlatform remains an "open" standard (freely downloadable from the GlobalPlatform website) that is offering high standards of multi-application smart card management functionality.

It looks like GlobalPlatform is becoming the de facto standard in downloading and managing smart card applications. For instance, ETSI GSM 03.19 standards rely on GlobalPlatform for smart card application downloading.

It also looks as if the battle of the giants, between Visa and MasterCard, has been settled, at least to some extend, when MasterCard joined the GlobalPlatform association. Furthermore, within the recent GlobalPlatform card specification Ver 2.2.2 there are specific references on how some of its functionality can coexist within the Multos operating system. It appears that GlobalPlatform card specification is heading along an increasingly successful path.

However, the GlobalPlatform association has realised that looking good on paper is not enough. Therefore, it is putting great effort to make sure that GlobalPlatform implementations are properly tested and that GlobalPlatform developers provide accurate product implementations.

3.4 Multos

In this section we highlight the main characteristics of the Multos smart card operating system.

3.4.1 The MULTOS Consortium

The Multos consortium is a group of independent organisations that possess a common interest in multi-application smart card standards and in particular for the future development of the Multos smart card operating system. Once more, there different membership fees depending on the level of influence each organisation may require.

Table 3.4 MULTOS Consortium Members

Company Names	
• ACI Worldwide	• MasterCard Worldwide
• Bell ID	• NBS Technologies
• Dai Nippon Printing	• Oberthur Card Systems
• Datacard Group	• Samsung SDS
• Fujitsu	• StepNexus
• Gemalto	• Techtrex
• Hitachi (including Renesas)	• Thales
• Infineon Technologies	• Trueb
• Keycorp	• UBnics

The current members[4] of the MULTOS consortium are presented in Table. 3.4.

3.4.2 MULTOS Specification

In this section we present an overview of the Multos smart card operating system.

3.4.3 The Multos Card Architecture

During the 1990s Natwest put a lot of effort into the development of the Mondex electronic purse [5, 8]. It is often stated [27, 52] that the Multos [36] smart card operating system originated from the Natwest development team in their attempt to provide a secure and reliable platform for the Mondex electronic purse.

The Multos name is believed to originate from the terms Multi-application Operating System. It was designed from scratch by focusing on security along with the specific details of the underlying smart card micro-processors. It is considered among the very few non military products that managed to obtain an ITSEC [22] E6 certification, which corresponds to EAL7 under Common Criteria [4] security evaluations.

At an early stage of its development, it was almost impossible to obtain access to the Multos specification. This partially explains why was Multos not as widely utilised as Java Card. A few years later an independed consortium MAOSCO was created in order to promote and manage the specifications.

The internal architecture of a Multos card is described in Fig. 3.5. At the bottom of the architecture we encounter the smart card microprocessor. The Multos operating system, offering the basic required functionality (e.g. I/O, file management, crypto), is located immediately above. This functionality, for example, will allow the Multos operating system to dispatch received commands and load and delete applications.

The Multos Application Abstraction Machine (i.e. the interpreter) provides the necessary functionality that will enable smart card applications to remain agnostic to the underlying hardware.

3.4.4 Multos Executable Language (MEL)

The Multos applications were originally written in a byte code assembly language called Multos Executable Language (MEL). MEL byte code is the only code that can be executed by the Multos operating system. Therefore, all Multos applications will

---

[4] As of August 2007

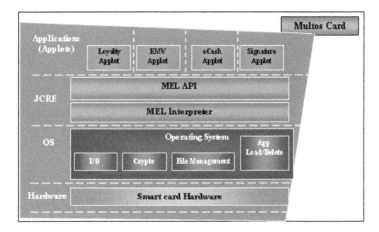

Fig. 3.5 The Multos Smart Card Architecture.

have to ultimately be executed as MEL bytes codes. According to [34], the Multos language is comprised of two languages, numerical one (which is interpreted by the operating system) and the assembly language (which is utilised by the developers).

The MEL language is interpreted by Multos and not directly by the undelying smart card hardware, and as a result, a secure environment for application execution is provided. In this way the applications remain independent from the underlying hardware as any differences are hidden away.

Apart from the MEL byte codes, Multos offers a number of operating system primitives that enable programmers to develop low level subroutines that could be called by the applications (even if they are written in high level langauges).

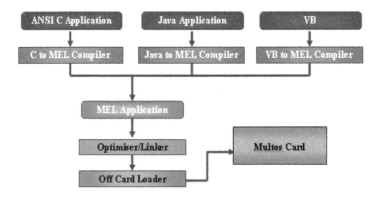

Fig. 3.6 Overview of Multos Application Development Cycle.

Multos applications can be developed, by using the MEL Application Programming Interface (API), in a number of high level languages (e.g. C, Java) and then compiled into MEL. As already mentioned in the previous types of technologies an optimiser and off-card loader are utilised in order to download the application into the smart card.

3.4.5 The Application Abstract Machine

As mentioned above, the Multos Application Abstract Machine (AAM) is located between applications and the Multos OS. It provides an API that will enable application developers to write applications that will be interoperable between different Multos implementations. It mainly defines how memory is managed and how applications receive APDU commands and responses.

The Multos memory is divided in code space (memory space for the application code) and data space (for all data that the applications may need). Code space and other static variables are stored in the EEPROM memory of the smart card. Each application is provided with its own memory space to hold data and code. Public data and stack data are stored in RAM. As an application will only have access in its own allocated memory, the public data functionality offers the ability for applications to share data. All these memory spaces are handled by different memory registers. It is worth mentioning that the memory space does not relate to physical memory which is invisible to application.

3.4.6 Application Loading and Deletion

Multos applications (i.e. the actual applications to be downloaded) are contained within Application Load Units (ALUs). The ALUs must also be accompanied by an Application Load Certificate (ALC) which is generated by the Multos Certification Authority (CA). Multos will only allow applications with a valid ALC to be downloaded in a Multos card.

Applications can also be deleted from a Multos card with the necessary authorisation. This is obtained in the form of a valid Application Delete Certificate (ADC). Therefore, similarly to GP, the Issuer remains in control of the card as at any stage all downloads and deletion must be pre-authorised.

From the developer point of view, the above strict controls, through the Multos CA, imposed a huge burden. However, this situation has changed recently as the Multos website (www.multos.com) allows the generation (in a more flexible way) of the above certificates [34].

3.4.7 Communicating with a Multos Smart Card

As explained in the previous sections, communication with a smart card is strictly defined within the ISO standards [17]. In a Multos card, either the Multos operating system will process the command or the command will be redirected to the corresponding (e.g. the default selected) application.

3.4.8 Multos Files

The Multos files are organised in the file structure defined within ISO 7816-4 [17]. According to this structure, files (e.g. elementary, transparent, fixed, linear and cyclic) are defined in a tree structure with the MasterFile (MF) at the root directory. Therefore, in order to access card data a file must first be selected and then the corresponding command should be executed.

3.4.9 Multos Security Features

Each Multos application is interpreted by the AAM. Therefore, each application is contained within very well defined boundaries. At the same time, Multos imposes well defined procedures as to how an application maybe downloaded or deleted from the card. Data and applications are controlled through dedicated registers (firewalls) and therefore, undocumented application interference will not be allowed. Actually, this was among the main claims during Multos evaluation.

Additionally, the existence of the Multos certification authority and the utilisation of public key cryptography for the load and delete certificates provides a stable and off-the-shelf set of tools and procedures, which is often a major requirement of card Issuers (mainly financial).

Multos can be encountered in contact and contact-less smart cards. It is mentioned [23] that code size for MEL is significantly smaller compared with other platforms. This can be attributed to the efficiency/inefficiency of the corresponding compilers. The same article also claims that MEL is "in general overall faster" than the other three tested platforms.

A cryptographic coprocessor was mandatory in Multos implementations. This was deemed necessary in order to perform the necessary application download and delete operations. Although the existence of a crypto coprocessor might improve security and speed, on the other hand it increases the overall cost of the chip.

Implementers of the Multos operating system must always adhere to the functionality already defined within the Multos standards. This is an attempt to make sure that all Multos implementations remain interoperable.

3.5 Smartcard.NET Card

Smartcard.NET [14] was developed by Hive Minded in an attempt to bring the functionality of the .NET platform into smart card devices. The platform was developed as close as possible to the international standardisation organisation ECMA335 [6] NET specifications and the .NET framework.

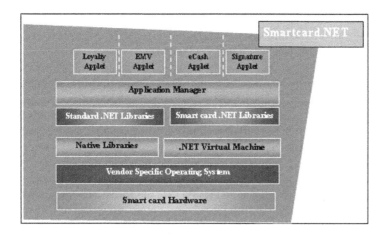

Fig. 3.7   Smartcard .NET Architecture [16].

It is defined as a multi-application, multi-language, environment that will offer smart card application interoperability. Thus, the .NET applications can be written in C#, C++, Visual Basic (VB), J#, JavaScript, etc. Since the applications written in the above languages will be compiled to the .NET code it becomes possible to combine one or more languages for the same smart card application.

The Smartcard.NET card offers a virtual machine that imposes [16] the concept of an "Application Domain" as a mechanism to isolate running applications and avoid undocumented data sharing. The platform also offers a garbage collection mechanism. A remoting mechanism (often referred as RPC in .NET) will enable inter-application communication. Finally, the latest Nectar [15] Smartcard.NET platform also support streams, 64-bit integers and card code verifications. At the time of writing [5] this chapter, it was not easy to obtain detailed information about the inner workings of the Smartcard.NET card. However a sample figure containing a pictorial view of the architecture is presented in Fig. 3.7. At the time of writing a visit to the Hive Minded web site, revealed that that it has been acquired by Step-Nexus [41].

---

[5] August 2007

3.6 BasicCard

The BasicCard [56] concept came into existence around 1996 through its inventor Wolfgang Salge and ZeitControl Cardsystems (www.zeitcontrol.de). The proposed architecture allowed smart card programmers to develop applications in the ZeitControl Basic language and through an integrated environment, download them in the BasicCard.

The syntax of the language contains all the major Basic commands, including strings, IEEE floating-point numbers and various user defined data types. At the heart of the card's operating system we encounter a Basic interpreter (occupying approx. 17Kb of ROM) which executes [3] P-codes.

The BasicCard concept relies heavily on the existence and availability of Basic as an easy to learn programming language. The concept of APDUs exists, but it is completely transparent in BasicCard. For example, the BasicCard programmers simply define their program functionality through functions and procedures and the BasicCard underlying functionality is responsible for translating the necessary calls and handling the APDUs.

The BasicCard offers a number of additional programming libraries (mainly cryptographic) that aim to support the development of advanced and dedicated applications. According to Wolfgang and Rankl [52] the BasicCard "program code is very compact and the execution speed is relatively high". However, among the most widely advertised features of the BasicCard are the low selling prices and by the fact that they can be obtained relatively easily through the ZeitControl website.

3.7 WfSC

The concept of Windows for smart cards was introduced by Microsoft around 1998, but it seems as if the whole concept has been abandoned. At that time, Microsoft realised that as they offered operating systems for PC/server computers and hand-held devices they should also be doing something around smart cards. The plan was to offer a version of Windows for smart cards.

The WfSC operating system (requiring an 8-bit CPU, 32Kb ROM, 32Kb or EEP-ROM and 1Kb of RAM [38]) was presented as a direct competitor to the other multi-application smart card platforms. But although the great efforts and overwhelmed publicity it appears that it never took-off and a couple of years later Microsoft withdraw its support.

WfSC came as a fully configurable smart card operating system, as developers had the flexibility to define its exact behaviour. This concept was further enhanced by the existence of a number of functional components offering additional support for a number of industries (e.g. GSM, and additional cryptographic support). The supported file system was based on the ISO 7816 standards [17, 21] and on the well known File Access Table (FAT) of the Microsoft desktop operating systems. Access control to files was enforced by Rule-Based Access Control Lists.

The proposed architecture was subject to security evaluation from Microsoft. Moreover, Microsoft introduced a smart card manufacturer licensing fee for each WfSC that would be developed.

Applications could be developed in VB, C++ and mainly via the closely coupled Visual Studio product. Communication to/from a WfSC card was accomplished by APDUs. The WfSC virtual machine was according to [26] among "the most well designed" of the smart card vitual machines. WfSC, like Java Card, did not specify how applications would be managed, i.e. downloaded, deleted, etc. It was suggested that GP would act as the controlling entity.

3.8 Conclusions

In the above sections, we covered the principle characteristics of the main multi-applications smart card platforms. One cannot easily compare one with another as some of them are platforms (residing at the top of an operating system) and some others are operating systems. Furthermore, there are constant improvements to the actual specifications and platforms and therefore indicative comparison factor might not be valid

However, it would be fair to state that the Multos smart card operating system was designed by taking security into very serious consideration. It has placed tremendous efforts in order to achieve high levels of confidence through smart card security evaluations. On the other hand its closed design, the secrecy around the whole concept and the difficulty in obtaining developments tools and cards, partially contributed towards its restricted deployment. Progressively, the entities promoting Multos have realised their mistakes and attempted to overcome some of the aforementioned problems.

The Java Card programming model is very widely utilised mainly in the banking and telecommunications sectors. The fact that the Java Card specifications were publicly available (along with simulators, documentation and cards) from an early stage, provided a great momentum towards its wider acceptance. Java Card suffered, and to some extend still suffers even today, through interoperability problems and a non verified security model. Both issues have been taken seriously by Sun and the smart card manufacturers and a number of common criteria Java Cards cards adhering to interoperability standards are in existence.

The GlobalPlatform card specification seems to becoming the defacto standard in terms of managing smart card applications in Java Card and perhaps also in Multos. From the very beginning it received the necessary attention from the banking industry and recent standardisation efforts [51] will bring it even closer to the GSM industry.

The WfSC operating system seems to have almost disappeared as it is very difficult to find information around its design or any major companies/industries supporting it. The situation appears to be slightly different with the SmartCard.NET and BasicCard platforms. They are both supported by their corresponding companies and it also relatively easier to find information around their supported infrastructures. However, it remains to be seen whether they will really take off and be utilised in large scale deployed projects that currently use Java Card, GP and Multos.

The battle for the winning platform is not yet over!

Acknowledgement

The author wishes to thank Vodafone, Giesecke and Devrient for their encouragement and support.

References

1. Andrew S. Tanenbaum. *Modern Operating Systems*. Prentice Hall, Upper Saddle River, N.J, 2001.
2. Bill Venners. *Java bytecode*. More Information Available via
   `http://www.javaworld.com`, Cited Jan 1996.
3. Brian Millier. *Basiccards 101, program your first smartcard*. Circuit Cellar, 164:22-27, March 2004.
4. Common Criteria. More Information Available via
   `http://www.commoncriteriaportal.org/`, Cited 03 Oct 2007.
5. E.K. Clemons, D.C. Croson, and B.W. Weber. Reengineering money: the mondex stored value card and beyond. In *System Sciences, 1996., Proceed-ings of the Twenty-Ninth Hawaii International Conference on ,,* volume 4, pages 254-261vol.4, 3-6 Jan. 1996.
6. ECMA. *Common Langauge Infrastrcure*. European Computer Manufactur-ers Association, More Information Available via
   `http://www.ecma-international.org/publications/files/ECMA-ST/`
   `Ecma-335.pdf`, `4thedition`, Cited 03 Oct 2007.
7. Frank Yellin Tim Lindholm. The java virtual machine specification. More Information Available via
   `http://java.sun.com/docs/books/jvms/second_edition/html/`
   `VMSpecTOC.doc.html`, Cited 03 Oct 2007.
8. G.R.L. Higgins. Electronic cash in a global world. In *Security and Detec-tion, 1997. ECOS 97., European Conference* on, page 86, 28-30 April 1997.
9. GlobalPlatform. *Card Specification v2.2*. More Information Available via
   `http://www.globalplatform.org`, Cited March 2006.
10. GlobalPlatform. *GlobalPlatform Card Security Requirements Specification*. GlobalPlatform, 1 edition, May 2003.
11. GlobalPlatform. *GlobalPlatform Smart Card Security Target Guidelines*. GlobalPlatform, 1.0 edition, October 2005.
12. GlobalPlatform. *Open Platform Specification*, Version 2.0.1. More Information Available via
    `http://www.globalplatform.org`, Cited 2000.
13. GlobalPlatform Association. *Introduction to globalplatform techology*. More Information Available via
    `http://www.globalplatform.org/showpage.asp?code=resourceedu`,
    Cited 2006.

14. Hive Minded. *Smartcard.NET Executive Overview*. Hive Monded, More Information Available via
    `http://www.hiveminded.com/docs/Smartcard.NET\%201.0\%20-\ %20Executive\%20Overview.pdf`, Cited 2003.
15. Hive Minded. *Nectar: Smartcard.NET 1.1*. Hive Minded, More Information Available via `http://www.hiveminded.com/whitepapers.htm`, 1.1edition, Cited Feb 2004.
16. Hive Minded. Smartcard.NET technology overview, November 24 2006.
17. ISO/IEC. ISO/IEC 7816-4 *Identification cards - Integrated circuit cards - Part 4: Organisation, security and commands for interchange*. International Organization for Standardization, More Information Available via `http://www.iso.org`, 2edition, Cited 2005.
18. ISO/IEC. ISO/IEC 7816-6 *Identification cards - Integrated circuit cards - Part 6: Interindustry data elements for interchange*. International Organization for Standardization, More Information Available via `http://www.iso.org`, Cited 2004.
19. ISO/IEC. ISO/IEC 7816-7 *Identification cards - Integrated circuit(s) cards with contacts - Part 7: Interindustry commands for Structured Card Query Language (SCQL)*. International Organization for Standardization, More Information Available via `http://www.iso.org`, Cited 1999.
20. ISO/IEC. ISO/IEC 7816-8 *Identification cards - Integrated circuit cards - Part 8: Commands for security operations*. International Organization for Standardization, More Information Available via `http://www.iso.org`, Cited 2004.
21. ISO/IEC. ISO/IEC 7816-9 *Identification cards - Integrated circuit cards - Part 9: Commands for card management*. International Organization for Standardization, More Information Available via `http://www.iso.org`, Cited 2004.
22. ITSEC. More Information Available via `http://www.cesg.gov.uk/`, Cited July 1996.
23. J. Elliot. The maos trap [smart card platforms]. *Computing & Control En-gineering Journal*, 12, Issue 1:4-10, February 2001. ISSN: 0956-3385.
24. Java Card Forum Objectives, More Information Available via `http://www.javacardforum.org/04_press-room/press4.html`, Cited 07 Oct 2007.
25. Jon Byous. *Java technology: The early years*. More Information Available via `http://java.sun.com/features/1998/05/birthday.html`, Cited January 1998.
26. Jurgensen T.M and Guthery S.B. *Smart Cards : The Developer's Toolkit*. 2002.
27. K.E. Mayes K. Markantonakis and Fred Piper. *Managing Information As-surance in Financial Services*, chapter Smart Cards for Security and Assur-ance. Idea Group Publishing, Information Science Publishing, IRM Press, 2007.
28. K. Markantonakis. Is the performance of the cryptographic functions the real bottleneck? In M. Dupuy and P. Paradinas, editors, *Trusted Informa-tion: The New Decade Challenge*, IFIP TC11 16th International Conference on Information Security (IFIP/SEC'01) June 11-13, pages 77-92. Kluwer Academic Publishers, 2001. Paris, France.
29. K. Markantonakis. Multiapplication smart card platforms, February 2006.
30. K. Markantonakis and K. Mayes. An overview of the globalplatform smart card specification. *Information Security Technical Report: Smartcard Security*, 8(1):17-29, 2003. Elsevier Science Ltd (ISSN:1363-4127).
31. M. Braentsch, P. Buhlier, T. Eirich, F. Horing, and M. Oestreicher. *Java Card - from hype to reality*. Mobile Computing - IEEE Concurrency, October 1999. IBM Zurich Research Labaoratory.

32. M.S.Jung D.W. Kim. *A Study on the Optimization of Class File for Java Card Platform*, volume Information Networking. Wired Communications and Management of *Lecture Notes in Computer Science*, chapter Lecture Notes in Computer Science, pages 563-570. Springer Berlin / Heidelberg, Dept. of Computer Engineering, Kyungnam University, Masan, South KOREA dwkim, msjung@eros.kyungnam.ac.kr, February 2004.

33. M. Tunstall D. Sauveron K. Markantonakis, K. Mayes. *Smart card Secu-rity, volume 50 of Studies in Computational Intelligence*, chapter Studies in Computational Intelligence, pages 205-237. 2007.

34. MAOSCO, *Mutlos Developers Guide*, 1.30 edition, 2000. More Information Available via www.multos.com, Cited 03 Oct 2007.

35. MAOSCO. The multos technology. Technical report, November 24 2006.

36. MAOSCO Ltd. Multos operating system specfication. Licensed Online Access,, 2006. More Information Available via
    http://www.multos.com/, Cited 03 Oct 2007.

37. Microsoft. Windows powered smart cards. More Information Available via
    http://www.microsoft.com, Cited 03 Oct 2007.

38. Peter Johannes. Maos platforms technical status report. Technical report, Europay International, November 1999.

39. Ruth Cherneff, John Griffin, Dave Outcalt, Dr. Carmen Pufialito, Rhonda Kaplan Singer, and Michelle Stapleton. Smart cards 97. More Information Available via
    http://www1.shore.net/bauster/cap/s-card/index.html, Cited November 1997.

40. Smartcard Trends. .NET brings web services to smart cards. In *Smart card Trends*, volume 1, page 12. April 2004.

41. StepNexus. *Nectar.NET 2.0 Virtual Machine for Secure ICs*. StepNexus, More Information Available via
    http://stepnexus.easycgi.com/home/UploadedFiles/
    Nectar-Product-Sheet.pdf, Cited 03 Oct 2007.

42. Sun Microsystems Inc. Java Card 2.0 Language Subset and Virtual Machnine Specification. More Information Available via
    http://www.javasoft.com/products/javacard/, Cited 1998.

43. Sun Microsystems Inc. Java Card 2.0 Programming Concepts. More Information Available via
    http://www.javasoft.com/products/javacard/, Cited 1998.

44. Sun Microsystems Inc. The Java Card API Ver 2.0 Specification. More Information Available via
    http://www.javasoft.com/products/javacard/, Cited 1998.

45. Sun Microsystems Inc. The Java Card API Ver 2.1 Specification. More Information Available via
    http://www.javasoft.com/products/javacard/javacard21.html, Cited 1999.

46. SUN Microsystems Inc. Overview of the java card protection profile collection. More Information Available via
    http://www.sun.com, Cited May 2006.

47. Sun Microsystems Inc. The Java Card API Ver 2.2.2 Specification. More Information Available via
    http://java.sun.com/products/javacard/specs.html, Cited August 2007.

48. Sun Microsystems Inc. *Runtime Environment Specification; Java Card Platform, Version 2.1.1*. More Information Available via
    http://java.sun.com, Cited 03 Oct 2007.

49. Sun Miscrosystems Inc. *Runtime Environment Specification; Java Card Platform, Version 2.2.1*. More Information Available via
    http://java.sun.com, Cited 03 Oct 2007.

50. Sun Miscrosystems Inc. *Java 2 Platform Standard Edition 5.0.* More Information Available via
    `http://java.sun.com`, Cited 2006.
51. Third Generation Partnership Project, *Security mechanisms for the SIM application toolkit; Stage 2* (Release 1999) TS 03.48 V8.9.0 (2005-06) More Information Available via
    `http://www.3gpp.org/`, Cited 03 Oct 2007.
52. W. Rankl and W. Effing. *Smart Card Handbook.* John Wiley & Sons, Ltd, 3rd edition, 2003. ISBN: 0470856688.
53. Walter A. Ettlin Gregory Solber. *Microsoft Basic Book/Macintosh Edition.* McGraw-Hill Osborne Media, 1985.
54. Wikipedia. Operating system. More Information Available via
    `http://en.wikipedia.org/wiki/Operating_system`, Cited 03 Oct 2007.
55. Z. Chen. *Java Card Technology for Smart Cards: Architecture and Pro-grammer's Guide.* The Java Series. Addison-Wesley, June 2000. ISBN: 0201703297.
56. ZeitControl. *Basiccard.* More Information Available via
    `http://www.basiccard.com/`, Cited 03 Oct 2007.

Chapter 4
Smart Cards for Mobile Communications

Keith Mayes and Tim Evans

Abstract There are well over 2 billion smart cards in use today within mobile communications devices. The cards known as Subscriber Identity Modules ((U)SIMs) represent some of the most technically advanced smart cards that have ever been deployed. Their original role was to safeguard the system security by providing authentication and confidentiality, but they have evolved to support additional security and value added functionality. The success of (U)SIMs has been largely due to the efforts of a number of standardisation bodies and indeed the technical evolution and standardisation is still progressing at pace. There are some exciting developments in the form of Near Field Communication (NFC), high-speed interfaces and high capacity smart cards that may radically expand the role of the (U)SIM and mobile device, but also challenge pre-conceptions about application architectures and protocols.

Key words: SIM, USIM, UICC, R-UIM, SIM Toolkit, CAT, STK, JSR177, USB, Authentication, Mileage, NFC, Menu, GSM, UMTS, BIP, VAS

4.1 Introduction

One would have to lead a very secluded life to be unaware of at least one successful or publicised smart card application. It is therefore quiet surprising that the most successful application of all time, that uses the most technically advanced smart cards in widespread use today, is largely unknown to most of its users. The reason is that the users do not handle it as a conventional "card" and indeed may never have

Keith Mayes, Director of the ISG Smart Card Centre,
Royal Holloway University of London,
e-mail: keith.mayes@rhul.ac.uk ·
Tim Evans, (U)SIM Authority, Vodafone UK Ltd.
e-mail: Tim.evans@vf.vodafone.co.uk

seen it, although they may rely on it every day. The smart cards in question are found in every GSM [15] phone and the new 3G generation [10] of mobile phones. At the time of writing [1] this means that there are over 2 billion in daily-use. The smart card is mainly safe-guarding security, but it is also providing customer and network data storage as well as supporting value added services. It is also very well standardised and transferable between mobile devices and the fact that it does all this with the minimum of fuss or trouble to its users, is a good endorsement of standardisation and the use of smart cards in general.

The smart card in a GSM phone is usually called a SIM which stands for sub-scriber identity module, a strong clue to one of its functions. When an abbreviation has been around for a while it is sometimes given an alternative definition, which is not always complementary, as in the case of the NTSC television standard, which was referred to as "Never The Same Colour". Fortunately the alternatives for SIM tend to be complementary (and accurate) e.g. "Secure; In the subscribers hand; Managed [35]". As the SIM was originally designed as a standalone Smart card application, the term SIM refers to both the physical card and the software on it. However, around the same time as 3G networks were being standardised, it was envisioned that this new form of the SIM may sit in parallel with other Smart card applications (e.g. Banking, ticketing or loyalty applications). This created two new terms: the smart card physical/low level software when used for telecommunication use is now called a UICC and the application software on it that allows telecom-munication access is called a USIM. The USIM is the evolution of the SIM card and it replaces the SIM even for 2G network access. It is possible to have a UICC with both a SIM application and a USIM application on it. This is often the case if a network operator wants the UICC to work with the widest range of handsets possi-ble. Note that in this chapter when we do not wish to differentiate between SIM or USIM devices we will use the term (U)SIM.

The SIM has been standardised and in service for quite a long time. The European Technical Standards Institute (ETSI) [7] first defined the SIM back in 1990 and the 3GPP standards organisation defined the USIM in 1999. There was a smart card enabled telecoms system that just pre-dated even the SIM. This was the C-NET system that introduced cards in 1988.

The SIM in particular has done a very good job. Before it was introduced some networks were losing many millions of pounds revenue through cloning fraud which was running at around 15%. Since SIM introduction, cloning fraud has become negligible in networks that use robust algorithms on cards from quality vendors.

Making a reliable and secure solution is not easy as the (U)SIM must work in a wide range of mobile phones and there are thousands of different models in use. Even apparently identical makes/models of phones can behave differently across different software releases due to changes or to additional functionality. Fortunately the (U)SIM design has been comprehensively standardised and detailed confor-mance tests agreed. Understanding the standards bodies and the relevant standards

---

[1] As of August 2007

is absolutely vital to anyone wishing to understand or work with (U)SIMs and so the following is a brief introduction.

4.2 SIM/USIM Standards

There are several standardisation bodies and forums that create and maintain documents used to design and test telecommunications smart cards. Some of the most important bodies are shown in Fig. 4.1.

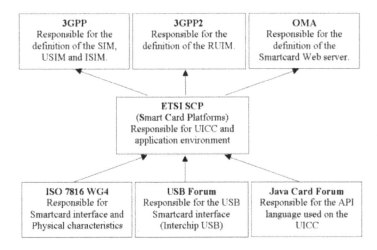

Fig. 4.1 Smart Card Standardisation for Telecommunications

In the centre of standardisation of telecommunications smart cards is ETSI SCP [6] (European Telecommunications Standardisation Institute Smart Card Platforms). ETSI has done some fine work in the area of telecommunications standardisation and the success of GSM can be regarded as largely due to the quality of these standards and the skills of the experts that wrote them. ETSI SCP meets at least four times a year (sometimes as much as eight times when significant developments are being agreed) and is attended by industry representatives (network operators, handset manufacturers, UICC manufacturers, smart card chip manufacturers and test equipment vendors). ETSI SCP has two subgroups which also meet four times a year; ETSI SCP REQ who agree requirements and ETSI SCP TEC who deliver technical solutions.

ETSI SCP has defined the common platform (called the UICC) with two types of access (ISO and USB), Secure Remote Management procedures for the UICC, an API set for the UICC and they also manage the allocation of identifiers for applications on this platform. To achieve this, the ETSI SCP standards, reference standards created and maintained by ISO 7816 WG4 [11], the USB forum [34] and the Java Card Forum [20]. As mobile communication is truly a global phenomenon with many global players, the main focus for telecommunication smart card innovation is in ETSI SCP. All ETSI standards are available free from the ETSI website; the smart card standards can be found by setting the relevant body to "SCP".

The Third Generation Partnership Project (3GPP) [21] is a world wide standardisation body that is now custodian of the GSM specifications and responsible for the further standardisation of the 3G successor system. It uses these specifications as the basis of the SIM and the USIM. The 3GPP CT6 committee design and maintain the files and applications needed to deliver services that are specific to 3GPP networks. In addition, 3GPP has developed a range of conformance test specifications to verify the USIM and 3GPP handsets.

The International Standards Organisation (ISO) [12] is another important standards body for smart card platforms. It considers the card for general applications such as banking and loyalty as well as telecommunications. For (U)SIMs the most widely referenced standards are the ISO7816 series [11]. The first four standards provide important information on physical/electrical aspects, protocols and inter-industry commands. There are various other ISO standards that become appropriate depending on the particular area of investigation. The biggest drawback to the interested reader is that the standards have to be purchased from ISO and there are strict rules about copying and re-distribution. It is quite easy to purchase the standards via the ISO web-site however the costs start to become significant if you need several documents.

The Open Mobile Alliance (OMA) [18] is also worth a mention. OMA evolved partly from the WAP Forum and is now also interested in Multimedia Message Service (MMS) and Device Management (DM). WAP is a Wireless Application Protocol that allows handsets to browse and access mobile services. Within WAP there is the concept of a WIM which stands for Wireless Identity Module and so is a kind of (U)SIM for the WAP world. In fact the WIM can be incorporated within the (U)SIM and so the OMA specifications become relevant. OMA also specifies and makes use of some data files that are stored on the (U)SIM in order to support various OMA services. The specifications can be found on the website.

The Java programming environment has become significant in the smart card and mobile device world. Smart Card applets are often written in a form of Java and the functionality developed for mobiles is often in the form of Java midlets. Given this converging approach it is perhaps not surprising that defacto standards exist to allow mobile device midlets to access functionality from the (U)SIM. This of course has to be standardised and the Java community process (JCP) [13] created the obscurely named JSR177 specification [14].

There are clearly several sources of (U)SIM relevant standards and if you visit their websites for the first time you may be bewildered by the sheer number of specifications and obscure document numbering conventions. To help the reader with some first steps in this area, the following tables identify some "must-have" GSM and 3G standards. In both cases we will use the modern numbering format although some of the most well used ETSI references will be noted in passing.

Table 4.1 Common 2G/GSM Standards

Standard	Description
3GPP TS 02.17	High level description of the standardised SIM services [22]
3GPP TS 11.11	Detailed technical requirement for the SIM-ME interface. Includes files and procedures (old GSM 11.11) [25]
3GPP TS 11.14	Detailed technical requirements for SIM Toolkit commands and processes (old GSM 11.14) [26]
ISO 7816	Detailed low level (Smart card) specification [11]
3GPP TS 03.48	Detailed protocol for the secure transfer of data to/from the SIM and a server in the network (old GSM 03.48) [23]
3GPP TS 03.20	Detailed definition of Security related network functions for GSM. [24]

Table 4.2 Common 3G/UMTS Standards

Standard	Description
3GPP TS 21.111	High level description of the standardised SIM services. [27]
3GPP TS 31.101 & 3GPP TS 31.102	Detailed technical requirement for the SIM-ME interface. Includes files and procedures [28, 29]
3GPP TS 31.111	Detailed technical requirements for SIM Toolkit commands and processes [30].
ISO 7816	Detailed low level (Smart card) specification [11]
3GPP TS 23.048	Detailed protocol for the secure transfer of data to / from the SIM and a server in the network [31]
3GPP TS 33.102	Detailed definition of Security related network functions for 3G [32]

Having given a quick introduction to the SIM/(U)SIM and drawn attention to various standards bodies and important specifications, it is now time to take a look at some of the important things that these devices do for us.

4.3 Subscriber Identity and Authentication

In the introduction chapter a brief overview was given of SIM authentication and we will now look at this in more detail. The main reason that GSM uses SIM authentication is to securely identify the user account and check that it is valid before allowing access to the network. The mechanism required three items to be available on the SIM card

1. The IMSI
2. The secret Key Ki
3. The authentication algorithm A3

The mobile telephone number of the account is not used as an identifier even though the international format is unique. The IMSI is used instead and only the network operator knows how to associate this to the actual telephone number. The format for the IMSI is shown in Fig. 4.2. and the fields uniquely identify a user account anywhere in the world.

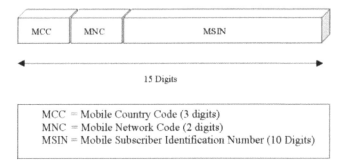

Fig. 4.2 IMSI Fields

Note that to further disguise the user's identity, the IMSI is rarely transmitted in clear and a temporary version (TMSI) is used instead. The IMSI is not a "strong" secret and if the SIM is not PIN locked it can be read direct from the card. Note also that depending on the registration procedures, the network operator might not even know who the actual user/person is, especially with pre-pay SIMs. This is in contrast to say Bank cards which are normally personalised to an individual.

The secret Ki is a very strong/sensitive secret and has to be stored in an attack and tamper-resistant manner by the smart card. It is the network operator's responsibility (although often delegated to vendors) to try and ensure that keys are randomly generated for each card. The size of Ki is 128 bits which according to current best practice reports [3], is still acceptable for symmetric key security systems. Getting the algorithm (A3) right is also the network operator's responsibility and it is a common misunderstanding to assume that the algorithm is a standard. What the algorithm has to do, and the messages used to run the algorithm, are standardised, but the actual algorithm is not. The standards are very flexible and allow for all networks to use different algorithms and indeed a single network might chose to support several authentication algorithms at the same time. In realty attempts have been made to limit the number of algorithms within a particular network, not necessarily because of card complexity but the fact that the algorithms and keys etc. must also be duplicated in the network. The server in the network is called an Authentication Centre (AuC) and this is logically associated with the Home Location Register (HLR) that is effectively a database holding account-related information. The algorithms tend not to be very processor intensive as after all they have to run on smart cards, but the AuC must satisfy the requests from the many millions of subscribers using the network without introducing unacceptable delay. How many requests that originate per user can be strongly influenced by operator configuration controls. For example, you could authenticate when you switch on the phone, when you make a call, when you change location area, or perhaps on a timeout basis. Operator policies vary, with some authenticating on a regular and event basis, whereas others may authenticate very rarely. The latter approach weakens security, particularly the confidentiality of ciphered data, which will be mentioned later. The main point, which is easy to overlook, is that having a good algorithm plus robust smart cards and servers may be less effective than you imagine, if you do not have an appropriate authentication policy and configuration.

4.3.1 So how does SIM Authentication Work?

When the phone powers up it attempts to read lots of useful information from the SIM. The information is stored in files that may be protected by various PIN codes (more about this later). The IMSI is stored in one of these files and can be read by the mobile. If the user as not enabled his PIN lock then there is no restriction on read-access to the IMSI, otherwise the user has to first enter his PIN to get the phone to start-up.

Basically, there is a message exchange between the mobile and the server. The mobile sends the IMSI on a radio signalling channel and requests to use the network. The network generates a 128 bit random challenge (RAND) that it uses together with the particular card key (Ki) to calculate a 32 bit expected response (XRES) using the A3 function and a 64 bit cipher key (K) using the A8 function. The network sends the RAND to the mobile phone that passes it to the SIM card in the form of an APDU containing a RUN_GSM_ALGORITHM command. The command is described in the GSM standards, but summarised in Table. 4.3. below.

Table 4.3 RUNGSM Command Structure

APDU Fields	Contents(hex)	Comments
Class;	A0	Class bytes common to GSM APDUs
Instruction:	88	RUN_GSM_ALGORITHM instruction code
P0:	00	Not-used
P1:	00	Not-used
P2:	10	Number of supplied bytes (in RAND)
Bytes 1-16(dec)		RAND

The response will contain 12 byes of data which includes the 4 byte subscriber response (SRES) and the 8 byte cipher key (Kc) calculated by the SIM in the same way that the corresponding parameters were calculated in the network. The break down of the data field is shown in Table. 4.4.;

Table 4.4 Response to RUNGSM Command

Bytes (dec)	Contents	Comments
1-4	SRES	SIM result from authentication using RAND
5-12	Kc	Cipher key

To finish off the GSM authentication part, the mobile sends the results including SRES to the network and if it matches XRES the device is authenticated and allowed to use the network. An important principle of the challenge response authentication mechanism is that the secret key (Ki) is never revealed to the mobile or untrusted parts of the network. Furthermore, the functions A3 and A8 should be designed in such a way that it is infeasible to determine Ki even if the attacker can observe or control the parameters RAND, SRES/XRES and Kc.

So far not much has been said about the cipher key (Kc), but it plays a very important role in ensuring confidentiality of mobile communications. Because of problems with earlier mobile phone systems, GSM was designed to cipher the radio transmissions and so it should not be possible for a third party to eavesdrop the calls. As the SIM is a hardware security module one might think that it could cipher the call data, however SIMs where historically too slow for handling real-time call data, both in terms of processing power and data I/O speed. The solution was to build a ciphering algorithm (A5) into all GSM mobile phones which made use of a temporary cipher key Kc (like a session key) from the SIM. This was a reasonable solution as the mobile was much faster and the Kc was changed at each authentication. As discussed earlier not all operators are as rigorous about authentication as others and that means that a Kc may be used for overly long time periods. In addition, the key length is starting to look a little short at 64 bits (if indeed the network operator is using the maximum key size available). The Kc is also vulnerable in other ways as it might be extracted from the mobile phone and indeed a copy of this key is stored in clear on the SIM card.

In summary SIM authentication and its support for ciphering have done a creditable job and there would not be 2billion+ GSM users and a thriving mobile communications industry if they had not. That is not to say there is no room for improvement and removal of potential vulnerabilities. This is in fact what the 3G standard sets out to do.

4.3.2 3G/USIM Authentication/Ciphering

The use of symmetric keys, algorithms and challenge response protocols can also be found in 3G and so the USIM should be considered as an evolution rather than a radical departure from the GSM/SIM approach. One of the potential vulnerabilities of GSM is the fact that only the SIM is authenticated and not the network. The SIM therefore has no way of knowing if the requests it receives are from a genuine source. This can lead to a man-in-the-middle attack as shown in Fig. 4.3.

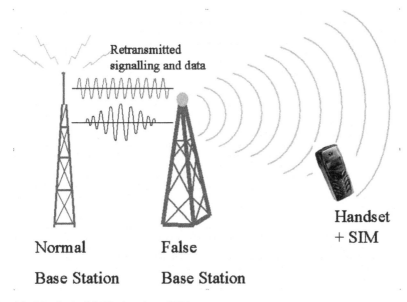

Retransmitted
signalling and data

Handset
+ SIM

Normal   False

Base Station   Base Station

Fig. 4.3 Man in the Middle Attack on GSM

Basically the false base station sits between the legitimate subscriber and network and relays the messages back and forth. It can create, change and suppress messages, so for example it may convince the mobile that ciphering is not enabled on the network and so voice transmissions could be sent in clear via the fake base station. How widespread this attack has been (if at all) is difficult to say, but with the appropriate equipment it is quite feasible. To remove this potential flaw, the 3G solution uses mutual authentication in combination with a mechanism for integrity protecting critical signalling messages, including the messages used to enable and disable ciphering.

The authentication challenge to the USIM now has a MAC that has been computed by the network with knowledge of the secret key (K). If the USIM finds that the MAC is correct then the source of the challenge is verified. As a further precaution a sequence number (SQN) is also provided to prevent an attacker copying and then replaying legitimate challenges. The sequence number has to follow an expected incrementing pattern if the USIM is to consider it valid.

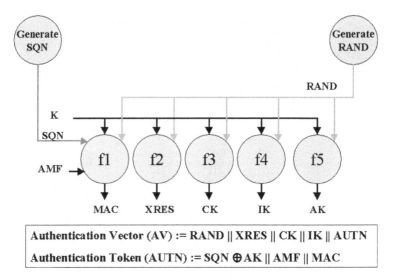

Fig. 4.4 UMTS Authentication - Network Challenge Calculations

The network calculations are shown in Fig. 4.4. Key K is logically equivalent to the GSM Ki and CK to Kc. You will note that there are two new keys. IK is the integrity key that is used to protect the integrity of signalling messages. AK is an anonymity key used as part of the protocol to disguise the sequence number. AMF is an Authentication Management Field that allows the network to communicate authentication control information to the USIM. The functions shown in the boxes are defined in the Milenage specification [5], which is the example implementation for the 3G algorithm.

The authentication vector (AV = Challenge) consists of 5 elements (quintuplet) compared to the 3 element (triplet) used for GSM. The new entries are the Authentication Token (AUTN) to support mutual authentication, management and counter replay attacks plus the Integrity Key (IK). The USIM receives only 2 of these fields i.e. the RAND and the AUTN whereas GSM only expects the RAND.

The processing steps taken by the USIM are shown in Fig. 4.5.

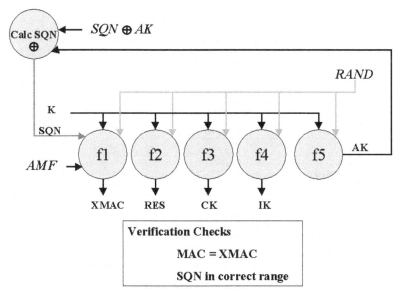

Fig. 4.5 USIM Authentication Calculations

The message exchange across the Mobile to USIM interface is shown in Table. 4.5.

Table 4.5 3G Authenticate Command Structure

APDU Fields	Contents(hex)	Comments
Class;	00	Class bytes common to 3G APDUs
Instruction:	88	AUTHENTICATE instruction code
P0:	00	Not-used
P1:	81	
P2:	22	Number of supplied bytes
Bytes 01	10	Number of bytes in RAND
Bytes 02-17		RAND
Bytes 18	10	Number of bytes in AUTN
Bytes 19-34		AUTN

A good response will typically contain 44 byes of data which includes the result calculated by the USIM (SRES) plus the cipher and integrity keys (CK and IK), as shown in Table. 4.6.

Table 4.6 3G Authenticate Good response

Bytes (dec)	Contents (hex)	Comments
01	DB	Good result
02	08	Bytes in result
03-10		SRES
11	10	Bytes in Cipher Key
12-27	CK	Cipher key
28	10	Bytes in Integrity Key
29-44	IK	Integrity Key

4.3.3 SIM/USIM Authentication Algorithms

So far very little has been said about the authentication algorithms used in the authentication, other than the standard defines the mechanism and message exchanges, but does not dictate the algorithms themselves.

There are many GSM authentication algorithms in use and they tend to be kept secret by the network operators. There was an example algorithm for GSM called COMP128 that was made available to members of the GSM MoU Association [9], but was otherwise expected to remain secret. A lot of mobile operators initially adopted the example algorithm. However the algorithm was weak and relied on secrecy of its design for protection. Unfortunately and indeed predictably, the secrecy could not be maintained and when a design document was "leaked" the algorithm was successfully attacked [4] and is no longer recommended for use. Because of the experiences with GSM, the ETSI SAGE [19] group adopted a more open approach with the specification of the 3G "Milenage" algorithm. The solution was based around the publicly proven AES algorithm and it was decided to publish Milenage so that there was no suggestion that its security relied on the secrecy of the design. There is also a version of Milenage for GSM called G-Milenage.

To conclude the discussion on the essential authentication and ciphering support functions provided by SIMs and USIMs, a comparison is presented in Table. 4.7.

Table 4.7 SIM USIM Authentication Comparison

GSM			UMTS		
Description	Bits	Alg	Description	Bits	Alg
Ki Subscriber authentication key	128		K Subscriber authentication key	128	
RAND random challenge	128		RAND random challenge	128	
XRES expected result	32	A3	XRES expected result	32-128	f2
Kc cipher key	64max	A8	CK cipher key	128	f3
			IK integrity key	128	f4
			AK anonymity key	48	f5
			SQN sequence number	48	
			AMF authentication mgmt field	16	
			MAC message auth. code	64	f1
			AUTN authentication token	128	
Example algorithm COMP128-1			Example algorithm Milenage		

It should be noted that whilst the security functionality discussed above are the
fundamental drivers for the use of (U)SIMs, there are many other general functionalities and indeed advanced applications that can be supported by these devices.

4.4 General Added Features

4.4.1 Phone Book

A phone book, or list of useful stored names and numbers has been a much used
(U)SIM functionality. In the early days of GSM this was perhaps even more important as you might regularly swap your SIM between say your embedded car phone
and your mobile handset. For a long time the SIM was the default place to store the
phonebook, although modern phones usually have an option to use a phone memory.
This tends to push the phonebook towards the phone storage, but with corresponding
loss of portability and handset vendor independence for the customer. In an attempt
to redress this balance, a new phonebook was designed that offers a more complex
set of contact details and requires more memory per entry. The basic situation is;

User Phone book - Before Release 99

- SIM storage for 3 types of entry:-

    - ADN (Abbreviated Dialling Numbers) - choose to call, user can edit.
    - FDN (Fixed Dialling Numbers) - call from list, parent/company to edit.
    - SDN (Service Dialling Numbers) - choose to call, operator edit only.

- Files are stored in a specified location.
- Operator chooses how many of each are available and their size.

  User Phone book - Release 99 and after

- Complex phone book possible which includes over 500 names with email addresses, alternate names, grouping and multiple numbers - See 3GPP TS 31.102 [29] for details.

4.4.2 Roaming list

The preferred roaming list is a very important feature that helps determine which mobile network you try to find when travelling away from your home country. Initially this list was designed to speed up the acquisition of a foreign network by directing the phone to networks that the home operator had an agreement with. Generally when you make a call abroad you are allowed to use a foreign network because your home network has made some kind of roaming deal with them which involves sharing of the call value. The choice of network may affect the available services, the reliability and quality but it also has a major effect on the cost of the call to the user and the profit made by the network operators. Deals vary and the final cost to the user can fluctuate greatly depending on the network selected. The list is meant to help you select the "best" network and is simply a sequential list of networks that you would like to try first if your own is not available. The list contents are initially defined by the network operator and so one would hope that the "best" choices are the most cost efficient for the customer. This is not always the case and the user has the right to modify the list (if he can find the appropriate phone menu) but bear in mind that the network operator is often able to remotely manage and update these lists. As most network operators now have roaming agreements with each other, the list is now used mainly to prioritise networks over each other to get the best level of service for the lowest cost. As these agreements change frequently, it is not uncommon for these lists to be updated remotely by the network operators as often as every 3 months.

4.4.3 SMS Settings and Storage

When a user sends an SMS message it does not go direct to the recipient but has to go to a network server/entity known as a Short Message Switching Centre (SMSC) which sits on the communication signalling network. Each network would normally have their own and other types of organisation could also have SMSCs. Therefore the signalling message must be addressed to the appropriate SMSC, however the phone and user do not know the address. Fortunately this information is stored within the (U)SIM card. The (U)SIM can also store the user's SMS messages.

4.4.4 Last Dialled numbers

Another useful function is to keep a list of the last numbers dialled by the mobile and a file is kept on the (U)SIM for this purpose.

4.4.5 Access Control Class

The access control class (ACC) is an important parameter stored on the card. When a mobile requests access to the network or to make a call, its class ACC maybe used to determine if this should be allowed. Each network cell lists the Access Overload Control (ACCOLC) classes that it can use and if the ACCOLC entry in the SIM does not match any of the 16 possible classes then the handset will not even attempt to use this cell. This can be used in cases of network congestion when new calls are stopped to manage overloading, but it can also be used to restrict usage for emergency services in the event of an incident.

4.4.6 GPRS Authentication and encryption files

In addition to all the authentication functions and data there is also similar functionality to support the GPRS packet data services. The principles are fairly similar and the reader is referred to the standards for a detailed explanation.

The functions listed above make use of information stored in files. The SIM supports a number of file types including Linear Fixed, Binary and Cyclic and these will be described next.

4.5 File Types

The UICC uses three file types as defined by ISO 7816 [11]: Linear Fixed, Transparent and Cyclic files. Table. 4.8. below summaries and compares the standard file types found in (U)SIMs

Just because a file exists on a (U)SIM does not automatically mean that you can access it. That is because access to files is protected by a hierarchy of PIN codes. A PIN has to be verified by the (U)SIM prior to the particular access taking place. If the verify fails a number of times (typically 3) then the PIN may become blocked. Some PINs can be unblocked with a PIN Unblocking Code (PUK), but this is not always the case and some higher level administrative PINs may not even allow one mistaken PIN entry. The user PIN is the most common, although it is often disabled. If disabled or correctly verified, the user PIN allows at least read access to many of

Table 4.8 SIM File Types

Linear Fixed	Transparent	Cyclic
Many records, all are the same length.	A single block of data.	Many records, all are the same length.
READ RECORD command reads.	READ BINARY command reads.	READ RECORD command reads.
UPDATE RECORD command writes.	UPDATE BINARY command writes.	UPDATE RECORD command writes.
Can only be resized by deleting file and creating a new one correctly sized.	Can only be resized by deleting file and creating a new one correctly sized.	Can only be resized by deleting file and creating a new one correctly sized.
Last Record does not wrap to first record.		Last Record wraps to first record.
Used mainly by the Phonebook	Used for most files	Used for Last Number Dialled
Supports absolute record, relative record and SEEK.	Can be read / written from any offset (P1,P2)	Supports relative record record only.

the files on the (U)SIM. The command structures to verify the user PIN (CHV1) is shown in Table. 4.9.

Table 4.9 Verify CHV1 (User PIN) Command

APDU Fields	Contents(hex)	Comments
Class;	A0	Class bytes common to GSM APDUs
Instruction:	20	Verify PIN command
P0:	00	Not-used
P1:	01	Selects CHV1 (PIN1)
Bytes 01-04		PIN code in ASCII
Bytes 05-08		RFU (some pin codes are longer than 4 bytes)

A "90 00" good response message should result from this and thereafter you and/or your mobile will be able to access files protected by CHV1.

PIN handling can get fairly complex and for USIMs there is the concept of a global pin as well as the normal local PINs. The reader is referred to ETSI TS 102.221 for more information. At this point it is also worth noting that network operators can remotely access the (U)SIM files and so there are also additional mechanisms and keys for this purpose. This is described within the chapter 11 on Over The Air (OTA) Systems.

4.6 SIMs and USIMs Some Practical Comparisons

A fairly detailed comparison was given to SIM and USIM authentication, but there are some other practical differences to be aware of. Recall that the SIM was originally defined as a single entity i.e. there was no distinction between a card platform and the application that ran on it. For USIMs the situation is different as the USIM is logically an application that runs on a general purpose platform (UICC). In fact the UICC can host other applications including a SIM or some custom functionality. Because there are potentially multiple applications there is a need to select the USIM and this alters the file access hierarchy. This is noted in table. 4.10 where we see that in GSM, one of the first steps is to select the master file as the Root Directory whereas with the USIM we select the USIM application.

Table 4.10 SIM/USIM Usage Comparison

Feature	SIM	UICC/USIM
Class Byte used	Class = "A0"	Class = "00"
Root Directory	MF (3F00)	ADF USIM (7FFF)
Support Multiple Channels	No	Yes
Authentication Command	RUN_GSM_ALGORITHM	AUTHENTICATE
Can be used for GSM access	Yes	Yes
Can be used for 3G access	Yes	Yes
Support SIM Toolkit	Yes	Yes
Specified in releases	Ph.1 to Rel.4	Rel.99 to Rel.7
Standards development	Frozen	On-going

It is not perhaps surprising that the SIM standards are now simply maintained rather than improved with the new features destined for the USIM. Perhaps a more surprising table entry is the one indicating that a SIM can be used for authentication to a 3G network. The standards allow for this to happen and so a network operator might sell 3G handsets with SIM cards. Fig. 4.6. and Fig. 4.7. show example start-up command sequences for a SIM and a USIM.

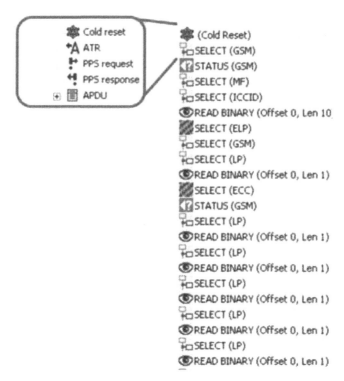

Fig. 4.6 SIM Start-up Sequence

Note that in the SIM start-up sequence shown in Fig. 4.6 the SIM is chosen by the use of the 'A0' Class Byte in the APDUs. The terminal will then begin access to the various files by direct selection of the Master File (MF) directory.

By contrast with the SIM, the USIM is communicated to via the Class Byte '00'. The files are now indirectly selected by selecting the USIM application as can be seen in Fig. 4.7. This is a necessary change as we recall that the USIM is designed assuming that it is one of several applications hosted on a UICC platform. The use of additional applications on the UICC needs to be treated with care as the platform is not normally multi-threaded i.e. only one application runs at a time. The USIM has some real-time duties to perform even when the terminal appears idle and so these must not be adversely affected by running additional applications.

One of the obvious questions is why would anyone want to run additional applications on the (U)SIM? The answer is not hard to find, especially as the extra functionalities are often referred to as Value Added Services. They provide something that has value to the user, which equates to an extra service offering and revenue generation for the network operator. There are of course many ways to provide a mobile service by exploiting network servers and handset capabilities that are often way beyond those of (U)SIMs, but remember our alternative definition for the SIM; "Secure, In the subscribers hand, Manageable". The (U)SIM has proven itself to

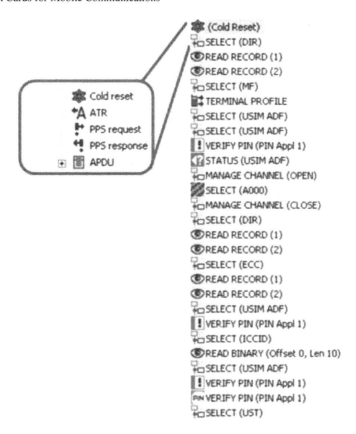

Fig. 4.7 USIM Start up Sequence

be a very well standardised and controllable platform that has provided real value added services across a wide-range of legacy handsets.

4.7 (U)SIM Value Added Services

In Chapter 1 a number of smart card application development and implementation routes were briefly mentioned. In this chapter we will focus on 2 favoured routes that that are relevant to (U)SIM application today i.e. SIM Toolkit and JSR177. Note that application development is considered in more detail within chapter.10.

We will start with SIM Toolkit (now called CAT, Card Application Toolkit) as it is the oldest and most well-proven route to provide value added services to the user. It is actually quite a departure from the original philosophy of the SIM, in that it was a slave to the handset merely satisfying its requests. SIM Toolkit turns the tables and allows the (U)SIM to be "proactive" and take temporary control to request the handset to carry out tasks in accordance with applications stored on the (U)SIM. The set of requests/commands that are standardised for the (U)SIM is quite powerful and summarised in Table. 4.11.

Table 4.11 SIM Toolkit Commands

User Interface	Network Interface	Handset Interface	Misc.
DISPLAY TEXT	SETUP CALL	PROVIDE LOCAL INFORMATION	TERMINAL PROFILE
GET INPUT	SEND SHORT MESSAGE	POLLING INTERVAL	CALL CONTROL
SELECT ITEM	SEND USSD	POLLING OFF	EVENT TRIGGERING
DISPLAY IDLE MODE TEXT	ENVELOPE (SMS-PP DOWNLOAD)	TIMERS	LAUNCH BROWSER
GET INKEY		MORE TIME	BEARER INDEPENDENT PROTOCOL

The most popular SIM Toolkit applications take the form of a simple menu. The user has access to an extra menu that appears to be part of the handset functionality, but is actually fully controlled by the SIM. Text screens are defined via the DISPLAY TEXT commands and the user inputs and menu selections are captured via the GET INPUT and SELECT ITEM commands. An example is shown in Fig. 4.8.

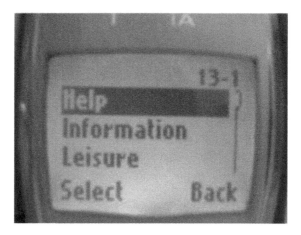

Fig. 4.8 SIM Toolkit Menu Screenshot

Most menus are geared around making a call or sending a message to request information and so they make use of the Network Interface command set. Note that SEND USSD (Unstructured Short Signalling Data) is a fast way to send information that does not need guaranteed delivery and the ENVELOPE command is used for direct server to (U)SIM communications via SMS. The handset can pass some of its operational data to the (U)SIM via the PROVIDE LOCAL INFORMATION command. This is very interesting as the information can include positioning in the form of cell ID and so enable the (U)SIM to offer location based services. How often the (U)SIM can get the handset to carry out a command depends on how often it gets the opportunity. The (U)SIM issues it commands via additional response to every other (U)SIM command. This additional response triggers the handset to fetch the next command. Once the command has been actioned, the handset will send a Terminal Response indicating the outcome of the command and passing any relevant data. The (U)SIM is only allowed to have one command running at a time so the handset will not fetch another command until the last one has been completed. As the (U)SIM has no internal clock or appreciation of elapsed time, the standards provide for timers hosted by the handset and controlled via the (U)SIM, which can be used to trigger an application after a set interval.

Perhaps one of the most powerful SIM Toolkit commands is CALL CONTROL. The principle is that as the handset is about to set-up a call or send an SMS, it first sends it to the (U)SIM card for checking. The (U)SIM can examine the impending communication action and decide based on its own functionality and intelligence whether it is correct and appropriate. The options open to the (U)SIM are enormous. For example, it could simply allow the communications to proceed, it could block the action or modify it. As an example to illustrate the power of this capability, consider a roaming scenario in which an inexperienced UK traveller takes a foreign holiday and tries to use his/her mobile phone. He selects a number from the phone book, but as it lacks the country code, the call fails. The intelligent (U)SIM using CALL CONTROL knows which country it is in (as it is provided by the handset in the CALL CONTROL message) and spots the error and so substitutes the correct international number before placing the call. Event triggering is another way of informing the (U)SIM that something is happening in the handset. It is fast and direct (compared to polling) and allows the (U)SIM to take action. The event could be that the handset has just changed location, or there is an incoming call, or perhaps a call has been dropped.

Bearer Independent Protocol(BIP) is another extremely powerful capability. Normally most (U)SIM based applications use the SMS bearer for communicating with network servers, however with BIP you could setup a much faster GPRS or 3G connection. Equally interesting is the ability to set-up and control local connections e.g. via Bluetooth or Infrared as this then extends the influence and control of the (U)SIM into a whole new area of applications.

Launching a WAP browser may sound a little odd, as historically there has been some competition between the SIM Toolkit/SIM Browsers and WAP. However WAP can provide access to useful services if it is properly configured for the user. Launching the WAP browser from the (U)SIM is a way of ensuring that this will work without requiring the user to manually change local settings and allows an network operator to integrate the two services seamlessly. Furthermore, when a new technology called Smart Card Web Server (SCWS) becomes available, it will likely use this command to start the browser and point back to a URL hosted within the (U)SIM!

Hopefully the foregoing explanation of SIM Toolkit commands has illustrated just how powerful they can be and why (U)SIMs are regarded as the most advanced smart cards is widespread use. However the great disappointment of SIM Toolkit has been the poor and inconsistent support from handsets. This is not the fault of standardisation as the (U)SIM standards are well written and mature, but more due to the decisions of handset vendors to implement the various features. In the early days of GSM one might argue that it was technically difficult to accommodate all the extra functionality, however enough time has passed for this no longer to be the case. One must appreciate that there has always been an uneasy relationship between network operators and handset vendors when it came to the (U)SIM card. The (U)SIM is an embodiment of the network operator's control of security, customers, brand, applications and indeed revenues. The handset vendors on the other hand would like to see their brands more to the fore and more value added applications leveraged and controlled by the handset. The result of this, is that even after many years of stable standards, the most advanced SIM Toolkit features such as CALL CONTROL are not yet widely supported. However as the (U)SIM is required to work reliably in any handset that it is placed in, there is a requirement for the (U)SIM to determine the capabilities of the handset and this is achieved via the TERMINAL PROFILE command. Note that the handset will already be well aware of the (U)SIM capabilities from the (U)SIM Service Table that is read during the normal start-up sequence.

Considering the problems with handset support for advanced SIM Toolkit features one might reasonably question whether SIM Toolkit services have been feasible and successful. The answer is a resounding yes and there have been many business examples that have successfully exploited the core user and network interface commands that are supported on most handsets. SIM Toolkit "Operator Menus" are therefore found on many of the (U)SIMs that are issued today. Much of the value comes from making available services more obvious and easier to use and this has a dramatic effect on their usage. If for example a service can be accessed by manually editing code words and sending SMS messages, then changing this to a SIM Toolkit Menu driven service can increase usage by ten-fold. If the network operator revenue is taken from SMS messages then the revenue from the service can also increase ten-fold. Understandably, companies are rather sensitive about presenting actual service revenue statistics and so Fig. 4.9. is presented as an anonymous example. The graph shows the dramatic improvement in usage of an information service moving from a manual SMS approach to a SIM Toolkit Menu.

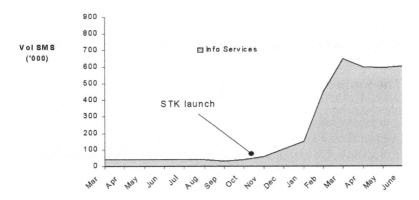

Fig. 4.9   The Effect of SIM Toolkit on the Usage of a SMS Based Information Service

4.8 The (U)SIM as a Handset Security Module

One of the arguments against the SIM Toolkit approach is that modern handsets are more sophisticated and media rich and so the user service experience (& revenues) can be further enhanced by hosting the functionality on the handset and not the (U)SIM. If the capable handsets represent a large proportion of the deployed base and they are consistent, controllable and reliable, then there is some justification for this viewpoint. Sometimes functionality has ended up in the handset simply because the (U)SIM has not had the necessary memory, processing speed and interface speed. These limitations may be challenged by new technology developments (described later), but there are always likely to be applications that are hosted in the handsets. In this scenario the (U)SIM can still be of great value by providing security functionality and information to the handset.

Handsets are very good at providing user interfaces and have powerful data processing and communication capabilities. However, they have a very poor record when it comes to tamper resistant security, whereas (U)SIMs are primarily designed as tamper-resistant security modules. A good marriage of capabilities would therefore be to put much of the application in the handset, but exploit the security algorithms and secure storage capabilities of the (U)SIM. It is also important that the interface is "open" to prevent the introduction of proprietary techniques that ultimately would deter developers from using the (U)SIM capabilities. For this reason the JSR-177 [14] de-facto standard was written. It includes a set of Java methods (classes) that allow Java MIDlets on the handset to call routines on the (U)SIM. The (U)SIM routines can be called by name or by issuing APDUs and a typical use could be for cryptographic functions such as PKI Signing. JSR-177 is not yet well supported by handsets but the fact that it supports a handset application rather than tries to compete with it, may drive future support. It is also attractive from a development point of view because familiar Java tools could be used for both handset midlet and (U)SIM/UICC applet development.

4.9 The Future Evolution of the (U)SIM

Trying to predict the future, especially in the fast moving hi-tech world of mobile communications is a good way to ensure future embarrassment. This is rather like the old prediction that the UK mobile phone market could be as high as one million subscribers, which at the time was derided as a wildly optimistic target. Nevertheless there are some (U)SIM developments that must be mentioned, as they could have a radical effect on the future capabilities of (U)SIMs and how they are used within system solutions. Most of these features were "on-the-horizon" when this book was being planned, however such is the pace of change that a number of them are now in main-stream standardisation.

We will start with something that is relatively straightforward (at least at the (U)SIM). This is the concept of adding a R-UIM [1] to the UICC/(U)SIM. To explain what a R-UIM is, requires a brief history lesson. There were two main camps in the 2G mobile communications world i.e. GSM and IS-95 (CDMAOne) [8]. The former was a driven by European standardisation and used SIM cards, whereas the latter was more USA driven and relied on handset security. There were a lot of technical differences between the technologies and so the opportunity for harmonisation only arrived with the 3G standard development. Unfortunately, for political and commercial reasons, it was not possible to have a single world-wide 3G standard, despite a lot of technical similarities. The result is that in addition to the 3GPP standardisation body there is also a 3GPP2 group [33] looking after CDMA2000 (the successor to CDMAOne). Clearly the multiple standards can present a problem to the roaming user because even if the handset could cope with the various radio interfaces, the user authentication would only work on the home standard. Fortunately CDMA2000 has the possibility of authentication via a Smart Card based application called the R-UIM. As the UICC found in a normal 3G phone is a multi-application platform, it is possible to have USIM, SIM and R-UIM applications present. Therefore at the UICC level a roaming solution appears possible, however it should be noted that the more difficult problems have to be solved at the network signalling level.

The idea of adding additional authentication handlers does not need to stop with the R-UIM. In principal you can authenticate to almost anything and the linkage to the (U)SIM means that you may also have a simple billing solution via the normal mobile phone account. If the applications have a strong linkage to a user's identity (which is not necessarily the case with (U)SIMs) then a whole range of identity management options also present themselves.

One of the most interesting and exciting developments is the support of Near Field Communications (NFC) [17] in mobile phones. In smart card jargon this is a contact-less smart card/RFID interface for handsets. One of the reasons to get excited about this is because it enables the handset to behave as if it is a contact-less smart card. At the time of writing we have a rapidly expanding set of contact-less card services, including passports, health cards, travel tickets and the recent introduction of touch and pay purchasing. Using the phone and (U)SIM instead of a physical card could not only reduce deployment costs and improve convenience but also provide additional capabilities. The (U)SIM is after all a remotely managed platform linked to a billing system that can also be location aware and take advantage of additional communications channels when necessary. It is left to the reader to imagine all the possible new service combinations that could result from these capabilities, however the second reason for getting excited about NFC could leave this in the shade.

There are lots of ideas for smart card based services and the business cases may easily support the deployment of smart cards to the customer base. Where the propositions grind to a halt is in the deployment of the reader infrastructure. Even when free smart card readers are sent to end-users they are very rarely capable or indeed inclined to install and use them correctly. However, if you have an NFC capable mobile phone you are carrying around an advanced reader system with sophisticated user interface, remote communications interface and embedded security module ((U)SIM). Not only does it mean that some smart card service ideas may be resurrected, but the NFC reader handset can interact with all kinds of contact-less devices including e-tickets, bank cards, passports and RFIDs. The opportunities from reading RFIDs are not to be underestimated as they will find themselves in all sorts of everyday objects and products.

For example a stranger arrives in town and sees a poster that says "CINEMA".

- He holds his phone against the poster and reads the embedded RFID.
- The location is known either directly from the RFID identity or the phone positioning and triggers the phone to browse the website of the nearest cinema.
- The user selects a film.
- The user pays, either from his phone account or holds his contact-less payment card against the handset.
- The service provider downloads an e-ticket to the phone (Virtual RFID)
- User is guided to the cinema using mapping software
- At the cinema the user holds his phone against an access gate and as the e-ticket/RFID is valid, is allowed in to watch the film

The possibilities for NFC appear endless, however it is not the only radical and exciting development in the world of smart cards for mobile telephony. The prospect of fast High Density/Capacity (U)SIMs [16] could revolution the way that these devices are used.

When deciding how to partition a system solution across servers, handsets and (U)SIMs, careful consideration is given to the capabilities and limitations of the various elements. Normally you would not tend to use the (U)SIM for bulk data storage or fast real-time processing. Typically the (U)SIMs have been small compared to memory cards and at the time of writing[2] a high-end (U)SIM card has about

---

[2] As of August 2007

128 kilobytes EEPROM storage, whereas a flash memory card is about 2GB. One of the reasons that the (U)SIM has remained small is because the chip size is restricted due to some ISO bend and twist tests, but it is also strongly influenced by cost. One could argue that these are not fundamental reasons for avoiding larger (U)SIM card chips. Firstly the modern (U)SIM is never used as a card as it spends its life in a slot within the handset and so providing the card can be delivered and installed without damage, there is no need for the ISO restriction. Secondly if you need a lot of memory, you have to pay for it somehow, whether it is in the (U)SIM, embedded in the phone or a separate flash card. There may be differing production costs but there is also an element of "who pays?" rather than "how much?". Some things that are stored in mobile devices have little importance, but increasingly there is valuable multi-media such as music files and pictures as well as business, personal and private information. The prospect of storing this information on a security device has some appeal both from a user and content provider perspective. In response to this, some smart card and memory card companies have proposed and indeed demonstrated Gigabyte (U)SIM cards. Increasing the memory alone does not help matters greatly as the conventional ISO 7816 interface between the handset and (U)SIM is far too slow to allow the extra memory to be exploited. Therefore a high speed (USB) [34] interface is also implemented. The combination of large memory and fast I/O really challenges the pre-conceived ideas about what a (U)SIM should or should not be used for. It can also have an impact on data encryption. Conventionally the (U)SIM and its interface is too slow to cipher/decipher real-time data such as digitized audio and so this is performed by the handset using a temporary session key produced by the (U)SIM. However if the interface and the (U)SIM processor is fast enough, the ciphering and deciphering could be performed within the tamper-resistant device. This would probably require more power to be drawn from the handset , but then the handset has to work less hard.

Whether we will actually see the widespread deployment of these high capacity and high performance (U)SIMS will depend on handset support, which is strongly influenced by the general wishes of network operators. If network operators consider only the conventional and restricted role of the (U)SIM card it is unlikely that they would consider paying extra for the high capacity version. On the other hand if some influential operators considered security and service delivery from a more radical and bigger-picture perspective, it might provide justification for these advanced devices.

One radical idea is to put web-servers onto the cards so that all the smart cards become part of an IP network. This is perfectly feasible and has been demonstrated by smart card vendors. Putting an IP stack on the (U)SIM is a natural thing to do as the old ISO 7816 interface was never designed for high performance communications. Indeed the (U)SIM operating systems and file structures would probably also become outmoded and need redesign.

At this point it is probably worth adding a word of caution. The reason that (U)SIMs have been very successful at protecting mobile communications is that they are restricted and highly controlled platforms. Once the (U)SIMs start looking like IP platforms or indeed PCs then they may inherit their security problems. The key to avoiding these problems is to have well defined standards right from the outset. Fortunately the issues are already being dealt with by ETSI and at the time of writing the features shown in Table. 4.12. are being standardised.

Table 4.12 New UICC Features ETSI SCP Rel.7

Feature	Description
High Speed Interface	This adds an 8Mb/s USB channel, based on USB, which will eventually replace the ISO interface. Will have an IP layer.
Contact-less Interface	Allows the UICC to act as a contact-less smart card via the terminal.
Secure UICC - Terminal Interface	Secures the terminal to UICC interface so secure transactions can take place such as DRM.
Smart Card Web Server	Specifies how the SIM card can act as a Web server.

Note that the Secure UICC Terminal Interface is not so much a new service but a security improvement that will make other services more feasible. Although physical access to the UICC to terminal interface is a little tricky, it is not impossible and so one must assume that the protocol transmissions can be eavesdropped. Indeed it is possible to buy powerful test equipment that performs exactly that purpose [2]. For normal (U)SIM interaction this does not matter too much, but for DRM applications it might be a route to discover a content decryption key that could be used to break copyright protection measures. Encrypting the transmissions is a solution to this but may shift the point of attack from the interface to the handset itself.

4.10 Conclusions

Mobile communications has provided one of the great success stories for smart cards both in terms of the sheer numbers used, the rigorous standardisation and the technical sophistication. Authentication, confidentiality and security in general have always been at the heart of the GSM SIM and the enhancements made for the 3G USIM have resulted in an even stronger and more flexible security solution. Whereas the SIM was historically a single application card, the UICC platform concept now allows the SIM, USIM and indeed many other applications to flexibly co-exist on the same card. The (U)SIM has always represented a value added service enabler and there are some very powerful and standardised SIM Toolkit commands. These facilities have been used to great advantage but never to their full potential, as handset support for SIM Toolkit has always lagged behind the standards. The handset developers are perhaps more interested in ways of exploiting (U)SIM functionality within their mobile applications e.g. via JSR177. Exactly how the (U)SIM will interact with the handset and indeed other entities in the long-term future is quite difficult to predict as some radical leaps forward in (U)SIM functionality are proposed.

Adding NFC, a high speed interface, server-on-card and high capacity storage challenge many of the past limitations of (U)SIMs. Aside from rethinking application architectures it may also be necessary to rethink the protocols, file structures and operating systems. As a final remark it is worth noting that despite its success, the (U)SIM is not very card-like and might be better described as a removal security token. Whether it will look the same in future and whether it will remain removable is perhaps less important than ensuring than the tamper-resistant security functionality and service enabling features continue to underpin the integrity and usefulness of mobile communications.

References

1. 3GPP2, Removable User Identity Module (RUIM) for Spread Spectrum Systems, 3GPP2 CS0023-C V1.0 May 2006
2. Comprion, IT3 Move Datasheet, More Information Available via http://www.comprion.com/products_it3move.html, Cited 03 Oct 2007
3. Damien Giry (2007), *Cryptographic Key Length Recommendations*, Keylength.com (with extracts from Ecrypt report 2007) More Information Available via http://www.keylength.com/en/3/, Cited 03 Oct 2007
4. David Wagner and Ian Goldberg (1998), GSM Cloning, ISAAC Berkley More Information Available via http://www.isaac.cs.berkeley.edu/isaac/gsm.html, Cited 03 Oct 2007
5. ETSI SAGE Group (originally), 3G Security; Specification of the MILENAGE algorithm set: An example algorithm set for the 3GPP authentication and key generation functions f1, f1*, f2, f3, f4, f5 and f5*; Document 1: General, 3GPP TS 35.205 More Information Available via http://www.3gpp.org/, Cited 03 Oct 2007
6. ETSI SCP Group , *SCP Specifications*. More Information Available via http://docbox.etsi.org/scp/scp/Specs/, Cited 03 Oct 2007,
7. European Technical Standards Institute (ETSI). More Information Available via http://www.etsi.org/, Cited 03 Oct 2007.
8. Garg V.K, *IS-95 CDMA and cdma 2000*, Prentice Hall 2000.
9. GSM Association, More Information Available via http://www.gsmworld.com/, Cited 03 Oct 2007
10. GSM & UMTS - *The Creation of Global Mobile Communication* - Wiley 2002
11. International Organization for Standardisation, ISO 7816 Parts 1-4, More Information Available via http://www.iso.ch/, Cited 03 Oct 2007
12. International Standards Organisation. More Information Available via http://www.iso.org/, Cited 03 Oct 2007
13. Java Community Process (JCP), More Information Available via http://jcp.org/en/home/index, Cited 03 Oct 2007
14. Java Community Process, JSR177 More Information Available via http://jcp.org/en/jsr/, Cited 03 Oct 2007
15. M. Mouly, M-B Pautet, *The GSM System for Mobile Communications*, Cell & Sys. Correspondence 1992
16. Mayes K and Markantonakis K On the potential of high density smart cards, Elseivier Information Security Technical Report Vol11 No3 2006
17. Near Field Communication (NFC) Forum More Information Available via http://www.nfc-forum.org/, Cited 03 Oct 2007

18. Open Mobile Alliance OMA, More Information Available via
    http://www.openmobilealliance.org/, Cited 03 Oct 2007
19. Security Algorithms Group of Experts (SAGE), More Information Available via
    portal.etsi.org/sage/, Cited 03 Oct 2007
20. The Javacard Forum More Information Available via
    http://www.javacardforum.org/, Cited 03 Oct 2007
21. Third Generation Partnership project (3GPP), More Information Available via
    http://www.3gpp.org/, Cited 03 Oct 2007
22. Third Generation Partnership Project, Digital cellular telecommunications system (Phase 2+);
    Subscriber Identity Modules (SIM);Functional characteristics (GSM 02.17 version 8.0.0 Re-
    lease 1999) More Information Available via
    http://www.3gpp.org/, Cited 03 Oct 2007
23. Third Generation Partnership Project, *Security mechanisms for the SIM application toolkit;
    Stage 2* (Release 1999) TS 03.48 V8.9.0 (2005-06) More Information Available via
    http://www.3gpp.org/, Cited 03 Oct 2007
24. Third Generation Partnership Project, *Security related network functions* (Release 1999) TS
    03.20 V8.5.0 (2007-09) More Information Available via
    http://www.3gpp.org/, Cited 03 Oct 2007
25. Third Generation Partnership Project, *Specification of the Subscriber Identity Module-Mobile
    Equipment (SIM - ME) interface* (Release 1999) TS 11.11 V8.14.0 (2007-06) More Informa-
    tion Available via
    http://www.3gpp.org/, Cited 03 Oct 2007
26. Third Generation Partnership Project, *Specification of the SIM Application Toolkit for the
    Subscriber Identity Module - Mobile Equipment (SIM - ME) interface* (Release 1999) 3GPP
    TS 11.14 V8.18.0 (2007-06) More Information Available via
    http://www.3gpp.org/, Cited 03 Oct 2007
27. Third Generation Partnership Project, *USIM and IC card requirements* (Release 7) TS 21.111
    V8.0.0 (2007-03) More Information Available via
    http://www.3gpp.org/, Cited 03 Oct 2007
28. Third Generation Partnership Project, *UICC-terminal interface; Physical and logical charac-
    teristics* (Release 7) TS 31.101 V7.0.1 (2007-06) More Information Available via
    http://www.3gpp.org/, Cited 03 Oct 2007
29. Third Generation Partnership Project, *Characteristics of the Universal Subscriber Identity
    Module (USIM) application* (Release 7) TS 31.102 V7.10.0 (2007-09) More Information
    Available via
    http://www.3gpp.org/, Cited 03 Oct 2007
30. Third Generation Partnership Project, *Universal Subscriber Identity Module (USIM) Appli-
    cation Toolkit (USAT)* (Release 7) TS 31.111 V7.8.0 (2007-09) More Information Available
    via
    http://www.3gpp.org/, Cited 03 Oct 2007
31. Third Generation Partnership Project, *Security mechanisms for the (U)SIM application
    toolkit; Stage 2* (Release 5) TS 23.048 V5.9.0 (2005-06) More Information Available via
    http://www.3gpp.org/, Cited 03 Oct 2007
32. Third Generation Partnership Project, *3G Security; Security architecture* (Release 7) TS
    33.102 V7.1.0 (2006-12) More Information Available via
    http://www.3gpp.org/, Cited 03 Oct 2007
33. Third Generation Partnership Project 2 (3GPP2) More Information Available via
    http://www.3gpp2.org/, Cited 03 Oct 2007
34. Universal Serial Bus (USB) Forum, More Information Available via
    http://www.usb.org/, Cited 03 Oct 2007
35. Vodafone, *SIM/USIM Cards Applications & Security for Mobile Telephony*, Masters Lecture
    Slides at Royal Holloway University of London 2006.

Chapter 5
Smart cards for Banking and Finance

Konstantinos Markantonakis and Keith Mayes

Abstract The banking industry enjoyed the benefits of magnetic stripe card technology for a long time. However, over the last decade, fraud levels were on the increase and the magnetic stripe card technology, at least for the banking sector, appeared to have reached the end of its life time. The major credit card scheme operators realised that they had to act and introduce a new card medium that would be in a position to better safeguard their interests. This resulted in the Europay-MasterCard-Visa (EMV) specifications. This chapter looks into the EMV specifications along with other initiatives that aim to offer additional security in e-commerce and enhanced smart card based authentication, necessary for Cardholder Not Present transactions.

Key words: Payment Cards, Magnetic Stripe Cards, EMV, Chip, PIN, Dynamic Passcode, CNP, 3D Secure, E-commerce, Token Authentication

5.1 Introduction

History reveals that ancient Greece was amongst the first nations that started to use more complex banking structures. They were accepting deposits and offering loans that could be exchanged for gold or other valuables; these exchanges were taking place between various merchants at different cities other than those of their origin. This provided customers and merchants with the mechanisms that would improve mobility. Similarly, Romans had an extremely well developed monetary

Konstantinos Markantonakis, Lecturer,
Information Security Group Smart Card Centre,
Royal Holloway University of London,
e-mail: k.markantonakis@rhul.ac.uk
Keith Mayes, Director of the ISG Smart Card Centre,
Royal Holloway University of London,
e-mail: keith.mayes@rhul.ac.uk

society which was relying on a relatively well developed banking system. This system allowed individuals and credit offering institutions to keep detailed records of financial transactions and charge interest on loans and deposits.

Since then, financial institutions have evolved significantly, became regulated and played an important role in our societies by lending and borrowing money to/from individuals and organisations. It was around the 17th century that paper based currency was introduced. Shortly afterwards, the concept of credit through paper cheques and "money-orders" also came into existence.

The banking industry is constantly investigating new, more convenient and secure ways for allowing the ever growing customer demand for convenience and flexibility. As a result, during the 1950s in the USA, the concept of credit cards received enormous attention and growth.

This book chapter is organised into the following subsections. Section 5.2 provides an introduction to the concept of payment cards, including magnetic stripe cards. Section 5.3 introduces smart card technology and the EMV standards. Section 5.4 introduces various issues around electronic commerce and, in particular, 3-D Secure and Token Authentication. Finally, some concluding remarks are presented in section 5.5.

5.2 Payment Card Technologies

In 1951, the "Franklin National Bank became the first bank to issue credit cards to customers of rival banks" [21]. The first credit card is often attributed to have been developed 50 years ago by an American called Frank McNamara. He came with the idea of issuing credit cards to the Diners Club (for their VIP members) as a symbol of identity and status. The card could be used in a small number of restaurants and hotels, as alternative means of payment for cash. The cardholders were charged an annual fee and they were billed monthly for any purchases [21].

The term "payment card" is linked with different types of card products (e.g. debit, credit), but they have a common denominator; that all these products are linked with the cardholder through bank accounts and/or detailed transaction records. It is estimated that today there are "nearly 2 billion cards used in some 30 million merchant locations" [6].

A typical credit card payment scheme involves four entities; the Client, the Merchant, the Acquiring bank (merchants' bank) and Issuing bank (credit card Issuer). A typical credit/debit card infrastructure is presented in Fig.5.1 below.

Assume that a customer (Client) wants to pay, using his credit/debit card issued by the card Issuing Bank, for some goods offered by a merchant. Therefore, the customer has a relationship with his card Issuing Bank. The merchants must also have a relationship with an Acquirer Bank, in order to be able to accept card transactions. The large financial institutions (e.g. Visa and MasterCard) do not issue cards, but they support the Acquirer bank and the Issuing bank to achieve transaction clearing and settlement. Therefore, these financial institutions offer the building blocks

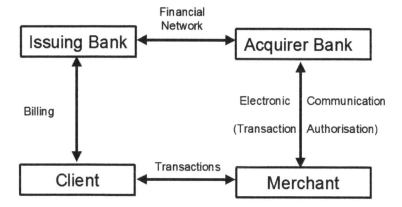

Fig. 5.1 Typical Credit/Debit Card Infrastructure.

to facilitate both contractually and technically the relationship between the entities participating in the transaction. This is achieved mainly through powerful computer networks, rules of operation and support for their member banks.

One feature of the early payment cards, which still remains operational today, is that they contained embossed information (e.g. customer, account and bank details) at the front of the card. A customer, that wanted to pay for services or goods, would hand in his card to the retail assistant. The retail assistant would have to use the so-called "zip-zap" swipe machine, in order to obtain a paper record of the transaction, amount and the customer's signature for authorisation. The cardholder would keep a copy of the record and the merchant would have to manually supply a copy of this record to his Acquirer Bank, in order to receive payment. In case the transaction was done smoothly, a record would be created in the customer's account and the card Issuing Bank would have to eventually obtain the money from the customer.

Although this system was used for many years, it had a major disadvantage. The cardholder authentication method was relying heavily upon the sales assistants checking the customer's signature. In case the transaction involved a large amount, or the merchant was suspicious about the card or the cardholder, he needed to call his clearing institution, in order to obtain further authorisation. However, this system left enormous gaps for fraud. It is worth noting that it may still be used in various countries, especially by merchants that do not have high numbers of transactions or the cost of obtaining extra authorisations maybe high.

5.2.1 Magnetic Stripe Cards

Among the most notable additions to the original plastic cards was the introduction of a magnetic stripe at the back of the cards, in order to allow merchant terminals to electronically read the cards.

The introduction of the magnetic stripe allowed the point-of-sale terminals to be able to read the information (at the back of the card) electronically. Some terminals could also connect (often via a normal telephone line) to the corresponding clearing (or Acquirer) bank and submit all the card transactions. This introduced significant savings (in the transaction settlement process) over the manual submission of credit card slips.

Since the terminals had the capability to connect to their Acquirer banks for settlements purposes, they could also connect in order to obtain an additional authorisation for individual transactions. For example, a terminal could decide to go on-line depending on the transaction type, the value, or other specific transaction details.

The introduction of magnetic stripe cards was also accompanied by the introduction of the Personal Identification Number (PIN). The PIN (typically 4 digits) was mainly used in the Automated Teller Machines (ATMs), in order to ensure that a transaction was authorised based on something the cardholder owned (i.e. a valid card) and something "secret" that only he knew about (i.e. the PIN).

However, as technology evolved and information along with cards and magnetic stripe card reading/writing devices became more widely available, the levels of counterfeit fraud increased substantially. This was possible, as the data in the magnetic stripe of the card was not highly protected. Therefore, it was relatively easy for a criminal to obtain a valid card, copy the magnetic stripe data and, subsequently, write the information in another legitimate looking card. Even easier a criminal could simply obtain card information from receipts or statements and embed them in legitimate-looking cards.

5.2.1.1 Magnetic Stripe Card Security

In an attempt to avoid the aforementioned types of fraud, the credit card industry (e.g. Visa and MasterCard) introduced some protection mechanisms. The PIN number, when included in the Authorisation Messages, was cryptographically protected. Additionally, the data included in the magnetic stripe of the card was followed by a cryptographically generated check value. This check value was generated by the card Issuer and the main aim behind it, was to make it more difficult for criminals to create valid magnetic stripe information from details copied from paper receipts.

When the card was used in an ATM, the PIN number had to travel to the Issuing bank, in order to be verified. In this case, as mentioned above, the PIN is cryptographically protected. However, if the same key is used during all PIN transmissions, and the messages are intercepted, it will then be possible to launch a dictionary attack that will match the encrypted PIN messages to unencrypted PINs.

This is a well-known issue within cryptography and it can be avoided by adding some extra information to the message that will be encrypted. In our case, the PIN is XORed with the unique Primary Account Number (PAN), some padding is added in order to bring the message to the appropriate length, before it is encrypted. This ensures that different cards that have the same PIN will result in different encrypted PIN messages.

The PIN protection and transmission process between the Issuer and the Acquirer is summarised in the following paragraphs. The PIN is formatted into a PIN block and it is encrypted using the unique ATM symmetric algorithm key (e.g. DES or triple DES). Subsequently, it is appended in an authorisation request message send to the Acquirer (with which the ATM is connected and maintained). Upon receiving the message, the Acquirer will decrypt it and, subsequently, format a new message and encrypt it with the Acquirer Working Key (AWK) which is shared between the Acquirer and the financial institution (e.g. Visa or MasterCard). The encrypted message is then forwarded to the financial institution. Upon receiving the message, the financial institution will decrypt it, and, if everything is fine, it will encrypt it with the Issuer Working Key (IWK). The encrypted message is forwarded to the card Issuer for decryption and further processing. The Issuers and Acquirers can update their financial institution working keys by using Zone Control Master Keys (ZCMKs, which are not changing frequently) that are exchanged between the participating entities. The above procedure is summarised in Fig.5.2.

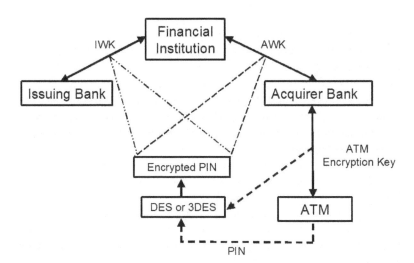

Fig. 5.2 PIN Encryption and Cryptographic Key Relationship

5.3 Smart Cards and EMV

The banking industry realised that it needed to provide a better alternative to the magnetic stripe cards that were resulting in unacceptably high fraud levels. It became evident that individual patches were contributing towards reduced fraud levels, but only for a relatively short period of time. This was mainly due to the underlying card medium (i.e. magnetic stripe) rather than the communications infrastructures.

It was around 1990 that the obvious type of technology for migrating the relatively out of date (at least for the financial industry) magnetic stripe cards, was chip cards or smart cards. Smart cards became widely known in the UK through payphone cards introduced by British Telecomm during the mid 1990s. The relative tamper resistance, accompanied with recent advances in cryptographic algorithms and improvements in performance and memory sizes, led to the conclusion that smart cards would be the natural succesor to the magnetic stripe.

As soon as the smart card was identified as the carrying medium, the actual processes and applications were realised in the form of the Europay-Mastercard-Visa (EMV) standards [5]. The EMV standards were developed, as their name suggests, by Europay, MasterCard and Visa and cover a wide range of card characteristics, including the exact behaviour of the smart card application responsible for realising payments.

Among the main aims of the EMV specifications is to overcome some of the disadvantages of the magnetic stripe card technology and, at the same time, to offer a more secure and reliable carrying medium for payment applications. Due to the nature of the smart card microprocessor, the actual payment application can take decisions based on risk management policies. Equally important is to authorise transactions off-line and, therefore, to provide significant reductions in telecommunications and processing costs.

EMV draws its baseline security from the underlying security functionality and tamper-resistance of the actual smart card microprocessors. The smart card allows the storage of cryptographic keys and other sensitive information within the card, which was not possible with the previous carrying mediums. In summary, EMV offers the following enhanced functionality:

- Terminal/Card Risk Management
- Offline PIN Management
- Online Transaction Processing
- Authentication of Card Resident Data

The main EMV processes, relating to authentication, are described in the following sections.

5.3.1 Card Authentication

Card authentication involves the terminal performing certain checks to identify whether the card has been changed, in an unauthorised way, since it was issued. When the smart card is inserted in the card terminal, the two entities begin a dialogue, in order to identify whether the current transaction needs to go on-line or not. The decision is based on a number of parameters such as the cost of the transaction, the number of off-line transactions etc. The EMV specifications defined three main card authentication methods, summarised in the following subsections.

5.3.1.1 Static Data Authentication (SDA)

The whole process of SDA is based on the existence of a certification authority (e.g. Visa, MasterCard, etc.) often referred to as the scheme operator. The Issuer creates a Public and Private Key pair. The scheme operator maintains a highly secure cryptographic facility and creates its own Private and Public key pair. The scheme operator, using the scheme's Private Key, certifies the Issuer's Public Key (placed in the EMV card). It is worth noting that corresponding scheme's Public Key is placed in every EMV card terminal. Subsequently, the Issuer signs certain card resident data using its Private Key and places the resulting signature in the card (during the personalisation phase). In the case when an EMV card is presented in a terminal

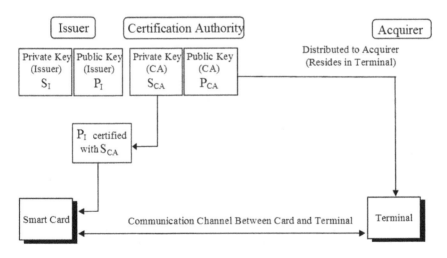

Fig. 5.3 Static Data Authentication

and SDA is selected, then the terminal retrieves the schemes public key in order to verify the Issuers public key. Subsequently, it uses the Issuer's Public Key, in order to verify the Issuer's signature on card resident data. If the process is completed without any problems, the terminal obtains the necessary reassurance that the card data have not been modified during the card's lifetime. This process is described in Fig.5.3

5.3.1.2 Dynamic Data Authentication (DDA)

The Dynamic Data Authentication (DDA) process is summarised in Fig.5.4. If we suppose that an EMV smart card is presented in a smart card terminal, this smart card along with the Issuer and the scheme operator all have their own unique pairs of Private and Public keys. The data verification process begins with the terminal

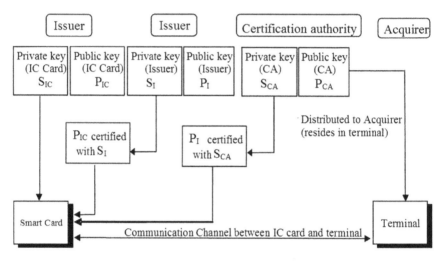

Fig. 5.4 Dynamic Data Authentication

having access to the scheme's Public Key. This key is used in order to verify the Issuer Public Key (contained within the Issuer Public Key Certificate and stored within the card). Following on from that, the terminal verifies the card's Public Key by using the Issuer Public Key (which was in turn verified in the above step). During this stage the terminal challenges the card and requests the card to sign some data. At this stage, the terminal uses the card's verified Public Key, in order to confirm that the signed card data originated from a legitimate card.

5.3.1.3 Combined Data Authentication (CDA)

A further enhancement in data authentication is the combined data authentication (CDA). CDA combines a dynamic signature and an application cryptogram. The main difference between CDA and DDA is that part of the data that will be signed by the smart card also includes an Application Request Cryptogram (ARQC) and the random number provided by the terminal.

5.3.1.4 Off-line PIN Check

There are two main variants of off-line PIN checking. The simple version requires that the PIN is transmitted (with the *VERIFY* command) in clear from the terminal to the smart cards, for verification. There is also the option of encrypting, using the cards Public Key, the PIN and subsequently, sending it to the card through the *VERIFY* command. The card will then use its Private Key, in order to decrypt the message and verify the PIN.

5.3.1.5 Card/Issuer Authentication

Card authentication takes place in an on-line terminal and aims to prove to the Issuer that the card contains a key that is valid and genuine for that particular card. The whole process requires the terminal requesting from the card an Application Cryptogram (AC).

One form of an application Cryptogram can be the Authorisation Request Cryptogram (ARQC) which is requested from the card by the terminal. Along with the request, the terminal also sends a challenge to the card. If the card decides to proceed on-line, it uses the symmetric key that is shared with the Issuer and appends a Message Authentication Code (MAC) to the minimum set of data presented in Table 5.1. The ARQC message is forwarded to the terminal which in turn forwards it to the Issuer.

Table 5.1 Typical Values Supported Within the ARQC

Value	Source
Amount, Authorised (Numeric)	Terminal
Amount Other (Numeric)	Terminal
Terminal Country Code	Terminal
Terminal Verification Results	Terminal
Transaction Currency Code	Terminal
Transaction Date	Terminal
Transaction Type	Terminal
Unpredictable Number	Terminal
Application Interchange Profile	smart card
Application Transaction Counter (ATC)	smart card

The Issuer uses the shared key, in order to verify the ARQC. Subsequently, it informs the terminal whether the transaction is authorised or not. The latter will depend on the successful verification of the ARQC, whether the card account has enough funds and other typical checks (e.g. the card is not reported stolen). By including the data presented in Table 5.1, within the AC (MACed by the card), the Issuer can confirm that the data has not changed in transit and, more importantly, authorise the transaction at the same time as authenticating the card.

The Application Transaction Counter (ATC) is maintained within the card and it is incremented every time a transaction is taking place. Since the ATC is different for every transaction the resulting cryptogram will also be different. The main aim of the ATC is to avoid reply attacks. For example, if the Issuer receives an ARQC and all the data (including the ATC) are the same (as a previously received ARQC), it can safely assume that the transaction is replayed (presented twice).

The Authorisation Response Cryptogram (ARPC) may be sent in the authorisation response by the Issuer to the card via the terminal. The ARPC is a triple-DES MAC applied to the 8-byte ARQC generated by the smart card, the 2-byte (padded accordingly to achieve 8-bytes) Authorisation Response Code ARC (typical values appear in Table 5.2), by using the 16-byte Application Cryptogram Session Keys.

Table 5.2 Typical Values Supported Within the ARC

Typical ARC Indicators
Online approved
Online declined
Referral (initiated by Issuer)
Capture card

When the card receives the ARPC, and it is verified correctly, it is able to verify that it is a response to its message and that it comes from the Issuer. The ARPC is linked with the ARQC (and the ATC), therefore, any attempts to manipulate the card by replaying already issued ARPC commands will fail.

5.3.1.6 Transaction Certificate

The other form of the AC is the Transaction Certificate (TC) which indicates whether a transaction was approved or not. The TC also provides additional information about a transaction along with evidence that a particular card was present during a transaction. All this information will be particularly helpful in case of a dispute.

The whole process is accomplished by requesting the card to generate a DES cryptogram on certain transaction data (e.g. whether the terminal performed SDA or DDA, ARQC, was an on-line authorisation, etc.). This information is provided by the card to the Issuer via the terminal.

5.3.1.7 EMV in Practice

Migrating from magnetic stripe cards to smart card technology is not trivial. As soon as the banks began to come to terms with all the issues involved they also began to seek assistance from the scheme operators. The scheme operators are responsible for providing their member banks with all the necessary guidelines for a proper EMV implementation. In certain cases this includes assisting them in realising the financial benefits from fraud reduction, and the successful creation of a robust business case. In some regions the scheme operators also provided chip incentive plans. For example, offering to cover part of the cost of every chip card that will replace a magnetic stripe card.

It should be mentioned that until 2001 the majority of issued EMV cards were supporting SDA. DDA was available, but the cost of the card was relatively prohibitive. The Issuers also had to take into account the overall cost of the required changes in the terminals, mainly in the form of new applications and the communications link with the Acquirer. Therefore, it was decided that SDA would be used as an entry point. As soon as the necessary experience was gained and telecommunication and card (supporting Public Key cryptography) costs were reduced, alternative options could be adopted.

Among the forerunners for the adoption of smart card technology and EMV was France. The rest of the European countries were a bit reluctant to bear the cost of migrating to chip, although fraud at a national level was on the increase.

The decision to migrate to chip was assisted further by the national banking associations putting forward certain mandates and incentives for migrating to chip. These chip incentive programs and the liability shift were among the driving forces. For example, the 2005 liability shift in the UK stated that, in case something goes wrong in a transaction, the cost will be taken by the party (i.e. Issuer, Acquirer or merchant) that does not have the capability to process an EMV transaction.

Irrespectively of all the above initiatives and mandates, it appears that the main driving force behind chip migration is fraud. Therefore, it remains to be seen whether the fraud levels will drop to such a level that will justify the investment.

5.4 Cardholder Not Present Transactions

If we cast our minds back just a few years ago then our perception of banks, banking and financial transactions was quite different to what it is today. Banks were in the high street, in real buildings, with real people and generally inspired some awe, but also confidence. It is doubtful that anyone stepping through the front door would have questioned whether he was entering a genuine branch, or that deposited funds where kept in any other form than cash or bullion, locked in an impressive looking vault. Similarly, when spending our hard-earned cash, we would wander into a real shop and walk away with a bag of physical items. For the customer, the distinction and level of risk between buying from a brand name store and a shady looking market trader was clear to see. Similarly the merchant had some clues to the authenticity of the customer and his presented credentials, because the "Cardholder was Present". Fast forward back today and there is a much greater proportion of transactions when the "Cardholder is Not Present" (CNP). One immediately thinks of the Internet as the driving force for this, but we have in fact being generating CNP transactions for a long time by purchasing items over the telephone. One might expect that in an age of smart cards and even smarter and smarter technology, that the CNP problem is reducing, but alas, technology has made CNP transactions an even more attractive target for criminals. One reason for this, is that EMV [4] Chip & PIN has tightened the security around normal cardholder present transactions and so criminals are switching to the softer target of CNP for telephone sales and of course internet purchases. In CNP not only is the entire chip solution bypassed, but so too is the relatively week electronic security of the magnetic-stripe and indeed even the customer signature. As a starting point, let us consider some of the ways in which this can be exploited.

5.4.1 Purchase from a Genuine Merchant Using Someone Else's Payment Details

In the first instance let us assume that we have found an old-style purchase receipt, made using the victim's card. The receipt was in the rubbish bin outside the victim's home - so we also know where he lives. If we can determine the card number, name, and expiry date, we could try and order something over the telephone or via the Internet. One of the initial barriers to this was that purchased goods could only be delivered to the same address as the card was registered to, but this has been relaxed and many valuable items today are not physical e.g. software, e-books and music downloads. To improve the situation most receipts no longer include the full card number and a merchant may challenge the purchaser to state the Cardholder Verification Value (CVV2) [18], a three digit code printed on the back of the payment card. These measures may make it less attractive to search through dustbins for receipts, however the measures can be undermined by anyone who has seen the physical card just once. Considering how many times and in how many places, a payment card is presented, the opportunity to make a note of the details or just take a quick photo with a phone camera, is hardly limited.

5.4.2 Genuine Purchaser Buying from a Rogue Merchant

It seems that we are buying more and things on-line or via the telephone, but how do we know we are dealing with genuine merchants? The transaction has to start with a telephone number or a website address and so the question is how the purchaser obtained it. If it is trusted information (used before) or closely linked to another trusted source (e.g. obtained from your bank) then there is less likely to be a problem, however we are often first time buyers following on from a directory or Internet search. The contact information may have come from a quality publication and so some confidence can be taken from the publisher's policing of advertisers and indeed the significant expense involved in placing the advertisements. Information from the Internet is less certain and although some sites have certificates that may be checked, very few customers are sufficiently knowledgeable to do this. Whatever safeguards we take and however careful we are selecting merchants, there comes a point when we hand over our details including name, address, card owner, card number, expiry date and indeed the CVV2. If we click on the save details box then this information is stored on the merchant's database and if we buy from many merchants the details end up on many databases. With so many merchants in the fast moving competitive world of Internet and telephone sales, it is perhaps naïve to expect them all to have perfect processes for the management of stored transaction data. It only takes one rogue merchant or employee to use/sell our customer details for fraudulent purposes [2].

5.4.3 Third Party Attacker

A third party attacker or hacker may seek to discover the transaction information. Whilst bribing a merchant's employee might be the most effective method, we will focus on the more technical possibilities. For a telephone purchase, anyone within earshot can learn your transaction details, however the criminal is unlikely to rely on such a lucky break. The odds can be tipped in the criminals favour in locations where lots of telephone transactions take place e.g. at airport payphones when new arrivals book hotels, hire cars etc. It is possible to physically tap a conventional telephone line, but this is a lot of trouble for an attacker and to make it worthwhile he would need to tap into a point of concentration e.g. a telephone switch or perhaps an Integrated Voice Recognition (IVR) system used for transactions. Increasingly, with the popularity of cheap IP telephony our voice calls are handled just like any other IP traffic that it trusted to the mercies of the Internet. The Internet hacker could try and grab IP data in transit, but this may still be too much trouble and so customers are encouraged to send the information direct to the attacker. This may sound like an odd thing to do, but that is what "Phishing" [2] is all about. For example, a customer receives a genuine looking email suggesting that he re-submits his payment details to his "bank", as part of a routine check. Of course there is no bank except for one safeguarding the ill-gotten gains of the criminal. Phishing is a major problem and it can be combined with attacks against the customer's Personal Computer (PC). If the customer clicks on an attachment to a fraudulent email, it may install unpleasant software known as "malware" [13] onto the computer. The malware could capture keystrokes and screen information for reporting to the criminals. Merchant servers also come under attack and although better defended than PCs, the attackers only have to win occasionally to capture sensitive transactional data on a great many customers. For an individual customer this would be very distressing, but it could well bring about the end of the merchant, because of the bad publicity, compensation claims and loss of customer confidence.

It would seem from the foregoing examples that some paranoia over one's card and transactional details is quite justified for CNP transactions, however the situation may be even worse than that. The information that is sneaked, copied or stolen might be used to make counterfeit cards for cardholder present transactions in countries that do not yet use Chip & PIN.

Clearly the CNP transactions fall way short of the security that we are becoming accustomed to with Chip & PIN and so the search is on to find a way to improve the situation. An obvious strategy is to try and use our EMV enabled payment cards to try and secure CNP transactions and one such approach uses "dynamic passcode authentication"

5.5 Dynamic Passcode Authentication

There are many authentication and transactional systems that make use of static passcodes, for example, a log-on password could be regarded as a static code. The major problem with this, is that once discovered, a static code can offer no further security. Furthermore, if the code has to be memorised by a user it tends to limit its length and complexity and most likely a dictionary attack [16] would identify the code in far fewer attempts than the code length would theoretically imply. One approach is to make the code dynamic so that once discovered it quickly loses its value, however humans are not great at remembering codes, especially if they have to change them regularly. If IT Security managers had their way then passcodes might be changed on every transaction, whereas users would never want to change them. A working compromise for a single system log-on might be a monthly change, which is still a huge window of opportunity for a hacker. If we remember that there are many systems and merchant sites that a user may need to log into with different credentials then the human-reliant dynamic passcode approach is a non-starter. We therefore need some computing technology to help us and if Chip & PIN works for cardholder present transactions then why not for CNP too?

The first problem when seeking to exploit our EMV cards in say an Internet access application is that the card obviously has no user-interface, so we need to insert it in something that does. A PC is a prime candidate, however not many of them have in-built smart card readers. As readers today can cost less than eight Euros [22] one solution is to simply issue them to customers, but unfortunately, such attempts often meet with limited success, as customers either have limited IT skills to install the readers correctly, or they simply cannot be bothered to do it. Another solution, which is being given serious consideration by banks, is to issue a small standalone reader device that is relatively easy for the customer to use. The use of the reader plus the EMV card and user PIN, goes under various names including Dynamic Passcode Authentication [19], Chip Authentication Programme (CAP) [10] or simply Token Authentication. In classical security terms it is known as a two-factor [8] security solution i.e. something you have (the card) and something you know (the four digit PIN).

If we are to expect the customer to carry the reader around with him then it needs to be quite small and in fact not much bigger than the EMV card. An example of a typical device is shown in Fig.5.5. Using the Token Reader is a little more trouble

Fig. 5.5   Token Reader

for the user than a normal Chip & PIN transaction as there is no computer interface. More precisely it has no electronic interface, because there are still information flows to and from the card, but it is up to the user to enter them on the reader keypad and computer keyboard when prompted. The positive aspect of this is that the reader, as an off-line device, will not be subjected to the normal range of Internet hacking attempts e.g. spyware, malware etc. As far as the user in concerned the method of use is as shown in Fig.5.6

As a means to enhance the security of the authentication it is possible for a website to also present an initial challenge that they user can key into the reader as input to the cryptogram generation. However this is more inconvenience for the user and we must not lose sight of the fact that we are offering a solution that fits with user behaviour and capabilities e.g. patience, memory, typing errors etc.

The use of the token reader and the user typing in passcodes may not seem very novel and indeed similar looking systems such as the Racal Guardata "Watchword" [15] have been around since at least 1992 - albeit without a separate card. Most systems to-date have been proprietary in nature which tends to ultimately limit their roll-out and compatibility with other systems. The advantage of taking the EMV approach is that in countries like the UK, banks have already issued such cards to their customers. The usage of Chip & PIN is now embedded in the mentality of EMV users so perhaps it is not too much of a leap to get them to operate the reader device and type passcodes at the PC. This is of course ignoring the obvious problem that the token readers have to find their way into customer hands. On the plus

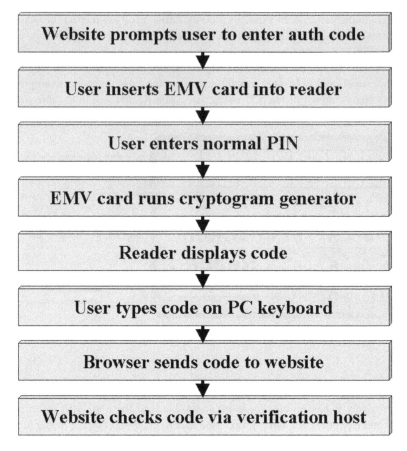

Fig. 5.6 Using Dynamic Passcode Authentication

side the readers are not doing anything particularly clever because the cryptographic generation is performed within the tamper-resistant EMV card, however deploying anything at all to millions of customers is a major challenge. There is also the issue of where customers would want to use these devices. If it is always in one place then a fixed location reader is fine, but more than likely, users will need to authenticate themselves in several locations. Some users might carry the readers around with them if they are small and lightweight, but others probably would not want to. It is worth noting at this point that the reader is not usually a user-personalised device, which means that you could own or borrow multiple reader devices. Borrowing a reader could potentially expose a user to some risk as there may be no proof that it is a legitimate device and whilst this may not result in any violation of the passcode approach, the reader could be used to capture and store sensitive data such as the user PIN. This may be of added interest as the PIN used for passcode authentication is probably the same as for normal EMV transactions, in order to avoid confusion to the user. Sharing PINs across applications is one of several concessions and simplifications to make the solution practical and convenient for the user.

The card itself is not necessarily much different to an EMV card designed without token authentication in mind. There is some added personalisation data and key management to take care of, but nothing major. This also means that the host systems that normally handle EMV transactions can cope with token authentication, with only minor functional modifications. The fact that there is any difference at all is to reduce the amount of data going into the cryptogram generator, which needs to be carried by the card and also the number of digits in the response that the user will have to type at the PC. The way that the cryptogram is reduced to make it practical for the user, makes use of a bit filter that is implemented within the token reader and which is proprietary to the Issuer. This is shown in the example of Fig.5.7.

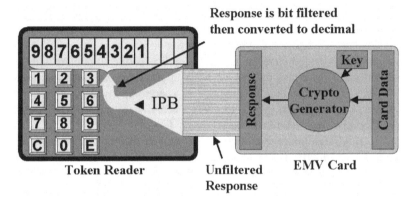

Fig. 5.7 Passcode Generation

The Issuer Proprietary Bitmap (IPB) is used to filter the data generated by the card in response to the Generate Application Cryptogram command. It has as many bits as there are in the response and each bit acts as a simple switch e.g. if the IPB bit is set to logic '1' then the response bit is retained in the output. As most users aren't likely to be too impressed by binary output, there is a binary to decimal mapping prior to display. Typically the passcode is eight or nine decimal digits long.

5.6 Could a Mobile Phone be a Token Reader?

Considering the examples shown above, one might be tempted to think that perhaps the mobile phone could be used to replace both the token reader and the EMV card. After all, a mobile phone has a display and keyboard and hosts a sophisticated smart card in the form of a SIM or USIM (see chapter 1). It also has the advantage that almost everyone has one and whilst we may forget our keys, coats and umbrellas, we rarely leave home without our mobile phones. So it seems as if we have a ubiquitous, portable device with all the functional capabilities that we require. That is, until we start thinking about the security and logistics of the solution. The smart card within a mobile is quite sophisticated and increasingly based on multi-application Java Cards and so ignoring any cross-industry politics, it could in theory host the EMV application. However EMV cards undergo very formalised security evaluation e.g. common criteria to EAL5+ (see chapter 8), whereas telecommunications cards do not. This would be a show-stopper for many financial organisations. Other potential issues are that SIMS/USIMs ((U)SIM) don't universally have crypto-coprocessors and they do not have expiry dates. The latter is interesting as it is a mandatory field for Internet purchases and it also means that it can take a very long time to roll out new (U)SIM card capabilities across a large proportion of the customer base. There is however some encouragement on the horizon as the introduction of Near Field Communication (NFC) [3] technology will allow mobiles to interact with external contactless smart cards. So if we have a contactless version of our EMV card, the phone is then rather like our token reader. The big difference is that mobile phones are connected devices and increasingly are becoming mobile computers with Internet connections. This means that all the nasty attacks, malware and spyware that beset our PCs may be heading for the phones. Therefore, when we enter our PIN code via the phone keyboard, who is to say if it is really secure? Looking to the future, the PIN code may not always be necessary for some transactions (see section 5.9) and so if we can improve mobile phone security, perhaps through the introduction of Trusted Platform Modules (see chapter 7) then a whole host of mobile transaction services may be possible. Indeed if we have sufficient confidence in the mobile phone itself we can use it as a combined passcode generator. Mastercard already has a mobile authentication solution [10] that implements a passcode generator on some Java Mobile (J2ME) enabled mobile phones and Personal Digital Assistants (PDAs).

5.7 Token Authentication Examples

Just having an EMV card and a token reader does not automatically mean that we have improved the security of CNP transactions, it really depends how these resources are integrated within the system solution. Because of the phishing problems, one of the main drivers for token authentication has been for securing user access to remote banking facilities.

The log-on procedure to e-bank accounts varies considerably depending on the bank in question. Some require a simple username, static password and the answer to a pre-registered personal question. Others require entering a long account code, a passcode and randomly selected characters form a pre-stored pass phrase. The former is reasonably convenient for the user, but presents a relatively easy target for a phishing attack. The latter appears to offer more security, but is more difficult for the customer to remember and use. When security processes are difficult for users they tend to write the security information on slips of paper or store it in their phones and PDAs, creating indirect risks to their account security [7]. None of the log-in processes are ideal and so any technology that can improve security without further annoying or confusing the user is highly desirable. Token authentication could therefore be very helpful as it offers two-factor authentication without the user risking his long-term secret code (PIN) on a connected and untrusted PC or terminal platform. The process would be similar to that shown in Fig.5.6. Prior to the website challenge, the user would probably still have to enter the account information, but he may be saved the static password and pass phrase interrogation.

Not all users are able and willing to access their bank accounts via the Internet and so telephone banking is still an important service. Fortunately, the token authentication can also help here, by providing (via the phone keypad) the service operator with a passcode instead of a static password.

5.8 E-Commerce Solutions

E-banking and telephone banking are vital services to protect, but one would imagine that banks with their resources and security know-how will eventually get this under control. However, the really big issue is how to control Internet transactions in general. A workable solution is needed that satisfies the needs of the banks and merchants, whilst being practical and safe for customers to use. One example of this is called "3D-Secure" that is known under various brand names such as "Verified by Visa" [20] and "MasterCard SecureCode" [11]. It is not necessarily dependent on a chip card or the token authentication method, but as it is a process that delays a transaction and inconveniences the customer (albeit for good security reasons), combination with token authentication helps to restore convenience as well as improve security.

5.8.1 3D-Secure

The 3D Secure solution breaks up the Internet transaction into a number of conceptual domains. There are in fact three domains such that each entity or supporting system sits within one or more domains. The interrelation of the domains is shown graphically in Fig.5.8

Within the Issuer Domain (ISD) we see that the Issuer has the relationship with the cardholder. This implies that previously a cardholder registration process has been completed and so the Issuer is well placed to authenticate the cardholder by manual means, but also by the electronic server means (logically contained within the domain) necessary for e-commerce. The ISD contains the Access Control Server (ACS) that fulfils this purpose. The Acquirer Domain (AQD) contains the merchant and the linkage/systems of the acquiring bank. Again this implies a pre-registration procedure such that the Acquirer is well placed to authenticate the merchant via electronic server means. So that the merchant's servers can communicate with the Acquirer server during automated transactions, it is necessary to add the Merchant Server Plug-in (MPI). This leaves the Interoperability Domain (IND) which is basically the "plumbing" used to connect the Issuer and Acquirer Domains (& hence the cardholder and merchant) together, for the purpose of secured e-commerce transactions. One of the responsibilities of the IND is to host a Directory Server (DS) so that it can determine which Issuer server to query when a particular card is involved in a transaction. The directory is effectively a mapping of participating/registered cards to the appropriate ACS server address. Another responsibility of the IND is to maintain a log of authentication history for the purposes of dispute resolution and this is achieved by means of the Authentication History Server (AHS). Although not shown in Fig. 5.8 there is an implied and secure communications link between the Issuer and Acquirer under the particular card scheme. The detailed connections between the server equipment is beyond the scope of this chapter, but the reader can assume that best practice IT security protocols are in use (e.g. SSL [9]).

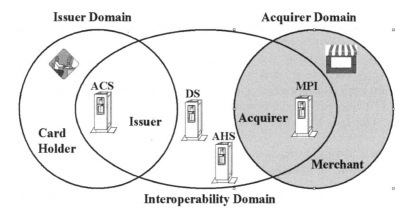

Fig. 5.8   3D-Secure Domains

The way that all these entities work together and the associated message flows is best illustrated by an example. Fig.5.9 represents the basic protocol steps when a cardholder buys a product via a merchant's website. Note that the MPI would normally be managed by the merchant but for the purposes of explanation we will treat it as an Acquirer element that simply acts as a conduit for website generated authentication requests and responses.

The explanation for the sequence of message flows is given in Table 5.3

Table 5.3 Sequence of Message Flows

Flow Number	Description
(1)	This simply represents the cardholder browsing for products on a merchant's website and beginning the "check-out" for on-line purchase.
(2)	After the cardholder has entered his normal payment details, such as card type/number etc, the website needs to determine, if this card has been enrolled in the 3D-Secure scheme. It does this by generating (via the MPI) a Verify Enrolment Request query, which is sent to the DS.
(3)	The DS can recognise the issuing bank from the number range of the payment card and so forwards the request to the appropriate ACS.
(4)	The ACS looks up the particular card number in its database and determines whether it is registered for the scheme and then returns the Verify Enrolment Response to the DS.
(5)	The response is then returned to the merchant via the MPI and the merchant's action depends on the status and local policy e.g. • Not registered - allow the transaction to proceed anyway • Not registered - suggest that the cardholder registers but allow the transaction to proceed • Not registered - force the cardholder to register or abort the transaction • Registered - follow the steps below to complete the transaction
(6)	The merchant (via the MPI) now needs to "POST" a Payer Authentication Request to the ACS via the cardholder's terminal. The cardholder will see a new browser window on the screen that is controlled via the ACS. Note that the MPI is aware of the ACS address, as the URL was received within the Verify Enrolment Response.
(7)	The Payer Authentication Request is effectively forwarded by the cardholder terminal/PC to the appropriate ACS
(8)	The ACS creates the content of the cardholder's browser window, which will include some kind of authentication request such as entry of a username or ID code plus password(s)
(9)	The ACS checks the information from the cardholder and uses it as input to a Payer Authentication Response. The response also contains an Accountholder Authentication Value; the details of which vary depending on the card scheme. MasterCard uses UCAF (Universal cardholder Authentication Field) and Visa uses CAVV (cardholder Authentication Verification Value). The response is digitally signed and then returned to the MPI via the cardholder browser and the authentication window is closed.
(10)	The ACS also sends a copy of the Payer Authentication Response to the AHS for use in dispute handling
(11)	When the Payer Authentication Response reaches the merchant via the MPI, the result would normally be to abort the transaction or more likely to proceed with the transactions as normal, seeking authorisation for financial transaction via the Acquiring bank. The Acquirer will pass on the request to the Issuer who is now more likely to approve the request, as it will obtain the Accountholder Authentication Value obtained via the 3D-Secure process.

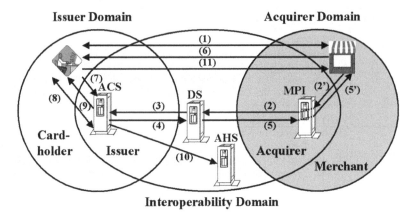

Fig. 5.9 Example Message Flows in 3-D Secure

5.8.2 Thoughts on 3D Secure

The real test of 3D Secure is whether customers and merchants like it. At present cardholders don't get a lot of choice, because if they need to buy from a participating merchant they are driven into using the scheme. Perhaps they are allowed one or two transactions when they can opt out, but then the next time they are compelled to register. Having registered, the customer then has to go through the 3D secure process at other participating merchant sites. Even registering is not necessarily a good experience for the cardholder. In a world where our banks are continually warning us about phishing and keeping our transaction details safe, 3-D Secure pops up an unexpected window asking us to enter sensitive financial information. In use, the 3D secure experience depends on the complexity of the authentication challenges that the issuing bank decides is appropriate. For example the cardholder may be asked to submit randomly positioned letters from a long pass phrase, which is by no mean trivial unless the phrase has been written down. Whilst there are good security reasons for all of this it seems to be heading in the opposite direction to merchant strategy, who would really like us to buy something instantly on an impulse click of the mouse button. It also seems to conflict with the financial industry's drive toward new wave/touch and pay methods of purchasing.

5.9 Just Wave Your Card to Pay

The financial industry seems to be getting quite excited about contactless payment cards. The main reason is that there are various schemes around the world [14] that have proved very popular with customers. Although the UK is just gearing up for these services, the success of the London Oyster [17] card e-ticket has shown just how popular contactless card solutions can be. In fact one of the pioneering solutions is a combined EMV, Oyster and contactless payment card all in one. Barclays launched this in September 2007 as the "OnePulse" card [1], which allows, PIN-less purchase for items costing £10 or less. Mastercard also have a "PayPass" [12] contactless card that is similar to the Barclays product, but currently without the Oyster card capability.

Dropping down to single factor authentication from two factor, is of course a risk, although offset by the cap on transaction value. The service is likely to be popular with customers once enough merchants have signed up for the scheme. The avoidance of PIN handling will mean fast transactions and perhaps a resurgence of interest in using mobile phones as the reader devices, perhaps via NFC technology.

5.10 Concluding Remarks

We examined some of the early attempts of the banking industry to offer flexibility and enhanced security through the use of magnetic stripe cards and PINs. As the magnetic stripe card technology (within the banking industry) reaches the end of its lifetime, we also examined the introduction of smart card technology as the replacing medium. More importantly we reviewed the main security functionality of the EMV specifications.

We have seen how the technology to secure cardholder present transactions has improved, however there has been less progress with cardholder not present (CNP) transactions. As CNP transactions are the norm for Internet and telephone purchases, there is clearly a requirement to improve their security. Current implementations of 3D Secure are a step in the right direction, but they are not as customer friendly as might be desired. The use of token readers and EMV cards for dynamic passcode authentication may ease this problem, but there is still the issue of deploying the readers and whether customers can really be relied on to use them. One thing that is evident is that customers like contactless cards where you just wave the card past a reader and the "OnePulse" and "PayPass" cards will be a good test for contactless payment in the UK. NFC in mobile phones might ensure that we would all carry the reader part for the contactless payment, but it will be some years before this could be a mass-market solution.

References

1. Barclaycard "OnePulse", http://www.barclaycard-onepulse.co.uk/cardDetail.html (accessed Oct 13th 2007)
2. Card Watch "Types of Card Fraud" http://www.cardwatch.org.uk/ (accessed Oct 13th 2007)
3. ECMA (Standard ECMA-340) Near Field Communication Interface and Protocol NFCIP-1 2nd Edition 2004

4. EMV Books 1-4 Version 4.1 2004. http://www.emvco.com/specifications
5. Europay-MasterCard-Visa. Emv'96 integrated circuit card specification for payment systems", version 3.0, from. http://www.europay.com/Pdf/EMV_card.pdf.es, 1996.
6. Karl Brinkat David Main. Smart cards for secure banking & finance. Presenattion in the MSc in Infor-mation Security, Royal Holloway University of London.
7. Keith Mayes, Konstantinos Markantonakis, "Are we Smart about Security?", Elsevier Information Security Technical Report, Volume 8, No. 1, pp.6-16 (2003), ISSN:1363-4127.
8. Konstantinos Markantonakis, Keith Mayes, Fred Piper, "Smart Card Based Authentication-Any Future", Computers & Security (2005), Elsevier Issue No 24, pages 188-191.
9. Mel H and Baker D., "Cryptography Decrypted" chapter 20 pages 215-227, Addison Wesley ISBN 0-201-61647-5, 2001
10. Mastercard, "Mastercard Authentication Solutions", http://www.mastercard.com/us/company/en/docs/Authentication%20Sell%20Sheet_FINAL_April_2006.pdf (accessed 13th Oct 2007)
11. Mastercard, "Mastercard SecureCode", http://www.mastercard.com/us/personal/en/cardholderservices/securecode/how_it_works.html (accessed Oct 13th 2007)
12. Mastercard, "Madtercard PayPass", http://www.paypass.com/ (accessed Oct 13th 2007)
13. Microsoft, "Antivirus Defense-in-Depth Guide", Chapter 2 malware threats, Microsoft technet 2004, http://www.microsoft.com/technet/security/guidance/serversecurity/avdind_2.mspx#E6F (accessed Oct 13th 2007)
14. Octopus, http://www.hong-kong-travel.org/Octopus.asp (Accessed Oct 13th 2007)
15. Racal Guardata "Watchword datasheet" 1992, http://www.anagram.com/berson/watchword.pdf (accessed 13th Oct 2007)
16. Schneir B, "Applied Cryptography", page 170-173, Wiley ISBN 0-471-12845-7 1996
17. Transport for London "What is Oyster Card?" http://www.tfl.gov.uk/tickets/oysteronline/2732.aspx (accessed Oct 13th 2007)
18. Visa, "Card-not-present security" http://www.visaeurope.com/aboutvisa/security/paymentsecurity/cardnotpresentsecurity.jsp (accessed Oct 13th 2007)
19. Visa, "Dynamic Passcode Authentication", http://www.visaeurope.com/aboutvisa/products/dynamicpasscode.jsp (Accessed Oct 13th 2007)
20. Visa, "Verified by Visa", http://www.visaeurope.com/personal/onlineshopping/verifiedbyvisa/main.jsp (accessed 13th Oct 2007)
21. Wonglimpiyarat. Strategies of Competition in the Bank Card Business: Innovation Management in a Complex Economic Environment. Sussex Academic Press, 2004.
22. Xiring "Teo reader", http://www.teobyxiring.com/ (accessed 13th Oct 2007)

Chapter 6
Security For Video Broadcasting

Allan Tomlinson

Abstract This chapter presents an overview of a well known application of smart card technology, namely that of pay-TV systems. The focus is on the security issues of this particular application and the mechanisms available to meet the security requirements. The chapter begins by establishing the requirements for the application and then looks in detail at the security mechanisms provided by current broadcast standards.

Key words: Smart Cards, Pay-Tv, Digital Video Broadcast, Conditional Access, Security

6.1 Introduction

Smart cards have been associated with pay-TV systems for some time now. This chapter will describe this particular application, focusing on the system design constraints and, of course, on the security issues. Although there are many different pay-TV systems in the market, and each one has its own idiosyncrasies and security secrets, the general security problem addressed by these systems is common across all of these applications. It is the general application security that will be discussed rather than the details of any specific solution.

The first objective of this chapter is to provide some understanding of the commercial motivation to provide content protection. A second objective is to show how the overall security solution takes this into consideration to provide a degree of flexibility sufficient to cover as many commercial requirements as possible. The

Allan Tomlinson,
Information Security Group,
Royal Holloway, University of London,
e-mail: Allan.Tomlinson@rhul.ac.uk

third, and main, objective is to provide an overview of how a typical digital pay-TV system operates and the mechanisms used to control access to content.

The general security problem alluded to above is that of securely delivering content from a *single source* to thousands, or more often millions, of receivers in such a way that no illegal receivers can access the content. Although data integrity is important, the main security concern is the provision of confidentiality. This problem applies to all broadcast networks – satellite, cable TV, and terrestrial broadcasts – and the mechanisms described in this chapter are applicable to all types of broadcast networks.

All broadcast networks require the establishment and maintenance of a network infrastructure. These networks may require video play-out and scheduling equipment; distribution networks between broadcast sites; and the broadcast network itself, which may require leasing transponders on a satellite. All of this incurs cost to the broadcaster. Another cost is the cost of the content. The broadcaster often has to pay a content provider a license fee to be able to broadcast the content. In addition to this fee, the license may place restrictions on the broadcaster requiring the content to be broadcast only at specific times or dates; the number of times it can be broadcast; and perhaps the geographical location of the broadcast. So in addition to the cost of the infrastructure and the cost of the content, there is a cost associated with managing the distribution of the content. The broadcaster's business model relies on recouping these costs, either through advertising, or charging the consumer. Content protection is therefore an important aspect of most digital TV broadcast businesses.

To conclude this introduction it is useful to consider the differences between broadcast networks and the more familiar TCP/IP networks – particularly in terms of the security constraints.

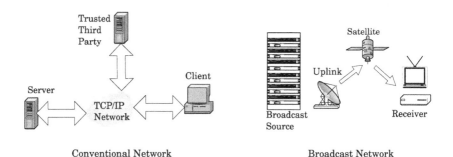

Fig. 6.1   A Comparison Between Broadcast and Conventional Networks.

If the networks shown in Fig. 6.1 are compared, the following observations can be made about broadcast networks. First of all, in a broadcast network there is no return path. The communications channel is one-way only, which makes key sharing and key management more difficult than in a conventional network where two way communication is available. Secondly, the broadcast network is dealing with constantly streaming, often live, video. This creates important constraints on key synchronisation. The keys must be changed at *exactly* the same instant at the play-out centre and at all receivers to avoid temporary loss of service. Finally, there is no way to control who connects to a broadcast network. Thus pirates have access to all broadcast content, without the need to take precautions against being detected by the network operator.

The foregoing has described the environment in which pay-TV systems operate. Before delving into the details of how the security issues are addressed and the role of the smart card, it is first necessary to look in a little detail at the structure of the content we are tying to protect.

6.2 Digital Video Basics

The motivation behind digital transmission is commercial, and lies in the ability to apply digital compression techniques to the signal. Compressing the amount of data that needs to be transmitted provides the ability to broadcast, typically, about five or six digital TV programmes, at VHS quality, in the bandwidth normally used for a single analogue programme. Additional benefits of digital transmission are that more flexible packages of content can be constructed, offering a choice of audio channels for example; the quality of the received signal is often better, up to the point where it fails completely; and finally, it provides the opportunity to secure the content using digital, rather than analogue, techniques.

After converting the analogue video and audio signals MPEG compression [6, 8] is applied to produce digital content. This results in multiple compressed *elementary streams*. In addition to the video elementary stream, there may be one or more audio streams, and perhaps a data stream. This collection of elementary streams is used to reconstruct the programme at the receiver. Several collections of elementary streams representing several programmes are usually combined to form a *digital multiplex* or *transport stream* [7]. When transmitted, this multiplex will occupy the same bandwidth as a single analogue video channel so, as mentioned earlier, it typically carries around five or six programmes in a single channel. The situation is illustrated in Fig. 6.2.

Although the elementary streams are continuously streaming content, in the construction of the transport stream these elementary streams are split into discrete packets. Each packet contains 188 bytes and the stream to which it belongs is identified by a unique Packet ID or PID. Fig. 6.2 illustrates how a collection of programmes, or services, may be transmitted. Service 1 represents a standard TV programme with an associated text service; service 2 has multiple audio streams; and service 6 is a simple programme with one audio stream and one video stream.

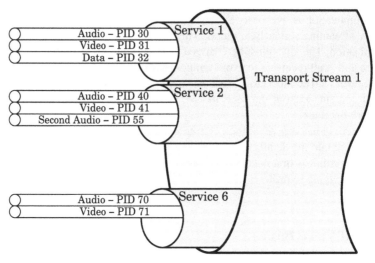

Fig. 6.2 Basic Transport Stream

6.3 Scrambling

Dividing the elementary stream into uniform packets simplifies the scrambling process. Unlike a continuous stream we now have a well defined block of data with a fixed length. This means that we can use a block cipher over a fixed block length, or apply a stream cipher to a stream of known length using a key stream re-initialised for each packet.

The scrambling algorithm used is defined in an ETSI standard (ETR 289) [5] and is known as the *Common Scrambling Algorithm* or CSA. Although this algorithm has been standardised, the details are subject to a non-disclosure agreement. However, it is widely known that the algorithm applies both a block cipher and a stream cipher to the payload of the packet. When scrambling, the block cipher is applied first, using cipher block chaining on 8 byte blocks. The result is then scrambled again using a stream cipher based on non-linear feedback shift registers. The algorithm was designed by a committee of the Digital Video Broadcast[1] (DVB) group. Both the block cipher, and the stream cipher use the same *Common Key* (CK), hence the name Common Scrambling Algorithm.

Descrambling is the reverse. The stream cipher is applied first, followed by the block cipher. The algorithm was designed to be most efficient when descrambling since this will be carried out in the consumer equipment where cost is important.

---

[1] www.dvb.org

6.4 Synchronisation

For any given elementary stream the Common Key changes rapidly, as often as once every 5 seconds, and typically around once every 30 seconds. New keys must therefore be delivered *in advance* of this change, and key changes synchronised *exactly* at transmitter and all receivers. Remember, this is continuously streaming content and any failure to synchronise will result in corruption of the received service.

Another key synchronisation issue arises when channel changes are considered. Typically each continuously streaming programme, or service, is scrambled with a unique key. This leads to a potential problem if someone is "channel surfing" – flicking through each channel, looking for a programme to watch. Even if keys are changed every 5 seconds no one would be happy to wait this length of time for a new key to be delivered each time they changed channel. So, although the CK may change every 5 seconds, it must be repeatedly broadcast every 100 ms. or less, to reduce delay when switching channels.

To address the synchronisation problem it was mentioned that while the current key was being broadcast, the next key is delivered in advance. The DVB standards [1, 4] introduce the the concept of a *crypto-period* as the duration of a valid current key (5 seconds in our example). The standards also introduce the idea of odd crypto-periods, and even crypto-periods, switching from odd to even (and back) with every key change. This leads to the notion of having odd and even keys. So while an elementary stream is being scrambled with an odd key, the next even key is being delivered in advance.

Now, for each packet scrambled, an indicator can be set in the packet header to say whether this packet was scrambled with an odd or even key. This indicator is provided by the *transport scrambling control* bits shown in Fig. 6.3. The first bit indicates whether the packet is scrambled or in the clear; the second bit indicates whether the packet was scrambled with an odd or even key. The meaning of the transport scrambling control bits is summarised in Table 6.1.

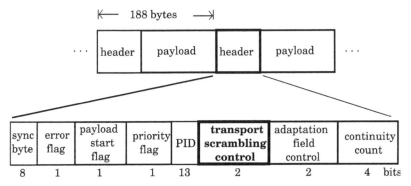

Fig. 6.3 The Location of Transport Scrambling Control Bits within the Packet Header.

Table 6.1 The Meaning of Transport Scrambling Control Bits.

Bit values	Description
0 0	Payload not scrambled
0 1	Reserved
1 **0**	Payload scrambled with **even** key
1 **1**	Payload scrambled with **odd** key

So now, when a packet arrives at the receiver, if there is a change from odd to even indicated in the packet header, the descrambler will know to use the next (even) key which it should have received in advance of the key change at the transmitter. Thus, key changes can be synchronised precisely without relying on any timers or counters.

The synchronisation process at the receiver may be illustrated with reference to Fig. 6.4. When a packet arrives the receiver inspects the transport scrambling control bits in the header to see if it is scrambled or not. If the packet is scrambled, the receiver then checks whether it has been scrambled with an odd or even key. It then selects the appropriate key, and descrambles the packet.

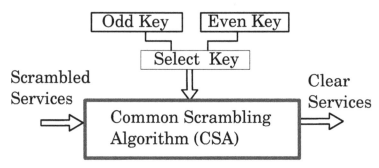

Fig. 6.4 Synchronisation at the Receiver.

6.5 Key Delivery

The Common Key is cryptographically derived from a 64-bit *Control Word* (CW). Since there is no return channel or any means of negotiating the CW, it has to be delivered to each receiver in the broadcast signal itself. Since the CW is broadcast in the transport stream, it has to be encrypted. This encrypted Control Word is delivered in a special stream within the multiplex known as an ECM or *Entitlement Control Message* stream. The structure of an ECM packet is defined by the MPEG standards [4,7], and it usually carries two encrypted Control Words per message: the current and next. Although the ECM structure is standardised, the algorithms used to encrypt the CW remain proprietary. This allows different vendors to distinguish their products in the marketplace.

Each ECM stream is usually associated with a complete service. In other words the same Control Word is used to scramble all elementary streams associated with a complete service. The standards do however allow an ECM to be associated with single elementary streams too. This allows, for example, an additional audio stream, perhaps a second language, to be encrypted separately from the main service. Thus the broadcaster is able to provide this second audio service only to subscribers who have paid for it. ECMs may also be associated with groups of services if cost is an issue for the broadcaster. Grouping services in this way could reduce the need for expensive specialist encryption hardware. However, most broadcasters use one ECM stream per service as illustrated in Fig. 6.5 where service 6 has now been scrambled.

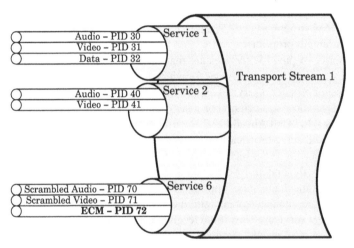

Fig. 6.5 ECM Stream

6.6 Access Requirements

ECM messages also contain *access requirements*. These access requirements, also known as access criteria, identify what "packages" the user must be subscribed to before they can access the service. For example, a football match might require that the user has paid their subscriptions to the "sports package" before they can view the programme. Access requirements may also place a constraint on the geographical region that a receiver is in. Again to use the football example, there may be a restriction on viewing a football match in the city where the game is being played. Each receiver therefore has a set of viewing rights, depending on the subscriptions paid.

Only those receivers with rights that match the access criteria are able to recover the CW from the ECM and view the programme.

Before any attempt is made to decipher the CW delivered in the ECM, the access criteria are checked and compared with the *rights* that the receiver has. These rights are held in secure storage on the receiver, typically on a smart card, and may be updated by the service provider depending on the subscriptions paid by the user. Thus each receiver may have a different set of rights, giving access to different sets of services.

The rights that each receiver has are updated by the service provider by sending a second type of entitlement message: the *Entitlement Management Message*, or EMM. This type of entitlement message is different from the ECM because where the ECM is associated with a service and must be delivered to all receivers, the EMM is associated with an individual receiver and the rights delivered should not be available to all receivers in the broadcast network. The way this is managed is by means of a key hierarchy as discussed in section 6.7. As was the case with the ECM, the EMM structure is standardised [4, 7], but the algorithms used to encrypt the contents remain proprietary.

The majority of pay-TV services are managed on a subscription basis. That is, the user subscribes to a set of services for which a monthly fee is paid for continuous access to a set of broadcast services. A more flexible mechanism to manage payment for services is to allow subscription on a per programme basis. This is known as pay-per-view (PPV). In "Call Ahead PPV" the user calls the service provider in advance of the programme being broadcast and buys a subscription for that programme only, for example a sporting event such as a football match. Once payment has been made, the broadcaster will send an EMM to the individual receiver to update its rights. A more convenient mechanism is "Impulse PPV" where instead of calling the service provider each time, the receiver contains a certain amount of credit which is used to pay for such PPV services. Thus if the receiver is in credit, the event can be viewed, and the credit level adjusted accordingly.

The model of service delivery may now be updated to include the EMM stream as shown in Fig. 6.6.

6.7 Key Hierarchy

In section 6.5 we saw that the ECM message delivered an encrypted CW. If the CW is encrypted under the control of a key K_0, $ECM = \{CW\}_{K_0}$, then it is clear that all receivers that are authorised to view the programme must have K_0. K_0 however is not permanent, it may be changed on a per-programme basis, or per day, or week, depending on the service provider's requirements. When K_0 is changed, the new key must be delivered to all receivers. This is accomplished by another type of EMM message which, instead of delivering rights, delivers keys to the receivers.

Of course the keys being delivered by the EMM must be encrypted before being broadcast. Thus K_0 will be encrypted under a more long term key, say K_1. Each

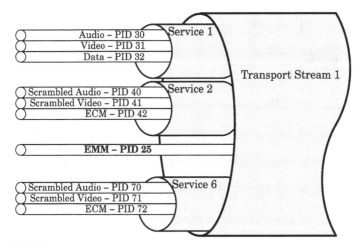

Fig. 6.6 EMM Stream

receiver could then have its own unique K_1 and a unique EMM generated and broadcast for each receiver. In large networks this may be impractical since the bandwidth required to continuously broadcast individual EMM messages for a period of time long enough to ensure all receivers are updated, will become too large. Especially if K_0 is changing at a relatively high rate, say once per programme.

In practice receivers are often organised into groups so that they can be updated on a group basis rather than an individual basis. Each group will share K_1, which will be delivered to each group member encrypted under another key, say K_2 which this time may be unique to each receiver.

Thus we have a key hierarchy as illustrated in Fig. 6.7. In a broadcast network it is not practical to duplicate scrambled content, scrambling it with keys unique to each receiver. Therefore at the bottom level, the content itself must only be scrambled once under one key: the CK derived from the CW. This CW changes rapidly and is delivered in an ECM associated with the scrambled service. Higher level keys change less rapidly and are delivered in EMM messages. The longer update interval allows more time to ensure all receivers are updated with new keys. Ultimately, at the top of the key hierarchy, all receivers are updated one at a time with keys encrypted under the *unique key* for that receiver.

6.8 Implementation

Prior to standardisation, all aspects of the previously described architecture were proprietary. The DVB standards body however defined specifications [1,4,5] which, if followed, will allow scramblers and receivers to operate with *any* proprietary system. These standards isolate scrambling functionality from higher layers of the key

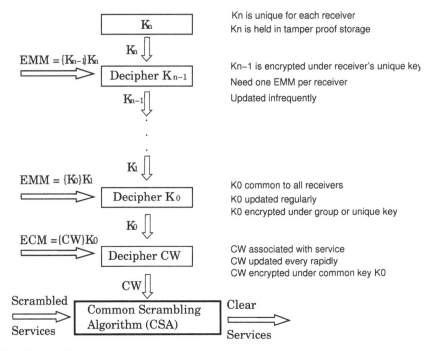

Fig. 6.7 Key Hierarchy

hierarchy, and define the scrambling algorithm to be used. The standards also define the interface between the scrambler and higher layers of the key hierarchy. Thus the higher layers can still remain proprietary allowing vendors to design their own systems, known as *Conditional Access* (CA) systems, while at the same time allowing broadcasters to switch CA systems if they require to do so.

In addition to the commercial benefit of defining the interface between proprietary and standard parts of the key hierarchy, there is also a security gain. If the whole key hierarchy was standardised then there would be greater incentive for pirates to attack the system. Whereas with the standard–proprietary split, a successful attack may compromise one CA system, but the others will remain secure. Moreover, the ability to choose from a number of CA systems provides an incentive to the CA vendors to constantly monitor and improve their systems if they are to compete in an open marketplace.

Fig. 6.8 illustrates how content is scrambled at the broadcast play-out centre [4]. The CW used to scramble the content is passed to the CA system and used to construct the ECM messages. An Event Information System is often used to schedule when to apply scrambling and what access criteria to use. The CA system also generates the EMM messages and delivers them to individual receivers or groups of receivers based on data held in a Subscriber Management System. The ECMs, EMMs, and scrambled content are then combined to form the digital multiplex prior to transmission on the broadcast network.

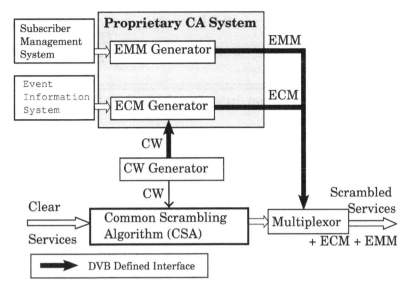

Fig. 6.8 Scrambling at the Broadcast Centre.

The descrambling process at the receiver is illustrated in Fig. 6.9. The *Common Interface Module*, or CIM is a PC Card module that the user may plug into a compatible receiver. The interface between this module and the receiver is defined by a CENELEC standard [1], and the CIM also has a standard ISO smart card interface. The CIM typically contains the hardware to descramble the content in real time, and a smart card, initialised with the unique key at the top of the key hierarchy, is typically used to recover and store higher level keys. Thus the smart card stores the high level keys in a tamper resistant location and generally only provides the CW to the CIM as required. This hardware architecture raises a potential security issue: since the interface between the smart card and the CIM is standardised, it is vulnerable to eavesdropping. In other words, an attacker who is familiar with the CENELEC standard will have access to the Control Words as they pass across this interface. To counter this vulnerability a shared key is often established between a smart card and the descrambling hardware, and used to set up a secure communications channel to protect the CW in transit.

Therefore the CIM and smart card will be unique to each different type of Conditional Access system, implementing not only the content descrambling algorithm, the CSA, but the algorithms used throughout the key hierarchy. The exact details of these algorithms remain proprietary to each Conditional Access system vendor. The smart card, in addition to securely storing the high level keys, will also implement some of these proprietary algorithms. The division of processing between smart card and CIM will depend on the particular CA system in use.

The receiver, once tuned to a particular frequency, will receive the complete digital multiplex containing all scrambled services, ECM and EMM messages. This data stream will be de-multiplexed, based on packet ID to reconstruct the elemen-

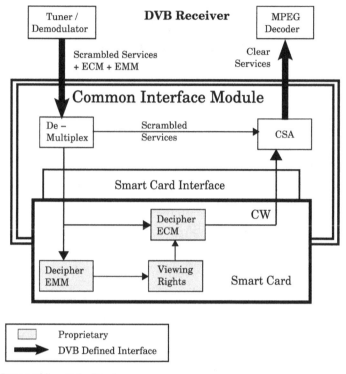

Fig. 6.9 Descrambling at the Receiver.

tary streams. The EMM stream will be processed to recover viewing rights and keys delivered to that particular receiver. These rights and keys will typically be stored on a smart card. When a viewer selects a service to watch, the corresponding ECM stream will be de-multiplexed, processed by the smart card and any Control Words returned to the descrambler. Thus the CIM will be able to descramble the content in real time.

The advantage of providing a standard interface at the receiver is that a CIM for one Conditional Access vendor may be replaced by a CIM for another vendor. This gives the consumer wider access to services without the need for multiple receivers. Some receivers have multiple CIM slots, allowing modules to be daisy chained as illustrated in Fig. 6.10. This provides greater user convenience, since the modules will not need to be swapped to receive services scrambled by multiple service providers with different CA systems.

Taking user convenience one step further, and removing the need for a hardware CIM altogether led to the idea of emulating the CIM in software. This is the concept behind the DreamBox [2] which is a sophisticated DVB receiver that has much of the functionality of a powerful PC, including an Ethernet interface. This type of receiver supports the implementation of the CIM in software, with the aim of providing as much flexibility as possible to the user. However, this opens up the

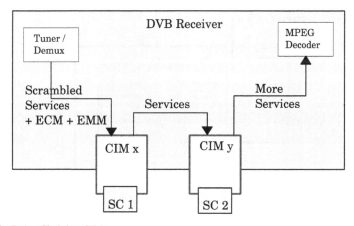

Fig. 6.10 Daisy Chaining CIMs

possibility of cloning a genuine CIM in software and distributing this over the Internet to many illegal receivers. Since the CIM is not a tamper resistant device it may be possible to extract any secret key that is shared with a genuine smart card. Moreover, a genuine receiver may be modified to recover the Control Words from its CIM and distribute these over the Internet too. The pirate receivers will then be able to recover the CW and illegally access the scrambled content. If a smart card is completely reverse engineered it too could be simulated on the DreamBox. Details of these attacks together with proposed safeguards based on behavioural analysis built into a smart card are described by Francis et al. [9]. An alternative may be to use trusted computing technology to ensure that the host platform has not been tampered with before the descrambler is enabled [3].

At the transmission site, the DVB standards define the interface between the scrambler and the Conditional Access system [4]. This allows broadcasters to change CA systems if they desire, or to use multiple CA systems simultaneously. The latter is referred to as "simulcrypt" and is illustrated in Fig. 6.11.

In Fig. 6.11, although the service is only scrambled once, with one CW, the standard interface allows this CW to be passed to *two* Conditional Access systems, CAS 1 and CAS 2. Thus *two* ECM message streams are generated for each scrambled service, both containing the encrypted CW, but the CW will be encrypted with a different algorithm and a different key in each ECM. In addition to the two ECM streams there will be a second EMM stream to manage entitlements controlled by the second CAS as shown in Fig. 6.12. The benefit this brings to the broadcaster is that he can now provide services that can be accessed by receivers designed with two different Conditional Access systems, thus giving access to a wider potential market.

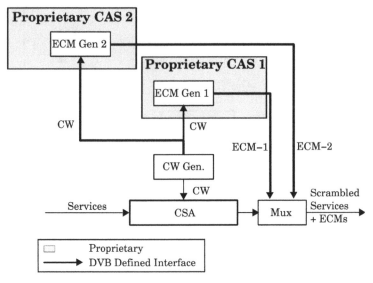

Fig. 6.11 Simulcrypt

6.9 In Conclusion

In this chapter the construction of a digital TV multiplex has been briefly described. As far as security is concerned, the services carried in this multiplex may be scrambled by a standard "Common Scrambling Algorithm", CSA [5], using a key derived from a Control Word, CW. This Control Word is delivered to receivers in an ECM message which also contains access criteria. Changes in CW are synchronised by setting bits in the packet header to indicate which CW was used to scramble the packet. Since the CW must be encrypted before being broadcast another key must be made available to the receiver to allow recovery of the CW from the ECM. This key is delivered in an EMM message. Again, this key must be encrypted, which leads to a key hierarchy. At the top of the key hierarchy is a key *unique* to each receiver which will be stored in a tamper proof area on a smart card. The EMM message is also used to deliver rights to the subscriber, which again must be stored in tamper proof memory. These rights are compared with the access criteria in the ECM before any attempt is made to recover the CW.

Although the bulk encryption, or scrambling of content, uses a standard algorithm, protection of the higher level keys remains proprietary. This led to two standards being developed by DVB to allow interoperability. At the receiver the "Common Interface" standard [1] defines the interface between a PC Card Common Interface Module and the receiver. This allows the consumer to swap Conditional Access systems by swapping CIM modules. At the transmission site, the "Simulcrypt" standard [4] defines the interface between the scrambler and the Conditional Access system. Not only does this allow the broadcaster to swap systems, if required, but it

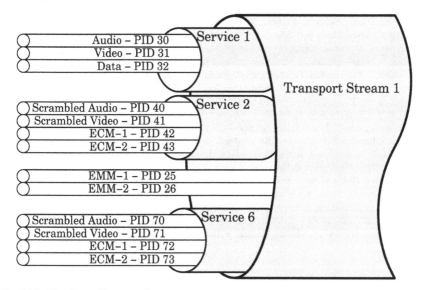

Fig. 6.12 Simulcrypt Transport Stream

allows the broadcaster to use several systems simultaneously, thus providing access to more receivers.

In any secure system some residual vulnerabilities remain, and the Pay TV system described here is no exception. Many attacks on Pay TV systems exploit vulnerabilities in smart cards to create clones. Moreover, with the advent of the DreamBox, the CIM can also be cloned and Control Words distributed over the Internet. The size of the key used with CSA is only 64 bits, although there is provision to increase this. However, this vulnerability may be mitigated to some extent by frequent changes of the CW. A final vulnerability is the fact that proprietary mechanisms are used to manage the higher level keys in the Conditional Access systems. Since these mechanisms have not been subject to public scrutiny little can be said about their security except that some are, no doubt, more secure than others.

References

1. CENELEC, "Common Interface Specification for Conditional Access and other Digital Video Broadcasting Decoder Applications," CENELEC Standard 50221, European Committee for Electrotechnical Standardization (CENELEC), Brussels, Belgium, Feb. 1997.
2. D. Multimedia TV GmbH, Dreambox DM7000S user manual., 2004.
3. E. Gallery and A. Tomlinson, "Conditional Access in Mobile Systems: Securing the Application," in The First International Conference on Distributed Frameworks for Multimedia Applications DFMA 05, (Los Alamitos, CA, USA), pp. 190–197, IEEE Computer Society, February 2005.
4. ETSI, "Digital Video Broadcasting (DVB); Head-End Implementation of DVB Simulcrypt," ETSI Standard TS 103 197 V1.3.1, European Telecommunications Standards Institute

(ETSI), Sophia Antipolis, France, Jan. 2003.

5. ETSI, "Digital Video Broadcasting (DVB); Support for use of Scrambling and Conditional Access (CA) within Digital Broadcasting Systems," ETSI Technical Report ETR 289, European Telecommunications Standards Institute (ETSI), Sophia Antipolis, France, Oct. 1996.

6. ISO/IEC, "Information Technology – Generic Coding of Moving Pictures and Associated Audio: Audio," International Standard ISO/IEC 13818-3, International Organization for Standardization (ISO), Geneva, Switzerland, 1994.

7. ISO/IEC, "Information Technology – Generic Coding of Moving Pictures and Associated Audio: Systems," International Standard ISO/IEC 13818-1, International Organization for Standardization (ISO), Geneva, Switzerland, 1995.

8. ISO/IEC, "Information Technology – Generic Coding of Moving Pictures and Associated Audio: Video," International Standard ISO/IEC 13818-2, International Organization for Standardization (ISO), Geneva, Switzerland, 1995.

9. L. Francis, W. Sirett, K. Markantonakis, and K. Mayes, "Countermeasures for attacks on satellite tv cards using open receivers," in Australasian Information Security Workshop 2005 (AISW2005) (R.Buyya, P. Coddington, P. Montague, R. Naini, N. Shepperd, and A. Wendelborn, eds.), vol. 44, pp. 53–158, Australian Computer Society Inc., 2005.

Chapter 7
Introduction to the TPM

Allan Tomlinson

Abstract The Trusted Platform Module (TPM) and smart card devices have many features in common. Both are low cost, tamper resistant, small footprint devices used to provide the basis of a secure computing environment. This chapter presents an introduction to the security mechanisms provided by the TPM highlighting those not typically found on a smart card. The concept of "ownership" is one of the major differences between the TPM and a smart card and this is described in some detail before concluding with a review of some of the security services uniquely provided by the TPM.

Key words: Smart Cards, Trusted Computing, TPM, Security

7.1 Introduction

Smart cards provide a wide range of functionality from simple storage media to complex processors. A common design goal across this diversity however, is the provision of some degree of secure processing, implemented in secure hardware. The Trusted Platform Module, or TPM, is similar to a smart card device in that it is a small footprint low cost security module typically implemented as a tamper resistant integrated circuit (IC). The TPM however, has been specifically designed to be a building block for trusted computing. So although there are many similarities, the different design goals have resulted in a number of differences between the two types of device. One major difference is that the TPM is considered to be a fixed token bound to a specific platform, whereas a smart card is a portable token traditionally associated with a specific user across multiple systems. This is not to

Allan Tomlinson,
Information Security Group,
Royal Holloway, University of London,
e-mail: Allan.Tomlinson@rhul.ac.uk

say that the two technologies are mutually exclusive, but rather that they may be considered as complementary.

The details of smart card architectures and applications are discussed elsewhere in this book so this chapter will focus on the TPM and expand on the "complementary" aspects of this device, describing the specific mechanisms where the TPM differs from a typical smart card IC. In order to fully understand the rationale behind these mechanisms it is important to understand the underlying design goals of trusted computing that guided the development of the TPM.

This chapter therefore begins with some background on trusted computing to explain the features that the TPM is designed to support and the rationale behind the design decisions that were made. The fundamental features of the TPM that emerged from these design constraints are described in section 7.3. This section focuses on the functionality of the basic TPM building blocks to expose some of the differences between the design of smart card ICs and the TPM. Many of the differences that appear, arise from the contrasting requirements for ownership and management between the two types of device. Section 7.3 therefore looks at these concepts in some detail. The differences between the two types of device result in differences in functionality, and section 7.4 looks at some of the security services not found in typical smart card devices, which are fundamental to the operation of the TPM.

7.2 Trusted Platforms

Where smart cards may be considered as general purpose security processors, the TPM has been designed specifically to support trusted computing platforms. Therefore, in order to understand the TPM design requirements, it is first necessary to understand what the desirable features of a trusted platform are. To do this, a definition is required as to exactly what is meant by the term "trusted platform".

The concepts of trusted computing, and a Trusted Computing Base, or TCB, are not new and are described in many publications ranging from the Orange Book [3] through to more recent material that describe these ideas within the context of contemporary developments in computer security [2, 5, 15]. One such development is the emergence of the Trusted Computing Group[1] (TCG) that has attempted to define what is meant by a trusted computing platform and that has produced a series of standards that can be used to design trusted platforms. The TCG defines trust to be "the expectation that a device will behave in a particular manner for a specific purpose" [16]. The TCG's definition of a trusted platform therefore, is a platform that behaves in such a manner. This is, necessarily, a rather high level definition: but what this means is that any entity that interacts with such a trusted platform can be given some degree of assurance that the platform (system or computer) will behave in the way that entity expects it to. Providing assurance of expected behaviour does not in

---

[1] https://www.trustedcomputinggroup.org

itself provide any security. To achieve that, the entity relying on this assurance still has to ascertain that the "expected behaviour" is indeed secure. However, assuming that the relying entity is satisfied that the expected behaviour is secure then he may, for example, be assured that any data given to the system is kept confidential, or that no malware is running on the platform.

There are many ways to design trusted computing platforms that allow statements about expected behaviour to be made [15], but the approach taken by the TCG is to have some physically secure trusted component that can be used as a foundation upon which trust in the rest of the system can be built. The purpose of the TPM is to provide this foundation. For this chapter, a more appropriate definition of a trusted platform is provided by Pearson [13] who states that:

> "A Trusted Platform is a computing platform that has a trusted component, probably in the form of built-in hardware, which it uses to create a foundation of trust for software processes"

or Balacheff et al. [1] who say:

> "A trusted platform (TP) is defined as a computing platform that has a trusted component, which is used to create a foundation of trust for software processes."

It is perhaps appropriate at this point to make a subtle distinction between what is meant by a *trusted component*, such as the TPM, and a *trustworthy component*. One generally accepted definition of these terms is given by Anderson [9, 10] who states that:

> "The proper definition is that a *trusted* system or component is one whose failure can break the security policy, while a *trustworthy* system or component is one that won't fail"

By implementing this trusted component, the TPM, as a tamper proof IC; and binding it to the platform, usually on a printed circuit board containing a more powerful processor capable of running software applications; the TPM can be used as the foundation of trust for higher level processes that run on the main processor.

7.2.1 Fundamental Features of a Trusted Platform

In order to establish this foundation of trust, the TPM is expected to provide a fundamental set of security features which have been defined by the TCG. The minimum set of features that a trusted platform should have are: protected capabilities; integrity measurement; and integrity reporting [16]. Providing support for these features leads to the definition of the security requirements of the TPM.

Protected Capabilities

To meet the requirements of a trusted platform, according to the TCG [16], the system should provide some form of protected capabilities. In the TPM design prin-

ciples specification, the concept of protected capabilities is used to "distinguish platform capabilities that must be trustworthy" [17].

These trustworthy protected capabilities are abilities to execute a command or
set of commands on the TPM which access *shielded locations* where it is safe to operate on sensitive data [16]. Examples of protected capabilities in the TPM include
protection and reporting of integrity measurements (described below); and storage
and management of cryptographic keys.

Integrity Measurement and Storage

Any trusted platform will need some means of measuring how it is configured and
what processes are running on that platform. The increasing complexity of personal
computers and software applications has resulted in an increase in the number of
processes that run on a typical PC. Many of these processes are launched implicitly,
rather than explicitly by the user. Under such circumstances it is difficult to tell if
the code being executed on a particular platform is a legitimate process or not, and
consequently, if this particular platform can be trusted. It is important therefore, if
a platform is to be trusted, that it has some means of measuring the integrity of the
processes it is running. This measurement should result in some form of *integrity
metric* [16] which Pearson defines as "a condensed value of integrity measurements"
[14]. This integrity metric can then be compared with acceptable values for a trusted
platform. Having obtained an integrity metric for the platform it is often useful to
store that value somewhere for later use. Of course such data needs to be held in
secure storage locations such as would be provided by the protected capabilities
described above.

In measuring platform integrity in this manner there has to be a starting point.
It may be acceptable for a particular application to perform integrity measurements
provided that the application itself is trustworthy. Even if the operating system can
verify the integrity of this application, the integrity of the operating system too has
to be verified. Ultimately there will be some integrity measurement process that
exists which cannot itself be verified. This process is known as the Root of Trust
for Measurement, or RTM. This is the starting point in the chain of integrity measurements, and ideally this process should run on tamper proof hardware, with the
execution code being stored in secure storage.

Integrity Reporting

The third requirement for a trusted platform [16] is that it should be able to report
its configuration to a challenger who requires this information in order to decide
how much trust to place in the platform. In other words, the platform should have
some means to report its integrity metrics and to vouch for the accuracy of this
information. This attestation requires the generation of evidence that the challenger
can rely on in making its trust decision. The implication here is that the integrity

metrics can be signed by the trusted platform and that the challenger has a certificate that can be used to verify the signature.

7.2.2 Additional Features

While the above features would allow the implementation of a basic trusted platform as defined by the TCG, there are other features that would be required to create a more flexible implementation of a trusted platform. These include: confidentiality and integrity protection; secure storage; and process isolation.

Confidentiality and Integrity Protection

In addition to the protection of integrity metrics, a trusted platform should provide both confidentiality and integrity protection to any data as required by the user. This could include both user data, and application code. Moreover, these security services should be available to protect this data while it is being stored, and during the execution of any process.

Secure Storage

The provision of confidentiality requires that a trusted platform is able to encrypt any user data for secure storage. Access to the data is controlled by a securely stored cryptographic key. Similar to encryption is the concept of sealing. In this case access to the data is controlled by platform state, the use of a cryptographic key is optional. This means that data can be sealed to a set of integrity metrics that reflect the platform state. The data will then only be accessible when the platform is in the desired configuration. The sealing mechanism can be used, for example, to ensure that no rogue applications are running before access is granted to sensitive data.

Process Isolation

The secure storage and integrity checking mechanisms will protect data during storage. To protect data during execution the provision of process isolation is necessary. The concept here is to provide an isolation kernel between the hardware and any operating system. This isolation kernel is used to create and manage multiple secure compartments. These compartments exist in parallel, on the same machine, and access is managed exclusively by the isolation kernel. Each compartment can then run its own operating system and applications in isolation from any other processes that are executing in parallel. In this way, application code and data can be protected during execution. Furthermore, the use of an isolation kernel greatly simplifies the validation of acceptable integrity metrics: by isolating processes, the set of acceptable platform configurations can be reduced to one operating system and one application only.

7.3 TPM Features

The previous section described the main security requirements for the TPM and the rationale behind these requirements. These high level requirements for a trusted platform provided some of the input to the development of a series of standards which are published by the TCG, including the specification of the TPM. This specification is written as a collection of three documents, currently at version 1.2. The documents describe the TPM design principals [17], which will be reviewed in more detail in the following section; and the data structures [18] and commands [19] used to control the TPM. A discussion of TPM structures and commands is beyond the scope of this chapter but may be found in other work [4, 12].

7.3.1 TPM Components

When comparing the TPM to smart cards, an important point to note is that the TCG specifications do not mandate that the TPM is implemented as an IC. The standards define TPM *functionality*, leaving it open for developers to implement this functionality as they wish, either in hardware or software. Having said that, most commercially available implementations of the TPM are hardware based and produced by the major IC manufacturers. The main building blocks of the TPM are shown in figure 7.1.

The TPM itself, however implemented, must be physically protected from tampering. In PCs, for example, this may be accomplished by physically binding the TPM to the motherboard to make it difficult to disassemble or transfer to a different platform. This is not a requirement for the TPM to be tamper proof, but tamper resistant. The TCG also require that tamper evidence measures should be deployed to enable detection of any tampering by physical inspection.

It is important to note when looking at figure 7.1, that the TPM standards do not specify the communications interfaces or bus architecture, leaving these decisions to be made by the developers.

7.3.2 I/O Block

The TCG do, however, specify an interface serialisation transformation that allows data to be transported over virtually any bus or interconnect. This is one of the

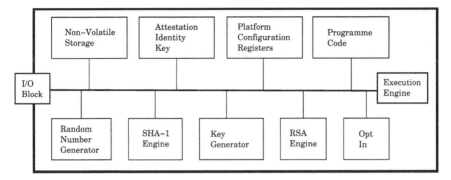

Fig. 7.1 TPM Building Blocks

functions of the I/O block. This block manages information flow between the components illustrated in Fig. 7.1, and between the TPM and the external bus. Since the I/O block is managing data flow, it is also able to control access to the various TPM components. The access rights are determined by flags maintained by the Opt-In block.

7.3.3 Non-Volatile Storage

As with a smart card IC, a TPM has some non-volatile memory to store long term keys. Two long term keys are stored in non-volatile memory on the TPM. The first of these is the Endorsement Key (EK); the second key is the Storage Root Key (SRK) which forms the basis of a key hierarchy that manages secure storage.

The TPM also uses non-volatile memory to store *owner* authorisation data. This authorisation data is, in effect, the owner's password and is set, not by the manufacturer, but during the process of taking ownership of the TPM. There are also a number of persistent flags related to access control and the Opt-In mechanism, discussed in section 7.3.12, that need to be stored in non-volatile memory.

Endorsement Keys

The Endorsement Key (EK) is a fundamental component of a TPM. It is also something unique to the TPM which is not found on a smart card device. It is therefore important to consider how the TPM uses this key in a little more detail.

For the TPM to operate, it must have an endorsement key embedded in it. To be more precise, it must have an endorsement key pair, of which the private key is embedded in the TPM and *never leaves* it. The public EK is contained in a certificate and is only used in a limited number of procedures. The reason for limiting the use of the EK certificate is because the EK is unique to each TPM and consequently may be used to identify the device, and by extension the platform. Therefore, to protect user privacy when interacting with other entities, the use of the EK is restricted and internally generated aliases, the Attestation Identity Keys, or AIKs, are used for routine transactions.

TPM manufacturers will provide the endorsement key pair and store this in tamper resistant non-volatile memory before shipping the TPM. A certificate, or *endorsement credential,* can then be created which contains the public EK and information about the security properties of the TPM. This endorsement credential should be signed by a certification authority, known as the TPME or Trusted Platform Module Entity, who can attest to the fact that the key contained in the certificate is a public EK whose corresponding private EK is stored in a TPM that conforms to the TCG standards. This TPME may be a third party or, if authorised to do so, it may be the manufacturer themselves.

Some organisations who wish to use the TPM may, for security reasons, prefer to use their own endorsement keys. To accommodate this, the standards allow the EK to be deleted and re-installed by the user. Of course if the user generated endorsement credential is not signed by a TPME, its use may be limited.

The purpose of the endorsement credential is to prove that the corresponding private EK is stored in a genuine TPM. So, in keeping with policy to control exposure of the public EK, the private EK is *never used to generate signatures.* Thus, the public EK is never required to verify signatures so it does not have to be widely distributed. The public EK is only used for encrypting data sent to the TPM during the process of taking ownership and the process of creating AIK certificates. These processes are described in sections 7.3.12 and 7.4.4. Encrypting data with the public EK ensures that the plaintext can only be recovered by the particular TPM identified in the endorsement credential.

7.3.4 Attestation Identity Keys

As mentioned above the TPM Endorsement Key and Storage Root Key are stored in non-volatile memory. These keys never leave this secure storage during normal operation. A third type of key, the Attestation Identity Key (AIK), may also be stored within the TPM. This key may be regarded as an alias for the Endorsement Key. Each TPM can support many AIKs, thus the user can have many unlinkable keys that can be used to maintain anonymity between different service providers who require proof of identity. These AIKs must, therefore, be persistent and although they could be stored on the TPM non-volatile memory, for practical reasons the standards recommend keeping the AIK keys in secure external storage. The TPM however must provide a volatile storage area where one or more AIK keys can be loaded when in use.

7.3.5 Platform Configuration Registers

The Platform Configuration Registers (PCR) are unique features of the TPM architecture and are used to store *integrity metrics*. The integrity metrics stored in these
registers measure the integrity of any code, from BIOS to applications, typically before the code is executed. Platform Configuration Registers may be implemented in
volatile or non-volatile storage. However, these registers *must* be reset whenever the
system loses power or re-starts. If the registers were not reset then old integrity metrics might remain in the PCRs after a platform is re-booted and reconfigured. The
standards specify that a TPM must have at least 16 Platform Configuration Registers
and that each register stores 20 bytes. Registers 0 to 7 are reserved for exclusive use
by the TPM, the remaining registers are free for use by the operating system and
any application.

7.3.6 Programme Code

In common with smart cards, the TPM requires storage for the firmware that is used
to initialise the device.

If the programme code is stored permanently on the tamper proof TPM then
it would be reasonable to assume that it is trustworthy. Thus there would be no
need to check its integrity making this the obvious location to store the code that
carries out the integrity checks on all other platform devices and code. That is to
say, the programme code on the TPM is the obvious "root of trust" for integrity
measurements described in section 7.2. The TCG refer to such a root of trust as
the CRTM, or Core Root of Trust for Measurement. Although the TPM programme
code is the obvious choice for the CRTM, implementation decisions often require
the CRTM be located in other firmware such as the BIOS boot block. Regardless
of where the CRTM resides it should be considered as a *trusted component* of the
system since if it fails all security policy based on integrity measurements will be
broken.

7.3.7 Execution Engine

Like many smart cards, the TPM has an execution engine which runs the programme
code described above. The execution engine responds to external commands by selecting the required programme code and executing it on the TPM.

7.3.8 Random Number Generator

Another unique feature of the TPM is the inclusion of a *true* random bit stream generator. Again the implementation is left to the developers so long as some random source is used, rather than a deterministic method. Having a true random bit generator is extremely valuable in any security application. In the TPM, random bit streams are used to seed a random number generator. The random numbers produced by this generator may then be used to construct keys for symmetric cryptographic applications. The random numbers may also be used to provide nonces and, by mixing with user input, to increase the entropy in pass phrases

7.3.9 SHA-1 Engine

The SHA-1 message digest engine is an implementation of the Secure Hash Algorithm [6] SHA-1. This algorithm hashes the input data and produces a 20-byte digest. It also forms the basis of an HMAC [7, 8] (Hash Based Message Authentication Code) engine, and is used in a number of cryptographic procedures carried out by the TPM, for example: in the computation of digital signatures and for creating key objects where a hash of the key may be required as part of an integrity protection mechanism.

7.3.10 RSA Key Generation

Generating keys suitable for use with the RSA algorithm [11] can be a computationally intensive task and since such keys are widely used in the TPM, for signing and providing secure storage, the standard specifies that the TPM should include a module specifically for this task [16]. The standard requires that a TPM is able to support keys *up to* a 2048 bit modulus. Moreover, there are certain keys used with the TPM that must have *at least* a 2048 bit modulus.

In other words, all implementations of the TPM are required to support up to 2048 bit RSA. Some keys are allowed to have a smaller modulus than this, depending on what they are used for. However there are certain keys that must have a 2048 bit modulus - or greater. Of course if the modulus is greater than 2048 bits there is no guarantee that all implementations of the TPM will support this since the only requirement is that the TPM is able to support keys with up to a 2048 bit modulus.

7.3.11 RSA Engine

Just as the generation of RSA keys is computationally complex, so is the execution of the algorithm itself. Therefore, the standards also require the TPM to have a dedicated RSA engine used to execute the RSA algorithm. The RSA algorithm is used for signing, encryption, and decryption. Maintaining the principle of key separation, the TPM uses dedicated signing keys for signing data, and separate storage key pairs for encryption and decryption. It is worth noting that the TPM does not mandate the use of any symmetric crypto-engines. According to the TCG [16], "The TCG committee anticipates TPM modules containing an RSA engine will not be subject to import/export restrictions."

7.3.12 Opt-In

The Opt-In component and the concept of ownership, represent one of the biggest differences between smart cards and the TPM. Smart cards are in general, owned and customised by the Issuer before the consumer receives the device. The TCG, however, conscious of the perception that TPM enabled platforms will somehow be controlled by large remote organisations, have been very careful to provide mechanisms to ensure that it is *the user* who takes ownership and configures the TPM. The TCG policy is that the TPM should be shipped "in the state that the customer desires" [16]. Thus, it is up to the user to opt-in to use the TPM. Users are not compelled to use trusted computing, they only opt-in if they choose to do so by taking ownership of the device.

During the process of taking ownership, the TPM will make transitions through a number of states depending on the initial state in which the device was shipped. The state in which the TPM exists is determined by a number of persistent and volatile flags. Changing the state of these flags requires authorization by the TPM owner, if he exists, or demonstration of physical presence. Proving ownership is discussed below, but the means of proving physical presence is determined by the platform manufacturer. The key point is that no *remote* entity, other than the TPM owner, should be able to change the TPM state [17].

The function of the Opt-In component is to provide mechanisms and protection to maintain the TPM state via the state of these flags.

TPM Operational States

There are several mutually exclusive states in which the TPM can exist, ranging from disabled and deactivated through to fully enabled and ready for an owner to take possession [16]. In the *disabled* state, the TPM restricts all operations except the ability to report TPM capabilities and to accept updates to the PCRs. Once a TPM is *enabled*, all it's features are made available, provided ownership has been established. If an owner has not already been established then the transition from disabled to enabled requires proof of physical presence.

A second state variable indicates whether the device is *activated* or *deactivated*. The deactivated state is similar to the disabled state. The difference is that when deactivated, a TPM may still switch between different operational states, for example to change owner or to activate. Once activated, all features are available [16].

A third state variable relates to ownership and determines whether the TPM is *owned* or *unowned*. For a TPM to be owned by a user, it must have an endorsement key pair, and a secret *owner authorisation data* known by the owner. Once in the owned state, the owner of the TPM may perform all operations including operational state change. The TPM needs to have an owner and be enabled for all functions to be available [17].

Depending on the configuration, cases may arise where different states have overlapping influence. As explained in the TCG architectural overview specification [16], in such situations, where TPM commands are available by one mode and unavailable by another mode, precedence is given to making the command unavailable.

Taking Ownership

When a user takes ownership of a TPM they establish a shared secret, referred to as *owner authorisation data*, and insert this data into secure storage on the TPM. This is, in effect, the owner's password and being able to demonstrate knowledge of this secret provides proof of ownership. Once owned, the TPM can control access to certain protected operations by requiring proof of ownership which can be demonstrated by entering the *owner authorisation data* to authenticate the owner.

The process of taking ownership requires that the owner authorisation data is protected from eavesdropping or theft by a malicious third party. This is one case where the endorsement credential is used, since the EK is the only key an un-owned TPM has. It is the EK that establishes the secure channel to transmit the authorisation data to a genuine TPM. So, during the process of taking ownership, the owner requests the endorsement credential and after verifying this credential, retrieves the public EK and uses this to encrypt the shared secret. Only the TPM identified in the endorsement credential has access to the private EK, therefore the shared secret is only made available to the intended TPM. The process of taking ownership is completed by the creation of the Storage Root Key (SRK) which is generated by the TPM and stored in non volatile memory. The SRK forms the root of a key hierarchy used to provide secure storage and, as with the private EK, the SRK *never leaves* the TPM.

7.3.13 Other Features

The TPM provides several other useful security features that are not always available in smart cards. One of these is the provision of monotonic counters which can, for example, provide a secure mechanism to prevent replay attacks. A second feature is the provision of time-stamping, although it is important to note that no absolute measure of time is possible, only measurement of time intervals. Finally, the TPM should provides mechanisms to create and manage audit trails

7.4 TPM Services

To conclude this chapter, this section presents an overview of the TPM operation to illustrate the basic security services provided. The foundation for the provision of these services is the concept of a "root of trust" from which other services such as authenticated boot, secure storage, and attestation can be constructed.

7.4.1 Roots of Trust

As defined in section 7.2, a trusted platform has at is foundation some trusted component. Since all other trust is built upon this foundation it is known as a *root of trust*. An analogy may be made with root certification authorities (CA) in a public key infrastructure (PKI). Although users may not trust the public key presented in a certificate, or even the authority who signed the certificate, so long as there is someone at the top of the certificate chain whom the user trusts, then it is reasonable to trust the key - assuming of course that all signatures are verified. The entity at the top of the certificate chain is often referred to as the *root CA* and his certificate referred to as a *root certificate*. In most web browsers, many root certificates are installed with the application and trusted implicitly by the users. Failure of this component, the root certificate, breaks the security policy of the PKI.

In the trusted platform architecture defined by the TCG, there are three distinct roots of trust: a Root of Trust for Measurement (RTM), a Root of Trust for Storage (RTS) and a Root of Trust for Reporting (RTR).

The Root of Trust for Measurement (RTM) must be trusted to generate integrity measurements for the processes that are running on the platform. This should ideally be a tamper proof component that boots very early in the boot process and therefore is able to measure all other components that are loaded after it. The TPM is an ideal candidate for the CRTM, but in practice the CRTM is more likely to be found in the BIOS boot block. This has been discussed in sections 7.2 and 7.3.6.

The Root of Trust for Storage (RTS) is a trusted component that provides confidentiality and integrity protection. The RTS can then be trusted to store either data, e.g. PCRs, or keys such as the SRK that allow data to be securely stored in external locations. Finally, the Root of Trust for Reporting (RTR) is a trusted component that provides reports of any integrity measurements that may have been made - attesting to the platform configuration. Both the RTS an RTR are provided by the TPM.

7.4.2 Boot Process

Figure 7.2, taken from the TCG Architectural Overview [16], shows the system boot process. The BIOS boot block, or Trusted Boot Block (TBB) as shown in the diagram, contains the CRTM, and is the first process to boot. The CRTM is a trusted component and its integrity is not measured by any external code, but it may perform a self-check of its own integrity. Although not illustrated in the diagram, the CRTM should measure the rest of the BIOS before loading it. Once the BIOS is loaded it takes control and measures the integrity of the OS Loader as shown in step 1 of the diagram. Control then passes to the OS Loader in step 2, and the OS Loader measures the integrity of the operating system. This process continues until the applications are loaded and executed in step 6.

The integrity measurements at each stage are made by creating a SHA-1 digest of the code to be loaded. This digest is stored in one of the PCR registers, which are initialised to zero. The new integrity metric however does not simply overwrite the old PCR value. The process of updating (or extending) the PCR value concatenates the 20 bytes of data already held in the PCR with the 20 bytes of new data calculated by hashing the new code. These 40 bytes of data are then hashed again using the SHA-1 algorithm and the result written to the original PCR. In pseudo code: $PCR \leftarrow hash(PCR \parallel hash(new\,code))$. This way the PCR can store an unlimited number of measurements.

In order to interpret the value contained in the PCR, it is necessary to know the individual digests that have been added to it. These data are stored externally in what the TCG refer to as the Stored Measurement Log. Thus, if the data in the stored measurement log is known, and the PCR values are known, and trusted, then a challenger can verify the state of the platform.

7.4.3 Secure Storage

In section 7.3.12 it was mentioned that the process of taking ownership resulted in the creation of a Storage Root Key, or SRK. This key is generated by the TPM and never leaves the device. It can only be accessed by demonstrating knowledge of a shared secret, in this case the *SRK authorisation data*. This shared secret is similar to the *owner authorisation data* and loaded into the TPM at the same time, during the process of taking ownership. As with the *owner authorisation data,* the *SRK authorisation data* is encrypted by the endorsement key before being sent to the TPM.

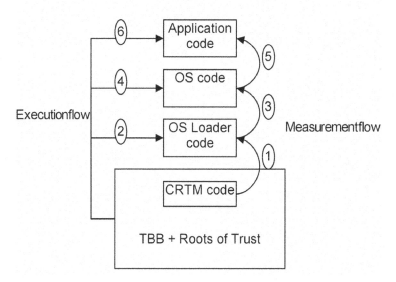

Fig. 7.2 Boot Process [16]

The SRK forms the root of a key hierarchy as illustrated in figure 7.3 which has also been taken from the TCG Architecture Overview [16]. This key hierarchy allows data, or keys, to be encrypted such that they can only be decrypted by accessing the TPM. In the diagram, the opaque data is encrypted under a specific storage key. The storage key is also encrypted and stored external to the TPM. To access this data the encrypted storage key is loaded into the TPM, via the key cache manager, and deciphered by the storage root key. Since the SRK never leaves the TPM, and the TPM is physically bound to the trusted platform, the opaque data can only be deciphered on that platform.

The TPM provides two mechanisms for secure storage: binding and sealing. The *binding* operation encrypts the data using a key that is managed by a particular TPM as described above. The *sealing* process adds to this by only allowing the deciphering process to proceed if the platform is in a specific configuration. This configuration is determined by data held in the PCR registers. Thus, when data is sealed, not only must the same platform be used to unseal the data, but that platform must be in a predetermined configuration before the data can be recovered.

7.4.4 Attestation

The AIK keys shown in figure 7.3 are the Attestation Identity Keys mentioned in section 7.3.1. The purpose of an AIK is to provide user privacy when communicating with different sources. Although EK could be used to secure communications

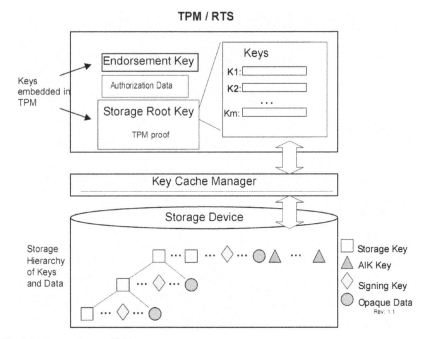

Fig. 7.3 Secure Storage [16]

with different sources, since the EK is unique to the TPM, this could potentially allow the platform's identity to be linked between each source it chose to communicate with. The idea of the AIK is to provide a unique unlinkable identity for the TPM, for use with each different source. In each case the AIK acts as an alias for the EK. The AIK credential is a certificate containing the AIK public key which proves that the corresponding private key is bound to a genuine TPM. This proof is guaranteed by a signature on the credential created by a trusted third party known as a "privacy CA".

To obtain an AIK a request is sent to the privacy CA together with the endorsement credential. This the second case where the public EK is exposed. The endorsement credential proves to the privacy CA that the request came from a genuine TPM. In response to the request, the privacy CA creates and signs the AIK credential, and encrypts this under the public EK contained in the endorsement credential. Thus the AIK is cryptographically bound to the TPM that contains the private EK. The users can create as many AIK keys as they wish and provided the privacy CA is trustworthy, these keys will remain unlinkable and provide the privacy required when communicating with different sources.

The private AIK key is managed by the TPM as illustrated in 7.3 and may be freely used to generate signatures. In particular, the private AIK can sign the contents of the PCR registers. This is how the TPM can be used to attest to the platform configuration. A relying party in possession of a public AIK can now challenge the trusted platform, and the attestation mechanism can be used to provide an integrity report describing the platform state.

7.5 In Conclusion

This chapter has reviewed the structure of the TPM and identified several unique features that distinguish it from a typical smart card. One of the main differences between the two is the concept of ownership. Where smart card cards are usually owned and customised by the Issuer, the TCG have been careful to ensure that the TPM is owned by the user.

The TPM is designed to provide a number of security services to a platform which differ from those services provided by smart cards. These services include secure storage that can be used to protect data in a hostile environment and, when used with integrity reporting, can ensure that this data is only accessed in a controlled manner. The TPM also provides the mechanisms to implement authenticated boot processes. Perhaps the most unique feature of the TPM is the attestation mechanism. This allows challengers to verify the state of the platform, and which applications are running. It remains, however, the challenger's responsibility based on this attestation, to decide whether or not the platform is actually trustworthy.

References

1. B. Balacheff, L. Chen, S. Pearson, D. Plaquin, and G. Proudler, *Trusted Computing Platforms: TCPA Technology in Context*. Prentice Hall, 2003.
2. C. Mitchell, ed., Trusted Computing. London, UK: IEE Press, 2005.
3. D. of Defense, "DoD 5200.28-STD: Department of defense trusted computer system evaluation criteria", tech. rep., Department of Defense, 1985.
4. E. Gallery, "An overview of trusted computing technology", in Trusted Computing (C. J. Mitchell, ed.), IEE, 2005.
5. E. Gallery and C. J. Mitchell, "Trusted mobile platforms", in FOSAD '07, International School on Foundations of Security Analysis and Design, vol. 4677 of LNCS, (Bertinoro, Italy), Springer-Verlag, Sep 2007.
6. FIPS, "Specifications for the Secure Hash Standard", Tech. Rep. 180-2, Federal Information Processing Standards, National Technical Information Service (NTIS), 5285 Port Royal Road, Springfield, VA 22161, Aug 2002.
7. H. Krawczyk, M. Bellare, and R. Canetti, "HMAC: Keyed-hashing for message authentication", RFC 2104, IETF, 1997.
8. M. Bellare, R. Canetti, and H. Krawczyk, "Keying Hash Functions for Message Authentication", in Advances in Cryptology - Crypto '96 (N. Koblitz, ed.), vol. 1109 of Lecture Notes in Computer Science, Springer-Verlag, 1996.
9. R. Anderson, "Cryptography and competition policy: issues with 'trusted computing'", in PODC '03: Proceedings of the twenty-second annual symposium on Principles of distributed computing, (New York, NY, USA), pp. 3V10, ACM Press, 2003.
10. R. J. Anderson, Security Engineering - a Guide to Building Dependable Distributed Systems. Wiley, 2001.

11. R. L. Rivest, A. Shamir, and L. M. Adelman, "A method for obtaining digital signatures and public-key cryptosystems", Communications of the ACM, vol. 21, pp. 120V126, 1978. More Information Available via. `http://citeseer.ist.psu.edu/rivest78method.htm`. Cited on 3rd Oct, 2007

12. S. Kinney, Trusted Platform Module Basics: Using TPM in Embedded Systems. Elsevier, 2006.

13. S. Pearson, "Trusted computing platforms, the next security solution", Technical Report HPL-2002-221, Hewlett-Packard Laboratories, Nov 2002.

14. S. Pearson. (ed.): "Trusted Computing Platforms: TCPA Technology in Context", Prentice Hall, 2003.

15. S. W. Smith, Trusted Computing Platforms: Design and Applications. Springer-Verlag, 2005.

16. TCG, "TCG Specification Architecture Overview", TCG Specification Revision 1.4, The Trusted Computing Group, Portland, OR, USA, Aug 2007.

17. TCG, "TPM Main, Part 1 Design Principles", TCG Specification Version 1.2 Revision 103, The Trusted Computing Group, Portland, OR, USA, Jul 2007.

18. TCG, "TPM Main, Part 2 TPM Data Structures", TCG Specification Version 1.2 Revision 103, The Trusted Computing Group, Portland, OR, USA, Jul 2007.

19. TCG, "TPM Main, Part 3 Commands", TCG Specification Version 1.2 Revision 103, The Trusted Computing Group, Portland, OR, USA, Jul 2007.

Chapter 8
Common Criteria
A brief history and overview

John Tierney

Abstract This paper will consider how Common Criteria evolved, how it is defined and how it is used in practice. As an example we will look at how Common Criteria is applied to smart card evaluations. This paper will not attempt to define in detail Common Criteria, nor should the reader expect to understand it in sufficient detail to be able to immediately participate in evaluations. It will, however, give a gentle introduction to what is a complex and demanding evaluation methodology.

Key words: Smart Card, Common Criteria, Security Evaluation

8.1 Introduction

Security costs. It costs time and it costs money. In a world where new IT security threats are identified on an almost daily basis there is a common question: "Do I need security?"The answer is almost always the same: "It depends". In order to determine whether or not I need security I need to perform an analysis of the risks I perceive against the costs of implementing countermeasures to protect against them. This is not a straightforward task, since some risks may not be easy to clearly define (or, indeed, may be unknown); in addition the cost of implementing countermeasures may also be difficult to determine, especially if there is no off-the-shelf solution readily available. The subsequent cost/benefit analysis aims to show whether or not the selected countermeasures can provide cost-effective protection against the defined risks.

If we are looking to purchase, rather than develop, security solutions, it is difficult to compare like with like unless there is a framework which permits vendors to define their solutions in a common language. Common Criteria provides this framework - a methodology whereby vendors can certify their products and consumers

John Tierney, MasterCard UK Management Services Limited
e-mail: John_Tierney@mastercard.com

can interpret such certifications in order to compare competing solutions. Moreover Common Criteria is an international standard, allowing what was originally a national solution to become international.

This paper will consider how Common Criteria evolved, how it is defined and how it is used in practice. As an example we will look at how Common Criteria is applied to smart card evaluations. This paper will not attempt to define in detail Common Criteria, nor should the reader expect to understand it in sufficient detail to be able to immediately participate in evaluations. It will, however, give a gentle introduction to what is a complex and demanding evaluation methodology.

8.2 Evolution of National and International Standards

The first publicly available standards for security evaluations were the TCSEC[1] standard - Trusted Computing Security Evaluation Criteria - which were published in the US in 1985. These provided a defined methodology for assessing security, ranging from D (Minimal Protection) to A1 (Verified Design).

In the late 1980s the UK Government introduced the UK Confidence Levels, ranging from L1 (lowest) to L6 (highest). Both US and UK schemes were essentially aimed at the government market and not at commercial products.

In the early 1990s a European Initiative combined the UK scheme with similar German and French criteria to form ITSEC - Information Technology Security Evaluation Criteria. This was a European standard with the UK, Germany, France and the Netherlands participating to give a well-defined set of security evaluation criteria. For the first time there was an international security evaluation standard available and, in addition, it was seen as a potential marketing tool - hence commercial products started to be evaluated for the first time.

The first version of ITSEC stimulated new Canadian and draft US criteria in 1993; however by then it was recognised that there was both a need and opportunity to define a truly international standard.

Version 1.0 of Common Criteria was released in 1996, followed by version 2.0 in 1998. At the time of writing the current version of Common Criteria is v2.3 (see [1–4]), which will be superceded by v3.1 in 2008 (see [5–8]). Common Criteria became an ISO standard (15408) in 1999 (v2.1) and subsequent releases have all been published as ISO standard, whilst at the same time being freely downloadable from the Common Criteria Portal website. Note that [4,8] are respectively the current and new versions of the Common Evaluation Methodology - a companion document which defines the precise nature of deliverables for the lower levels of evaluation.

In a relatively short period of time an international standard was developed, arising from existing national and European scheme - a difficult task given the protective nature governments have when it comes to national security. What Common Criteria gives today is a framework for security evaluations of government, defense and

---

[1] Also known as the "Orange Book"due to the colour of its cover.

commercial products - a common language enabling cross-border certifications and product evaluations.

8.2.1 International Recognition

Although Common Criteria provides an internationally recognised framework for security evaluations, cross-border recognition is, in practice, potentially limited. The Common Criteria Recognition Agreement (CCRA) is intended to ensure the cross-border re-use of certificates, but is limited to EAL4 - a medium level[2] of evaluation. Current signatories of the CCRA are:

- Australia*
- Austria
- Canada*
- Czech Republic*
- Denmark
- Finland
- France*
- Germany*
- Greece*
- Hungary*
- India
- Italy
- Japan*
- Republic of Korea*
- Netherlands*
- New Zealand*
- Norway*
- Singapore
- Spain
- Turkey
- UK*
- USA*
- Israel

Those countries marked with an asterisk in the above list have evaluation schemes in place - the other countries do not currently support an evaluation scheme, but recognise certificates produced in the countries which do have a scheme. This provides a global, but limited (to EAL4) scheme for certificate recognition. So if a vendor has a product evaluated in one country that certificate should be recognised in any of the other countries.

---

[2] But roughly equated to "good commercial practice".

SOGIS provides a European scheme for wider certificate recognition. This provides for mutual recognition up to EAL7 (the highest level of evaluation) between the following countries:

- Finland
- France*
- Germany*
- Italy
- Netherlands*
- New Zealand*
- Norway*
- Portugal
- Spain
- Sweden
- Switzerland
- UK*

Again those countries providing a certification scheme are marked with an asterisk.

It is interesting to note that Portugal and Switzerland are signatories to SOGIS, but not CCRA. In addition several European countries participate in CCRA, but not SOGIS.

8.2.2 The need for security benchmarks

As we have seen earlier, initial evaluation criteria such as TCSEC and the UK Confidence Levels were primarily aimed at providing assurance for products supplied to government and defense organisations. Common Criteria provides a scheme which permits commercial organisations to certify their products.

In determining whether or not to certify a product, the developer must ensure they develop a suitable business case. Evaluations (just like security) cost time and money, especially when the higher levels of assurance are used. Any prudent commercial organisation will therefore wish to ensure that they assess the costs and benefits involved before undertaking an evaluation.

Issues to consider in this process from a vendor/developer perspective include:

- Do the organisations that we wish to sell this product to mandate Common Criteria certification to a specified level? (This is typically a requirement for supplying product to government or defense organisations, but can also apply to financial products).
- Do we consider that a Common Criteria certificate will give us sufficient differentiation from our competition? (If two products are similar in specification, can a certification support increased sales and/or an increased price?).
- Do we believe that developing to Common Criteria will improve the quality of our development process and, ultimately, our product? (Developing a product

to Common Criteria standards will ensure that there is a rigorous focus on the design, implementation and testing of security functionality).

There is also the consumer perspective to consider. As a potential purchaser of one or more products implementing security I would like to know:

- What security features does a product implement?
- Are they implemented properly?
- What confidence do I have that they cannot be subverted or fail?

8.3 Evaluation Practicalities

From a developer perspective there are a number of practical issues to consider before embarking on an evaluation. These include:

- An evaluation will cost money - the evaluation laboratory will charge a fee, and the Certification Body[3] may also charge.
- An evaluation will take time - especially at the higher levels of assurance, which can typically take more than a year. An assessment needs to be made as to whether a certificate that is not available immediately for product launch is worthwhile. A product could theoretically be obsolete before a high-level assurance evaluation is completed.
- An evaluation will use up internal resources. There will typically be at least one person dedicated to managing the evaluation process internally and there will be evaluation-specific documentation to produce. In addition the development process must ensure that it provides all the required documentation and processes that meet the requirements of the chosen assurance level.
- The developer will have to liaise with at least the evaluation laboratory and Certification Body, and possibly other participants in the evaluation. These entities may be located in different time-zones and there may be language differences.
- Evaluations typically include a site audit for the developer.
- The developer needs to consider whether to perform the evaluation in parallel with the development (potentially delaying the product release) or to "retrofit"the evaluation at a later stage. In evaluations I have performed, I have found that the most efficient way to perform evaluations is to do them in parallel with development. In fact the most efficient way I have found to develop and evaluate is to ensure that the evaluation lags behind the development slightly - e.g. the requirements are produced and are evaluated while the High Level Design is being developed, which is then evaluated while the Low Level Design is being developed, etc. In this way any changes required as a result of the evaluation can be made with a minimal cost, since it is widely recognised that making changes are more expensive the later in the development cycle they are discovered.

---

[3] The Government Body which runs the certification and evaluation scheme in a particular country. Examples are NIST, CESG, DCSSI, BSI, etc.

8.3.1 Types of evaluation

There are three types of evaluation defined within Common Criteria:

- Protection Profile
- Security Target
- Product or System

Once any of these evaluations is successfully completed, the subject of them is "certified".

Protection Profiles are optional within Common Criteria, but if they are used they need to be evaluated to have any formal meaning. Protection Profiles are essentially templates for subsequent evaluations and contain a lot of content that is common to a Security Target based on them. Protection Profiles define the security functionality that a product or system is required to have. Protection Profiles can be mandated as a requirement for subsequent evaluations. In this way they are a useful tool for purchasers, who can assess them and stipulate that products should meet specific Protection Profiles. Protection Profiles do not specify how security features should be implemented - just what features must be provided. An uncertified Protection Profile should be treated with caution, as it may not be Common Criteria compliant. Protection Profiles define the required Evaluation Assurance Level (see below) together with the required Security Functionality.

Meeting the requirements of a Protection Profile usually means that the product or system under evaluation must be designed to meet its requirements up front - retrofitting a product to a Protection Profile after the product has been designed is usually problematic.

A **Security Target** is a mandatory requirement for all evaluations. A Security Target may optionally be based on an existing (and certified) Protection Profile, in which case it will share a lot of common contention with the latter, but add details of how security is implemented. If a Security Target is not based on a Protection Profile there are no restriction on its content other than it must be compliant with Common Criteria (and this is no trivial restriction as we shall see later). The Security Target forms the basis of the subsequent Product or System evaluation, but is certified separately and is the lynchpin of the entire evaluation process. Getting the Security Target right is critical for an evaluation's success and is the focus of most of the early work from both developer and evaluation lab.

A **Product** or **System** is the subject of an evaluation and is referred to as the TOE or Target of Evaluation. The difference between the two subjects is that a Product is a standalone entity whereas a System is a combination of separate products into a multi-component entity. Product evaluations are typically more straightforward than System evaluations due to their single-entity nature. However note that an evaluated product can be part of a larger system, the rest of which may not necessarily be (formally) evaluated.

8.3.2 Evaluation Assurance Levels

Common Criteria defines 7 EALs (Evaluation Assurance Levels) as follows:

- EAL1 - functionally tested
- EAL2 - structurally tested
- EAL3 - methodically tested and checked
- EAL4 - methodically designed, tested and reviewed
- EAL5 - semiformally designed and tested
- EAL6 - semiformally verified, designed and tested
- EAL7 - formally verified design and tested

EAL1 gives the lowest level of assurance and EAL7 the highest.

More details can be found in [3] and p196 of [3] gives a table which provides an overview of the various deliverables required to support each EAL. This table illustrates that the assurance requirements (i.e. evidence) become more and more demanding as the EAL increases.

The following table gives an approximate mapping of Common Criteria and IT-SEC assurance levels:

Table 8.1 CC vs ITSEC

Common Criteria	ITSEC
-	E0
EAL1	-
EAL2	E1
EAL3	E2
EAL4	E3
EAL5	E4
EAL6	E5
EAL7	E6

Because of the different ways that these criteria are designed and are used, the above table can only ever be a rough guide.

8.3.3 Augmentation of Assurance Levels

The standard EALs can be "augmented"- this means that additional assurance components can be added to give an increase in selected areas. The effect is that a partial - but not complete - enhancement to a higher level EAL can be achieved.

As an example EAL4 can be augmented by adding an additional 3 assurance components: ADV_IMP.2 (which means that the entire software source code is supplied - rather than a sample), ALC_LCD.2 (which enhances the requirements on the development life-cycle) and AVA_VLA.4 (which enhances the requirements on the product to sustain attacks to the highest possible level). This particular augmentation is common in smart card evaluation requirements and Protection Profiles.

Augmented EALs are denoted by adding a "+"sign, so the above example would be denoted by EAL4+. *Note that unless the augmentation is defined precisely specifying EALX+ means nothing expect that at least 1 new assurance component has been added to EALX.*

8.4 Evaluation Roles

The Developer of the Target of Evaluation is responsible for the creation of the TOE itself, the Security Target and all the required deliverables. The Developer may be responsible for instigating and paying for the evaluation in the first place. Alternatively a Sponsor may take these responsibilities, working in collaboration with the Developer; otherwise the Sponsor and Developer are the same entity.

An Evaluation Laboratory performs the evaluation of the deliverables, providing reports to all participants (although these will differ in detail depending on the various roles participating). The Certification Body is responsible for validating the reports and also performing any cryptographic analysis required. The Certification Body issues the certificate once the evaluation is successfully completed.

Using an evaluation lab to provide the developer an independent, expert analysis of their product. Independence ensures that Common Criteria evaluations provide as level a playing field as possible and brings a different perspective to the product to that of a developer. It should be noted that the Developer provides all evidence and

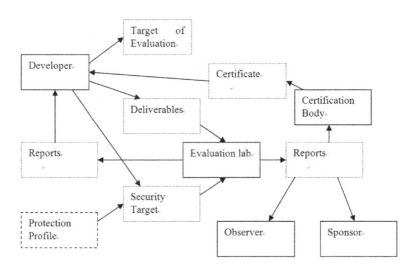

Fig. 8.1 Evaluation Roles

deliverables to the Evaluation Lab and therefore there is a requirement for these two parties to have a suitable agreement to maintain the confidentiality (and integrity) of the supplied information and for the lab itself to have suitable procedures to ensure that information is suitably protected. Indeed labs are regularly audited to ensure that they implement the requisite procedures to the satisfaction of the Certification Body. Finally labs need to ensure that their staffs are suitable for this type of task - as well as technical skills they are required to follow procedures and maintain confidences.

Finally there may be one or more Observers, who have an interest in the evaluation progress. Observers are optional.

8.4.1 Performing Evaluations

As a developer, the question of whether to evaluate a product/system or not requires careful consideration. Evaluations cost time, money and resources and should not be lightly undertaken. Protection Profiles are optional and are normally developed by industry groups with an interest in defining generic requirements which can be met by specific products. But Security Targets and the product or system they cover must be formally evaluated in order to achieve certification under Common Criteria. A product or system evaluation requires a set of deliverables to be supplied and evaluated by the evaluation laboratory. The higher the EAL, the most rigour and detail is required for both deliverables and their evaluation. Hence higher level evaluations cost more and take longer.

Any cryptographic evaluation required is dealt with by the Certification Body involved, rather than the evaluation lab - Certification Bodies already have the expertise for this task and are heavily involved in the detail of defining national policies for encryption standards.

Evaluations may be linked. Using the example of a financial smart card product, a typical product configuration is:

1. Integrated Circuit (IC)
2. Operating System (OS)
3. Smart card application

In order to successfully evaluate the smart card application, links are required to IC and OS evaluations, and we will return to this subject later.

Evaluations take time to perform. Meetings are typically face to face and the formal evaluation process mandated by Common Criteria is rigorously followed by the evaluation lab and monitored by the Certification Body. Even low level (e.g. EAL1) evaluations will take several months to complete. Mid level (e.g. EAL4) evaluation will typically take between 6 and 9 months, perhaps longer. High level evaluations are unlikely to complete in less than 18 months. All these timescales are highly dependent on factors such as rework required, turnaround time for queries, etc.

Costs will, again, vary dependent on the EAL required, but cover:

- Direct fees to the evaluation lab and certification body
- Travel costs
- Internal resource costs
- Any external resource costs (e.g. consultancy, contractors)

8.5 Developing Protection Profiles and Security Targets

Protection Profiles and Security Targets have many common sections of content. Indeed a Security Target based on a Protection Profile will re-use much of the latter's content - the main additional requirements being that a Security Target includes details of how the required security functionality is implemented. Apart from that Protection Profiles and Security Targets can include vast swathes of very similar text. A Security Target can be seen as a specific instantiation of a Protection Profile, identifying the specific TOE and adding details of how it works.

This section will look in some details as to how specific sections of these documents are developed.

8.5.1 Establish the security environment

This task applies to both Protection Profiles and Security Targets.

There are 3 inputs to this phase:

- The TOE Physical Environment
- The purpose of the TOE
- The assets requiring protection

The **physical environment** of the TOE is, as is fairly obvious, the environment in which it will work. This may vary from a completely open environment to a secure location with very restricted access. In the former case attackers have uncontrolled access to the TOE and can spend as much time as they like attacking it, with any means at their disposal. In the latter case the TOE may be located in a secure location, perhaps with very restricted physical access and possibly no electronic link to the outside world. The environment will clearly have a bearing on the type of protection required.

The **purpose** of the TOE should be clear to the author(s) of the Protection Profile or Security Target. The former case may be more difficult if there is no existing product available and/or the Protection Profile is being developed for a new product or service. In the latter case the Security Target will state the purpose of the product or system under development.

The **assets** requiring protection may need some careful consideration. Assets are typically grouped into primary and secondary groups. Primary assets are those which require the highest level of protection, whereas secondary assets are those which are not as critical, but which still require protection. Assets may require protection in terms of disclosure, modification or both.

Once these three inputs have been defined, they are used to establish the TOE security environment. The TOE security environment described the security aspects of the intended environment and the manner in which it is expected to be used. The TOE security environment is defined in terms of:

- Assumptions
- Threats
- Organisational Security Policies

These form the inputs to the next phase of PP/ST creation.

8.5.2 Establish Security Objectives

This task applies to both Protection Profiles and Security Targets.
The inputs from the previous phase are:

- Assumptions
- Threats
- Organisational Security Policies

Assumptions define details about the intended use of the TOE and the environment it will be used in.

Threats to the TOE are defined in terms of the asset under attack, the attack method and the agent carrying out the attack. Threat agents are described in terms of level of expertise, available resources and motivation. Attacks are described in terms of the method used and any vulnerabilities or opportunities that are being exploited.

Organisational Security Policies define rules or policies with which the TOE usage must comply.

Assumptions, threats and organisational security policies are used to establish the Security Objectives for both TOE and its environment, which are the inputs into the next phase.

8.5.3 Establish Security Requirements

This task applies to both Protection Profiles and Security Targets.
The inputs to this phase are the TOE Security Objectives and the Security Objectives for the environment.

- **TOE Security Objectives** are fulfilled by the TOE itself.

- **Security Objectives for the Environment** reflect objectives that cannot be completely met by the TOE itself.

The Security Objectives are used in conjunction with the Common Criteria requirements catalogue [3, 7] to establish:

- TOE Security Functional Requirements
- TOE Security Assurance Requirements
- Requirements on the environment

These are used as inputs to the next phase for Security Targets only.

8.5.4 Establish TOE Summary Specification

This task applies to Security Targets only.

The inputs to this phase are the TOE Security Functional Requirements, the TOE Security Assurance Requirements and the requirements on the environment.

The TOE Security Functional Requirements define the functional requirements using definitions from Common Criteria. These define the requirements in a specific way using Common Criteria terminology and constructs.

The TOE Security Assurance Requirements define the assurance level required i.e. one of the predefined EALs, possibly augmented with additional assurance requirements as previously discussed.

Environment Security Requirements define any environmental requirements using Common Criteria terminology and constructs.

For the Security Target these inputs are used to establish the TOE Summary Specification. This defines, in sufficient detail (usually a side or more of text), how specific Security Functionality is implemented within the TOE.

8.5.5 Establish Rationale

This task applies to both Protection Profiles and Security Targets.

The Rationale ensures that all the elements developed in phases 1 - 4 above are constructed and used in a consistent way. Security Targets can re-use a rationale from any Protection Profile they are claiming compliance with, but will need to add a mapping for the Security Functions defined in the TOE Summary Specification. The rationale requires a comprehensive analysis of all the elements involved in the Protection Profile/Security Target and is non-trivial to develop and ensure the correctness of.

8.5.6 Claiming Compliance with Protection Profiles

Some evaluations will mandate compliance with a specific Protection Profile. For example the customer may require certain functionality and may have developed a Protection Profile to ensure this. In such cases the Security Target will need to be based on the Protection Profile. In addition the TOE must be designed to meet the required functionality - if this is not the case it is unlikely that an evaluation will succeed, as it will be akin to fitting a square peg in a round hole.

If meeting a Protection Profile is mandatory, the PP itself should be certified. If this is not the case, there is no guarantee that a Security Target based on it will be Common Criteria compliant and in this case it is possible that the ST evaluation will have problems or even fail.

Using a (certified) Protection Profile has the advantage that a lot of the Security Target content already exists and is Common Criteria compliant. However the potential disadvantage is that unless the product is designed to meet the PP, there are likely to be problems. A Protection Profile also defines the EAL required and Developers must ensure that they are capable of meeting all the deliverables required.

8.6 An Example

In order to see how the various components of a Security Target are generated, let us look at a realistic example. We will consider an implementation of a smart card application - in this case indexEMV EMV - running on an operating system, which in turn is implemented on an integrated circuit. The application can potentially be one of several present on the card and the configuration may be represented thus:

An EMV application is, in theory, familiar to most UK citizens as this is the implementation of Chip&PIN on UK-issued debit and credit cards. EMV is a stan-

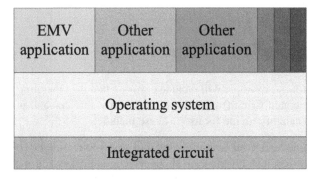

Fig. 8.2 Multi-application OS

dard which provides means of authenticating both card (using cryptography) and the cardholder (locally, using a PIN).

The use of cryptography implies the use of secret keys within the smart card.

We will now consider each stage required to construct the various elements of the Security Target and look at some examples based on an EMV card. These examples are not exhaustive; however the interested reader will be able to find examples of Protection Profiles and public Security Targets online on the websites of the various national Certification Bodies.

8.6.1 Establish the Security Environment

The **Physical Environment** of the TOE is open. Cardholders have total and private access to their cards - and can carry out whatever attacks they like, taking as long as they want.

The **Purpose** of the TOE is clearly defined by the EMV specifications and is to provide a secure implementation of EMV (see www.emvco.com for example).

Primary assets are:

* Secret Keys
* The PIN

Secondary assets are:

* Data used to make security decisions
* The application code itself

In the case of primary assets we need to ensure that they are protected in terms of both confidentiality and integrity. We may care less about the confidentiality of secondary assets, but we do care about its integrity - otherwise the security functionality could be subverted. Alternatively the confidentiality of the source code may be a requirement, which would make it a primary asset under these definitions.

8.6.2 Establish security objectives

Assumptions for our example will include ensuring that the Operating System (and underlying Integrated Circuit) provides the necessary services and protection that the application cannot provide for itself. These include:

* Data cannot be read from or modified within any type or memory or bus
* The chip does not leak information about cryptographic keys during calculations
* The operating system provides a secure, separate domain for an application to execute

Threats to the assets include:

- Unauthorised disclosure of primary assets
- Unauthorised disclosure of primary and/or secondary assets
- Replay attacks of EMV transaction data

An obvious example of an **Organisational Security Policy** is that:

- Cardholders will not disclose their PIN to anyone else (or write it down on the back of the card)

8.6.3 Establish Security Requirements

Security Objectives for the TOE can be easily derived from the threats:

- The TOE will prevent unauthorised disclosure of primary assets
- The TOE will prevent unauthorised modification of primary and secondary assets
- The TOE will prevent replay attacks on transaction data

Some **Security Objectives for the Environment** can be derived from the Assumptions:

- The chip will not leak information about cryptographic keys during calculations
- The chip will not permit data to be read or modified from any type of memory or bus
- The operating system will provide a secure, separate domain for an application to execute

Additional Security Objectives for the Environment may arise from services that the application relies on the Operating System to provide (in Common Criteria terminology such services are called Security Functional Requirements for the IT Environment). For example the application will probably require a library of (securely and correctly implemented) cryptographic functions to be provided, leading to:

- The operating system will provide RSA and DES cryptographic primitives

The security objectives are used to select the appropriate Security Functional Requirements and Security Assurance Requirements (together with any requirements on the environment). We have seen that the Security Assurance Requirements define the EAL to be used (together with any required augmentation). More complex is choosing the appropriate Security Functional Requirements (or SFRs). Common Criteria (part 2) provides a comprehensive set of SFRs grouped into the following classes:

- Audit
- Communication
- Cryptographic support
- User data protection
- Identification and authentication
- Security management

- Privacy
- Protection of TOE security functions
- Resource utilisation
- TOE access
- Trusted path/channels

Each class provides multiple definitions of security functionality which may be used, although there are dependencies within and between classes - interactions which limit the possible valid combinations of SFRs available.

An example from the Audit class (FDP_SDI.2) taken from cite3 is as follows:

- **FDP_SDI.2.1** The TSF shall monitor user data stored within the TSC for [assignment: *integrity errors*] on all objects, based on the following attributes: [assignment: *user data attributes*]
- **FDP_SDI.2.2** Upon detection of a data integrity error, the TSF shall [assignment: *action to be taken*]

(TSF means TOE Security Functionality and TSC means TOE Scope of Control).

The texts in square brackets are used to represent assignments - this is text that represents generic items which are replaced with TOE-specific entities within a Security Target. Protection Profiles may leave assignments generic or partially complete, or may complete them. Incomplete assignments from Protection Profiles must be completed within a Security Target.

This particular SFR deals with how data integrity is monitored and how errors are acted upon. A typical completion of this SFR within a Security Target for an EMV application might be:

- **FDP_SDI.2.1** The TSF shall monitor user data stored within the TSC for **checksum errors** on all objects, based on the following attributes : **checksum errors on secret key data**
- **FDP_SDI.2.2**Upon detection of a data integrity error, the TSF shall **abend and reject all subsequent commands**

This represents a TOE which monitors the secret keys for checksum errors and terminates execution of the application if one is detected. Furthermore the application takes the (perhaps drastic) step of rejecting all subsequent commands, which means that once an error is found, the application cannot be used any more. (It could potentially be deleted and reloaded, depending on the functionality provided by the Operating System).

8.6.4 Establish TOE summary specification

The TOE Summary Specification is relevant for Security Targets only, as it defines how the **Security Functions** of the TOE are implemented. Security Functions must support all the SFRs defined in the Security Target (although this is not necessarily a one-to-one mapping). To complete our data integrity example from the previous section, here is a potential Security Function:

- The TOE will monitor all secret key data for checksum errors whenever key data is accessed. The 4-byte checksum is calculated over all the secret key data and is updated whenever key data is updated. If the checksum fails to verify the system will set the checksum_error flag in EEPROM and abend. Upon start-up the checksum_error flag is checked and if set all commands will be rejected.

8.6.5 Establish Rationale

Finally the Security Target must complete the Rationale, which maps the threats, assumptions, objectives, SFRs, etc. together to show complete consistency. In addition the Security Target will give an overview of how deliverables will provide the assurance evidence required.

8.7 Deliverables

Common Criteria provides a series of classes supporting the delivery of evidence for the evaluation. These classes are grouped and summarized as follows:

- ACM class - configuration management

  - Procedures and processes
  - Automated CM system
  - Unique identification of TOE

- ADO class - delivery and operation

  - Installation, generation and start-up procedures/processes

- ADV class - development

  - Functional specification
  - High Level Design
  - Implementation (e.g. source code)
  - Internals (modularity of design)
  - Low Level Design
  - Representation Correspondence
  - Security Policy Model

- AGD class - guidance documentation

  - Administrator guidance
  - User guidance

- ALC class - life cycle support

  - Security of development environment
  - Development life cycle
  - Tools and techniques

- ATE class - testing

  - Coverage of (functional) testing
  - Depth of testing
  - Functional testing
  - Independent testing by evaluator

- AVA class - vulnerability assessment

  - Covert channel analysis
  - Misuse analysis
  - Strength of function analysis
  - Vulnerability analysis

Deliverable requirements for evaluations (currently) up to and including EAL4 are defined in great details in the Common Evaluation Methodology [4] document. This defines what evaluators look for in deliverables and so is a great help to developers as they can see precisely what it is that the evaluators will expect. A limitation of [4] is that as it only covers up to EAL4 any evaluations using a higher assurance level (including any augmentations to EAL) are not included.

As an aside, Common Criteria terminology and language can take some getting used to. Take this example from [4] paragraph 1406:

> To demonstrate consistency, the evaluator verifies that the functional specification correspondence shows that the functional description in the functional specification of the functions identified as implementing the policy described in the security policy model identify the same attributes and characteristics of the security policy model and enforce the same rules as the security policy model

Familiarity with Common Criteria - perhaps combined with a few read-throughs of the text - render this a perfectly reasonable explanation of how the functional specification and security policy model must be consistent.

8.8 Evaluation Composition

Returning to our example of a smart card product which consists of three elements - application, operating system and integrated circuit - we will now look at how evaluations of such products are performed in practice.

Expertise involved in the development (and therefore evaluation) of such a product will include:

- Software development (application and operating system)

- Hardware
- Cryptography
- Security
- Product Development
- Design Methodology
- Configuration Management

Such a product is typically developed as follows:

- The Integrated Circuit is developed
- The Operating System is implemented on the IC, taking into account any user guidance provided by the IC developer
- The Application is implemented on the OS, taking into account any user guidance provided by the OS developer

These developments are - again, typically - performed by separate companies who specialise in each particular type of product, although there may be - for example - companies who develop both Operating System and Applications. However taking the general case, there will be three separate companies involved in developing these elements. Each company will therefore know the intimate details of their own product (and its development, testing, vulnerabilities, etc.) - but will only have information about the other components provided to them (potentially under confidentiality agreement). Therefore the OS developer will not know precisely how the IC ensures data is not easily extracted from the chip. Similarly the Application developer will not have details of how the OS ensures that Applications cannot interfere with each others' secure data. Specifically developers will wish to maintain confidentiality of their products and will not typically make this available to other parties. When an evaluation of the final product is considered, it quickly becomes clear that co-operating between the developers is required.

Another factor to consider is modularity and re-use of evaluations. If the combined product is evaluated in a single project, any change to any part of the product will require the whole product to be re-evaluated. This will be time-consuming and costly.

A way to make such evaluations tractable is evaluation composition. Using this technique the evaluation of the final product is constructed in an analogous way to that sketched above for product development, namely:

- The Integrated Circuit is evaluated
- The Operating System is evaluated in isolation and then a composition evaluation of the OS on the IC is performed
- The Application is evaluated in isolation and then a composition evaluation of the Application on the (previously composed) OS + IC is performed.

The main issues considered during the composition phases of this process include:

- Ensure that the security functions of the product being composed cannot be subverted

- Ensure that the user guidance of the underlying product (IC or OS) has been followed in the product being composed (OS or Application respectively). If this is not the case vulnerabilities may exist.
- Ensure that combining products does not introduce new vulnerabilities.

Segregating IC, OS and Application evaluations and later combining them has advantages:

- It gives a modular approach - evaluations can be re-used as required.
- Each developer can focus on their own evaluation and does not need to share the details of their product's security with other developers
- Composition evaluations are typically short - and therefore relatively cheap

However there is some additional work required when undertaking evaluations of this nature - for example:

- Composed Security Targets need to be generated, which means that some details of relevant security functions will need to be shared between developers (e.g. the Application Developer will need to be aware of how some of the OS functionality is implemented).
- Evaluation plans will need to be aligned - a degree of co-operation between developers will be required and an overseeing role will need to be played by the evaluator and certification body.

Composition evaluations bring a pragmatic method of evaluating smart card products, which are necessarily modular in design.

8.9 In Conclusion

Common Criteria is an international standard which uses high-quality, independent evaluation laboratories to perform security evaluations in a rigorous and well-defined manner. Evaluations can be used as marketing tools, but also ensure that developers focus attention during the development process to ensure that product security features are correctly implemented and tested.

Successful evaluations can be crucial tools in ensuring product sales, however obtaining them comes at a price - costs and timescales for evaluations always need to be considered.

Finally Common Criteria is an evolving standard. At the time of writing version 2.3 is current; however version 3.1 is already published and valid for new evaluations and will be mandatory from 2008. The interested reader is encouraged to use the Common Criteria Portal website for information on the latest developments.

This paper is the result of the author's experience of security evaluations and represents the author's personal views only and not necessarily those of Master-Card International Incorporated or any of its affiliates.

Useful Websites

The reader may find the following websites useful:

- `www.commoncriterialportal.org` - the main site for Common Criteria (and the best place to start)
- `csrc.nist.gov/cc/html` - the US NIST site
- `www.cesg.co.uk` - the UK CESG site
- `www.ssi.gouv.fr/fr/confiance/evalcertif.html` - the French DCSSI site
- `www.bsi.bund.de/cc` - the German BSI site
- `www.emvco.com` - for information about EMV

Glossary

CB	Certification Body
CC	Common Criteria
CCRA	Common Criteria Recognition Agreement
DES	Data Encryption Standard
EAL	Evaluation Assurance Level
EMV	Europay, MasterCard, Visa
IC	Integrated Circuit
ISO	International Standardisation Organisation
IT	Information Technology
ITSEC	Information Technology Security Evaluation Criteria
OS	Operating System
OSP	Organisational Security Policy
PIN	Personal Identification Number
PP	Protection Profile
RSA	Rivest, Shamir and Adleman
SFR	Security Functional Requirement
SOGIS	Senior Officials Group Information Systems Security
ST	Security Target
TCSEC	Trusted Computing Security Evaluation Criteria
TOE	Target Of Evaluation
TSF	TOE Security Functionality
TSC	TOE Scope of Control

References

1. Common Methodology for Information Technology Security Evaluation - Part 1 Introduction and General Model, August 2005 Version 2.3 CCMB-2005-08-001
2. Common Methodology for Information Technology Security Evaluation - Part 2 Security Functional Requirements, August 2005 Version 2.3 CCMB-2005-08-002
3. Common Methodology for Information Technology Security Evaluation - Part 3 Security Assurance Requirements, August 2005 Version 2.3 CCMB-2005-08-003
4. Common Methodology for Information Technology Security Evaluation - Evaluation Methodology, August 2005 Version 2.3 CCMB-2005-08-004

5. Common Methodology for Information Technology Security Evaluation - Part 1 Introduction and General Model, September 2006 Version 3.1 Release 1 CCMB-2006-09-001
6. Common Methodology for Information Technology Security Evaluation - Part 2 Security Functional Components, September 2006 Version 3.1 Release 1 CCMB-2006-09-002
7. Common Methodology for Information Technology Security Evaluation - Part 3 Security Assurance Components, September 2006 Version 3.1 Release 1 CCMB-2006-09-003
8. Common Methodology for Information Technology Security Evaluation - Evaluation Methodology, September 2006 Version 3.1 Release 1 CCMB-2006-09-004

Chapter 9
Smart Card Security

Michael Tunstall

Abstract In this chapter, a description of the various attacks and countermeasures that apply to secure smart card applications are described. This chapter focuses on the attacks that could affect cryptographic algorithms, since the security of many applications is dependent on the security of these algorithms. Nevertheless, how these attacks can be applied to other security mechanisms is also described. The aim of this chapter is to demonstrate that a careful evaluation of embedded software is required to produce a secure smart card application.

Key words: Embedded Software, Fault Analysis, Side Channel Analysis, Smart Card Security.

9.1 Introduction

The implementation of secure applications on smart cards is different to the development on other platforms. Smart cards have limited computing power, comparatively small amounts of memory and are reliant on a smart card reader to provide power and a clock. There are security considerations that are specific to smart cards, that need to be taken into account when developing a secure smart card-based application.

In this chapter, attacks that are specific to smart cards, and other devices based around a secure microprocessor, will be described. There are other considerations that need to be taken into account when implementing a secure application, but these are generic and beyond the scope of this chapter.

Michael Tunstall, Coding and Cryptography Research Group,
Department of Electrical & Electronic Engineering,
University College Cork, Cork, Ireland
e-mail: miket@eleceng.ucc.ie

There are three main types of attack that are considered in smart card security. These are:

1. **Invasive Attacks:** These are attacks that require the microprocessor in a smart card to be removed and directly attacked through a physical means. This class of attacks can, at least in theory, compromise the security of any secure microprocessor. However, these attacks typically require very expensive equipment and a large investment in time to produce results. Invasive attacks are therefore considered to be primarily in the realm of semiconductor manufacturers and students at well-funded universities.

   An example of such an attack would be to place probes on bus lines between blocks of a chip (a hole needs to be made in the chip's passivation layer to allow this). An attacker could then attempt to derive secret information by observing the information that is sent form one block to another.

   At its most extreme this type of attack could make use of a focused ion beam to destroy or create tracks on the chips surface. In theory, this could, for example, be used to reconnect fuses. Traditionally, chip manufacturers typically used a test mode where it was possible to read and write to all memory addresses whilst a fuse was present. Once the fuse was blown inside the chip (before the chip left the manufacturer's factory) this mode was no longer available. In modern secure microprocessors this test circuit is typically removed when the chip is cut from the die and this attack is no longer possible.

   Further information on invasive attacks is available in [3, 28].
2. **Semi-Invasive Attacks:** These attacks require the surface of the chip to be exposed. An attacker then seeks to compromise the security of the secure microprocessor without directly modifying the chip.

   Some examples of this type of attack include observing the electro-magnetic emanations using a suitable probe [16,40] and injecting faults using laser light [6] or white light [43]. More details on these attacks are given in later sections.

   A description of numerous semi-invasive attacks is available in [44].
3. **Non-Invasive Attacks:** These attacks seek to derive information without modifying a smart card, i.e. both the secure microprocessor and the plastic card remain unaffected. An attacker will attempt to derive information by observing information that leaks during the computation of a given command, or attempt to inject faults using mechanisms other than light.

   Some examples of this type of attack would be to observe the power consumption of a microprocessor [27], or to inject faults by putting a glitch into the power supply [3].

   Further descriptions of power analysis attacks can be found in [29], and fault attacks in [6].

This chapter will focus on semi-invasive and non-invasive attacks, as the equipment required to conduct these attacks is more readily available. Invasive attacks are of interest but are extremely expensive to conduct. This chapter will focus more on what can be achieved in a reasonably funded laboratory. However, some information is given on invasive attacks where relevant.

Organisation

Section 9.2 contains a description of the cryptographic algorithms that will be used in later sections to give examples of attacks. Section 9.3 describes certain hardware security features that are typically included in a smart card. Section 9.4 describes the different forms of side channel analysis and how they can be applied to smart card implementations of cryptographic algorithms. Section 9.5 describes how fault attacks can be applied to smart cards. Section 9.6 describes how the techniques given in Sections 9.4 and 9.5 can be applied to other security mechanisms. Section 9.7 summarises the chapter.

Notation

The base of a value is determined by a trailing subscript, which is applied to the whole word preceding the subscript. For example, FE_{16} is 254 expressed in base 16 and $d = (d_{\ell-1}, d_{\ell-2}, \ldots, d_0)_2$ gives a binary expression for d.

In all the algorithms described in this chapter, ϕ represents Euler's totient function, where $\phi(N)$ equals the number of positive integers less than N which are coprime to N. In particular, if $N = p \cdot q$ is an RSA modulus then $\phi(N) = (p-1)(q-1)$.

9.2 Cryptographic Algorithms

Some of the attacks detailed in later sections will assume a detailed knowledge of some of the commonly used cryptographic algorithms. Specifically, the Data Encryption Standard (DES) and RSA, are detailed in this section to provide a reference, and to describe the notation that will be used.

9.2.1 Data Encryption Standard

The Data Encryption Standard (DES) was introduced by NIST in the mid 1970s [37], and was the first openly available cryptography standard. It has since become a worldwide *de facto* standard for numerous purposes. It is only in recent years that it has been practically demonstrated that an exhaustive search of the keyspace is possible, leading to the introduction of triple DES and the development of the Advanced Encryption Standard (AES) [38].

DES can be considered as a transformation of two 32-bit variables (L_0, R_0), i.e. the message block, through sixteen iterations of a round function, as shown in Fig. 9.1, to produce a ciphertext block (L_{16}, R_{16}). The Expansion permutation selects eight overlapping six-bit substrings from R_n. The P-permutation is a bitwise permutation on the 32-bit output of the S-box function. For clarity of expression, these

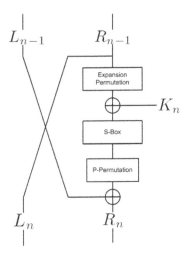

Fig. 9.1 The DES Round Function for Round n.

permutations will not always be considered and the round function will be written
as:

$$R_n = S(R_{n-1} \oplus K_n) \oplus L_{n-1}$$
$$L_n = R_{n-1}$$

(9.1)

where S is the S-box function. The subkeys K_n, for $1 \leq n \leq 16$, are each 48 bits
generated from the 56-bit secret key, by choosing 48 bits from the 56-bit key. This
is done by initially conducting a bitwise permutation on the key, referred to as Permuted Choice 1 (PC1). Each round bit shifts are conducted on the key, and 48 bits
are chosen from this shifted key to form each subkey using the Permuted Choice 2
(PC2) function.

Eight different S-boxes are applied in each round to sets of six bits, thereby reducing the 48-bit output of the XOR with K_n to 32 bits. Each S-box is a substitution
table that is addressed using six bits of information, and each entry is a 4-bit number.

The algorithm also includes an initial and final permutation (these permutations
are referred to as IP and IP^{-1} respectively), where the final permutation is the inverse of the initial permutation. More precisely the permutation at the end of DES
is conducted on (R_{16}, L_{16}) rather than (L_{16}, R_{16}). These permutations will be ignored in this chapter, as they do not contribute to the security of the algorithm. The
permutations IP and IP^{-1} were included since this was the most convenient way of
introducing the bits into the chip use to calculate the DES algorithm (at the time
software implementations were not considered because of the complexity of the
algorithm) [33].

9.2.1.1 Triple DES

In order to mitigate the key length problem, a modification to DES was proposed to make an exhaustive key search prohibitively complex. Triple DES is a construction that uses two different DES keys and is defined in [37]. In the algorithm below these are labelled K_1 and K_2, and in order to generate a ciphertext block C from a plaintext block M the following calculation is performed:

$$C = \text{DES}(\text{DES}^{-1}(\text{DES}(M,K_1),K_2),K_1) \qquad (9.2)$$

where $\text{DES}(M,K)$ denotes the output of the DES encryption algorithm applied to message block M with key K. Deciphering the ciphertext block C uses the function,

$$M = \text{DES}^{-1}(\text{DES}(\text{DES}^{-1}(C,K_1),K_2),K_1) \qquad (9.3)$$

The structure of triple DES allows for backward compatibility as if K_1 and K_2 are equal the resulting ciphertext will the equivalent to that produced with a single DES. The triple DES requires that three instantiations of the DES algorithm are used, since it has been shown that two instantiations of DES only increase the security of the algorithm by one bit (see meet-in-the-middle attacks [31]).

Another version of triple DES is proposed in [37], in which three different keys are used rather than two.

9.2.2 RSA

RSA was first published in 1978 [41], and was the first published example of a public key encryption algorithm. The security of RSA depends on the difficulty of factorising large numbers. This means that RSA keys need to be quite large, because of advances in factorisation algorithms and the constantly increasing processing power available in modern computers.

To generate a key pair for use with RSA, two prime numbers, p and q, typically of equal bit length, are generated; they are then multiplied together to create a value N, the modulus, whose bit length is equal to that desired for the cryptosystem. That is, in order to create a 1024-bit modulus, $2^{511.5} < p,q < 2^{512}$[1] (if values of p or q are chosen from $\{2^{511}+1,\ldots,2^{511.5}\}$ the product of p and q is not guaranteed to have a bit length of 1024 bits). A public exponent, e, is chosen that is coprime to both $(p-1)$ and $(q-1)$.

---

[1] This is possibly overly strong, as it typically recommend that the bit lengths of p and q are approximately equal. However, it will provide the most security for a modulus of a given bit length assuming that $p-q$ is sufficiently large to prevent an attacker from guessing their values by calculating $\sqrt{N}$.

A private exponent, d, is generated from the parameters previously calculated, using the formula:

$$e \cdot d \equiv 1 \quad (\text{mod } (p-1)(q-1)), \text{ or equivalently}$$
$$e \cdot d \equiv 1 \quad (\text{mod } \phi(N)) \tag{9.4}$$

where ϕ is Euler's Totient function.

9.2.2.1 The RSA Cryptosystem

In the RSA cryptosystem, to encrypt a message, M, and create ciphertext, C, one calculates:

$$C = M^e \bmod N \tag{9.5}$$

The value of e is often chosen as 3 or $2^{16} + 1$, as these value are small, relative to N, and have a low Hamming weight, which means that the encryption process is fast (see below). To decrypt the ciphertext, the same calculation is carried out but using the private exponent, d, which generally has the same bit length as N:

$$M = C^d \bmod N \tag{9.6}$$

9.2.2.2 The RSA Signature Scheme

The RSA digital signature scheme involves the reverse the operations used in the RSA cryptosystem. The generation of a signature, S, uses the private exponent d. By convention, this is expressed as:

$$S = M^d \bmod N \tag{9.7}$$

The verification therefore uses the public exponent and is expressed as:

$$M = S^e \bmod N \tag{9.8}$$

9.2.2.3 Padding Schemes

Applying the RSA primitive to a message, as described above, will not yield a secure signature or encryption scheme (for reasons beyond the scope of this chapter). To achieve a secure scheme it is necessary to apply the RSA operation to a transformed version of the message, e.g. as can be achieved by hashing the message, adding padding, and/or masking the result. This process is termed padding, and the interested reader is referred to [31] for a treatment of padding schemes.

Some of the attacks presented in this chapter will not be realistic when a padding scheme is used, since padding schemes mean that an attacker cannot entirely control a message. However, it is important that an implementation of RSA is secure against all possible attacks. If a given implementation does not use padding or, more realistically, contains a bug that allows an attacker to remove the padding function, the implementation should still be able to resist all the attacks described in this chapter.

9.2.2.4 Computing a Modular Exponentiation

Many different algorithms can be used to calculate the modular exponentiation algorithm required for RSA. In practice, a large number of algorithms cannot be implemented on smart cards, as the amount of available memory does not usually allow numerous intermediate values to be stored in RAM. The manipulation of large numbers is usually performed using a coprocessor (see Section 9.3), as implementing a multiplication on an 8-bit platform would not give a desirable performance level.

The simplest exponentiation algorithm is the square and multiply algorithm [31], and is given below for an exponent d of bit length ℓ:

The Square and Multiply Algorithm
Input:
$M, d = (d_{\ell-1}, d_{\ell-2}, \ldots, d_0)_2, N$
Output:
$S = M^d \bmod N \{$
    $A := 1$
    for $i = \ell - 1$ **to** 0 $\{$
        $A := A^2 \bmod N$
        if $(d_i = 1)$ $\{$
            $A := A \cdot M \bmod N$
        $\}$
    $\}$
    return A
$\}$

The square and multiply algorithm calculates $M^d \bmod N$ by loading the value one into the accumulator A and d is read bit-by-bit. For each bit a squaring operation modulo N takes place on A, and when a bit is equal to one A is subsequently multiplied by M. It is because of this multiplication that e is typically chosen to as 3 or $2^{16} + 1$, as both values only have two bits set to one; therefore minimising the number of multiplications required. It is not possible to only have one bit set to one as it is necessary for e to be an odd number in order for it to have an inverse modulo N. The most significant bit of a number will always be set to one, and the least significant bit will need to be set to one to produce an odd number.

9.2.2.5 Using the Chinese Remainder Theorem

The RSA calculation using the private exponent (i.e. where $S = M^d \bmod N$ and $N = p \cdot q$) can be performed using the Chinese Remainder Theorem (CRT) [25]. Initially, the following values are calculated,

$$S_p = (M \bmod p)^{(d \bmod (p-1))} \bmod p$$
$$S_q = (M \bmod q)^{(d \bmod (q-1))} \bmod q \tag{9.9}$$

which can be combined to form the RSA signature S using the formula $S = aS_p + bS_q \bmod N$, where:

$$\begin{array}{cc} a \equiv 1 \pmod{p} & b \equiv 0 \pmod{p} \\ a \equiv 0 \pmod{q} & \text{and} \quad b \equiv 1 \pmod{q} \end{array}.$$

This can be implemented in the following manner:

$$S = S_q + ((S_p - S_q) q^{-1} \bmod p) \cdot q \tag{9.10}$$

This provides a method of calculating an RSA signature that is approximately four times quicker than a generic modular exponentiation algorithm, i.e. two exponentiations, each of which can be computed eight times faster than an exponentiation using d (the bit length of $d \bmod (p-1)$ and $d \bmod (p-1)$ will be half that of d). This advantage is offset by an increase in the key information that needs to be stored. Rather than storing just the value of d and N, the values of $(p, q, d \bmod (p-1), d \bmod (q-1), q^{-1} \bmod p)$ need to be precalculated and stored.

9.3 Smart Card Security Features

This section will detail some of the features of smart cards that are pertinent when considering their security. Smart cards have traditionally been based on 8-bit Complex Instruction Set Computer (CISC) architectures [35]. Usually built around a Motorola 6805 or Intel 8051 core, often with extensions to the instruction set. More sophisticated smart cards are emerging based on 32-bit Reduced Instruction Set Computer (RISC) architecture chips, containing dedicated peripherals (cryptographic coprocessors, memory managers, large m memories, ...) [34].

9.3.1 Communication

A smart card has five contacts that it uses to communicate with the outside world defined in the ISO/IEC 7816-2 standard [22]. Two of these are taken by the power supply (usually 3 or 5 volts), referred to as Vcc, and the ground used to power the chip. Another contact is used to supply a clock, which is allowed to vary between 1 and 5 MHz but is typically set to 3.57 MHz. The remaining two contacts are used to communicate with the microprocessor. A sixth contact was originally used to provide a higher voltage to program the EEPROM (referred to as Vpp), but is no longer in use for reasons described in Section 9.6. The location of the different contacts is shown in Fig. 9.2.

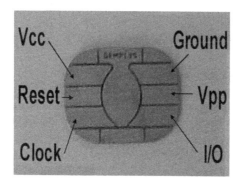

Fig. 9.2 The Contacts Used to Power and Communicate with a Smart Card.

One of the contacts, called the I/O, is used for communication and to send commands to the chip in a smart card. The protocols used to communicate with a smart card are referred to as T=0 and T=1 and are defined in the ISO/IEC 7816-3 standard [21]. This section will describe both protocols, as they are nearly identical. The extra requirements of T=1 are detailed where relevant.

The remaining contact is used to reset the smart card (there are a further 2 contacts defined in the ISO/IEC 7816-3 standard but they are not currently used). This is a physical event (i.e. moving the voltage applied to this contact from 0 to 1) that will always provoke a response from the smart card. A user can apply the reset at any time. The smart card will respond by sending an Answer To Reset (ATR) to the I/O contact, which is a string of bytes that defines the protocols the smart card can use, the speeds at which the smart card can communicate and the order in which bits are going to be sent during the session (i.e. most or least significant bit first).

9.3.2 Cryptographic Coprocessors

Traditionally, smart cards have been based around 8-bit architectures. In order to manipulate large numbers, e.g. to calculate the RSA algorithm, dedicated coprocessors can be appended to the CPU. In more modern 32-bit chips [34] this is no longer necessary, as efficient software implementations can be achieved. DES is also often implemented in a coprocessor to help increase performance, and AES implementations should be available in the near future. These coprocessors can increase the smart card's performance, as hardware implementations of secret key algorithms can be expected to require one or two clock cycles per round of the block cipher. However, the inclusion of coprocessors also increases the size of the chip and the overall power consumption. This means that chips with coprocessors are usually more expensive and are not ideal in environments where the amount of available current is limited.

9.3.3 Random Number Generators

Random number generators are usually included in smart cards, as unpredictable numbers are an important element in many secure protocols. A true random number generator is typically based on a signal generated by an analog device which is then treated to remove any bias that may exist, or has been induced, in the bits generated. The correct functioning of all aspects of a smart card chip under varied environmental conditions is important, but is critical for random number generation because the quality of the generated random values can have a profound effect on cryptographic schemes. Random number generators are therefore designed to function correctly in a large range of environmental conditions, including temperature, supply voltage, and so on. However, if an attacker succeeds in modifying the environmental conditions such that the physical source of randomness is affected, the subsequent treatment is included so that an attacker will not be able to determine if the change in conditions had any effect.

Pseudo-random number generators are also often included in a secure microprocessor. These are typically based on Linear Feedback Shift Registers (LFSRs) that are able to generate a new pseudo-random value every clock cycle, but are deterministic over time and are not usually used for critical security functions.

Where random values are required in cryptographic algorithms, a true random number generator is used when the quality of the random value is important, e.g. for use in a cryptographic protocol. Where the quality of the random value is less important, a pseudo-random number generator can be used. In some secure microprocessors only pseudo-random number generators are available. In this case, mechanisms that combine a random seed (that can be inserted into the chip during manufacture) with pseudo-random values can be used to provide random values.

An example of this latter type of random number generator is given in the ANSI X9.17 [2, 19] standard, that uses DES to provide random values based on a random seed generated during the initialisation of a given device and another source of pseudo-random information. This functions by taking a 64-bit pseudo-random input (X), a 64-bit random seed (S) and a DES key (K). X is usually generated by calculating $X = \mathrm{DES}(D, K)$, where D is a the date and/or time, but this information is not available to a smart card and is therefore replaced with values provided by a pseudo-random number generator.

To output a random value R the following calculation takes place:

$$R = \text{DES}(X \oplus S, K), \tag{9.11}$$

and the random seed is updated using:

$$S = \text{DES}(R \oplus X, K). \tag{9.12}$$

For increased security the DES function can be replaced with triple DES, as the key length used by DES has proven to be too short to entirely resist an exhaustive key search.

9.3.4 Anomaly Sensors

There are usually a number of different types of anomaly detectors present in smart cards. These are used to detect unusual events in the voltage and clock supplied to the card, and the environmental conditions (e.g. the temperature). These enable a smart card to detect when it is exposed to conditions that are outside the parameters within which it is known to function correctly. When unusual conditions are detected, the chip will cease to function until the effect has been removed (i.e. initiate a reset or execute an infinite loop when the sensor is activated). However, it is considered prudent not to rely solely on these sensors and to implement further countermeasures (see Section 9.5).

9.3.5 Chip Features

The surface of the chip used in a smart card can be uncovered by removing the plastic body of the card and using fuming nitric acid to remove the resin used to protect the microprocessor. Once the chip has been revealed the easiest form of analysis is to simply look at it under a microscope. The various different blocks can often be identified, as shown in Fig. 9.3.

Reverse engineering can target the internal design to understand how a given chip or block functions. An attacker can use such information to improve their knowledge of chip design and find potential weaknesses in the chip, which may allow them to compromise the chip's integrity.

In modern smart cards, various features used to inhibit reverse engineering are implemented using glue logic: important blocks are laid out in a randomised fashion that makes reverse engineering difficult. This technique increases the size of the block, and is therefore not used in the design of large blocks such as ROM and EEPROM.

Another common technique to prevent this sort of identification and targeting is to overlay the chip with another metal layer that prevents the chip's features being

Fig. 9.3 A Chip Surface with Readily Identifiable Features.

identified. This can be removed using hydrofluoric acid that eats through the metal layer; this reaction is then stopped using acetone before further damage is done and the chip surface can be analysed. The chip becomes non-functional but the layout of the chip can be determined, so that other chips of the same family can be attacked. The result of such a process is shown in Fig. 9.4.

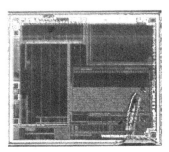

Fig. 9.4 A Chip with a Shield Present and Removed.

Discovering the layout and functioning of a chip is particularly important when using a laser as a fault injection mechanism (see Section 9.5). Different areas of a chip can be targeted through the metal layer once the layout of a chip is known.

9.4 Side Channel Analysis

Side channel attacks are a class of attacks where an attacker will attempt to deduce what is occurring inside a device by observing information that leaks during the normal functioning of the device. If this information can be related to any secret information being manipulated the security of the device can be compromised. It should be noted that side channel analysis is a passive form of attack, i.e. an attacker will simply observe what is occurring when a device is functioning. In the case of smart cards the message being manipulated can be controlled, but this is not necessary to construct a valid side channel attack.

The first publication that mentions a side channel attack is described in [45]. In 1956 MI5 mounted an operation to decipher communications between Egyptian embassies. The communications were enciphered using Hagelin machines [24]. These machines did not function by using a key value as described in Section 9.2. Enciphering occurred by routing electronic signals from a keyboard through seven rotating wheels to generate a ciphertext. The "key" was the initial setting of these seven wheels. The machine was reset every morning by the clerk who would be sending messages. MI5 managed to plant a microphone in close proximity to one of these machines. This allowed the initial settings to be determined by listening to the initial settings being made every morning. This would have allowed them to decipher intercepted communications with another Hagelin machine set to the same key. In practice MI5 was only able to determine a certain amount of wheel settings because of the difficulty of distinguishing the noise of the wheels being set from background noise. This made deciphering more complex, but not impossible, as the number of possible keys was significantly reduced by the partial information.

9.4.1 Timing Analysis

The first modern example of a side channel attack was proposed in [26]. This involved observing the differences in the amount of time required to calculate a RSA signature for different messages to derive the secret key. This attack was conducted against a PC implementation but a similar analysis could potentially be applied to smart card implementations. It would be expected to be more efficient against a smart card as more precise timings can be achieved with an oscilloscope or proprietary readers. An example of a trace acquired with an oscilloscope that would provide this sort of information is shown in Fig. 9.5. The I/O events on the left hand side of the figure represent the reader sending a command to the smart card. The I/O events on the right hand side of the figure show the response of the smart card. The time taken by a given command can be determined by observing the amount of time that passes between these two sets of events.

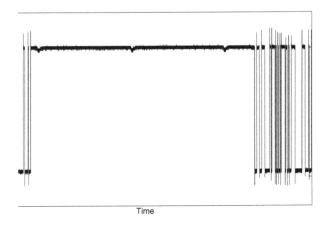

Time

Fig. 9.5 The I/O of a Smart Card Command.

9.4.2 Power Analysis

The most common form of side channel attack, when considering smart cards, is the analysis of the instantaneous power consumption [27]. This is measured by placing a resistor in series with a smart card and the power supply (or ground), and measuring the potential difference across the resistor with an oscilloscope. The acquired information can be analysed *a posteriori* to attempt to determine information on what is occurring within a secure microprocessor. There are two main types of power attack; these are Simple Power Analysis (SPA) and Differential Power Analysis (DPA).

9.4.2.1 Simple Power Analysis

A powerful form of power analysis is to search for patterns within the acquired power consumption. An attacker can attempt to determine the location of individual functions within a command. For example, Fig. 9.6 shows the power consumption of a smart card during the execution of DES. A pattern can be seen that repeats 16 times, corresponding to the 16 rounds that are required during the computation of DES.

This analysis can be further extended by closely inspecting the power consumption during the computation of one round, to attempt to determine the individual functions within each round. This is shown in Fig. 9.7 where the functions in the second round of a DES implementation are evident from the power consumption trace. This may not be immediately apparent, as close inspection of the trace's features is necessary to identify the individual functions. For example, if an attacker is seeking to determine where in a command the compression permutation (PC2) is

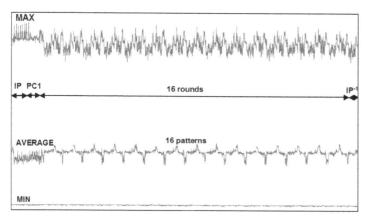

Fig. 9.6 The Power Consumption of a DES Implementation Showing the Rounds of the Algorithm.

computed. An attacker will look for eight patterns of six events. This is because the compression permutation selects 48 bits from the 56-bit DES key, where the 48-bit result is divided into segments of 6 bits (for use in the S-box function). The natural method of implementing this permutation will, therefore, be to construct a loop that will repeat eight times. Each loop will move six bits from the DES key to the 48-bit output. This should therefore produce eight patterns of six events because of the individual bits being selected and written.

The use of this information is not necessarily immediately apparent; an attacker can use this information to improve the effectiveness of other attacks. The efficiency of the statistical treatment required for Differential Power Analysis (DPA) [27] can be increased by taking more precise acquisitions. This is because the area that needs to be analysed can be defined, and therefore reducing the amount of data that needs to be acquired. A more detailed analysis is given below.

The same is true for fault injection techniques, detailed in Section 9.5, as it is often necessary to target specific events. If arbitrary functions can be identified using the power consumption, the point in time at which an attacker wishes to inject a fault can be discovered. This can greatly decrease the time required to conduct a successful attack, as less time is wasted injecting faults into areas of the computation that will not produce the desired result.

The examination of the power consumption can also be used to determine information on the private/secret keys used in naïve implementations of cryptographic algorithms. For example, if the power consumption of a smart card during the generation of an RSA signature using the square and multiply algorithm is analysed, it may be possible to determine some bits of the private key. An example of the power consumption during the generation of an RSA signature is shown in Fig. 9.8.

Looking closely at the acquired power consumption, a series of events can be seen. There are two types of event at two different power consumption levels, with a short dip in the power consumption between each event. This corresponds well to

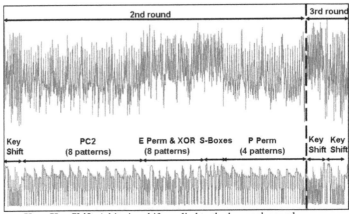

Key: **Key Shift** A bitwise shift applied to the key each round.
PC2 PC2 used to generate a 48-bit round key each round.
E Perm Expansion permutation applied to R_i,
for $1 \leq i \leq 16$, to produce a 48-bit output.
XOR The XOR with the round key.
S-boxes Eight substitution tables reducing 48 bits to 32 bits.
P Perm The P permutation, a bitwise transformation.

Fig. 9.7 The Power Consumption of a DES Implementation Showing the Round Functions.

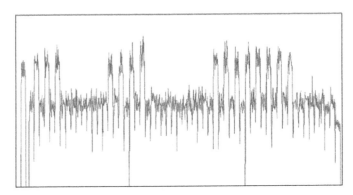

Fig. 9.8 The Power Consumption of an RSA Implemented Using the Square and Multiply Algorithm.

the square and multiply algorithm described in Section 9.2. Given the ratio of the two features, it can be assumed that the feature with the lower power consumption represents the squaring operation and the higher power consumption represents the multiplication. From this, the beginning of the exponent can be read from the power consumption, in this case the exponent used is $F00F000FF00_{16}$.

It should be noted that all the examples given in this section have been taken from chips that display the differences in an obvious manner. Modern secure microprocessors rarely display the functions being executed as clearly as in the examples given.

9.4.2.2 Differential Power Analysis

The idea of statistically treating power analysis traces was first presented to the cryptographic community in [27], and is referred to as Differential Power Analysis (DPA). DPA is based on the relationship between the power consumption and the Hamming weight of data being manipulated at a given point in time. The differences in power consumption are potentially extremely small, and cannot be interpreted individually, as the information will be lost in the noise incurred during the acquisition process. The small differences produced can be seen in Fig. 9.9, where traces were taken using a chip where the acquisition noise is exceptionally low.

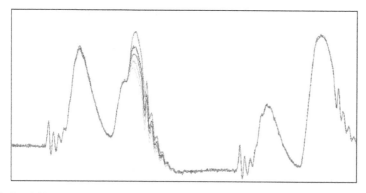

Fig. 9.9 Overlaid Acquisitions of the Power Consumption Produced by the Same Instruction but with Varying Data.

Differential Power Analysis (DPA) can be performed on any algorithm in which an intermediate operation of the form $\beta = S(\alpha \oplus K)$ is calculated, where α is known and K is the key (or some segment of the key). The function S is typically a non-linear function, usually a substitution table (referred to as an S-box), which produces an intermediate output value β.

The process of performing the attack initially involves running a microprocessor N times with N distinct message values M_i, where $1 \leq i \leq N$. The encryption of the message M_i under the key K to produce the corresponding ciphertext C_i will result in power consumption waveforms w_i, for $1 \leq i \leq N$. These waveforms are captured with an oscilloscope, and sent to a computer for analysis and processing.

To find K, one bit of β is chosen which we will refer to as b. For a given hypothesis for K this bit will classify whether each trace w_i is a member of one of two possible sets. The first set S_0 will contain all the traces where b is equal to zero, and the second set S_1 will contain all the remaining traces, i.e. where the output bit b is equal to one.

A differential trace Δ_n is calculated by finding the average of each set and then subtracting the resulting values from each other, where all operations on waveforms are conducted in a pointwise fashion, i.e. this calculation is conducted on the first point of each acquisition to produce the first point of the differential trace, the second point of each acquisition to produce the second point of the differential trace, etc.

$$\Delta_n = \frac{\sum_{w_i \in S_0} w_i}{|S_0|} - \frac{\sum_{w_i \in S_1} w_i}{|S_1|}$$

A differential trace is produced for each value that K can take. In DES the first subkey will be treated in groups of six bits, so 64 (i.e. 2^6) differential traces will be generated to test all the combinations of six bits. The differential trace with the highest peak will validate a hypothesis for K, i.e. $K = n$ corresponds to the Δ_n featuring a maximum amplitude. An example of a differential trace produced by predicting one bit of the output a DES S-box, with a correct key guess, is shown in Fig. 9.10.

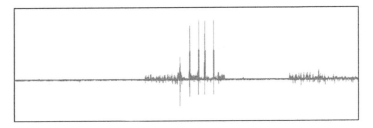

Fig. 9.10 A Differential Trace.

The differential trace in Fig. 9.10 shows a large difference in the power consumption at five different points, which are referred to as DPA peaks. The first peak corresponds to the output of the S-box, i.e. where the output of the S-box function is determined and written to memory. The four subsequent peaks correspond to the same bit being manipulated in the P-permutation. This occurs because the output of each S-box consists of four bits, and the memory containing those four bits will be accessed each time one of those bits is required in the output of the P-permutation.

A more complete version of this attack uses Pearson's correlation coefficient to demonstrate the correlation between the Hamming weight and the instantaneous power consumption. This can be used to validate key hypotheses in an identical manner to DPA. Details of this method are beyond the scope of this chapter, but the interested reader is referred to [11].

9.4.3 Electromagnetic Analysis

An alternative side channel to measuring the power consumption of a smart card is to measure the instantaneous electromagnetic emanations as a cryptographic algorithm is being computed [16, 40]. This is typically implemented using a small probe, an example of which can be seen in Fig. 9.11. Such probes can measure the electromagnetic emanations for different blocks of a chip, as such probes are an equivalent size to the chip's features. This means that the probe can be placed just above a given feature to try and get a strong signal from that part of the chip, e.g. the bus between two areas of the chip, while excluding noise from other areas of the chip.

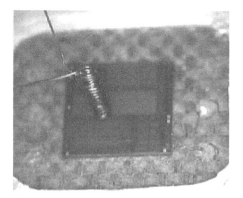

Fig. 9.11 Electromagnetic Probing of a Chip.

Unfortunately, it is a much more complicated attack to realise, as the chip needs to be open, as shown in Fig. 9.11. If the chip surface is not exposed the signal is not usually strong enough for any information to be deduced. The tools required to capture this information are also more complex, as the power consumption can be measured by simply reading the potential difference over a resistor in series with a smart card. To measure the electromagnetic field involves building a suitable probe (the probe in Fig. 9.11 is handmade) and the use of amplifiers, so that an oscilloscope can detect the signal.

The signals that are acquired using this method are also different to those acquired by reading the instantaneous power consumption. The signals acquired during two executions of a selected command by an 8-bit microprocessor is shown in Fig. 9.12. The black traces show the acquired power and electromagnetic signals when the chip manipulates FF_{16}, and the grey traces shows the same command where the microprocessor is manipulating 00_{16}. The difference in the black and grey traces representing the power consumption can be seen as a increase in the power consumption for short periods. The difference in the traces representing the electromagnetic emanations is caused by sudden changes in the electromagnetic field, shown by spikes in the signal at the same moment in time the difference in the power consumption can be observed.

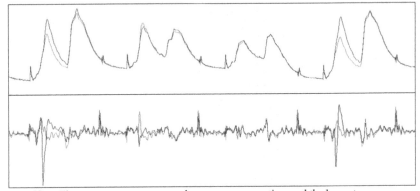

Key: The upper traces represents the power consumption, and the lower traces represent the electromagnetic emanations during the same command. The black traces were taken were FF_{16} is being manipulated, and the grey traces where 00_{16} is being manipulated.

Fig. 9.12   Power and Electromagnetic Measurements.

The traces acquired from measuring the instantaneous electromagnetic emanations can be treated in exactly the same way as power consumption acquisitions [16, 40]. The acquisitions can be analysed individually, referred to as Simple ElectroMagnetic Analysis (SEMA), or treated statistically, referred to as Differential ElectroMagnetic Analysis (DEMA).

9.4.4 Countermeasures

There are several countermeasures for protecting cryptographic algorithms against side channel attacks. Some countermeasures can either be implemented in hardware or software; only software implementations are considered here for simplicity. These countermeasures are listed below:

Constant Execution can be used to fix the time taken by an algorithm, so that no deductions on secret information can be made though timing analysis or SPA. This extends to individual processes being executed by a smart card. If a process takes different lengths of time depending on some secret information and the difference in time is made up by a dummy function, there is a good chance that this will be visible in the power consumption or electromagnetic emanations. It is therefore important that an algorithm is written so that the same code is executed for all the possible input values.

Random Delays can be inserted at different points in the algorithm being executed, i.e. a dummy function that takes a random amount of time to execute can be called. The algorithm can no longer be said to comply with the constant execution criteria given above, but any variation is completely independent of any secret information. This does not prevent any attacks, but creates an extra step for an attacker. In order to conduct any power analysis an attacker needs to synchronise the power consumption acquisitions *a posteriori*. The problem of attempting to conduct side channel attacks in the presence of random delays is described in [14].

Randomisation (or data whitening) is where the data is manipulated in such a way that the value present in memory is always masked with a random value. This randomisation remains constant for one execution, but will vary from one acquisition to another. This mask is then removed at the end of the algorithm to produce the ciphertext. Some ideas for implementing this countermeasure were proposed in [12], and an example of this sort of implementation applied to block ciphers can be found in [1].

The size of the random value used in block ciphers is generally limited as S-boxes need to be randomised before the execution of the block cipher. This is generally achieved by creating an alternative S-box in memory for each execution of the cryptographic algorithm using the algorithm given below:

Randomising S-box Values
Input:
$S = (s_0, s_1, s_2, \ldots, s_n)_x$ containing the S-box, $\mathbf{R}$ a random $\in \{0, 1, \ldots, n\}$,
and r a random $\in \{0, 1, \ldots, x-1\}$
Output:
$RS = (rs_0, rs_1, rs_2, \ldots, rs_n)_x$
{
    for $i = 0$ **to** n {
        $rs_i := s_{(i \oplus \mathbf{R})} \oplus r$
    }
    return RS
}

The random value used for masking the input data can be no larger than n, and the random used for the output value can be no larger that x. In an implementation of DES $\mathbf{R} \in \{0, 1, \ldots, 63\}$ and $r \in \{0, 1, \ldots, 15\}$. The rest of the algorithm needs to be a carefully designed to produce values masked with R, and to be able to manipulate returned values masked with r.

This is not possible in the case of RSA, where the calculation methods do not facilitate the method described above. A method for randomising the calculation of an RSA signature is given in [23], where the signature generation can be calculated using the formula:

$$S = \left((M + r_1 \cdot N)^{d + r_2 \cdot \phi(N)} \bmod (r_3 \cdot N) \right) \bmod N \qquad (9.13)$$

where ϕ is Euler's totient function and, r_1, r_2 and r_3 are small random values. The effect of the each of the small random values does not change the outcome, but the order of the squaring operations and multiplications required to compute S is randomised. This does not provide a totally secure algorithm as the modular exponentiation itself also has to be secured against SPA attacks. A discussion of these algorithms is given in [13].

Randomised Execution is the manipulation of data in a random order so that an attacker does not know what is being manipulated at a given moment in time. If, for example, n bytes are being XORed with n key bytes then it is prudent to do it in a random order. If an attacker wishes to determine which byte has been XORed at any particular time this will be infeasible given that the order that bytes are being manipulated is unknown.

This also inhibits any statistical analysis of a side channel (i.e. using DPA), as this relies on the same unknown variable being treated at the same point in time. As an attacker cannot know the order in which the data has been treated, this provides an extremely efficient countermeasure when combined with randomisation. An discussion of this technique applied to DES is described in [32].

9.4.4.1 Remarks

The above list gives the countermeasures that would need to be applied to a cryptographic algorithm to render it secure against side channel analysis. An attacker would, therefore, have to overcome the combination of all these countermeasures. For an extensive treatment of side channel analysis, the interested reader is referred to [29].

9.5 Fault Analysis

The problem of faults occurring in microprocessors has existed for a relatively long time. One of the initial observations of faults being provoked in microprocessors was accidental. It was observed that radioactive particles produced by elements naturally present in packaging material caused faults in chips [30]. Specifically, these faults were caused by Uranium-235, Uranium-238 and Thorium-230 residues present in the packaging decaying to Lead-206 and releasing α particles. These particles were energetic enough to cause bits stored in RAM to change.

Further research involved the analysis of the effect of cosmic rays on semiconductors [46]. While cosmic rays are very weak at ground level, their effect in the upper atmosphere and outer space is important for the aero-spacial industry. This provoked research into integrity measures that need to be included in semiconductors utilised in the upper atmosphere and space.

In 1997 it was pointed out that a fault present in the generation of an RSA signature, computed using the Chinese Remainder Theorem, could reveal information on the private key [10] (this attack is detailed below). This led to further research into the effect of faults on the security of implementations of cryptographic algorithms in secure microprocessors, and the possible mechanisms that could be used to inject faults in a microprocessor.

9.5.1 Fault Injection Mechanisms

There are a variety of different mechanisms that can be used to inject faults in microprocessors. These are listed here:

Variations in Supply Voltage [3, 9] during execution may cause a processor to misinterpret or skip instructions.

Variations in the External Clock [3, 4, 28] may cause data to be misread (the circuit tries to read a value from the data bus before the memory has time to latch out the correct value) or an instruction miss (the circuit starts executing instruction $n + 1$ before the microprocessor has finished executing instruction n).

Extremes of Temperature [10, 18] may cause unpredictable effects in microprocessors. When conducting temperature attacks on smart cards, two effects can be obtained [6]: the random modification of RAM cells due to heating, and the exploitation of the fact that read and write temperature thresholds do not coincide in most Non-Volatile Memories (NVMs). By tuning the chip's temperature to a value where write operations work but read operations do not, or the other way around, a number of attacks can be mounted.

Laser Light [15, 20, 39] can be used to simulate the effect of cosmic rays in microprocessors. Laser light is used to test semiconductors that are destined to be used in the upper atmosphere or space. The effect produced in semiconductors is based on the photoelectric effect, where light arriving on a metal surface will induce a current. If the light is intense, as in laser light, this may be enough to induce a fault in a circuit.

White Light [3] has been proposed as an alternative to laser light to induce faults in microprocessors. This can be used as a relatively inexpensive means of fault induction [43]. However, white light is not directional and cannot easily be used to illuminate small portions of a microprocessor.

Electromagnetic flux [42] has also been shown to be able to change values in RAM, as eddy currents can be made strong enough to affect microprocessors. However, this effect has only been observed in insecure microprocessors.

9.5.2 Modelling the Effect of a Fault

The fault injection methods described above may have many different effects on silicon. They can be modelled in ways that depend on the type of fault injection that has been used. The following list indicates the possible effects that can be created by these methods:

Resetting Data: an attacker could force the data to the blank state, i.e. reset a given byte, or bytes, of data back to 00 or FF_{16}, depending on the logical representation.

Data Randomisation: an attacker could change the data to a random value. However, the adversary does not control the random value, and the new value of the data is unknown to the adversary.

Modifying Opcodes: an attacker could change the instructions executed by the chip's CPU, as described in [3]. This will often have the same effect as the previous two types of attack. Additional effects could include removal of functions or the breaking of loops. The previous two models are algorithm dependent, whereas the changing of opcodes is implementation dependent.

These three types of attack cover everything that an attacker could hope to do to an implementation of an algorithm. It is not usually possible for an attacker to create all of these possible faults in any particular implementation. Nevertheless, it is important that algorithms are able to tolerate all types of fault, as the fault injection methods that may be realisable on a given platform are unpredictable. While an attacker might only ever have a subset of the above effects available, if that effect is not taken into account then it may have catastrophic consequences for the security of a given implementation.

In the literature one-bit faults are often considered. This is a useful model for developing theoretical attacks, but has proven to be extremely difficult to produce on a secure microprocessor. The model given above is based on published descriptions of implementations of fault attacks.

9.5.3 Faults in Cryptographic Algorithms

The faults mechanisms and fault model described above can be used to attack numerous cryptographic algorithms. Two examples of fault attacks on cryptographic algorithms are described below.

9.5.3.1 Faults in RSA Signature Generation

The first published fault attack [10], proposed an attack focused on an implementation of RSA using the Chinese Remainder Theorem (CRT). The attack allows for a wide range of fault injection methods, as it only requires one fault to be inserted in order to factorise the RSA modulus.

The technique requires an attacker to obtain two signatures for the same message, where one signature is correct and the other is the result of the injection of a fault during the computation of S_p or S_q (see above). That is, the attack requires that one of S_p and S_q is computed correctly, and the other is computed incorrectly.

Without loss of generality, suppose that $S' = aS_p + bS_q' \bmod N$ is the faulty signature, where S_q is changed to $S_q' \neq S_q$. We then have:

$$
\begin{aligned}
\Delta &\equiv S - S' \pmod{N} \\
&\equiv (aS_p + bS_q) - (aS_p + bS_q') \pmod{N} \\
&\equiv b(S_q - S_q') \pmod{N} \ .
\end{aligned}
\tag{9.14}
$$

As $b \equiv 0 \pmod{p}$ and $b \equiv 1 \pmod{q}$, it follows that $\Delta \equiv 0 \pmod{p}$ (but $\Delta \not\equiv 0 \pmod{q}$) meaning that Δ is a multiple of p (but not of q). Hence, we can derive the factors of N by observing that $p = \gcd(\Delta \bmod N, N)$ and $q = N/p$.

In summary, all that is required to break RSA is one correct signature and one faulty one. This attack will be successful regardless of the type or number of faults injected during the process, provided that all faults affect the computation of either S_p or S_q.

Although initially theoretical, this attack stimulated the development of a variety of fault attacks against a wide range of cryptographic algorithms. A description of an implementation of this attack is given in [5].

9.5.3.2 Faults in DES

A type of cryptanalysis of ciphertext blocks produced by injecting faults into DES was proposed in [8], based on using techniques used in differential cryptanalysis [31]. One-bit faults were assumed to occur in random places throughout an execution of DES. The ciphertext blocks corresponding to faults occurring in the fourteenth and fifteenth round were taken, enabling the derivation of the key. This was possible as the effect of a one-bit fault in the last three rounds of DES is visible in the ciphertext block when it is compared with a correct ciphertext block. This allowed the key to be recovered using between 50 and 200 different ciphertext blocks. It is claimed in [8] that, if an attacker can be sure of injecting faults towards the end of the algorithm, the same results could be achieved with only ten faulty ciphertext blocks, and that, if a precise fault could be induced, only three faulty ciphertext blocks would be required.

This algorithm was improved upon in [17]. When searching for a key, the number of times a given hypothesis is found is counted. This means that faults from earlier rounds can be taken into account. It is claimed in [17] that faults from the eleventh round onwards can be used to derive information on the key, and that in the ideal situation only two faulty ciphertext blocks are required.

The simplest case of a fault attack on DES involves injecting a fault in the fifteenth round, and such an attack is well-known within the smart card industry.

The last round of DES can be expressed in the following manner:

$$R_{16} = S(R_{15} \oplus K_{16}) \oplus L_{15}$$
$$= S(L_{16} \oplus K_{16}) \oplus L_{15}$$

If a fault occurs during the execution of the fifteenth round, i.e. R_{15} is randomised by a fault to become R'_{15}, then:

$$R'_{16} = S(R'_{15} \oplus K_{16}) \oplus L_{15}$$
$$= S(L'_{16} \oplus K_{16}) \oplus L_{15}$$

and

$$R_{16} \oplus R'_{16} = S(L_{16} \oplus K_{16}) \oplus L_{15} \oplus S(L'_{16} \oplus K_{16}) \oplus L_{15}$$
$$= S(L_{16} \oplus K_{16}) \oplus S(L'_{16} \oplus K_{16}) \ .$$

This provides an equation in which only the last subkey, K_{16}, is unknown. All of the other variables are available from the ciphertext block. This equation holds for each S-box in the last round, which means that it is possible to search for key hypotheses in sets of six bits, i.e. the 48-bit output after the XOR is divided into eight groups of six bits before being substituted with values from the S-boxes.

All 64 possible key values corresponding to the XOR just before each individual S-box can be used to generate a list of possible key values for these key bits. After this, all the possible combinations of the hypotheses can be searched though, with the extra eight key bits that are not included in the last subkey, to find the entire key.

If R'_{15} is randomised by a fault, then the expected number of hypotheses that are generated can be predicted using the methods given in [7]. The Table 9.1 shows the statistically expected number of key hypotheses E_k that would be returned by a fault producing a difference across each S-box in the last round. This is an average of the non-zero elements in the expected number of hypotheses that are generated using the tables defined in [7].

Table 9.1 The Expected Number of Hypotheses Per S-Box for One Faulty Ciphertext Block.

S-box	E_k
1	7.54
2	7.67
3	7.58
4	8.36
5	7.73
6	7.41
7	7.91
8	7.66

The expected number of hypotheses for the last subkey will be the product of all eight expected values E_k; this gives an expected number of around 2^{24}. This is just for the last subkey, an actual exhaustive search will need to take into account the eight bits that are not included in the last subkey, giving an overall expected keyspace size of 2^{32}.

This substantially reduces the number of possible keys that would need to be tested to try and determine the secret key used. The size of the keyspace can be further reduced if the fault attack is repeated and the intersection of the two resulting keyspaces is determined.

The same attack can also be applied if small faults occur in the last five rounds of DES, but the treatment is statistical in nature and requires many more faults to determine information on the key. Further details of this attack, and a brief description of an implementation, are given in [17].

9.5.4 Countermeasures

The countermeasures that can be used to protect microprocessors from fault attacks are based on methods previously employed for integrity purposes. However, countermeasures only need to be applied in processes where an attacker could benefit from injecting a fault, although a careful analysis of a given application is required to determine where countermeasures are required. This has proven to be true even where algorithms are based on one-time random numbers, as it has been shown that the manipulation of the random number can compromise the security of an cryptographic algorithm [36]. The list of countermeasures is given below:

Checksums can be implemented in software or hardware. This prevents data (such as key values) being modified by a fault, as the fault can be detected followed by appropriate action (see below).

Execution Randomisation can be used to change the order in which operations in an algorithm are executed from one execution to another, making it difficult to predict what the machine is doing at any given cycle. For most fault attacks this countermeasure will only slow down a determined attacker, as eventually a fault will hit the desired instruction. However, this will thwart attacks that require faults in specific places or in a specific order.

Random Delays can be used to increase the time required to attack. As with execution randomisation a determined attacker can attempt to inject a fault until the moment the fault is injected coincides with the target. However, this can take significantly more time than would otherwise be required, especially if an attacker is able to identify a target through a side channel (e.g. using Simple Power Analysis).

Execution redundancy is the repeating of algorithms and comparing the results to verify that the correct result is generated. This is most effective when the second calculation is different to the first, e.g. the inverse function, to prevent an attacker form trying to inject an identical fault in each execution.

Variable redundancy is the reproduction of a variable in memory. When a variable is tested or modified the redundant copy is also tested or modified. This is most effective when the copy is stored in a different form to the original, e.g. the bitwise complement, to avoid a fault being applied to each variable in the same way.

Ratification counters and baits can be included to prevent an attacker from successfully completing a fault attack by rendering a microprocessor inoperative once a fault attack is detected. Baits are small (< 10 byte) code fragments that perform an operation and test it's result. A typical bait writes, reads and compares data, performs XORs, additions, multiplications and other operations whose results can be easily checked. When a bait detects an error it increments a counter in Non-Volatile Memory (NVM), and when this counter exceeds a tolerance limit (typically three) the microprocessor ceases to function.

9.5.4.1 Remarks

Many of the countermeasures in this list can be implemented in either hardware or software. A more complete list of the countermeasures (in hardware and software), along with a description of certain fault attacks, is given in [6].

9.6 Embedded Software Design

The attacks described in the previous sections of this chapter have focused on attacking cryptographic algorithms to determine a secret or private key. In this section some example of how the attack methods presented in Sections 9.4 and 9.5 can be applied to other security mechanisms are described. This is to demonstrate that implementing a secure application on a smart card is not trivial, and requires the careful evaluation of every implemented function. It should also be noted that the attacks described below are only possible where no specific countermeasures are implemented.

9.6.1 PIN Verification

As described in Section 9.3, the first smart cards included a contact that was called Vpp used to supply power to the microprocessor so that it could program the EEPROM present in the chip. At the time the voltage supply (Vcc) did not supply enough power to allow a microprocessor to modify EEPROM and a higher voltage needed to be applied to the Vpp contact. The Vpp contact is no longer used as it led to security problems, as described below.

If the Vpp contact was masked (e.g. covered with nail varnish) then no power would be available for the microprocessor to program the EEPROM, but power would be available through the Vcc to run every other function of the smart card. This meant that an attacker could try every single PIN number without decrementing the PIN counter (typically a PIN counter is set to three and decremented with every false PIN presentation, once the PIN number is zero a smart card will render itself non-functional). This process could be automated using a standard PC and a smart card reader to determine a PIN number in matter of minutes.

After the Vpp contact was removed further problems were encountered. The most natural way to implement a PIN verification would be as follows:

Insecure PIN Verification Algorithm
```
{
    if (PINcounter > 0) {
        PIN := RequestPIN();
    }
    else {
    return false;
    }
    if (PIN ≠ UserPIN) {
        PINcounter := PINcounter − 1;
        return false;
    }
    else {
        return true;
    }
}
```

---

where the PIN entered by a user is returned by the RequestPIN function and compared with the PIN in Non-Volatile Memory (NVM). If the entered PIN is not equal to the stored PIN, the PINcounter will be decremented.

It was observed that the power consumption increased when a smart card modified the value of the PIN counter, i.e. it was visible using the SPA techniques described in Section 9.4 as an increase in the power consumption. Attackers then developed tools to cut the power being supplied to a microprocessor once this increase in power consumption was detected. This allowed automated tools to attempt every PIN number until the correct PIN was found. The correct PIN would be the only value where the command would finish as the microprocessor would not attempt to modify the NVM.

This made it necessary to change the algorithm used to verify a PIN number. Typically, a secure PIN verification will be implemented in the following manner:

where the PINcounter is decremented before it is tested, and only incremented if the PIN is entered correctly. The power supply can be removed at any point during the command without producing a security problem. However, further modifications would need to be made to render it resistant to fault attacks. An example of a fault attack against an operating system is described below.

Secure PIN Verification Algorithm

```
{
    if (PINcounter > 0) {
        PIN := RequestPIN();
    }
    else {
    return false;
    }
    PINcounter := PINcounter − 1;
    if (PIN = UserPIN) {
        PINcounter := PINcounter + 1;
        return true;
    }
    else {
        return false;
    }
}
```

9.6.2 File Access

Another possible target within a smart card operating system is the file structure. All personalisation information, e.g. PIN numbers etc., is stored in a file structure situated in NVM. Each file will have a set of access conditions that determine who can read and write to each file or directory. For example a user's PIN number on a SIM card, unless intentionally disabled, will grant access to the files that contain SMS messages once verified. If the PIN is not verified access to these files will be denied. There are often administrator identification codes (essentially eight digit PIN numbers) that grant access to more files and allow the modification of files that the end user is not able to directly modify, e.g. the user's PIN number.

If an attacker wishes to attempt to access information stored in files without any of the codes mentioned above, a fault attack could be attempted. An attacker can attempt to inject a fault at the moment a smart card is evaluating whether the right to read a file, for example, should be granted. If successful, the evaluation will be erroneous and the right to access the file will be temporarily granted.

In order to determine the point in which a fault would need to be injected, an attacker can use SPA (see Section 9.4). An attacker could compare a trace of the power consumption where file access is granted with a trace where file access has been denied. An example of this is shown in Fig. 9.13. The black trace represents the power consumption where access has been denied. The grey trace represents the power consumption where access has been granted. It can be see at the point indicated in the figure that the two traces diverge. This should represent the moment at which the access conditions are evaluated and will, therefore, be the targeted area for a fault attack.

On a smart card there are typically files that contain serial numbers and such information, which can be read by anyone. Finding two files to attempt to read in order to generate traces, as shown in Fig. 9.13, should be straightforward.

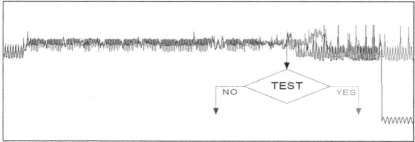

Key: **Black** Power consumption where file access is denied.
        Grey Power consumption where file access is granted.

Fig. 9.13 Determining the Moment File Access is Granted Using the Power Consumption.

This type of fault attack means that the access conditions to files, and other security mechanisms such as PIN verification, need to include redundancy in their tests to ensure that a fault attack is not possible. The various countermeasures that can be implemented are described in Section 9.5.

9.7 In Conclusion

This chapter presents the particular security considerations that need to be taken into account when implementing a secure smart card-based application. Implementations of all the commands on a smart card need to be subjected to careful analysis to prevent power analysis and fault injection techniques from compromising the security of the smart card.

Research in the domain of smart card security is typically a cyclic process. New attacks are developed against algorithm implementations, standards, etc. and countermeasures are proposed. The modifications are then reviewed for potential vulnerabilities and further countermeasures proposed if required. The aim of this process is to remain sufficiently ahead of what can be achieved by an individual attacker that smart cards remain secure throughout the period that they are active.

References

1. Akkar, M.-L. and Giraud, C. (2001). An implementation of DES and AES secure against some attacks. In Koç, C. K., Naccache, D., and Paar, C., editors, *Cryptogaphic Hardware and Embedded Systems — CHES 2001*, volume 2162 of *Lecture Notes in Computer Science*, pages 309–318. Springer-Verlag.
2. American National Standards Institute (1985). *Financial Institution Key Management (Wholesale)*. American National Standards Institute.

3. Anderson, R. and Kuhn, M. (1996). Tamper resistance — a cautionary note. In *Proceedings of the Second USENIX Workshop of Electronic Commerce*, pages 1–11.
4. Anderson, R. and Kuhn, M. (1997). Low cost attacks on tamper resistant devices. In Christianson, B., Crispo, B., Lomas, T. M. A., and Roe, M., editors, *Security Protocols*, volume 1361 of *Lecture Notes in Computer Science*, pages 125–136. Springer-Verlag.
5. Aumüller, C., Bier, P., Hofreiter, P., Fischer, W., and Seifert, J.-P. (2002). Fault attacks on RSA with CRT: Concrete results and practical countermeasures. In Kaliski, B. S., Koç, C. K., and Paar, C., editors, *Cryptographic Hardware and Embedded Systems — CHES 2002*, volume 2523 of *Lecture Notes in Computer Science*, pages 260–275. Springer-Verlag.
6. Bar-El, H., Choukri, H., Naccache, D., Tunstall, M., and Whelan, C. (2006). The sorcerer's apprentice guide to fault attacks. *Proceedings of the IEEE*, 94(2):370–382.
7. Biham, E. and Shamir, A. (1991). Differential cryptanalysis of DES-like cryptosystems. In Menezes, A. and Vanstone, S., editors, *Advances in Cryptology — CRYPTO '90*, volume 537 of *Lecture Notes in Computer Science*, pages 2?-21. Springer-Verlag.
8. Biham, E. and Shamir, A. (1997). Differential fault analysis of secret key cryptosystems. In Kaliski, B. S., editor, *Advances in Cryptology — CRYPTO '97*, volume 1294 of *Lecture Notes in Computer Science*, pages 513–525. Springer-Verlag.
9. Blömer, J. and Seifert, J.-P. (2003). Fault based cryptanalysis of the advanced encryption standard (AES). In Wright, R. N., editor, *Financial Cryptography — FC 2003*, volume 2742 of *Lecture Notes in Computer Science*, pages 162–181. Springer-Verlag.
10. Boneh, D., DeMillo, R. A., and Lipton, R. J. (1997). On the importance of checking computations. In Fumy, W., editor, *Advances in Cryptology — EUROCRYPT '97*, volume 1233 of *Lecture Notes in Computer Science*, pages 37–51. Springer-Verlag.
11. Brier, E., Clavier, C., and Olivier, F. (2004). Correlation power analysis with a leakage model. In Joye, M. and Quisquater, J.-J., editors, *Cryptographic Hardware and Embedded Systems — CHES 2004*, volume 3156 of *Lecture Notes in Computer Science*, pages 16–29. Springer-Verlag.
12. Chari, S., Jutla, C. S., Rao, J. R., and Rohatgi, P. (1999). Towards approaches to counteract power-analysis attacks. In Wiener, M., editor, *Advances in Cryptology — CRYPTO '99*, volume 1666 of *Lecture Notes in Computer Science*, pages 398–412. Springer-Verlag.
13. Chevallier-Mames, B., Ciet, M., and Joye, M. (2004). Low-cost solutions for preventing simple side-channel analysis: Side-channel atomicity. *IEEE Transactions on Computers*, 53(6):760–768.
14. Clavier, C., Coron, J.-S., and Dabbous, N. (2000). Differential power analysis in the presence of hardware countermeasures. In Koç, C. K. and Paar, C., editors, *Cryptographic Hardware and Embedded Systems — CHES 2000*, volume 1965 of *Lecture Notes in Computer Science*, pages 252–263. Springer-Verlag.
15. Fouillat, P. (1990). *Contribution à l'étude de l'interaction entre un faisceau laser et un milieu semiconducteur, Applications à l'étude du Latchup et à l'analyse d'états logiques dans les circuits intégrés en technologie CMOS*. PhD thesis, University of Bordeaux.
16. Gandolfi, K., Mourtel, C., and Olivier, F. (2001). Electromagnetic analysis: Concrete results. In Koç, C. K., Naccache, D., and Paar, C., editors, *Cryptographic Hardware and Embedded Systems — CHES 2001*, volume 2162 of *Lecture Notes in Computer Science*, pages 251–261. Springer-Verlag.
17. Giraud, C. and Thiebeauld, H. (2004). A survey on fault attacks. In Deswarte, Y. and Kalam, A. A. El, editors, *Smart Card Research and Advanced Applications VI — 18th IFIP World Computer Congress*, pages 159–176. Kluwer Academic.
18. Govindavajhala, S. and Appel, A. W. (2003). Using memory errors to attack a virtual machine. In *IEEE Symposium on Security and Privacy 2003*, pages 154–165.
19. Gutmann, P. (2004). *Security Architecture*. Spinger.
20. Habing, D. H. (1992). The use of lasers to simulate radiation-induced transients in semiconductor devices and circuits. *IEEE Transactions On Nuclear Science*, 39:1647–1653.
21. International Organization for Standardization (1997). *ISO/IEC 7816-3 Information technology – Identification cards – Integrated circuit(s) cards with contacts – Part 3: Electronic signals and transmission protocols*. International Organization for Standardization.

22. International Organization for Standardization (1999). *ISO/IEC 7816–2 Identification cards – Integrated circuit cards – Part 2: Cards with contacts – Dimensions and location of the contacts.* International Organization for Standardization.
23. Joye, M. and Olivier, F. (2005). Side-channel attacks. In van Tilborg, H., editor, *Encyclopedia of Cryptography and Security*, pages 571–576. Kluwer Academic Publishers.
24. Kahn, D. (1997). *The Codebreakers: The Comprehensive History of Secret Communication from Ancient Times to the Internet.* Simon & Schuster Inc., second edition.
25. Knuth, D. (2001). *The Art of Computer Programming*, volume 2, Seminumerical Algorithms. Addison–Wesley, third edition.
26. Kocher, P. (1996). Timing attacks on implementations of Diffie-Hellman, RSA, DSS, and other systems. In Koblitz, N., editor, *Advances in Cryptology — CRYPTO '96*, volume 1109 of *Lecture Notes in Computer Science*, pages 104–113. Springer-Verlag.
27. Kocher, P., Jaffe, J., and Jun, B. (1999). Differential power analysis. In Wiener, M. J., editor, *Advances in Cryptology — CRYPTO '99*, volume 1666 of *Lecture Notes in Computer Science*, pages 388–397. Springer-Verlag.
28. Kommerling, O. and Kuhn, M. (1999). Design principles for tamper resistant smartcard processors. In *USENIX Workshop on Smartcard Technology*, pages 9–20.
29. Mangard, S., Oswald, E., and Popp, T. (2007). *Power Analysis Attacks — Revealing the Secrets of Smart Cards*. Springer-Verlag.
30. May, T. and Woods, M. (1978). A new physical mechanism for soft erros in dynamic memories. In 16*th* International Reliability Physics Symposium.
31. Menezes, A., van Oorschot, P., and Vanstone, S. (1997). *Handbook of Applied Cryptography.* CRC Press.
32. Messerges, T. S. (2000). *Power Analysis Attacks and Countermeasures for Cryptographic Algorithms.* PhD thesis, University of Illinois, Chicago.
33. Meyer, C. (2000). Private communication. Carl Meyer was one of the designers of the DES algorithm.
34. MIPS-Technologies (2001). MIPS™architecture for programmers volume I: Introduction to the MIPS32™architecture. Technical Report MD00082, Revision 0.95.
35. Murdocca, M. and Heuring, V. P. (2000). *Principles of Computer Architecture.* Addison-Wesley.
36. Naccache, D., Nguyen, P. Q., Tunstall, M., and Whelan, C. (2005). Experimenting with faults, lattices and the DSA. In Vaudenay, S., editor, *Public Key Cryptography — PKC 2005*, volume 3386 of *Lecture Notes in Computer Science*, pages 16–28. Springer-Verlag.
37. NIST (1999). *Data Encryption Standard (DES) (FIPS–46-3).* National Institute of Standards and Technology.
38. NIST (2001). *Advanced Encryption Standard (AES) (FIPS–197).* National Institute of Standards and Technology.
39. Pouget, V. (2000). *Simulation expérimentale par impulsions laser ultra-courtes des effets des radiations ionisantes sur les circuits intégrés.* PhD thesis, University of Bordeaux.
40. Quisquater, J.-J. and Samyde, D. (2001). Electromagnetic analysis (ema): Measures and counter-measures for smart cards. In Attali, I. and Jensen, T. P., editors, *Smart Card Programming and Security, International Conference on Research in Smart Cards — E-smart 2001*, volume 2140 of *Lecture Notes in Computer Science*, pages 200–210. Springer-Verlag.
41. Rivest, R., Shamir, A., and Adleman, L. M. (1978). Method for obtaining digital signatures and public-key cryptosystems. *Communications of the ACM*, 21(2):120–126.
42. Samyde, D., Skorobogatov, S. P., Anderson, R. J., and Quisquater, J.-J. (2002). On a new way to read data from memory. In *Proceedings of the First International IEEE Security in Storage Workshop*, pages 65–69.
43. Skorobogatov, S. and Anderson, R. (2002). Optical fault induction attacks. In Kaliski, B. S., Ç. K. Koç, and Paar, C., editors, *Cryptographic Hardware and Embedded Systems — CHES 2002*, volume 2523 of *Lecture Notes in Computer Science*, pages 2–12. Springer-Verlag.
44. Skorobogatov, S. P. (2005). *Semi-Invasive Attacks — A New Approach to Hardware Security Analysis.* PhD thesis, University of Cambridge. available at http://www.cl.cam.ac.uk/ TechReports/.

45. Wright, P. (1987). *Spycatcher*. Heineman.
46. Ziegler, J. (1979). Effect of cosmic rays on computer memories. *Science*, 206:776–788.

Chapter 10
Application Development Environments for Java and SIM Toolkit

Gary Waite and Keith Mayes

Abstract The smart card is a very popular component of many commercial and government system solutions. The ability of the smart card to store data securely and resist a great deal of physical tampering is part of the attraction, but so too is the ability to run algorithms and protocols. Whilst there are successful and popular systems that make use of fairly simple cards with fixed function algorithms, the true potential of the smart card can only be realised when it represents a flexible platform for general application hosting and management. Fortunately such functionality is becoming commonplace on modern cards and so the focus moves to how applications may be practically developed to exploit it. There are a range of ways this can be done, but by way of illustration this chapter restricts itself to Java as one of the most popular development methods and applies it to (U)SIMs; perhaps the most powerful of the mass deployed smart cards.

Key words: Development, API, Java, Java Card, Java SIM, Java Framework, SIM Toolkit, SATSA, JSR177, Applet, Midlet, Events, Tools, Testing, DRM, Software

10.1 Introduction

A modern state-of-the-art smart card is a powerful multi-application platform incorporating sophisticated and secure management functionality. This enables applications to be added, deleted or modified both during the pre-issuance and post-issuance phases. Indeed it is possible to have a sophisticated hierarchy of security rights and permissions that delegate management authority to third parties. Most of the important features of smart card platforms have been well standardised, but

Gary Waite, Technology Manager Devices & SIM, O2 UK.
e-mail: Gary.waite@o2.com ·
Keith Mayes, Director of Crisp Telecom Ltd.
e-mail: keith.mayes@crisptele.com

the application platform has evolved into a few variants, as discussed in Chapter 3. Similarly there are different ways of designing smart card applications such as the browser approach mentioned in Chapter 1. In a single book chapter it is not possible to go into detail on every possible variant of platform, application and development method. Choosing a platform to focus on is not difficult as Java Card [20] is a popular de-facto standard and the Java language and tools are familiar to developers. Selecting the card type is a little more open, but as discussed in Chapter 4, the Subscriber Identity Module (SIM) [9] a good choice, being one of the most advanced smart cards in widespread use. This chapter will therefore focus on application development for Java Card based SIMs [9], but as a first step it will revisit some of the fundamental characteristics of the smart card that make it interesting as an application host. Note that where there is no need to differentiate between a SIM and a 3G USIM, the terms (U)SIM will be used for the device and SIM Toolkit for the Toolkit capabilities.

10.2 Smart Cards Characteristics

The experienced software developer, used to Personal Computers (PCs) and giant servers might wonder what makes the concept of a smart card so special for use in development? Well, there are in fact a number of useful attributes that normally go unnoticed or are simply taken for granted. Firstly a smart card is small, flat and portable. This in itself may not seem particularly special, but it is when you consider that all of its functionality is contained in a flat piece of plastic that can fit inside a wallet and be carried around to interact with a wide range of devices and readers. It is also a secure hardware platform, which essentially means that although the smart card may hold sensitive data it will not divulge this to just anyone (or any machine). The data is protected by sophisticated measures within the chip and various security policies, from Personal Identification Number (PIN), to mutual authentication challenges. Of course attacks are attempted against smart card security (as described in Chapter 9), but unless something has been badly designed or implemented, the associated time, effort cost and expertise are not usually merited by the value of the data discovered. The smart card also benefits from a global standard interface [15], which in real terms means that it will inter-operate with most terminal equipments around the world. This is an important point, as so many technologies coming to market these days promise powerful and compelling services, but fail due to lack of a widely-agreed standard interface. Smart cards are also very reliable, which is a vital attribute for any deployed or issued device. They seem to work way beyond their warranted lifespan and can take all manner of abuse including being dropped from great heights, repeatedly sat on, withstanding low and high temperatures, surviving duty as a windscreen ice scraper and even being submerged in beer! Whilst some cards such as credit cards have a controlled lifetime before re-issue, (U)SIM cards do not and there are still many in regular use that are over 10 years old. Smart cards can also be branded, for example with the issuing organisation. Now this may not seem particularly noteworthy especially in a chapter about application development, but branding is a hot issue even for single application cards and so one can imagine the difficulties with multi-application cards, especially if the applications are not all loaded or even known pre-issuance. The Issuer of a smart card e.g. a bank or network operator, is in a prime position to control the branding and indeed general functionality of the issued card, however the influence and control does not stop there. Often in the fine print of a user agreement you will find that ownership of the card remains with the Issuer and that the user is merely a temporary custodian. This means that the Issuer can manage, change and generally control the card post-issuance, using secure mechanisms that are usually denied to other parties. Having a smart card, in your wallet or mobile phone makes it very personal, especially as you have a measure of control over stored data and functionality, by means of your user PIN code. This brings us to an often forgotten attribute of a smart card in that despite its role in security and sensitive data handling it is not regarded as a threatening technology. Because smart cards have been in use by the general public for many years now (moreover: used by the general public for trusted services), and because they're small and flat, people are not too worried about having or using them. The user is ultimately in charge, as a pair of scissors can easily bring about the demise of a smart card, if required, which reminds us of another attribute; that smart cards are disposable. In the 21st century disposability and associated recycling are major concerns, however smart cards have a low waste factor and being essentially plastic can be recycled by the manufacturer. Finally, smart cards are relatively cheap, meaning that they can provide a cost effective solution for many services today.

With all these desirable attributes one might imagine that the smart card platform is a software developers dream, but alas that is not really the case as any application is constrained to work within a number of practical limitations described in the next section.

10.2.1 Limitations

Smart cards have very limited memory, typically anywhere between 16 kilobytes and 256 kilobytes. You can now buy cards with multi-Megabyte an even Gigabyte memory, but these are expensive and the technology is still being rolled out. So for now at least, any applications requiring vast amounts of local smart card memory are impractical.

Smart cards also have limited processing power. This is partly due to the size and vintage of the CPUs, but also to the power that they allowed to draw from a reader device. Generally, they are inappropriate for complex number-crunching or bulk data processing with the exception of cryptographic functions, where the chip may have a specialised co-processor for rapid execution. They also have limited Application Programming Interfaces (API)s, which in turn limit the creativity and flexibility for application developers. There is further disappointment as current smart cards have limited connectivity. Clearly there is no connectivity without a reader, but even when the reader is present, the connectivity is severely limited by the card-reader interface.

The very nature of the smart card being a secure device, means that the opportunities for developers are generally limited to those linked to the issuing organisations. This is because the security keys used to manage the device are generally not known to third parties. So even though the Java Card Open Platform (the most popular development environment) is a global standard, and specifications are freely available to any developer, practical open-access to such cards is difficult, if not impossible without permission by the Issuers.

Once cards are eventually deployed with one or more useful applications, there is limited opportunity for post-issuance management of the applications. Limited does not mean impossible and there are standardised protocols designed specifically to manage and/or change data and applications, however practical considerations often restrict management to minor changes. For example, in mobile-related applications there is the concept of Over The Air (OTA) management (see Chapter 11), but it is currently heavily bandwidth-restricted; mainly because of the SMS-data bearer used. Furthermore the sheer number of cards deployed makes any kind of management difficult. For example managing and maintaining the upgrade state of millions of smart cards of differing ages and capabilities, and when they may only be able to communicate at certain times and without annoying the user, is really quite a challenge.

Finally, one should not expect the latest and greatest smart card features and standards to be implemented overnight. Aside from the time to rollout new cards, the standards themselves tend to be slow to ratify new capabilities. It should also be noted that this is not simply due to technical debate, but also due to political and IPR interests. Indeed in some markets, including mobile communications, there is great pressure applied by some companies to limit what smart cards can do.

10.3 SIM Cards

SIM and USIM cards were introduced in Chapter 1 and described in detail within Chapter 4, so here we will just recap on some of the application relevant capabilities. A SIM card is essentially a smart card running at least a GSM application. For developers the main API is provided by a technology called SIM Application Toolkit (SAT or STK), but now generalised for all smart cards under the name of Card Application Toolkit (CAT). (Note the terms CAT, SAT and STK may be used interchangeably from now on)

CAT allows applications running on the (U)SIM card to access useful services on the mobile handset. These include the ability to send a short message, operate a simple UI with the handset, or perhaps to retrieve the handset's current location.

Some examples of currently deployed (U)SIM applications are:

Information on Demand Menus - here, traditional operator services such as receiving news headlines via SMS are made easier to access via a menu set up and controlled by a (U)SIM application. So for example, instead of having to re-member to send "FOOTBALL PREMIER MANCHESTER UNITED " to 80202 the customer can simply select the "Manchester United" item from the menu. Upon selection, the (U)SIM application will prepare and send an appropriate SMS message.

IMEI Trigger - it is very useful for the operator to know the particular hand-set that is being used by each customer (for example to ensure the correct GPRS/WAP/MMS settings are sent). An application on the (U)SIM is able to retrieve the International Mobile Equipment Identity (IMEI) from the handset when the (U)SIM is powered on, then compare it with a list of IMEIs stored on the (U)SIM. If the IMEI is new (i.e. not in the list), the operator is automatically notified via SMS, so that appropriate settings can be sent to the handset.

Phonebook backup - an application on the (U)SIM is able to monitor changes to phonebook data stored locally on the (U)SIM, then upload those changes pe-riodically to a central server so as to maintain a remotely synchronised copy of that data.

Preferred network selection - when roaming, some operators like to steer their customers to particular networks and this can be achieved using a (U)SIM appli-cation.

Digital rights management - in the same way that Universal Serial Bus (USB) dongles can be used to copy-protect software running on PCs, the (U)SIM can also be employed for a similar purpose.

The listed applications are only a small sub-set of what is possible and indeed in regular use today. The reader may have many other ideas for services and so an important question is how to write applications that can run on a (U)SIM. When considering multi-application (U)SIMs we are normally talking about a Java Card platform running a (U)SIM application and so we first need to recap on the that platform.

10.4 Java Card

As discussed in Chapter 3, a Java Card is a smart card capable of running Java programs, compliant to the Java Card specification issued and maintained by Sun Microsystems. For detailed information the reader is referred to the platform speci-fication [20]. Most smart card manufacturers licence Java Card product, and in 2007 alone it is expected that over a billion Java Card products will be shipped.

Recall that the architecture model for Java Card is as follows (see Fig. 10.1):

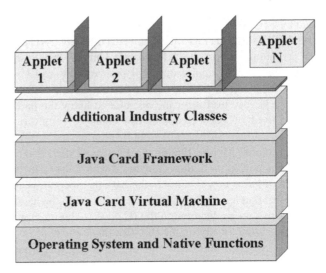

Fig. 10.1 Java Card Architecture Model

At the lowest layer the smart card manufacturer still provides a proprietary operating system which runs directly on the microprocessor and provides native functions to the next layer, the Java Card Virtual Machine or JVM. The JVM executes what is known as byte code, an abstracted machine code that makes the platform "open" so that code written once will operate on any product, no matter the machine language of the microprocessor itself. The next layer, the Java Card Framework, provides useful service APIs for smart card operations in general, including an Applet class, PIN class etc. The industry-add-on classes at the layer just below the applets provide further useful classes particular for that industry.

There are a few points worth noting with regard to Java Card technology:

- Java Card is referred to as a platform, not an operating system
- Unlike other Java platforms, the virtual machine in Java Card runs forever (i.e. when power is no longer supplied to the card, the Virtual Machine (VM) runs in an infinite clock cycle, and all non-transient objects created persist in EEPROM)
- Applets start their life when installed and registered in the system's registry, end their life when removed from the registry, and are held in an inactive state until explicitly selected by the terminal
- Garbage collection (i.e. memory recovery after applet or object deletion) is optional for Java Card and product-dependant
- Java Card currently does not support the following: Dynamic class loading, Security manager, Threads & synchronisation, Object cloning, Finalization, Large primitive data types (float, double, long)

10.4.1 The Java Card Framework

When developing an applet for a Java Card you make use of the Java Card Framework The Framework comprises four main package that you may see declared at the top of the applet source file:

- Java Card.framework

  - Core package
  - Applet, PIN, APDU, System and Util classes

- Java Cardx.framework

  - ISO-7816-4 file system
  - supports elementary files (EF), dedicated files (DF) and file-oriented APDUs
  - optional extension

- Java Cardx.crypto
- Java Cardx.cryptoEnc

  - Cryptographic functionality

Detailed information on these packages can be found in the API specification [2], but it is worth expanding a little on the Java Card Framework here, as this is the starting point for applet development. Indeed it includes the class that allows you to declare your application as an applet that you intend to load, install and run on a Java Card. Near the top of your source file you will have a statement something like;

"Public class ExampleApplet extends Java Card.framework.Applet;"

There are a number of methods associated with this class that you can use to install and register the applet, then select it when you want it to handle incoming APDUs. The method "process(APDU)" is a fundamental for an Java Card applet and is the first point to examine when determining the functionality of an applet, as it indicates the appropriate response to the various incoming APDU messages and their associated parameters. A simple example is shown in Fig. 10.2.

It is worth noting that the "Security Manager" class not supported on Java Card; instead language security policies are implemented by the virtual machine.

Although any applet can create objects that store and manipulate data, an object is owned by the applet that creates it, and even though an applet may have a reference to another object, it cannot invoke the object's methods unless it owns that object, or the object is shared (between applets). It is therefore possible for an applet to share objects with another or indeed all applets on the card. Overall, an applet is an independent entity within a Java Card. Its selection, execution and functionality are not affected by other applets residing on the same card; this construct is known as "firewalling".

The Java Card Runtime Environment (JCRE) comprises Java Card VM and classes within the Java Card Framework. Each applet on the card has unique Application Identifier (AID) assigned. The "install()" method (if successful) creates an instance of the application and registers it with the JCRE. It is generally expected that the developer will create all objects to be used during the life of the applet at installation. An Applet becomes active on a SELECT APDU command from the terminal. Any previously selected applet is immediately suspended (with its "deselect()" method being called so that the applet is informed), and the newly active applet has its "select()" method called. All APDU commands sent to the card (other than a SELECT command to select another applet) are routed through to the active applet where they are handled by the "process()" method of the selected applet.

```
package com.o2.JavaCard;

import javacard.framework.*;
import javacardx.framework.*;

public class MyFirstJavaCardApplet extends Applet
{
    byte[] buffer;

    private MyFirstJavaCardApplet()
    {
        register();
    }

    public static void install(byte[] bArray, short bOffset, byte bLength)
    {
        new MyFirstJavaCardApplet();
    }

    public void process(APDU apdu)
    {
        buffer = apdu.getBuffer();

        if (buffer[ISO.OFFSET_CLA] != (byte)0x80)
            ISOException.throwIt(ISO.SW_CLA_NOT_SUPPORTED);

        if (buffer[ISO.OFFSET_INS] != (byte)0x99)
            ISOException.throwIt(ISO.SW_INS_NOT_SUPPORTED);

        // Process command here!
    }
}
```

Fig. 10.2 A Simple Java Card applet:

The example shown in Fig. 10.2 is the equivalent of the "Hello World" program in conventional programming. The class supports the install method which effectively creates the new applet instance. The instance is registered with the JCRE and becomes available for use. The most interesting method for a developer is the "process (APDU)" as this is where all the message handling takes place. The message handler can decide what action is appropriate by examining a buffer containing the incoming APDU. The examination normally takes place in a structured manner, first checking that the APDU class byte is appropriate for the applet and then determining an appropriate handler based on the instruction byte. Individual command handlers would normally be implemented in separate sub-routines where more precise parameter checking would take place to determine the appropriate action and response.

A pre-requisite to examining the APDU fields, is to know how to navigate the message buffer array. As buffers could be implemented in a variety of ways the particular message bytes are found using defined "ISO" indexes. For example in Fig. 10.2. the index "ISO.OFFSET_CLA" is used to index the buffer array position where the APDU class byte has been stored. In the simple program example only commands are accepted with a certain class byte "(80)" and even then only commands with a certain instruction byte "(99)". Upon receipt of a valid command the applet completed normally and a good status "(90 00)" is send back to the terminal. Although this is a simple example, simplicity is not something that can be forgotten when developing software for a Java Card, even when fleshing out a fully functional application

Having knowledge of general Java programming is of course an advantage for anyone developing for Java Card, however it may come as a surprise that many of the classic Java features are to be avoided. Probably the first thing that a developer would notice looking at commercial-grade Java Card applet source code, is the complete absence of object-orientation! Although one of the foundations of Java, object orientation is not really used for Java Card, because memory is at such a premium. Object orientation on small platforms is often more trouble than it is worth and developers focus instead on trying to fit into one byte what they would normally have written an entire class for. Java Card developers also use the "new" keyword sparingly or not at all as an object created can never be destroyed to reclaim its memory, unless there is garbage collection available. Garbage collection may not always be supported and in any case the run-time creation and deletion of objects could lead to memory problems and errors that may not have been reproduced during applet testing. Pragmatically, most applications will have to create objects and so this should be done once only, during the applet installation phase. Furthermore if data buffers are created, these should be re-used as much as possible (and therefore given generic names). Comments of course don't consume any smart card memory at all, and therefore should be used as much as possible, especially given the lack of object-orientation.

Java Card is very strict on types (short, byte etc.) and generally this is a good thing, however, the fact that bytes are signed and not unsigned will give the novice developer no end of trouble. To get around the sign issue, source code may contain a surprising amount of casting and byte masking and sometimes a developer will have added utility functions to take care of unsigned byte manipulation.

On the plus side, exception handling is a blessing for Java Card development as it allows efficient data checking without exhausting too much memory. For example if the data supplied by the terminal is not correct (see the class and instruction tests in Fig. 10.2) then simply throw an exception. This will automatically generate the status message response with the SW1/SW2 status of your choice. There is no need to extract yourself from nested function calls, as the Java Card platform will automatically tidy up the stack etc.

So far we have talked about the generic Java Card but as we wish to focus on the telecommunications version we need to consider Java SIM.

10.5 Java SIM

Java SIM is simply a Java Card with pre-installed (U)SIM applet and (U)SIM-related APIs providing the same functionally as native GSM SIM or 3G USIM, governed by the 3GPP (originally ETSI) specifications. [3, 4]. On Java SIM each SIM Toolkit application exists as a separate Java Card applet.

GSM operators fought hard to get Java SIM for a number of reasons:

1. To make their dual/multiple smart card sourcing easier (e.g. develop once, deploy onto any card).
2. To encourage an open platform with lower cost products and remove barriers for new entrants to the market.
3. To create 3rd party development opportunities
4. To leverage from Java security and management functionality that had achieved high accreditation ratings in other business areas (banking)

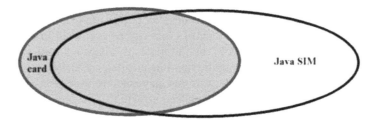

Fig. 10.3 Overlapping Scopes of Java Card and Java SIM

The Java SIM is represented by the large oval in Fig. 10.3. and can be considered (more or less) as an enlarged or superset of Java Card (in grey). From now on we will focus on Java SIM, and assume it covers both card technologies.

The Java SIM Framework is shown in context within Fig. 10.4.

In practice the additional functionality is accessed via two extra packages as defined in the standards [2];

- sim.toolkit
- sim.access

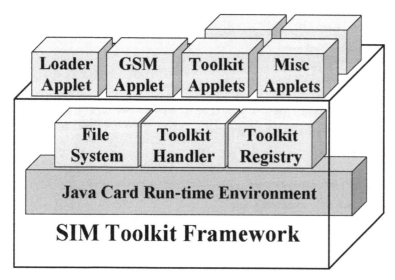

Fig. 10.4 Java SIM Architecture

10.5.1 sim.toolkit

This is the core package that manages SIM Toolkit-related activity, and provides a number of classes including;

- ProactiveHandler,
- ProactiveResponseHandler,
- ToolkitRegistry,
- EnvelopeHandler,
- EditHandler &
- ViewHandler.

The first two classes have "Proactive" in their names and this is quite significant. (U)SIMs can be used as slave devices simply satisfying requests from the network or mobile terminal but the proactive (U)SIM feature gives them the opportunity to take temporary control. This is a necessary capability for (U)SIM based applications to drive a sequence of actions although they still need some event(s) to trigger them to run. Events are processed by a SIM Toolkit handler process e.g.

"public void processToolkit(byte event)"

Rather like when "process(APDU)" is triggered by a general incoming APDU, "processToolkit()" is triggered by notification of an "event". This can be seen in the code segment of Fig. 10.5.

```
package com.o2.JavaSIM;

    import javacard.framework.*;
    import sim.toolkit.*;
    import sim.access.*;

    public class MyFirstJavaSIMApplet extends Applet
    {
        private byte[] text = { (byte)'H',(byte)'e',(byte)'l',(byte)'l',(byte)'o' };

        private MyFirstJavaSIMApplet()
        {
            register();
        }

        public static void install(byte[] bArray, short bOffset, byte bLength)
        {
            new MyFirstJavaSIMApplet();
        }

        public void processToolkit(byte event)
        {
            if (event == EVENT_PROFILE_DOWNLOAD)
            {
                ProactiveHandler ph = ProactiveHandler.getTheHandler();

                ph.initDisplayText((byte)0, DCS_8_BIT_DATA, text, (short)0, (short)text.length);
                ph.send();
            }
        }
    }
```

Fig. 10.5 Example SIM Toolkit Applet

The example is only interested in the PROFILE_DOWNLOAD event which informs the (U)SIM of the mobile terminal capabilities. This event occurs only once and early on during initialisation. When the event is triggered, the applet simply places an unoriginal text message "(Hello)" onto the handset display. There are quite a number of SIMToolkit events as shown in Table 10.1 and more fully described in the standards [2].

Table 10.1 SIM Toolkit Events

Received SMS Handling
FORMATTED_SMS_PP_ENV
FORMATTED_SMS_PP_UPD
UNFORMATTED_SMS_PP_ENV
UNFORMATTED_SMS_PP_UPD
FORMATTED_SMS_CB
UNFORMATTED_SMS_CB
Menu Selection Handling
MENU_SELECTION
MENU_SELECTION_HELP_REQUEST
Call and SMS Send Control
CALL_CONTROL
SMS_MO_CONTROL
Utility
UNRECOGNISED_ENVELOPE
STATUS_COMMAND
TIMER_EXPIRATION
Mobile Process Events
EVENT_DOWNLOAD
MT_CALL
CALL_CONNECTED
CALL_DISCONNECTED
LOCATION_STATUS
USER_ACTIVITY
IDLE_SCREEN_AVAILABLE
LANGUAGE_SELECTION
BROWSER_TERMINATION
CARD_READER_STATUS
Determining Terminal Capabilities
PROFILE_DOWNLOAD

As can be seen in Fig. 10.4 there can be multiple SIM Toolkit applets and so when one of the events in Table. 10.1 occurs, it has to be routed to the correct handler. The SIM Toolkit Framework takes care of this by using the Toolkit Registry. When a Toolkit applet is installed it not only registers itself to the JCRE but also to the Toolkit Framework, creating a Toolkit registry entry. The entry indicates the events that should be routed to the particular applet. Most commonly a Toolkit applet would register for the appropriate set of events only once but it is possible to change the set dynamically.

Whatever the purpose of the SIM Toolkit applet and the event(s) that it handles, it is likely that the applet will need to access some of the files stored in the (U)SIM and this requires an additional package.

10.5.2 sim.access

This package provides access to the GSM SIM file system on the card without compromising data integrity (i.e. an application accessing data at the same time as a terminal APDU command). It includes the SIMSystem and SIMView classes and provides methods for reading and writing to individual files, referenced by file identifier (FID) constants. The methods available in the SIMView class are listed in Table. 10.2 and one can see how they mirror the commands defined in GSM 11.11 [3]

Table 10.2 SIMView Methods Matching GSM 11.11 Commands

short **increase**(byte[] incr, short incrOffset, byte[] resp, short respOffset)
void **invalidate**()
short **readBinary**(short fileOffset, byte[] resp, short respOffset, short respLength)
short **readRecord**(short recNumber, byte mode, short recOffset, byte[] resp, short respOffset, short respLength)
void **rehabilitate**()
short **seek**(byte mode, byte[] patt, short pattOffset, short pattLength)
void **select**(short fid)
short **select**(short fid, byte[] fci, short fciOffset, short fciLength)
short **status**(byte[] fci, short fciOffset, short fciLength)
void **updateBinary**(short fileOffset, byte[] data, short dataOffset, short dataLength)
void **updateRecord**(short recNumber, byte mode, short recOffset, byte[] data, short dataOffset, short dataLength)

To use the methods provided by the SIMView to access the telecoms files, requires that a toolkit applet can obtain an overall view of the GSM File system. As the files are not stored within the toolkit applet it is first necessary to get a handle to the GSM file system. This is achieved by using the single method of the SIMSystem class; "getThe SIMView()". A simple example of using SIMSystem and SIMView is shown in Fig. 10.6.

```
...
GsmHandle = SIMSystem.getTheSIMView();
...
GsmHandle.select((short)SIMView.FID_DF_GSM);
```

Fig. 10.6 SIMSystem and SIMView Class Usage Example

Note there are several reasons why access to a file may be prevented or result in an error or failure, so there is also a SIMViewException class to handle these situations. In fact when developing (U)SIM card code in general, there are a lot of opportunities to introduce build-time and run-time errors. Because the platform does not have its own user interface to provide step by step diagnostics from a running applet it is hard to diagnose when something is going wrong. This is especially difficult for (U)SIMs because there are so many variations of handsets with different (U)SIM interface capabilities that are not always bug free. Bearing in mind that a new (U)SIM card may be deployed in its millions, it is vitally important that we have powerful tools to not only develop but also test and analyse card applications.

10.6 Application Development Tools

There are a number of dedicated tools on the market for those wishing to develop Java Card and Java SIM applets. These tools break down into the following categories:

- Compilers & Integrated Development Environments
- Simulators
- Protocol Analysers (Spy Tools)
- Utilities

10.6.1 Compilers & Integrated Development Environments

The starting point for any software development is the compiler and Integrated Development Environment (IDE). These tools allow you to create the source code for your application, with eventual compilation down to executable code for loading onto a smart card. One of the advantages of Java is that even though we are concerned primarily with the Java Card variant we can use nearly all of the mainstream Java IDE products on the market, together with a dedicated Java Card plug in (to support the particular semantics of Java Card). Two of the more popular and easily obtained IDEs are Eclipse [8] and NetBeans [17]. Both of these tools allow you to download and install plug-ins, to support Java Card development.

There are also some very powerful and specialist tools from the Java SIM Card Vendors. Giesecke & Devrient [12] have a range of tools including "UniverSIM Development Suite", which is a combined IDE and simulator for both SIM and USIM development. There are also similar tools from Gemalto [11] ("Developer Suite") and Sagem-Orga [19] ("JACADE"). The tools from Java SIM Card Vendors are not necessarily cheap to buy and are aimed at the serious smart card developer, which is often the customer for the cards i.e. the network operator. There are also specialist SIM IDEs offered by third parties, such as the SIM toolkit-based IDE (VurtuoSimo) from Bantry Technologies [6].

10.6.2 Simulators

Unlike other forms of software creation, the development and testing cycles on smart card platforms can be extremely tedious as the executable platform is not the same as the development platform. For example, the executable code (in this case Java bytecode, encapsulated in a CAP file) has to be downloaded onto a physical smart card placed in a reader and then the card is removed and placed into a terminal device (e.g. a GSM mobile phone) in order for the executable code to run. This process involves a high degree of physical card manipulation and potentially lengthy download times (in the order of a minute or two), greatly inhibiting the typical development flow of repeated code tests and modifications. It can also lead to a temptation to reduce testing, which raises the spectre of millions of faulty cards in customer hands. Fortunately the majority of IDEs come with some level of simulation and debug facility. Simulators are a real boon for Java Card development in that a software model of a Java Card (or Java SIM) allows near-instant download, installation and execution of Java Card applets. You still need to exercise the applet in some way and even the most basic simulators include or provide access to an APDU Scripter. The scripter allows systematic generation and issuing of APDU commands to the smart card and will record the responses. The more advanced scripter tools will react to the responses so that the next script depends on the result of a previous response. A Scripter tool gives very precise control over the commands and data sent to the card, however it is not well suited to the faithful generation of the many complex command and response sequences that would occur in real life. For example when a mobile phone powers up there are many hundreds of messages to and from the (U)SIM card. In order to cope with this problem and make the simulations as realistic as possible, the more elaborate (U)SIM card simulator tools also include a mobile phone simulator. Usually the phone appears as a realistic looking graphic on the computer screen allowing the computer operator to "press" the virtual buttons on the keypad and generally use the phone as if it was real. Exercising the normal phone functionality generates all the associated message exchanges between the phone and the (U)SIM card. The simulator would normally display and log these exchanges and offer the means to breakpoint the simulation at some point of investigation. A further enhancement is to simulate network and applications servers so that an entire system solution may be tested and debugged all from a simple and convenient computer interface.

Whilst simulators are tremendously useful, some words of caution are necessary. Simulation can speed up early development and test cycles, but it is definitely not a substitute for testing real (U)SIMs in real phones. A particular (U)SIM is likely to be a well-standardised device, however its behaviour is rarely identical to its virtual model. For example a CAP file that loads and runs nicely on the virtual card might be rejected by the real card loader tool or perhaps if loaded/installed, runs differently because of some differing assumptions about variable types. Perhaps a starker example is that you could load and script test a (U)SIM-like card application on a virtual T=1 protocol card, whereas it will never work in a GSM phone as the T=0 protocol is required. However, the big problem is not so much with the (U)SIM, but with the mobile phones. Their (U)SIM messaging sequences are surprisingly diverse and cannot be confidently modelled as they depend on make, model, capability, usage and software release. The great challenge when testing a new (U)SIM application is to ensure it will work with the thousands of phones used on the network in all possible sequence combinations e.g. authenticating, making calls, receiving SMS, using a menu etc. If simulation can't replace device testing it can ease the transition from the virtual to real World by some flexible options. For example you might test your virtual model with scripts then load a real card and use the same scripts. Alternatively if your simulated card works with a simulated phone, you could then move to a real card and exercise it from the simulated phone. Despite all this good work there will come a time when the simulations work fine but the real card in the real phone does not. Then it is time to reach for a different kind of tool.

10.6.3 Protocol Analysis (Spy) Tools

There is a problem when trying to diagnose a problem that involves mobile phone and (U)SIM interaction. The (U)SIM has no user interface to help you and although the mobile could display something, it has little or no debug and diagnostic facilities to tell you when things go wrong. Mobile phones also behave very differently when they have trouble communicating with the (U)SIM. Some lock-up completely, some report invalid (U)SIM present, others continue on as if nothing untoward has happened. Fortunately we have an accessible physical interface between the card and terminal, so it is possible to use a protocol analyser to effectively "spy" on all commands and associated responses. This is possible given the physical interface between the mobile phone and (U)SIM, which can be electrically probed without affecting communication. The tools tend to use a simple desktop computer for user interface functions with the specialist real time measurement and logging hardware in an external unit. These tools come with a range of adaptor leads that can plug into the (U)SIM socket of a mobile phone and lead the contacts to the measurement unit. The (U)SIM under test is then inserted into the external unit rather than the phone. Thereafter the phone works as if the (U)SIM was directly installed and all message and responses can be logged, displayed and analysed. There are several companies providing such spy tools, including Aspects Tools [5], Comprion [7] and Integri [14].

It should be emphasised that whilst these products are commonly referred to as spy tools there usage is quite legitimate, being aimed at commercial development and testing. Attackers could of course use the tools and so developers should ensure that their application security is not compromised by unauthorised access to the (U)SIM/mobile interface.

10.6.4 Utilities

Aside from sophisticated IDEs, simulators and spy tools there are lots of standalone utility programs that a developer may find useful. Good utilities are fast, easy to use and very importantly are card vendor independent. Some typical utilities are listed in Table 10.3.

Table 10.3 Utility Tools

Utility	Description
APDU Scripter	This allows the user to create custom APDUs, send them to the smart card and log the responses. This capability is often included in the main IDE, however the standalone versions can be less restrictive e.g. when controlling the class and instruction bytes.
File System Viewer	This is equivalent to a kind of Windows Explorer for the smart card file system. Depending on security permissions the user can normally see the overall directory structures, file contents and file headers.
Profile Editor	This is an extension to the File System Viewer and lets the user modify some files - when permitted by the security settings.
Profile Checker	The configuration and contents of a SIM are known as a profile. Profiles can become very complex, making them difficult to compare. A profile tool can capture and compare profiles from different cards providing the user with a clear report on the differences.
Applet Loader	A Java applet is loaded onto a smart card in the form of a CAP file, which is produced by the IDE. The loader handles the message exchange and security associated with loading the applet onto the card. An Applet Loader is often included with the IDE but there are also standalone versions.

Finally to conclude this section the reader is referred to Fig. 10.7. that attempts to show how and where the various tools are used. Note that it does not show any handset application development tools as there is often an assumption that the functionality (as far as the (U)SIM is concerned) is just fixed GSM/3G and just needs simulating. This assumption may have been true once but with modern mobile phones there can be additional functionality that makes use of the (U)SIM.

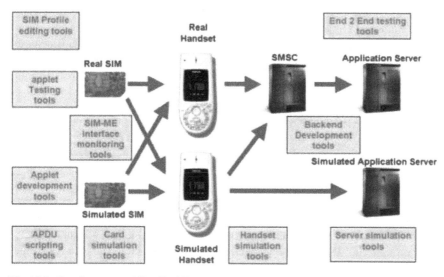

Fig. 10.7   Development and Test Tool Usage

10.7 Mobile Phone Applications and the (U)SIM

A modern mobile phone is a powerful multi-media computer platform with a wireless connectivity link for exchanging calls, messages and general Internet access. The functionality of these platforms is no longer fixed and it is possible to download new applications to support value added services. The technology is not as well standardised as in the smart card world, as aside from the far greater complexity of mobile phones compared to smart cards, user choice is greatly influenced by the functionality and style of a phone and so it is clearly a differentiator between manufacturers. Because of the commercial pressures and differences of opinion over what is the "best" platform there are number of variants in the market. The existence of these variants is rather a problem for application development and the associated widespread introduction of new value added services. Fortunately the Open Mobile Terminal Platform (OMTP) [18] organisation is trying to address these issues. Discussing the relative merits of say Nokia/Symbian, Windows Mobile or any other flavour is way beyond the scope of this chapter so we will stick with the Java approach to continue our description.

Some mobile phones support a Java environment called the Java Mobile Edition. It was once referred to as J2ME (Java 2 Platform Micro Edition). Whereas our applications on the Java SIM were called applets the phone based applications are called MIDlets. Now a good question is why would a mobile phone with all its processing, interface and communications capability want to interact with a lowly (U)SIM? Well the answer relates mainly to security related functionality, but also to control, configuration and management.

Mobile phones do not have a great reputation when it comes to security. The most common example is how GSM handset network locks can be removed for a small amount of money, or perhaps the theft of personal information via Bluetooth links. There may be little physical security to stop the better equipped attacker from examining and modifying both data and circuitry. Therefore, it would be useful to exploit the services of a hardware security module that has been designed to resist such attacks. As there is a (U)SIM designed for just such a purpose it is not surprising that a MIDlet API has been designed that can make use of it.

10.7.1 SATSA

SATSA stands for Security And Trust Services API. It is sometimes referred to as JSR177 [16] after the name of the expert group that defined it. It is not aimed solely at exploiting a (U)SIM, but a security element (SE) in general. The idea is that the SE will help provide secure data storage, some standard cryptographic primitives and an execution environment for custom security functionality. The API is split across four packages as shown in Table 10.4.

Table 10.4 SATSA API Packages

Package Name	Description
SATSA-APDU	This allows the MIDlet to communicate with the (U)SIM. As it is at the APDU level interface, it offers a great deal of control and flexibility
SATSA-JCRMI	This is Java Card Remote Method Invocation - basically it means that the MIDlet can remotely run a program (method) implemented within a Java SIM applet.
SATSA-PKI	This is intended for digital signing as part of a Public Key Infrastructure system
SATSA-CRYPTO	This is to provide a toolbox of useful cryptographic utilities; encryption/decryption, verification, hashes etc..

A complete explanation of the API packages is beyond the scope of this chapter and so our treatment will be restricted to the main features of SATSA-APDU and SATSA-JCRMI, which fit well with our previous discussions on Java SIM.

10.7.1.1 SATSA-APDU

To communicate with the (U)SIM, the MIDlet must establish a logical connection with it. This is done by using "APDUConnection()" and specifying the appropriate Application ID (AID). In fact if the (U)SIM supports it, the MIDlet can establish multiple logical channels. The standards also allow for the case of the MIDlet having access to multiple SEs and communications over the logical connection follows the conventional ISO7816-4 [15] standards. The main component of SATSA-APDU is the "javax.microedition.apdu" package that includes the "APDUConnection" interface, (additionally SATSA-APDU supports some exception classes).

The "APDUConnection" interface contains a number of methods as shown in Table 10.5.

Table 10.5 APDUConnection Methods

Method	Description
public byte[] changePin(int PinID)	Combined prompt/process for the user to enter a new PIN and update on SE
public byte[] enablePin(int PinID)	Combined prompt/process for the user to enable a particular PIN and update on SE
public byte[] disablePin(int PinID)	Combined prompt/process for the user to disable a particular PIN and update on SE
public byte[] unblockPin(int blockedPinID, int unblockingPinID)	Combined prompt/process for the user to unblock a particular PIN
public byte[] enterPin(int PinID)	Combined prompt to the user to enter a PIN and its subsequent verification by the SE
public byte[] exchangeAPDU(byte[])	Main method for APDU exchange
public byte[] getATR()	Provides the card Answer To Reset information supplied by the SE when it was last reset (also acts as a card present check)

The "exchangeAPDU()" method is of most interest and there are couple of points to note. Firstly the class byte field (CLA) in the APDU contains the logical channel number rather than some industry specific value. Secondly this method will block until the card responds and so an operational timeout/interrupt is need to stop the process hanging. An APDU level interface provides a lot of flexibility, however it does mean that the MIDlet (and the developer implementing it) has to know quite a lot about smart cards and protocols. A higher level interaction at the applet/method level is perhaps more appropriate and more in-keeping with the Java principle of being agnostic to the lower layers of implementation. Remote method invocation is a way to achieve this.

10.7.1.2 SATSA-JCRMI

SATSA-JCRMI provides an API to invoke a remote application implemented on the (U)SIM card. Aside from exception support and some general RMI functionality the main package is "javax.microedition.jcrmi". The package has two interfaces that are "Java CardRMIConnection" and "RemoteRef". The first interface is rather similar to the "APDUConnection" in that it establishes a logical channel for communicating with an application on the (U)SIM card, identified by its AID. There are also are similar range of PIN management functions. The method "getInitialReference()" is used to get an initial reference to the (U)SIM application so its methods may be used. The "RemoteRef()" interface represents a handle or reference to a remote object, whose most notable method is "invoke()", which as the name suggests is just what we were looking for; a means to invoke a remote method of an object stored within a smart card applet.

10.7.2 A Word on Testing

Anyone that develops smart card applications on a commercial basis will understand (often by painful experience) the mantra of testing, testing and more testing. Deploy millions of faulty cards and the cost, time and stress to recall and re-issue the cards, whilst pacifying angry customers, is too horrific to contemplate. Now if a lot of testing is needed for say a SIM Toolkit application on a relatively simple and well-standardised smart card platform, how much will be required for a mobile application plus a smart card application, working together by exploiting advanced APIs and functionality? Clearly the answer is "more", but it is worth noting some of the particular areas that might give cause for concern;

- Mobile phones are complex devices and different makes, models and releases have different capabilities and bugs. Often it seems as if the (U)SIM interface functionality and testing gets the least attention, being overshadowed by more exciting multi-media and UI features.
- The SATSA features rely on logical channels and the number of channels desired, supported and tested may not always match.
- Some (U)SIM activities have real-time duties to perform and disruption due to execution of say a remotely invoked method might cause problems.
- The state of an application and indeed its current position within a file system and access permissions needs to be preserved and synchronised in the various applet and MIDlet pairs.
- As mentioned earlier some methods may block on access to a smart card and so there could be problems with timeout mechanisms and periods.
- etc, etc...

Fundamentally, the source of the concern is the sheer number of possible device and event combinations, which makes it difficult if not impossible to fully anticipate and test them. Despite this, the considerable functional reward means it is well worth trying to get the mobile and (U)SIM combination working together. To illustrate this we will consider an application example.

Table 1. Solver Benchmarks with Test Data

Data Set	Beta	IP Solver Gap		MA Solver Gap		Imbalance[4]
		t_{CPU}	total/util	t_{CPU}	total/util	(avg., IP/MA)
random, $\|P\| = 1000$, $\|R\| = 200$	0	6'	-/-[5]	2'	0.0%/0.0%	200.0%/21.9%
	1	17'	**0.1%**/0.1%	32'	0.2%/0.2%	0.8%/0.5%
	10	24'	**0.2%**/0.1%	30'	0.4%/0.6%	0.7%/0.3%
	100	11'	0.6%/0.4%	41'	**0.2%**/1.6%	1.3%/0.2%
	1000	11'	0.7%/0.4%	28'	**0.1%**/3.4%	1.3%/0.2%
	10000	10'	0.7%/0.4%	26'	**0.1%**/3.5%	1.3%/0.2%
random, $\|P\| = 500$, $\|R\| = 100$	0	< 1'	-/-[5]	< 1'	0.0%/0.0%	200.0%/20.6%
	1	9'	**0.1%**/0.1%	2'	0.2%/0.2%	0.9%/0.6%
	10	3'	**0.2%**/0.2%	< 1'	0.5%/0.9%	0.6%/0.3%
	100	3'	0.3%/0.2%	18'	0.3%/2.3%	0.6%/0.2%
	1000	3'	0.3%/0.2%	13'	**0.1%**/3.8%	0.6%/0.2%
	10000	3'	0.3%/0.2%	3'	**0.1%**/5.2%	0.6%/0.1%
random, $\|P\| = 169$, $\|R\| = 66$	0	< 1'	-/-[5]	< 1'	0.0%/0.0%	200.0%/33.0%
	1	< 1'	0.2%/0.2%	6'	0.2%/0.3%	3.5%/2.3%
	10	< 1'	**0.6%**/0.5%	4'	0.9%/1.7%	1.6%/0.6%
	100	41'	0.7%/3.2%	2'	**0.6%**/3.2%	0.9%/0.6%
	1000	27'	0.6%/5.8%	4'	**0.3%**/8.1%	1.0%/0.4%
	10000	42'	0.4%/4.1%	7'	**0.2%**/13.2%	0.8%/0.4%
MIC 2001, $\|P\| = 137$, $\|R\| = 62$	0	< 1'	-/-[5]	< 1'	0.0%/0.0%	200.0%/119.5%
	1	< 1'	-/-[5]	2'	0.0%/0.0%	112.7%/112.7%
	10	29'	**0.0%**/2.4%	3'	0.1%/2.2%	71.8%/74.4%
	100	33'	**1.3%**/24.6%	3'	2.4%/27.7%	5.2%/5.2%
	1000	4'	1.3%/27.2%	43'	**1.2%**/41.1%	3.5%/2.0%
	10000	10'	0.7%/39.1%	18'	**0.6%**/42.5%	2.2%/2.0%
MIC 2003, $\|P\| = 90$, $\|R\| = 67$	0	< 1'	-/-[5]	< 1'	0.0%/0.0%	200.0%/117.3%
	1	< 1'	-/-[5]	< 1'	0.0%/0.0%	116.4%/116.0%
	10	40'	**0.0%**/3.6%	< 1'	0.1%/3.7%	71.8%/72.0%
	100	< 1'	**2.2%**/26.4%	6'	3.6%/33.3%	5.2%/3.9%
	1000	3'	2.0%/29.1%	7'	**1.8%**/39.1%	4.4%/3.1%
	10000	4'	1.9%/35.6%	< 1'	**1.5%**/41.6%	4.2%/3.4%
MIC 2005, $\|P\| = 169$, $\|R\| = 66$	0	< 1'	-/-[5]	< 1'	0.0%/0.0%	200.0%/121.9%
	1	< 1'	-/-[5]	< 1'	0.0%/0.0%	116.3%/116.3%
	10	30'	**0.1%**/3.4%	10'	0.2%/3.4%	64.9%/65.5%
	100	37'	**1.5%**/24.1%	11'	2.9%/30.1%	5.2%/3.8%
	1000	5'	1.5%/26.3%	10'	**1.2%**/39.8%	3.6%/1.9%
	10000	14'	0.9%/39.4%	3'	**0.7%**/44.0%	2.2%/1.8%

[4] 100% means $|l_r - l_r^*| = l_r^*$

[5] Optimal solution, gaps w.r.t. optimum

assignment set (i.e. for the actually realized solution), a total number of 14 iterations were performed.

Evaluation of Model Performance using Reviewer Feedback

In order to judge the overall quality of the solutions and to identify significant model parameters, a range of different solutions was created and sent out to reviewers. They should evaluate how good the given paper assignments would fit to them in terms of content. We received a strong response (about 50% of the questionnaires were returned), and the reviewers' marks show that the taken design decisions and parameter settings improved real-world solution quality.

The feedback data shows that the optimized solutions fit considerably better than a randomly generated reference solution. Further investigations show the positive effects of the second (continuous) matching calculation approach. Likewise, a relaxed exclusion list enabled the solver to find better matching assignments. Using manual tuning incorporated additional expert knowledge.

The evaluation results of selected solutions are reported in Table 2 and in Figure 7 and Figure 8. Solution "Random" represents a randomly generated reference solution. Solution "D-auto" was generated automatically without manual tuning using the discrete matching calculation approach, and solution "D-m14" is the published solution that was manually tuned for 14 iterations, starting from "D-auto". Likewise, we created solution "C-auto" and "C-m3" (3 manual iterations) using the continous matching approach. In the automatic solutions, only self-assignments (of a reviewer to papers that he/she is author of) were excluded. The other solutions' (initial) exclusion lists also prohibited all assignments of reviewers to papers where one of the paper's authors comes from the same country the reviewer comes from.

The degree to which the solution assignments fit the reviewers was evaluated by themselves. A grading scheme ranging from 1 to 5 (1 as worst and 5 as best mark) was applied. The average evaluation mark of each solution can be used to measure the solution quality in terms of overall reviewer satisfaction. As seen in Figure 7, the "Random" solution performs much worse than the optimized solutions. The manually improved solutions "D-m14" and "C-m3" perform best in terms of "real world performance", from the reviewers' point of view. The automatically generated solutions "D-auto" and "C-auto" are at about 80% relative performance (between the best performing "D-m14" and the "Random"

10.7.3 SIM Dongle Example

For the purposes of this example, a "dongle" is the name given to a hardware security module that is used in the PC world. Its purpose is to grant a user access to say a computer program and/or some restricted information or indeed viewing rights to a film or a football match broadcast. The hardware is used because the object or right that it protects is something of value, to the extent that a software only protection solution is not regarded as sufficiently secure. One of the advantages of the dongle is that it can be a standalone security solution and so the application does not have to assume Internet access or annoy the user with fussy set-ups and regular polling of licence servers. Fig. 10.8. presents the conventional concept of a dongle as used with PCs to protect software.

Fig. 10.8   Dongles in the PC World

Although dongles do a reasonable job at preventing the copying of software, they are not very user-friendly. They must be installed and physically connected to the right port every time the software is run. Furthermore, each piece of software usually has to have its own dongle, which can be inconvenient on a desktop computer, almost impractical on a laptop and a non-starter on a mobile phone.

As we know that modern mobile phones are indeed powerful portable computers and users are encouraged to exploit them to consume more and more services. So if we think dongles are a good idea then we need to find a solution for the mobile phone,

Fig. 10.9 graphically illustrates that the mobile phone already contains a hardware security module in the form of the (U)SIM that could be re-used as a dongle. In fact it would be a great platform for this, as customers would not need to carry anything else around and virtual dongles could be added/removed and securely managed by an Over The Air (OTA) applications server, connected to the communications network. Of course we also need some software in the mobile phone to interact with the dongles on the (U)SIM, but as we have already learnt,s we could use the SATSA API for this. An overall solution might look something like Fig. 10.10.

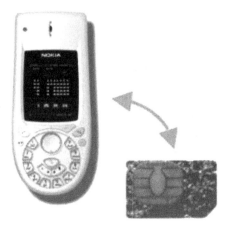

Fig. 10.9 A Mobile Dongle?

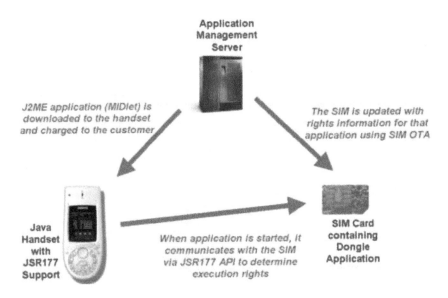

Fig. 10.10 (U)SIM Dongle System

Although Fig. 10.10 was presented simply as an example, it represents an attractive and practical technical solution, not only for software licence control but a whole range of Data Rights Management (DRM) scenarios. The commercial debate we will leave to others, but noting that it would centre around who owns, controls and benefits from the (U)SIM, the handset, the server and the valuable software or data content.

10.8 Looking To The Future

The ISO/IEC 7816 [15] interface and limited memory/processing constraints that have been with the smart card for over 20 years, has meant that development would always be a much more difficult proposition that on other platforms (e.g. desktop, enterprise or mobile). This is about to change however with the introduction of new technologies, including High Speed Interface (HSI) and Smart Card Web Server (SCWS). In 2006, the USB protocol was agreed to be the new communications interface to the smart card. One primary driver of this technology was to allow quick access to the increasing memory storage available on the card. The standard [10] took many years to ratify, but means that it is now possible to build standard internet protocols into the smart card architecture so that the smart card is seen simply as another computer platform, albeit a highly secure one. In addition, the Smart Card Web Server, provides the facility for the browser running in a mobile device to be served with HTTP content coming from inside the smart card (as opposed to an Internet server). Both these technologies mean that the world of the smart card is coming closer to that of standard development platforms, and therefore today's ubiquitous programming environments can be usefully employed with little change for smart card development. For example, it will not be long before Java Enterprise Servlets can be executed from with the smart card. Therefore you can expect server-based development tools to start providing plug-ins for that purpose.

10.9 Concluding Remarks

This chapter has attempted to provide the reader with a brief overview of a wide range of issues associated with smart card application development. The focus has been restricted to Java based technology and the reader is referred to chapters 1 and 4 for alternative technologies and development methods. The Java (U)SIM has been used as the primary platform, partly because (U)SIMs have a superset of Java Card capabilities, but also because a lot of Java (U)SIMs have been deployed in the market. We have seen that smart cards have historically been treated as very restricted application platforms, although support for Java is bringing them closer to mainstream development. In fact, the tools now available to developers are very sophisticated and advanced SIM Toolkit features such as event and file handling can be exploited by (U)SIM applications via the Java Card Framework, Unfortunately (U)SIM based applications have never fully realised their potential partly due to problems with mobile handset support of critical standards. However the most interesting service ideas see the handset and (U)SIM working together as parts of a system solution, underpinned by the (U)SIMs security qualities. Within Java mobiles supporting SATSA the problems of co-operating with the (U)SIM have already been addressed and standardised in the form of APIs, which permit application level and APDU message level interaction. Taking a common approach to development by using Java in both the mobile handset and also the (U)SIM makes life easier for developers and perhaps as the (U)SIM evolves towards a less restricted and IP based platform, the boundaries between phone and (U)SIM development may disappear.

It is clear that today's standards already contain very powerful features for both (U)SIM and mobile phone application development. There are more than enough sophisticated tools to exploit these features and so the challenge is to get consistency across the various types of mobile phone platform and the (U)SIM interface features that they support. This is well worth the effort as it could enable a broad range of value added mobile services underpinned by the hardware security module characteristics of the (U)SIM. In fact it looks as if the next decade is going to be an interesting time for smart cards in general, as their world is opened up to more mainstream development and their capabilities, including processing power and memory increase rapidly. With all this change, increased openness and added technical complexity, it is important that the inherent smart card characteristics remain. Security, reliability and controllability will be even more essential to future system solutions.

References

1. 3GPP, *Characteristics of the USIM Application Rel.7 3GPP TS 31.102* V7.10.0 (2007-09), More Information Available via
   `http://www.3gpp.org/`, Cited 03 Oct 2007.
2. 3GPP, *SIM API for Java Card Stage 2 Rel.99 3GPP TS 03.19* V8.5.0 (2002-09), More Information Available via
   `http://www.3gpp.org/`, Cited 03 Oct 2007.
3. 3GPP, *Specification of the SIM-ME Interface Rel.99 3GPP TS 11.11* V8.14.0 (2007-06), More Information Available via
   `http://www.3gpp.org/`, Cited 03 Oct 2007.
4. 3GPP. *Specification for the SIM Application Toolkit for the SIM-ME Interface Rel.99, 3GPP TS 11.14* V8.18.0 (2007-06), More Information Available via
   `http://www.3gpp.org/`, Cited 03 Oct 2007.
5. Aspects Tools Limited, More Information Available via
   `http://www.aspectstools.com/`, Cited 03 Oct 2007.
6. Bantry Technologies, More Information Available via
   `http://www.bantry-technologies.com/`, Cited 03 Oct 2007.
7. Comprion, More Information Available via
   `http://www.comprion.com/`, Cited 03 Oct 2007.
8. Eclipse, Open Development Platform, More Information Available via
   `http://www.eclipse.org/`, Cited 03 Oct 2007.
9. ETSI, SIM Technology, More Information Available via
   `http://www.etsi.org/WebSite/Technologies/SIM.aspx`, Cited 03 Oct 2007.
10. ETSI SCP Group, *SCP Specifications*, More Information Available via
    `http://portal.etsi.org/docbox/scp/scp/Specifications/`, Cited 03 Oct 2007.
11. Gemalto, More Information Available via
    `http://www.gemalto.com/`, Cited 03 Oct 2007.
12. Giesecke & Devrient, More Information Available via
    `http://www.gi-de.com/`, Cited 03 Oct 2007.
13. GSM & UMTS - *The Creation of Global Mobile Communication* - Wiley 2002.

14. Integri, More Information Available via
    http://www.integri.com/, Cited 03 Oct 2007.
15. ISO, ISO7816-X, *Identification cards*, More Information Available via
    http://www.iso.org/, Cited 03 Oct 2007.
16. JSR177 Experts Group, *Security and Trust Services API (SATSA) v1.0.1 for J2ME*, More Information Available via
    http://jcp.org/aboutJava/communityprocess/final/jsr177/index.html, Cited 03 Oct 2007
17. NetBeans, IDE 5.5.1, More Information Available via
    http://www.netbeans.org/, Cited 03 Oct 2007.
18. Open Mobile Terminal Platform (OMTP), More Information Available via
    http://www.omtp.org/, Cited 03 Oct 2007.
19. Sagem-Orga, More Information Available via
    http://www.sagem-orga.com/, Cited03Oct2007.
20. Sun Microsystems, *Java Card Platform Specification v 2.2.2*, More Information Available via
    http://java.sun.com/products/javacard/specs.html, Cited 03 Oct 2007.

Chapter 11
OTA and Secure SIM Lifecycle Management

Joos Cadonau

Abstract In the GSM mobile communication industry, the end user - called sub-scriber - is identified in the operator's network by the use of the Subscriber Identity Module SIM. In the third generation network 3G the equivalent application is called Universal Subscriber Identity Module USIM card. A (U)SIM card is a removable Smart Card for mobile phones. A mobile network operator is a telephone company that provides services for mobile phone subscribers.
The (U)SIM card is a managed platform, belonging to the operator's network. It offers to store operator specific but also subscriber related data. (U)SIM cards are in use for a long time, compared to the handset and other entities in the network. Therefore (U)SIM card data - operator or subscriber dependent - changes over time and needs over-the-air management. Customers can not be asked to visit an opera-tor shop for data management; Over-the-Air updates by the use of SMS as a bearer are the only possibility for mass updates. This implies certain security requirements which are specified in the 3GPP/ETSI standards. Also the current bandwidth offered by SMS limits the range of possible adaptations and requires the operator to have a flexible Over-the-Air system, adapted to his needs.
The Over-the-Air management is only one stage of the SIM lifecycle. To be able to launch new services during the lifecycle of a (U)SIM card, the whole (U)SIM lifecycle has to be planned carefully. There exist systems, supporting the operator in knowing in real-time the status of a (U)SIM card in all phases of the (U)SIM lifecycle.

Key words: Over-the-Air OTA; SIM Application Toolkit SAT / STK; SIM Lifecy-cle Management; SIM / USIM Card; OTA Performance Limitations; Public Land Mobile Network PLMN

Joos Cadonau, Product Manager, Sicap AG,
e-mail: joos.cadonau@sicap.com

11.1 Introduction

The (U)SIM card's properties as a tamper-proof device and as a unified storage facility for secure information, as well as its ability to access functions in the mobile handset and the network, makes it a key component. The (U)SIM is part of the operator's network and as such it holds vital information that must be managed and provisioned. Market requirements have introduced solutions that ensure that each and every card in circulation has the optimal configuration and set of services embedded at all times. The (U)SIM is the only linkage point between the network operator and the subscriber, thus making it imperative for the operator to have control over which networks their subscribers roam onto and to manage the subscriber's access to Value Added Services (VAS) via SIM based menus such as Dynamic SIM Tool Kit (DSTK).

The (U)SIM card holds not only operator specific data, it also stores subscriber related data like the subscriber's phonebook, the last numbers dialled or text messages. Subscriber based data is not static, but needs to be updated or saved regularly. This requires over-the-air management, as well as building additional services around the subscriber related data like a phonebook backup functionality.

As (U)SIM cards continue to evolve with more memory capacity and functionality, they will continue to be an important part of an operator's network. Over-The-Air (OTA) becomes essential in managing data on the (U)SIM such as Java applets, PLMN roaming lists, dynamic STK menus and the subscribers' personal information.

For the subscriber, (U)SIM is a personal, portable gateway to new services; for the operator, it's the key to security and differentiation in the world of 3G mobile services.

11.2 The SIM Card As A Managed Platform

The (U)SIM card is a key element in the operators network to identify the subscriber and to authenticate the (U)SIM in the network. There are a number of security features provided by the (U)SIM card to guarantee those processes and to cipher the information on the radio path. The (U)SIM card can therefore be seen as a secure element in the operators network which also makes it attractive to hold additional services requiring security such as Banking applications.

In addition to the security features, there is also a range of operator and subscriber data stored on the (U)SIM card.

11.2.1 Common Stored and Managed Data

The following list shall give an overview, (but not a complete list) about commonly stored and managed data[1]:

Table 11.1 Storage of Operator Information on a SIM Card

Name	File Name	Explanation
Service Provider Name	EF_ SPN	The Service Provider Name can be displayed on the handset. This file contains the name to be displayed as well as a flag indicating if the display of the name is required or not.
SMS Parameters	EF_SMSP	The Short Message Service header Parameters can be used by the handset for mobile originated SMS. Such parameters can be the service centre address, the Data Coding Scheme or the Validity Period of a message.
Preferred Networks	EF_PLMNsel	The entries held in this file represent the preferred roaming partners of an operator. When a handset is switched on in a foreign country, several mobile networks can be selected to roam with. If one of those networks is listed in the PLMNsel file, this network will be taken as the first choice.
Forbidden Networks	EF_FPLMN	In contradiction to the preferred networks, the forbidden networks represent the networks, which shall not automatically be chosen.

The (U)SIM card can also hold applications, called SIM Applets offering a certain service to the subscriber. A few examples of additional services can be found in the following table:

The examples mentioned above are based on the fact, that information is stored on the (U)SIM card in dedicated files and/or in applications. Since neither operator specific, nor subscriber specific data and services are static throughout the years of use, over-the-air management is necessary. A subscriber can not be asked to consult an operator shop in order to update files or applications on the SIM card. The operator costs would be too high and the subscriber's time would be too valuable to do so.

To be able to update over-the-air information stored in (U)SIM files, "remote file management" is necessary and dedicated security features have to be applied. To delete or install (U)SIM applications over-the-air, "remote applet management" processes are necessary. Chapter 3 is explaining technical possibilities and details regarding over-the-air management of files and applets.

In order to allow a (U)SIM application to communicate with the handset and with remote servers, a so called SIM Application Toolkit SAT interface between the

---

[1] The examples mentioned are only a subset of the SIM capabilities and are valid for a SIM card. For a USIM card, some of the examples may differ from the SIM card. File names are referenced to the 3GPP TS 11.11 [3].

Table 11.2 Storage of Subscriber Related Information on a SIM Card

Name	File Name	Explanation
Language Preference	EF_LP	The Language Preference can hold the preferred language of the user. The handset can read and use this language for displaying texts and menus.
Subscriber's Number	EF_MSISDN	The MSISDN field can store one or multiple mobile numbers for the subscriber. The entry can be used by the handset to be displayed or to be used in additional services.
Phonebook	EF_ADN	The Abbreviated Dialling Numbers represent the phonebook on the SIM card. This phonebook can be used beside of the handset based phonebook for storing the subscriber's personal contacts.
Restricted Phonebook	EF_FDN	The Fixed Dialling Numbers represent a phonebook, which can be used only when the handset is set into a dedicated mode. To set a handset into this mode, PIN2 is necessary. While in this mode, only numbers stored in the EF_FDN can be dialled.
Last Number Dialled	EF_LND	The Last Dialled Numbers are the numbers or service strings, which the user has dialled.
Text Messages	EF_SMS	Short Messages can be stored on the handset and on the SIM card. The SIM card storage can be seen as storage for more important messages, which shall not be deleted by cleaning the handset SMS buffer.

(U)SIM card and the handset is necessary. This interface is briefly reviewed in the next chapter.

11.2.2 SIM Application Toolkit Interface SAT

The SIM Application Toolkit interface between the SIM card and the handset offers a set of commands to build applications as mentioned in Table 11.3. By the use of the offered commands, the SIM card can send short messages, set up a call or display menu and text items. The SIM Application Toolkit interface is specified in a GSM specification called 3GPP TS 11.14[2]"Specification of the SIM Application Toolkit (SAT) [4] for the Subscriber Identity Module - Mobile Equipment (SIM-ME) interface".

A selection of the most commonly used commands can be found in the following list:

User Interface commands:

• *Set up Menu* supplies an item list to put in ME menu

---

[2] In this sub-chapter, only the SIM card is considered. For the USIM card exists a similar specification, called 3GPP TS 31.111 "Universal Subscriber Identity Module (USIM) Application Toolkit (USAT)" [7]

Table 11.3 SIM Applications Offering Additional Services

Name	Explanation
Dynamic STK Menu	Dynamic SIM Tool Kit applications on the SIM card can hold a menu structure and commands to access value added services. Value added services can be information about the weather, sport, entertainment and much more. Since the content and the menu structure can be changed, a mechanism has to be supported, to rearrange menus, to add, change or delete services.
Phonebook Backup	A SIM application can read the ADN file, pack it into single short messages and send it to a central OTA server. In case the subscriber is loosing the handset, the SIM card is broken or the user deleted important information, the phonebook can be restored from the OTA server.
Handset detection (IMEI detection)	The IMEI represents the serial number of a handset and its capabilities. To use additional non-voice services like GPRS (data), WAP or MMS, the handset has to be configured accordingly. Since the subscriber does not have the knowledge to configure a new handset, an automatic mechanism should be in place, where a device management system is configuring the handset accordingly. To let the device management system know, that a new - not configured - handset is attached to the mobile network, a SIM application reading the serial number of the handset can be used. The SIM application checks the IMEI of the handset every time when it is switched on and in case the number is different from any of the last numbers, a dedicated trigger is sent to the device management system.
Restricted Phonebook	The Fixed Dialling Numbers represent a phonebook, which can be used only when the handset is set into a dedicated mode. To set a handset into this mode, PIN2 is necessary. While in this mode, only numbers stored in the EF_FDN can be dialled.
Mobile TV application	Latest handsets are capable to receive Digital Video Broadcast signals (DVB-H). Since the video message can be encrypted, a key is necessary to decrypt the video signal. This key can be stored on the (U)SIM card. For security reason, this key can periodically be changed.
Call Control	When a subscriber dials a number, the handset can ask to the (U)SIM card to verify it and if necessary change the number or the format. With such functionality, calls into a foreign network can be rerouted to a cheaper number via a partner organization.
Banking application	Banking applications are offering services like access to personal bank account information or even executing transactions. Since the (U)SIM card is solely controlled by the operator and offers various security functionality, such banking applications can be stored on the (U)SIM card.

- *Display Text* displays text on screen
- *Get Inkey* sends text on display and get character answer
- *Get Input* sends text on display and get text answer
- *Select Item* supplies an item list to be displayed by ME to user
- *Play Tone* plays a tone

Network access commands:

- *Set up Call* initiate a call

- *Send SMS* sends a short message to network
- *Send SS* sends a supplementary string to network
- *Send USSD* sends an USSD string to the network
- *Send DTMF* sends a DTMF string after a call has been established

An application like Dynamic STK (DSTK) is making use of commands like "Set up Menu", "Display Text", "Send SMS" to display a menu on the handset's screen and to send the selected service to an external server. A phonebook backup application is reading the file EF_ADN, packing the content into single short messages and sending them to an external server.

By the use of the SIM Application Toolkit interface, the SIM card can get temporary control over the handset (proactive). Compared to the case where the handset sends a request to the SIM card and the SIM responds, the handset can fetch a SAT command from the SIM. The SIM card is issuing a SAT command towards the handset; the handset is reacting accordingly and sends the SIM a response back, if the command was executed successfully or not.

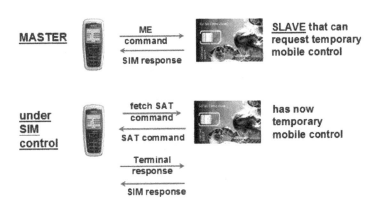

Fig. 11.1 Proactive SIM with SIM Application Toolkit

The 3GPP TS 11.14 [4] specification defines the SAT interface, which can be used by SIM applications, but does not define how the commands can be accessed in a unified way over various SIM card types from different SIM vendors. This means, an application written for one SIM operating system from one SIM vendor cannot be reused on another SIM operating system from another SIM vendor. This implies that the same applet has to be developed and tested for every operating system independently. Multiple developments and testing are resulting in high costs and additional risks.

Due to this fact, the Java Runtime Environment is also implemented on dedicated Java SIM cards. To be able to access the SAT functionality from Java SIM applications, the specification 3GPP TS 03.19³ [1] is applied.

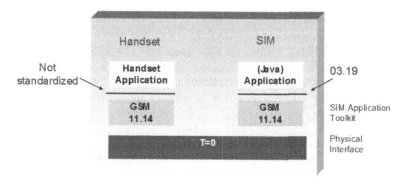

Fig. 11.2 SAT interface for Java SIM cards

The 3GPP TS 03.19 [1] specification allows developing a service based on a Java SIM card to be developed once and to be loaded onto different Java SIM cards from different SIM vendors. Although the access to SAT functionality from Java SIM applications is standardised, reality shows, that interoperability tests on every target SIM have to take place to guarantee error free functionality.

To achieve interoperable SAT applications on Java SIM cards, a number of specifications and documents should be considered. The following list mentions the most commonly used documents:

- 3GPP TS 03.19 [1] defines:

  - the events for triggering a SAT applet
  - how to access the SIM files from a SAT applet
  - how to implement the SAT commands (11.14) into Java classes

- 3GPP TS 03.48 [2] defines:

  - Security mechanism for SAT

- Open Platform Card Specification defines:

  - How to load, install, uninstall and delete an applet

- SIM Alliance Guideline

  - Useful hints how to make an applet interoperable

---

³ In this sub-chapter, only the SIM card is considered. For the USIM card exists a similar specification, called 3GPP TS 31.130 "(U)SIM Application Programming Interface (API)" [8]

11.2.3 Main Differences Between a SIM and a UICC/USIM Card

The SIM card for the GSM network contained one GSM application to authenticate the SIM towards the network. In case of a 3rd generation SIM card, the specifications were split into a UICC (Universal Integrated Circuit Card) and a SIM/USIM specification. Herewith the UICC defined the base, on which a SIM application and/or a USIM application can be placed. Like this, the base for future additional applications like ISIM (IP Multimedia Subsystem SIM) for new network authentication is given.

The UICC allows therefore multi application management, where the USIM can be one of them. The USIM application as another application has an enhanced phonebook supporting one name with multiple numbers assigned. Also the file structure and the files themselves follow a USIM specification which differs from the SIM file definition.

Due to the fact, that there is a split of the functionality into UICC and USIM specifications, there is not a one-to-one transition from the SIM to the UICC/USIM specifications possible. Some of the specifications were also transferred to ETSI. This is the main reason, why some 3GPP and ETSI specifications are referring to each other. Furthermore the GSM and 3GPP specifications were extended during time, resulting in multiple versions, which are bundled into Releases. For GSM specifications for example exists a Release 99, containing all necessary specifications to be followed by all network elements. For 3G there exists Release 4, followed by Release 5, 6 and 7. The Releases help to decrease interoperability problems due to the fact, that for a network element, a (U)SIM or a handset the support of a dedicated Release can be requested. On the other hand, due to the fact that multiple versions of a specification are available, one has to specify exactly the Release the implementation has to follow.

The most important specifications and its counterpart for UICC/ USIM used for remote file and applet management and for SAT application design are mentioned in the following table:

Table 11.4 Relation of Main GSM and 3GPP/ETSI Specifications

Name	GSM specification (Rel. 99)	3G/GSM specification (>Rel.4)
Security mechanism	3GPP TS 03.48 [2]	3GPP TS 23.048 [5]
(U)SIM/UICC specification	3GPP TS 11.11 [3]	ETSI 102 221 [10] (UICC definition) 3GPP TS 31.102 [6] (USIM definition) 3GPP TS 51.011 [9] (SIM definition)
(U)SIM Application Toolkit (U)SAT	3GPP TS 11.14 [4]	3GPP TS 31.111 [7]
Java API for (U)SAT	3GPP TS 03.19 [1]	ETSI 102 241 [13] UICC 3GPP TS 31.130 [8]

An overview of all specifications and Releases can be found on the 3GPP website:www.3gpp.org/specs/numbering.htm

11.3 OTA - Over-The-Air Management

As seen in chapter 2.1, there exist various cases where over-the-air management of files and applets is necessary. The most common used transport bearer for remote (U)SIM management are short messages "SMS". Commands, so called APDU (Application Protocol Data Unit) are encrypted and packed into SMS. The OTA server sends the SMS to the SMS Centre which is responsible for the delivery to the handset. In case a handset is not reachable, the SMS Centre is responsible for retrying to deliver the SMS until a certain time is reached, the "Validity Period". When the SMS is delivered to the handset, the handset recognises according the "Message Class" whether the SMS has to be handled by the handset or by the (U)SIM card. In case of a Message Class 2, the SMS is handed over to the (U)SIM card. The card decrypts the message and executes the included commands according to the specification 3GPP TS 11.11 [3]. Examples of commands to be executed by the (U)SIM card are:

- *Select*   selects the file with the given address
- *Read Binary*   reads the file type transparent
- *Update Binary*   updates a transparent file
- *Read Record*   reads one record of the file type linear fixed
- *Update Record*   updates a record of a linear fixed file
- *Envelope*   transfers 3GPP TS 11.14 coded data to the SAT application

In order to prevent, that any other party than the operator can remotely manage a (U)SIM card, security (according the specification 3GPP TS 03.48[4]) [2] is applied on top of the file and applet commands mentioned above. The security mechanisms are applied between the OTA server and the (U)SIM card. The main security features defined in the 3GPP TS 03.48 [2] specifications can be summarised in the following table:

Table 11.5 3GPP TS 03.48 [2] security mechanism

Name	Security mechanism applied
Message authentication	Cryptographic Checksum or a Digital Signature
Message integrity	Cryptographic Checksum
Message confidentiality	Message ciphering
Replay detection	Counter
Proof of receipt	Status code packed into response message

In order to apply security mechanisms to remote file or applet messages, a security header is included into the SMS. The security header defines, which of the above mentioned security mechanisms are applied. SPI defines the security applied to the message. KIc is defining the algorithm using a symmetric key - stored on the

---

[4] In this sub-chapter, only the SIM card is considered. For the USIM card exists a similar specification, called 3GPP TS 23.048 "Security mechanisms for the (U)SIM application toolkit" [5]

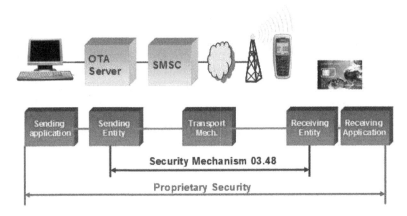

Fig. 11.3 SAT interface for Java SIM cards

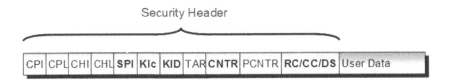

Fig. 11.4 OTA security header

OTA server and on the (U)SIM card - to cipher the message. Since multiple keys can be pre-stored in the U(SIM) and can be used for the ciphering, KIc also defines which key number shall be used by the encryption algorithm. KID represents the algorithm, also using a symmetric key, to calculate the Cryptographic Checksum and the Digital Signature. Also KID is additionally defining which key number to be used by the encryption algorithm. CNTR is the counter to detect, whether a message is received more than once. The counter has to be set in the security header. For every message, sent to the (U)SIM card, the counter is increased by the OTA server. The (U)SIM card checks towards the counter stored on the (U)SIM, whether the counter was increased compared to the last successfully received message. If the counter received from the OTA system is below or equal to the counter on the (U)SIM card, the received message is seen as a repetition of a previous message and is discarded.

During the definition phase of a (U)SIM card profile, it is agreed between the operator and the SIM vendor, whether the SIM supports one or multiple keys for Ciphering, Cryptographic Checksum and Digital Signature. According to the 3GPP specifications, up to 16 keys can be used.

11.3.1 OTA Server Capabilities

In case of over-the-air management, the extensive security features of a SIM card need to be supported as well on the OTA server side. The OTA keys for Ciphering, Digital Signature and Cryptographic Checksum (KIc, KID) have to be stored on the OTA platform in a secure way, protected from any misuse. The OTA keys can be used by different encryption algorithms, according the specification 3GPP TS 03.48 [2]. Before this specification was in place, every SIM vendor provided his own proprietary algorithms. Since (U)SIM cards are in use for a long time, such proprietary SIM cards are still in operation. A sophisticated OTA server therefore needs to also support the proprietary algorithms from different SIM vendors.

In addition to the security aspects of a (U)SIM card, an OTA server also needs to know how to build correct APDU and SMS with the header and security header according the 3GPP specifications.

Since the various (U)SIM cards on the market are supporting different features and are following different Releases of the 3GPP specifications, the OTA server has to know the capabilities for every (U)SIM card. The capabilities are summarised in a "(U)SIM Profile" and the OTA server needs to offer the functionality to configure the capabilities for every (U)SIM stored in the OTA system. By defining a (U)SIM Profile, the server knows which files exist on the (U)SIM card. Furthermore, additional information like the path, where the file is located, the length or the file type is defined. The same information has to be stored on the OTA server in order to create correct APDU commands. In addition, to prevent message duplication, counters accompany the APDU commands and are checked by the (U)SIM card for correctness. For every new message, the counter has to be increased. Messages containing a too low counter will be ignored by the (U)SIM card. The OTA server needs to manage the correct value of the counters and include within the messages.

The (U)SIM Profile also defines the remote applet management capabilities. To successfully execute remote applet management, not only do the applets have to be stored on the OTA server, but also various parameters according to the 3GPP TS 11.11 [3] and Global Platform Card Specification. The parameters are used to create correct remote applet download messages.

The starting point of an applet download is a Java application, which has to be converted by the use of standard Sun tools into a ".cap-file". The ".cap-file" has to be transformed into a ".jcl-file", which is downloaded by the OTA server according the Open Platform Card Specification. The applet can have different states on a (U)SIM card. It can be loaded, but not yet visible to the user (Status: Installed) or it can be installed and visible to the user (Status: Selectable). For the installation therefore two different commands are necessary. Similarly the removal can be handled in two steps, one for removing the visibility to the user or a complete removal from the (U)SIM card.

The above mentioned capabilities are essential in order to achieve successful remote file and applet management of (U)SIM cards, as used for the cases mentioned in chapter 2.1.

Since some of the remote file and applet management activities are done in an active mode, and some in a reactive mode, the OTA server needs to support both modes. Active remote management is mainly used to configure a whole subscriber base or a subset of it with new or changed data. Active mode means also to update several ten- or hundred thousand of (U)SIM cards in a certain time frame. For every target (U)SIM, the batch processing mechanism calculates the necessary APDU, applies the security and packs it into messages. The OTA server also has to handle the delivery of every single message to the SMS Centre and track the success of the delivery. Every target (U)SIM can be of a different (U)SIM Profile where different security has to be applied. In any case for every (U)SIM the OTA keys are different and every single SMS has to be encrypted independently. The OTA server has to provide such calculation capabilities and performance to reach an efficient remote update of the target (U)SIM cards.

Compared to batch processing, the reactive mode is dealing with single (U)SIM cards at a time. More important for the reactive mode is, that any user requests is immediately handled by the OTA server and an appropriate reaction has to be sent to the requesting (U)SIM card. An example for this mode is the request of a user to backup his phonebook. Or in case of Dynamic STK menus, the user can have to possibility to add or delete services himself. In this case, the user is waiting for an immediate response, which the OTA server needs to handle immediately.

11.4 Limitations and Improvements

Remote management of files and applets on a (U)SIM card can require from a few commands up to several kilobytes of data to be transferred over-the-air. Applets usually have a size from some kilobytes up to 20 kilobytes or even more. In an operators environment, applet download is performed for sizes up to 5 or 6 kilobytes. It is only in test environments that larger applets are practicable to be downloaded.

The main reason for this limitation is the available bearer. The only reliable bearer today is the short message SMS. Since an SMS has a size of 140 Bytes and due to header and checksum information, only a part of an SMS is containing data. The data part of an SMS is called payload. There exists SMS with reduced header information, so called concatenated SMS, allowing the payload to be increased slightly.

The more data that has to be downloaded, the more SMS have to be created, managed and sent. The more SMS that have to be sent to a single subscriber, the higher the risk of an incident. Heavy SMS load results in longer distribution time, which can be interrupted especially while changing location. Some of the necessary SMS might be not delivered in the correct order which might entail complicated retry mechanisms for some or even all the messages.

Due to those risks, large data downloads require alternative bearers to SMS. There exist some faster bearers, but due to several reasons these have so far seen limited use in the operator's environment.

Direct SS7 access:
Instead of using the operators SMS Centre, direct access to the signalling network (SS7) can be established. Direct SS7 access can be faster than using the operators SMS Centre, because the performance does not depend the SMS Centre, which might be temporarily loaded from other systems. By bypassing the SMS Centre, an increase of 10 to 20% in distribution time might be reached, however the commands still have to be packed into single SMS and the ordering and retry problems still exist.

SMS Cell Broadcast CB:
Cell Broadcast messages are generated once and distributed to all (U)SIM cards within an area. The configuration of every (U)SIM card determines, whether a CB message shall be treated by the receiving (U)SIM card or not. Cell Broadcast messages save time in the message creation since the same message is valid for all target (U)SIM cards. Cell Broadcast messages have a similar size to SMS, therefore the problems with the ordering and retry policy also exist here. Due to the fact that one message has to be valid for all target (U)SIM cards, the same security has to be applied for all (U)SIM cards. This implies a higher risk. If the uncertain situation would happen, that a OTA key is being hacked, the same OTA key could be used for all (U)SIM cards and this represents a high risk, that no operator is willing to take.

Unstructured Supplementary Service Data USSD:
Current (U)SIM cards in the operators use can send USSD strings, but not yet receive them. The main advantage of USSD is, the data is transferred in one of the signalling channel, which makes it fast. The package size on the other hand is similar to SMS. USSD has no store capability, which makes retry capabilities necessary in case the subscriber is not reachable. The problems with the ordering and its retry exist as for the direct SS7 access. USSD as a bearer might become more interesting, as the receiving of USSD data directly by the (U)SIM card is now in the latest 3GPP standards. On the other hand, experience has shown, that the widespread handset support of new features might take a long time. USSD might not be needed in the future since there is another solution with BIP/CAT_TP now slowly emerging.

Bearer Independent Protocol BIP with CAT_TP:
The Bearer Independent Protocol BIP with its overlaying Card Application Toolkit Transport Protocol CAT_TP has been in the 3GPP standards for several years. But it is only recently that the handset vendors have implemented BIP into their handsets. Currently there are more than 100 handsets on the market, which should theoretically support BIP. The (U)SIM vendors on the other hand have supported BIP for several years.
BIP allows the opening of a data channel from the handset to the OTA server and to the (U)SIM card, resulting in an end to end data channel. Compared to SMS, where one SMS has the size of 140 Bytes, a data package for BIP contains 1472 Bytes. Not only is the package size bigger, but also the transport - by using GPRS

or any advanced data channel from the handset - is much faster. BIP was designed not only to have a fast access channel towards an OTA server, but also local bearers like Bluetooth or Infrared would be possible.

A data channel via BIP can be opened by the (U)SIM card by sending an appropriate "open channel" command to the handset. When the OTA server wants to open a data channel, the command has to be packed into an SMS, which is sent from the OTA server to the (U)SIM card. As soon as the data channel is established, the (U)SIM card can send and receive data packages. CAT_ TP is the overlaying protocol to en-

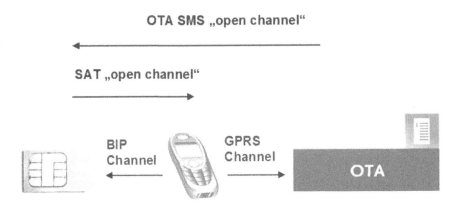

Fig. 11.5 BIP message flow

sure transport security and is based on UDP. Alternative solutions using TCP instead of CAT_TP are also studied. The market has not yet shown, which implementation will succeed. BIP is defined in the 3GPP TS 31.111 [7], CAT_TP in the ETSI TS 102 124 [11] and TS 102 127 [12].

11.4.1 Customer Managed Applications

Due to the security features that a (U)SIM card is offering, the OTA system requires access to the OTA keys for remote file and applet management. Since the (U)SIM card belongs to the operator, no other party than the operator has access to the OTA keys and can operate changes on a (U)SIM card.

New services could be provided by third party service providers, but the operator remains the only party to be able to download additional applets to the (U)SIM card. A dedicated restricted access to third party service providers could be granted by the operator, but it's the operator's responsibility to ensure that the applet is reliable and secure and doesn't open security holes.

In all known solutions, where a third party is involved in providing additional services, the operator is still heavily involved. Due to this fact, such implementations are rare and high costs for the operator and the service provider are the result. The applet as well as the interfaces has to be reliable and secure, requesting well proven processes.

Since there are also legacy (U)SIM cards in the field, the new services are not applicable to all (U)SIM cards. In order to address the whole customer base with a new service, (U)SIM card exchange might even be necessary, resulting in additional costs. Finally the memory management on (U)SIM cards from different vendors is not identically and might cause additional problems.

Future (U)SIM cards are more powerful and provide more memory and so the number of customer managed solutions might increase. On the other hand the increase of performance and memory on the handset is much greater than for the (U)SIM and due to the shorter lifecycle of a handset, it is also deployed much faster. The future of customer managed solution on the (U)SIM card is therefore not yet completely clear.

11.5 SIM Lifecycle Management

Over-the-air management of a (U)SIM card is used, when the (U)SIM card is active and in use by the customer. Since exchanging customers' (U)SIM cards due to malfunction or missing features is very cost intensive, the necessary features have to be planned and tested carefully. In order to successfully launch new (U)SIM cards with new services, a process needs to be followed. The process is illustrated as follows: Planning:

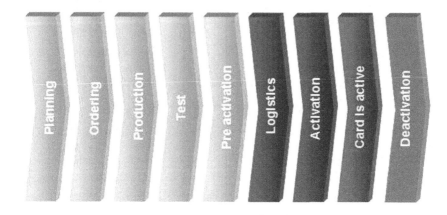

Fig. 11.6 The SIM lifecycle management process

Before a (U)SIM card can be ordered by an operator, the card profile has to be defined. This contains the electrical capabilities "the electrical profile", the security capabilities, but also the graphical profile with the definition of all general and individual card printing.

Ordering:
The operator orders (U)SIM cards from a vendor by the use of an "Input File". The Input File contains the profile information as well as (U)SIM card's serial number ICCID and the IMSI. In some dedicated cases also the MSISDN might be assigned already (possible in case of prepaid cards).

Production:
During production and personalisation, the (U)SIM manufacturer creates all secret data (Pin codes, OTA keys) and writes it into the card's memory. An "Output File" is generated, containing all necessary data to be loaded into the operator's network entities.

Test:

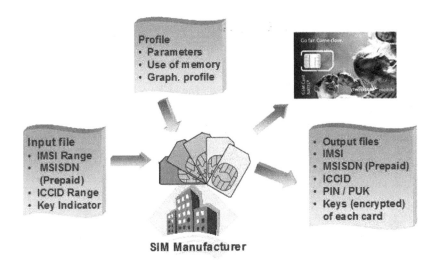

Fig. 11.7 SIM production I

In order to ensure, the (U)SIM will properly work when shipped to the customer and also to ensure, later over-the-air management is possible for fulfilling future changes, the (U)SIM card has to be extensively tested. The costs of replacing a set of several thousand (U)SIM cards already shipped to the customers is many times more expensive than ensuring its correctness during the test phase.

Pre-Activation:

The Pre-Activation phase is where the output file data has to be loaded into the operators' network systems in a secure manner. Systems to be issued with (U)SIM data include the HLR (Home Location Register), AuC (Authentication Centre), CCMS (Customer Care and Billing Systems) and OTA systems. Even after this process the card is still not active.

The process from the planning to the pre-activation can be supported by dedicated systems, in order to avoid manual provisioning and human errors. Systems supporting this phase are sometimes called as Resource Management Systems.

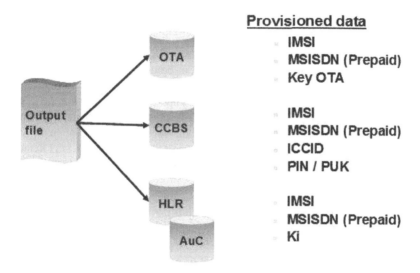

Fig. 11.8 SIM production II

Logistics:

The (U)SIM cards are shipped from the vendor to the operator and distributed to the operator's shops.

Activation:

When the (U)SIM card is shipped or handed over to the customer, the MSISDN is assigned and the card is activated in all systems, where the card data was provisioned. Many operators have a specific customer activation tool in their outlet that has an online connection to their customer management system, and which allows card activation once the subscriber has obtained the card.

Card is active:

The (U)SIM card is active and in use. Changes or additional services are managed remotely over-the-air by an OTA system.

Deactivation:
The (U)SIM card has no validity period as bank cards have. There are still cards in use which are more than 10 years old. Many operators worry about exchanging those SIM cards due to logical obstacles, low customer acceptance and high costs. Beside of the planned exchange of a (U)SIM card by the operator, also a lost or stolen (U)SIM or customer churn define the end of life of a card. The (U)SIM card is deactivated in all systems, where the card data was provisioned, but usually the card data remains in the systems in order to be able to track its history.

11.6 In Conclusion

The (U)SIM card with its security features can be used for various services. Services such as; storing the phonebook, managing the roaming list or configuring operator specific parameters. These services are kept in files, present on the (U)SIM card, which are specified by the ETSI and 3GPP standardization bodies. Additional services can also be added by loading or modifying applications (applets) on the (U)SIM card. Providing menus to access value added services via DSTK menus, backing up the phonebook on the (U)SIM card or configuring mobile TV applications are examples of such (U)SIM card applications.

Applets, in particular, can provide functionality to the subscriber that requests their interaction. Displaying data or requesting the input of subscribers data are based on functionality provided by a dedicated interface between the (U)SIM card and the handset. This is known as the SIM Application Toolkit (SAT) interface. In order to be able to load the same applet on several (U)SIM cards, Java applets are used. To unify the access by the Java applet to the SAT functionality, a dedicated specification provided by ETSI/3GPP is available. Nevertheless, interoperability tests between different (U)SIM cards are necessary to guarantee error free functionality.

Due to the variety of services provided by and due to the long lifecycle of the (U)SIM card, remote over-the-air (OTA) management is essential. Dedicated OTA systems exist to support this stage of the (U)SIM lifecycle. Whether single or a whole batch of (U)SIM cards are being updated over-the-air, the OTA systems need to follow certain rules for coding the messages, adding security to them and finally managing the messages until they are successfully executed on the (U)SIM card. The coding of the messages and the security to be applied is well defined by ETSI/3GPP specifications. Due to the security features offered by the (U)SIM card, it is seen as a trusted platform offering the storage and management of personal and sensitive data. On the other hand, to cope with the features offered by a (U)SIM card, the OTA system needs to be able to handle for every single (U)SIM card type its capabilities and its dedicated security features. Despite the wide standardisation of (U)SIM cards, the OTA system needs to be able to follow different versions of the standards to be able to execute remote file and applet management on a wide range of (U)SIM cards successfully. Coding can differ from one (U)SIM type to another, different security features might be applied and even proprietary security features still have to be supported.

Most of the remote over-the-air management in today's mobile telecom environment is made by sending Short Messages SMS to the (U)SIM card. Short Messages have a limitation in terms of speed and bandwidth. Therefore, alternatives like the Bearer Independent Protocol (BIP) are being specified and are starting to be used in order to replace Short Messages.

Due to the long lifecycle of a (U)SIM card and due to legacy performance limitations, the issuing of new (U)SIM cards and its services have to be planned carefully. To keep control of the features when a (U)SIM card is actively used, an OTA system is essential. To be able to manage the whole lifecycle of a (U)SIM card from the planning to the deactivation, a (U)SIM lifecycle management system is needed.

The (U)SIM card and its over-the-air management is very well standardised by organisations such as 3GPP and ETSI. OTA and (U)SIM lifecycle management systems are essential for keeping track of the valuable features and services offered by a (U)SIM card.

References

1. 3GPP TS 03.19 Subscriber Identity Module Application Programming Interface (SIM API) for Java Card
2. 3GPP TS 03.48 Security mechanisms for SIM application toolkit; Stage 2
3. 3GPP TS 11.11 Specification of the Subscriber Identity Module - Mobile Equipment (SIM-ME) Interface
4. 3GPP TS 11.14 Specification of the SIM Application Toolkit (SAT) for the Subscriber Identity Module - Mobile Equipment (SIM-ME) interface
5. 3GPP TS 23.048 Security mechanisms for the (U)SIM application toolkit; Stage 2
6. 3GPP TS 31.102 Characteristics of the Universal Subscriber Identity Module (USIM) application
7. 3GPP TS 31.111 Universal Subscriber Identity Module (USIM) Application Toolkit (USAT)
8. 3GPP TS 31.130 (U)SIM Application Programming Interface (API); (U)SIM API for Java Card
9. 3GPP TS 51.011 Specification of the Subscriber Identity Module - Mobile Equipment (SIM-ME) interface
10. ETSI TS 102 22 Smart cards UICC-Terminal interface Physical and logical characteristics
11. ETSI TS 102 124 Smart Cards; Transport Protocol for UICC based applications; Stage 1
12. ETSI TS 102 127 Smart Cards; Transport Protocol for CAT applications; Stage 2
13. ETSI TS 102 241 Smart cards UICC Application Programming Interface (UICC API) for Java Card (TM)

Chapter 12
Smart Card Reader APIS

Damien Sauveron

Abstract The aim of this chapter is to describe the main middlewares used to manage and access smart card readers. It is illustrated by samples[1] of code that the reader of this book will be able to reuse to quickly develop his/her first host applications to communicate with smart cards.

Key words: Smart Card Reader, Terminal, OCF, PC/SC, Wrappers, STIP

12.1 Terminology: Smart Card Reader, IFD, CAD and Terminal

Smart cards are becoming increasingly prevalent and in order to develop a host card-aware application it is fundamental to manage the readers enabling smart card communication.

A smart card reader is also known as a card programmer (because it can read data from and write data to a card), a card terminals, a Card Acceptance Device (CAD) or an InterFace Device (IFD). There is a slight difference between the card reader and the terminal. The term 'reader' is generally used to describe a unit that interfaces with a PC for the majority of its processing requirements. In contrast, a 'terminal' is a self-contained processing device.

As already shown in this book, smart cards are portable data cards that must communicate with an external device to gain access to a display device or a network. Thus, they can be plugged into a reader, commonly referred to as a card terminal, or they can operate using radio frequencies (RF).

Damien Sauveron, XLIM UMR Université de Limoges, FRANCE,
e-mail: damien.sauveron@unilim.fr

[1] All the examples of this book assume that there is on the card a default selected application with a Master File (MF, i.e. 3F00) that the host application tries to select it.

The reader provides a path for an application to send commands to the card and receive responses from it. There are many types of reader available and the easiest way to describe a reader is by the method of its interface to a PC:

- serial RS232;
- PCMCIA;
- USB;
- ExpressCard;
- floppy disk slots;
- parallel ports;
- infrared IRDA ports;
- keyboard wedge readers;
- built-in reader;
- etc.

Readers have many forms factors and capabilities. For example, some card readers come with advanced security features such as secure PIN entry, secure display or an integrated fingerprint scanner for the next-generation of multi-layer security and three-factor authentication.

As illustrated below, card readers can easily be integrated into a PC running one of common operating system (Windows 98/Me, 2000, XP, Vista, Linux, Unix, FreeBSD, Mac OS X).

To summarise the steps of the communication between the host application and a card:

- First; the application has to communicate with the reader. Each reader manufacturer providing a different protocol for communication between the host and the reader.
- Second; the reader communicates with the card, acting as the intermediary before sending the data to the card (communication with a smart card is based on the APDU format).
- Third; the card will process the data and return a response to the reader, which will then return the data to its originating source (i.e. the host application).

Unfortunately, as it is explained above, the ISO group was unable to provide a standard for communicating with the readers, so there is no one-size-fits-all approach to smart card reader communication. The most recent initiative in this field was launched by the USB Implementers Forum [25], with the CCID protocol which will be presented later in this chapter.

Nevertheless, in order to facilitate the development of the host application using the smart card, several software stacks to abstract these communication protocols and the management of the readers have been proposed. The two main stacks (OpenCard Framework and PC/SC) to communicate with a reader from a host are shown in Fig. 12.1. They are the topics of the following sections.

OpenCard Framework (OCF) [14, 27, 28] makes it possible to access readers on all systems supporting Java, whereas PC/SC provides access to the card readers through various programming languages. Therefore, even if PC/SC and OpenCard Framework share some similar concepts, they are two orthogonal standards [3, 13].

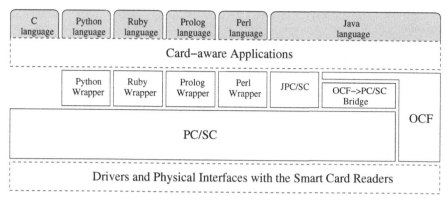

Fig. 12.1 The Two Main Stacks to Communicate with a Reader from a Host.

12.2 OCF: OpenCard Framework

OpenCard Framework is an open standard framework that provides interoperable smart cards solutions across many hardware and software platforms. Its architecture and its set of APIs enable application developers and service providers to build and deploy smart card aware solutions in any OpenCard-compliant environment.

12.2.1 Overview

The OCF project was initiated in 1997 by the OpenCard consortium which comprised Gemplus, Giesecke&Devrient, IBM, Schlumberger, Sun microsystems, Visa International, and others. The OCF makes it possible to access readers, smart cards and their applications in Java. The reference implementation of OCF, as presented in Fig. 12.2.1, includes a set of Java classes, packages and APIs that contains all the necessary functionality. The OCF architecture defines the `CardTerminal` and `CardService` classes and offers a standardised high-level interface to applications.

If the reader manufacturers want to make their readers available to applications, they just need to provide a `CardTerminal` class, which encapsulates reader behaviour, and a `CardTerminalFactory` class which has to be registered with the `CardTerminalRegistry`. It keeps track of all readers to the OpenCard Framework and it is used by the framework to create `CardTerminal` instances when the framework is initialised.

Card services offer smart-card functionality to application developers via high-level interfaces. Thus, card manufacturers have to provide `CardService` classes encapsulating the behaviour of their smart cards and a `CardServiceFactory` class which must be registered with the `CardServiceRegistry` (thereafter

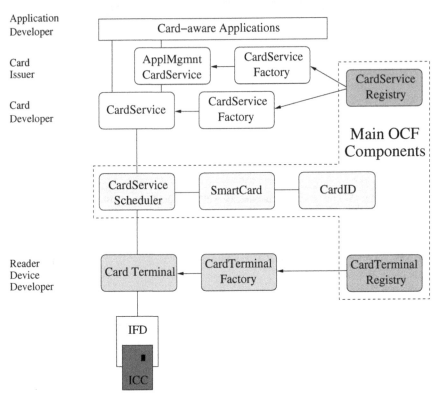

Fig. 12.2 The OpenCard Framework (OCF) architecture.

used by the framework to instantiate card services). For example such a service could be a `FileSystemCardService` for the cards hosting a file system. By the way, there is one default implementation of such an ISO file system provided in the optional package of OCF (`opencard.opt.iso.fs.FileAccessCard-Service`).

Application developers, they will mainly use card services already offered by the framework. However if they would like to propose their own smart card application to other developers they can also develop their own service. The example presented below will illustrate how it is possible to communicate with the card and thus develop a new service. OCF is described in much greater detail within the reference[27]. However it should be noted that the main problem with OCF is that maintenance and development was stopped in February 2000.

12.2.2 *Example*

The file `opencard.properties` should be configured as follows:

```
OpenCard.services =
                opencard.opt.util.PassThruCardServiceFactory
```

Hereafter is a code sample selecting the MF of the default selected application.

```java
package samples;

import opencard.core.service.SmartCard;
import opencard.core.service.CardRequest;
import opencard.core.terminal.*;
import opencard.opt.util.*;

public class SampleAPDUSent {
    public static void main(String[] args)
    {
        try {
            SmartCard.start();

            // Wait for smart card to be inserted
            CardRequest cr = new CardRequest();
            cr.setWaitBehavior(CardRequest.ANYCARD);
            SmartCard sc = SmartCard.waitForCard(cr);

            // Make sure card is available
            if (sc != null) {
              PassThruCardService ptcs = (PassThruCardService)
                  sc.getCardService(PassThruCardService.class, true);

              // Build an ISO command to select the MF
              byte[] apdu = { (byte)0x00, (byte)0xA4, (byte)0x00, (byte)0x00,
              (byte)0x02, (byte)0x3F, (byte)0x00 };
              CommandAPDU command = new CommandAPDU(apdu);

              // Send command and get response from card
              ResponseAPDU response = ptcs.sendCommandAPDU(command);

              // Print the SW of the response, but a more complex
              // handling could be done
               System.out.println("SW:" + Integer.toHexString(response.sw()));
              // We are done with this smart card.
              sc.close();
            }

        } catch (Exception e) {
            e.printStackTrace();

        } finally { // even in case of an error..
            try{
                SmartCard.shutdown();
            } catch (Exception e) {
            e.printStackTrace();
            }
        }

        System.exit(0);
    }
}
```

12.3 PC/SC

PC/SC is a standard of communication between an application on a host and a smart card terminal and consequently between the application and the card contained in the reader.

12.3.1 Overview

In order to standardise an architecture to interface the smart card with a PC, a consortium of companies formed the PC/SC Workgroup [15] in May 1996, the PC/SC Workgroup [15]. It gathered manufacturers of PCs, readers and smart cards industries, including Apple, Bull, Gemplus, Hewlett Packard, Infineon, Intel, Microsoft, Schlumberger and Toshiba.

The PC/SC Workgroup identified 3 parts to be standardised:

- the interface between the reader and the PC (Personal Computer);
- a high level API to use the functionalities of the card;
- mechanisms allowing several applications to share common resources, like the card or the reader.

The members of the consortium also wished to define an architecture and specifications allowing cards and reader manufacturers to independently develop their products while ensuring that they can work together.

In December 1997, the working group published the "Interoperability Specification for ICCs and Personal Computer Systems" [16], which is nowadays more commonly known under the name of PC/SC (PC/Smart Card).

Version 1.0 comprised eight parts each one detailing an aspect of the architecture. Version 2.0 was released in August 2004 followed by an update in January 2006 [17], which added support for contactless cards, enhanced readers (e.g. a keyboard, or a biometric sensor or a screen, etc.) and synchronous cards. It now comprises nine parts which are described in the following section.

12.3.2 Architecture

The Fig. 12.3.2 presents what each part of PC/SC 2.0 specifications covers:

- part 1 gives an overview of the architecture of the system and components defined by the working group.
- part 2 details the requirements to ensure interoperability between the smart card (i.e. ICC, Integrated Chip Card) and the reader (i.e. IFD, InterFace Device):
  - physical characteristics;

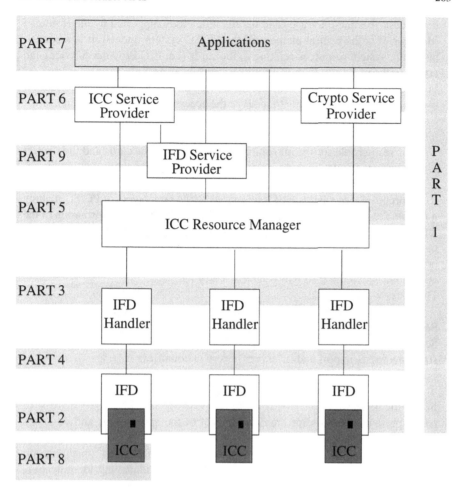

Fig. 12.3   The Architecture of PC/SC 2.0.

- communications protocols and the management of errors. They are mainly a copy&paste of the ISO 7816 and ISO 14443 standards in order to manage the contact and/or contactless synchronous and asynchronous cards.
- part 3 describes the interface which the driver of a reader (so-called IFD Handler) must implement so that the higher layers of PC/SC can independently communicate with it, without knowledge of the underlying connector (e.g. USB, serial) and protocols used. In particular, this driver must implement the sending of commands, the powering and unpowering, etc.
- part 4 presents the various types of interface with a reader (e.g. PS2, USB, serial, PCMCIA, etc.) and provides a certain number of recommendations which the readers should respect.

- part 5 describes the interfaces and the functionalities supported by the Resource Manager. It is the central element of the PC/SC system. Indeed, it is responsible to the system resources relating to the cards (i.e. ICC Provider Service) and access to the readers, and thus through them, to the cards.
  In theory, each operating system should provide its own Resource Manger. Moreover, it solves three problems to manage the access to various readers and cards:
    - it is responsible for the identification and the detection of the resources (e.g. insertion/withdrawal of a card, connection/disconnection of a reader, etc.);
    - it is responsible for the allocation of the resources: the cards and the readers for the various applications, by providing mechanisms for sharing or exclusiveness;
    - it proposes a mechanism of transactions to the high layers of PC/SC making it possible to carry out complex operations while ensuring that information of the intermediate states was not corrupted.
- part 6 proposes to hide the complexity of the underlying architecture while proposing to the application programmers a high level API corresponding to the operations which the card will be able to carry out.
  This part:
    - describes the models for the providers of service in a general way (i.e. ICC Service Provider) and for the providers of cryptographic services (i.e. Crypto Service Provider). Note that the separation of cryptography is related to the restrictions for its import and its export in certain countries;
    - identifies the necessary interfaces;
    - indicates how these models can be extended to meet the needs of applications in specific fields
- part 7 presents methods for the development of the applications and describes how to use the other components.
- part 8 describes the recommended functionalities for the cards which support cryptography. It contains best practice on the way of managing identification, authentication and protected storage, but also ways of ensuring the integrity of information, its traceability and confidentiality in a solution based on the card.
- part 9 which did not exist in the previous version of PC/SC, describes how to manage readers with additional features (i.e, IFD Service Provider): biometric sensor, screen, etc.

To summarise, in the PC/SC architecture, the card-aware applications are built on the top of one or several Service Providers and the Resource Manager. The provider of services encapsulates the expected functionalities for a specific smart card and makes them accessible through a high level API. The Resource Manager handles the resources relating to the cards and the readers inside the system. It allows, via a simple API, on the top of which the services of higher levels are built, to communicate with the readers and through them, with the smart cards.

12.3.3 Various Implementations

At the beginning, implemented exclusively by Microsoft, member of the consortium, PC/SC gave access to the card readers since various programming languages but only under Windows. Thus, few years ago a free project, pcsc-lite [18], initiated by David Corcoran – and in which the author of this chapter was an active developer – was born to give access to the readers on other operating systems.

12.3.3.1 Microsoft PC/SC

Microsoft as a member of the working group was the first to provide an implementation of the PC/SC specification. At the beginning, it consisted of an external program, the Resource Manager, and a high level library, the SCard API (for Smart Card) [10] making it possible to communicate with it.

The basic operations allowed by the API are:

- SCardEstablishContext This function establishes the resource manager context (the scope) within which database operations are performed.
- SCardReleaseContext This function closes an established resource manager context, freeing any resources allocated under that context.
- SCardListReaders This function provides the list of readers within a set of named reader groups, eliminating duplicates.
- SCardConnect This function establishes a connection, using a specific resource manager context, between the calling application and a smart card contained by a specific reader.
- SCardDisconnect This function terminates a connection previously opened between the calling application and a smart card in the target reader.
- SCardReconnect This function re-establishes an existing connection between the calling application and a smart card.
- SCardReleaseContext This function closes an established resource manager context, freeing any resources allocated under that context.
- SCardStatus This function provides the current status of a smart card in a reader. You can call it any time after a successful call to SCardConnect and before a successful call to SCardDisconnect.
- SCardGetStatusChange This function blocks execution until the current availability of the cards in a specific set of readers changes.
- SCardTransmit This function sends a service request to the smart card and expects to receive data back from the card.

More advanced operations are also possible:

- SCardBeginTransaction This function starts a transaction, waiting for the completion of all other transactions before it begins.
- SCardEndTransaction This function completes a previously declared transaction, enabling other applications to resume interactions with the card.

- `SCardControl` This function gives you direct control of the reader. You can call it any time after a successful call to `SCardConnect` and before a successful call to `SCardDisconnect`.

This API is an implementation of suggested API in part 5 of the PC/SC specifications. For a long time, the first versions of the Resource Manager had many problems. For example, it was only possible to communicate with one reader at a time. After having solved, some of these problems, Microsoft now integrates these components is all of its operating systems.

In this model, for each one of its reader types, each reader's manufacturer has to provide a driver (i.e. IFD Handler) respecting the Microsoft API for the support of the readers (e.g. an API similar to that defined in part 3 of the PC/SC specifications). Indeed, according to the part 4 of the specifications, various readers being able to use a specific protocol even if they use the same media (e.g. the USB), one driver per reader type or at least by family of reader type using the same protocol for the same media. Moreover, drivers need to pass tests of the Windows Hardware Quality Labs [29] in order to be approved.

However, in order to solve these worrying and expensive problems of installation of drivers and certification, an initiative aims at standardising a protocol on USB was launched within the USB Implementers Forum [25]. Thus, the CCID 1.0 specification (i.e. USB Chip/Smart Card Interface Device) [26] has been developed. Microsoft has implemented this specification in a driver distributed with its operating systems thus making it possible for any compliant CCID reader to work without requiring the installation of any additional driver at the time of its first connection. Obviously, not all readers follow this standard, but most of the manufacturers propose at least one. There is no doubt that the CCID standard is the future since it also considers readers with additional advanced features.

In the PC/SC model it is still the responsibility of the cards Issuers to provide adequate Service Provider (i.e. a high level API – part 6 of the PC/SC specifications) for its cards, in order to hide the complexity of the underlying protocol stack. For example, if an Issuer provides a card with a file system, it is probable that it will also provide a Service Provider, making it possible to read and write a file, to create a directory, to move it in the tree structure, etc. For the application programmer who will want to use these cards to store information, it will be more convenient to use this high level API rather than to communicate directly with the card in a rather obscure language.

If an ICC Service Provider could be related to a particular card of a particular manufacturer, it can also be related to a family of cards compliant with the same standard and thus to cards from various manufacturers. Once again, this example can be illustrated with cards having a file system compliant with the ISO7816-4 standard. If one ICC Service Provider exists for this type of card then the application programmer will be able to use it in a transparent way without having to be concerned with the particular card manufacturer. Of course the ICC Services Providers can co-exist without any problem. It should be noted that a clear goal for the working group is to promote adoption of PC/SC via a fair and open standards approach.

Crypto Service Providers (CSP) have a similar role to that of the ICC Service Providers and they are also standardised in part 6 of the PC/SC specifications. In certain countries, cryptographic algorithms are subject to very strict rules of import and export. Thus, there can be a CSP for a specific card or many general CSPs for a type of card.

To summarise the ICC Service Provider and Crypto Service Provider are provided in general by the cards Issuers or by vendors of interoperable solution components (e.g. file system , etc.). It will be noted in addition, that these CSPs are at the base of the cryptographic standard of Microsoft: CryptoAPI or CAPI [9].

12.3.3.2 pcsc-lite

The project pcsc-lite [18] was initiated in 2000 [1] by David Corcoran of the university of Purdue. This project was a free implementation of standard PC/SC 1.0 under BSD licence. The goal of the developers of this project was to provide a better support for the smart cards within the Unix environments. Their efforts were focussed within MUSCLE (Movement for the Use of Smart Card in A Linux Environment) [11].

In order to provide to the developers a simple API and to facilitate the porting of the card applications developed under Windows, it was decided to implement the SCard API proposed by Microsoft. Nowadays, pcsc-lite works on a great number of platforms: Linux, Solaris, Mac OS X, FreeBSD, HP-UX, etc. It could be noted that in 2000, Apple joined the PC/SC working group and decided to adopt pcsc-lite as implementation of reference for its Mac OS X system.

On the other hand, as the "lite" term in the name reminds us, pcsc-lite tries to implement the PC/SC specifications and specially the SCard API of Microsoft, but it does not yet include all its functionalities. The current functions of the SCard API implemented can be checked in reference material [19]. One of the reported reasons is that Microsoft provides little details about its implementation and associated behaviour.

Currently, the project includes a Resource Manager and a partial implementation of the SCard API, which respectively appear as a daemon and a shared library. The latter communicates with the manager through Unix sockets. The implementation is able to manage up to 255 readers simultaneously, or more exactly 255 slots (a reader can have several slots accepting simultaneously several cards). The pcsc-lite daemon can also manage by default, up to 16 applications using the cards/readers, but as the software is open source, it is enough to change the value of the limiting constant before compilation to manage more.

The basic operation of the daemon during its initialisation is as follows:

- allocation of the structures of data for the readers and creation of public memory space containing information on the state of the readers (though a shared memory mechanism);
- reading of the configuration file of the static readers (e.g. serial readers);
- creation of the main server and waiting of a client request;

- launching of a thread of detection for the added readers via "hotplug" mechanisms (e.g. USB, PCMCIA).

For each detected reader, if the driver of the reader (i.e. IFD Handler) allows it, the demon pcscd will create a thread to deal with the management of the communication and to give simultaneous access to the resources.

At the time of the first client request (i.e. SCardEstablishContext), through the shared library, pcsc-lite and thus through the Unix sockets, the daemon will create a thread which will start a dedicated server to deal with the context of the client. The subsequent requests will use this new Unix socket until the application decides to finish its dialogue with the daemon (i.e. SCardReleaseContext) or it dies (e.g. segmentation problem, termination, etc.).

Since 2003 the project pcsc-lite has played a major role in the smart card world, thanks to the work of Ludovic Rousseau. Indeed he has proposed a free implementation of an IFD Handler for the readers respecting the standard CCID [4] under a GPL licence. This drivers which also supports the readers having advanced features, puts the MUSCLE project at least at the same level as Microsoft, for the advanced use of cards.

12.3.4 Wrappers

An important difference and advantage of PC/SC is the existence of several *wrappers*. These middleware libraries make it possible to write applications communicating with the resource manager in different programming languages to that provided and imposed by the native library. For example, pcsc-lite only provides one library implementing the SCard API for the C language and this makes it possible only to write programs in this language or languages able to call C functions.

Thus, wrappers appeared for Perl [20], Python [21], Prolog [6], Ruby [22] and Java [7]. They use the mechanisms of FFI (Foreign Function Interfaces) [2] of these various languages. These middlewares contribute to the popularity of PC/SC while allowing more programmers to easily access to the low level functionalities of the PC/SC standard.

12.3.4.1 Solutions for Java: JPC/SC vs OCFPCSC

To access readers and cards with the Java language, there are two solutions based on PC/SC.

The first solution is a wrapper called JPC/SC and developed by Marcus Oestreicher of IBM BlueZ Secure Systems. The package supports basically two classes, Context and Card that are familiar to SCard API programmers, The Context and Card class methods are mapped, pretty much straight to native functions used in the SCard API, by the use of JNI (Java Native Interfaces) to return the calls of method and the Java arguments towards the native client library provided by the

PC/SC Microsoft or by `pcsc-lite`. With `Context`, the programmer establishes the communication with the PC/SC daemon, queries readers and set up a connection with a card. This results in a `Card` instance which is used to exchange APDUs with the card. Errors are typically signalled by `PCSCExceptions`. The `State` class wraps structures such as `READER_STATE` and is used to return the status of readers and card connections such as in `Context.GetStatusChange()` or `Card.Status()`. This solution has the advantage of being simple and low level. The latter point is an advantage and a disadvantage: it allows a greater freedom but it also requires the knowledge of certain underlying concepts to communicate with a card (APDU, etc.) that is not the case with the OCF card service.

The other solution is the OCFPCSC bridge [12], i.e. a bridge between the Open-Card Framework and PC/SC. Indeed, even if the OCF project makes it possible to access readers from Java, there are too few OCF drivers (i.e. Card Terminals) and using the bridge extends the set of the readers that can be used. From the OCF point of view, it is in fact a simple Card Terminal to declare in the configuration file `opencard.properties` and which is connected, through JNI calls, to the native client SCard library of the system to detect the presence of the readers, and to communicate with them

However, in Java if it is always necessary to use a layer of JNI calls to gain access to a hardware level (e.g. for the use of the serial or parallel port, `javax.comm` is used) or to access another native level (e.g. for the use of the solution OCFPCSC bridge), this latter solution has the disadvantage of adding additional layers in an already complex software stack.

For completeness, the `javax.smartcard` API [23] of Sun microsystems (which made it possible to communicate with a card from Java) could be cited, but it is now completely abandoned.

12.3.5 Examples

One of the best ways to understand how to communicate with a smart card via a reader, is to review software source code examples. The following example considers a JPC/SC approach, however Appendix A of this book also includes C Language and Perl Language examples. The source code is best read with reference to the SCard API.

12.3.5.1 JPC/SC

```
package samples;

import com.linuxnet.jpcsc.*;

public class Test{

    static final int PROTO=PCSC.PROTOCOL_T0|PCSC.PROTOCOL_T1;
```

```java
public static void main(String[] args){
    int j = 0;
    if (args.length != 0)
        j = Integer.decode(args[0]).intValue();
    System.out.println("EstablishContext(): ...");
    Context ctx = new Context();
    ctx.EstablishContext(PCSC.SCOPE_SYSTEM, null, null);

    // list readers
    System.out.println("ListReaders(): ...");
    String[] sa = ctx.ListReaders();
    if (sa.length == 0){
        throw new RuntimeException("no reader found");
    }
    for (int i = 0; i < sa.length; i++){
        System.out.println("Reader: " + sa[i]);
    }

        // get status change: wait the insertion of a card
        System.out.println("GetStatusChange() for reader "
        + sa[j] + ": ...");
        State[] rsa = new State[1];
        rsa[0] = new State(sa[j]);
        do{
            ctx.GetStatusChange(1000, rsa);
        }while((rsa[0].dwEventState & PCSC.STATE_PRESENT)
        != PCSC.STATE_PRESENT);
        System.out.println("ReaderState of " + sa[j] + ": ");
        System.out.println(rsa[0]);

        // connect to card
        System.out.println("Connect(): ...");
        Card c = ctx.Connect(sa[j], PCSC.SHARE_EXCLUSIVE,
        PCSC.PROTOCOL_T0|PCSC.PROTOCOL_T1);

        // card status
        System.out.println("CardStatus(): ...");
        State rs = c.Status();
        System.out.println("CardStatus: ");
        System.out.println(rs.toString());

        // select APDU for Master File (3F00)
        byte[] capdu = {
            (byte)0x00, (byte) 0xA4, (byte) 0x00, (byte) 0x00,  // select
            (byte) 0x02, // length
            (byte) 0x3F, (byte) 0x00 };

        // select MF, different Transmit() methods used
        try{
            System.out.println("Transmit(): try to select the MF ...");
            System.out.println("Command: " + Apdu.ba2s(capdu, 0, ...
            ... capdu.length));
            byte[] rapdu = c.Transmit(capdu, 0, capdu.length);
            System.out.println("Response: " + Apdu.ba2s(rapdu, 0, ...
            ... rapdu.length));
        }catch(PCSCException ex){
            System.out.println("REASON CODE: " + ex.getReason());
            System.out.println("TRANSMIT ERROR: " + ex.toString());
        }

        // disconnect card connection
        System.out.println("Disconnect() from card ...");
        c.Disconnect(PCSC.LEAVE_CARD);
    }

    // release context
    System.out.println("ReleaseContext() ...");
```

```
      ctx.ReleaseContext();
   }
}
```

12.4 STIP

To finish this illustration of smart card reader programming, the Small Terminal Interoperability Platform (STIP) will be overviewed.

The STIP Consortium was a grouping of secure transaction solution providers, including terminal manufacturers, payphone manufacturers, smart card manufacturers and others, formed to define a Java specification for Small terminals and transaction oriented devices.

The Consortium was initiated in 1999 by the Java Card Forum. Its principle objective was to enable interoperability of applications on a range of devices. Thus, the Consortium has chosen Java to provide the microprocessor independence and it has defined a Java API to provide secure transaction and multi-application capabilities. In May 2004, the STIP Consortium transferred all its assets (i.e. Intellectual Properties) to the GlobalPlatform consortium. Now, the release of version 2.2 of the API also takes into account the C# language and not only Java. The GDP/STIP API is focused on providing secure transaction capability in a multi-application environment, but non-secure transaction applications can be supported too.

Some of the secure transaction applications that can be supported are EMV, CEPS, ISO8583, APACS, Mondex, Proton, Visa Cash, Loyalty applications and Secure ID applications. The GDP/STIP API is designed to provide a high level of functionality and performance on devices with limited resources. The secure transaction capability of the API lends itself to EFT/POS terminals, payphones, parking meters, vending machines, mobile phones, PDAs and the like. In these APIs, the GDP/STIP Core Framework Technology API can be distinguished from other comprehensive set of service APIs that can form the basis of most "profiles". For example, one well-known profile is that defined by the FINREAD Consortium which consists of an API for PC-connected secure smart card readers.

More detailed information can be found on the GlobalPlatform website [5].

12.5 In Conclusion

This chapter has discussed the main middleware that can be used access smart cards via card readers plus the associated standards bodies and workgroups. Some example source was provided for clarity and more can be found in Appendix A. The are multiple routes to exploit smart card reader APIs but in the authors opinion a developer is well advised to use PC/SC (and a wrapper is needed) for the development of a host card-aware application. Moreover, PC/SC should be integrated in the next version of Windows Mobile and the porting of applications should become easier.

Acknowledgement

The author wishes to say thanks to Ludovic Rousseau for this kind authorization to reproduce some parts of the samples presented in this document and for his work in the MUSCLE community. The author would also like to thank Xiring[24] for providing the smart card readers used to test the source code examples.

References

1. David Corcoran. *M.U.S.C.L.E: porting the PC/SC architecture to Linux*. Gemplus Developers Conference 99, june 1999.
2. Design Issues for Foreign Function Interfaces. A survey of existing native interfaces for several languages and some suggestions. More Information Available via
   `http://xarch.tu-graz.ac.at/autocad/lisp/ffis.html`, Cited 8 Oct 2007.
3. Frank Seliger. *The OpenCard Framework and PC/SC V Two New Industry Initiatives for Smart Cards*, 1999. More Information Available via
   `http://www.opencard.org/docs/ocfpcsc.pdf`, Cited 8 Oct 2007.
4. Generic CCID IFD Handler home page. More Information Available via
   `http://pcsclite.alioth.debian.org/ccid.html`, Cited 8 Oct 2007.
5. GlobalPlatform. More Information Available via
   `http://www.globalplatform.org/`, Cited 8 Oct 2007.
6. GNU Prolog Wrappers for PC/SC. More Information Available via
   `http://www.musclecard.com/middleware/files/gplpcsc.tgz.`, Cited 8 Oct 2007.
7. Java Wrappers for PC/SC. More Information Available via
   `http://www.musclecard.com/middleware/files/jpcsc-0.8.0-src.zip`, Cited 8 Oct 2007.
8. JSR 177: Security And Trust Services API for J2ME. More Information Available via
   `http://jcp.org/en/jsr/detail?id177,2004`, Cited 8 Oct 2007.
9. Microsoft. CryptoAPI. More Information Available via
   `http://msdn.microsoft.com/library/default.asp?url=/library/en-us/seccrypto/security/cryptographyessentials.asp`, Cited 8 Oct 2007.
10. Microsoft. SCard API. More Information Available via
    `http://msdn.microsoft.com/library/default.asp?url=/library/en-us/secauthn/security/smartcardresourcemanagerapi.asp`, Cited 8 Oct 2007.
11. MUSCLE home page. More Information Available via
    `http://www.musclecard.com/`, Cited 8 Oct 2007.
12. OCF To PC/SC Shim. More Information Available via
    `http://www.musclecard.com/middleware/files/OCFPCSC1-0.0.1.tar.gz`, Cited 8 Oct 2007.
13. OpenCard Consortium. OpenCard Framework (OCF): Frequently Asked Questions: Positioning of OCF Versus PC/SC.
    `http://www.opencard.org/misc/OCF-FAQ.shtml#PCSC`, Cited 8 Oct 2007.
14. OpenCard Framework. More Information Available via
    `http://www.opencard.org/`, Cited 8 Oct 2007.
15. PC/SC Workgroup. More Information Available via
    `http://www.pcscworkgroup.com/`, Cited 8 Oct 2007.

16. PC/SCWorkgroup. PC/SCWorkgroup Specifications 1.0. More Information Available via http://www.pcscworkgroup.com/specifications/specdownloadV1.php, Cited 8 Oct 2007.

17. PC/SCWorkgroup. PC/SCWorkgroup Specifications 2.01.3.january2006. More Information Available via http://www.pcscworkgroup.com/specifications/specdownload.php, Cited 8 Oct 2007.

18. pcsc-lite home page. More Information Available via http://alioth.debian.org/projects/pcsclite/, Cited 8 Oct 2007.

19. pcsc-lite SCard API. More Information Available via http://pcsclite.alioth.debian.org/pcsc-lite/, Cited 8 Oct 2007.

20. Perl Wrappers for PC/SC. More Information Available via http://ludovic.rousseau.free.fr/softwares/pcsc-perl/, Cited 8 Oct 2007.

21. Python Wrappers for PC/SC. More Information Available via http://homepage.mac.com/jlgiraud/pycsc/Pycsc.html, Cited 8 Oct 2007.

22. Ruby Wrappers for PC/SC. More Information Available via http://raa.ruby-lang.org/project/pcsc-ruby/, Cited 8 Oct 2007.

23. Sun microsystems. Java Commerce/Smart Cards, 2001. More Information Available via http://java.sun.com/products/commerce/javax.smartcard/, Cited 8 Oct 2007.

24. Teo. More Information Available via http://www.teobyxiring.com/, Cited 8 Oct 2007.

25. USB Implementers Forum. More Information Available via http://www.usb.org/info, Cited 8 Oct 2007.

26. USB Implementers Forum. Universal Serial Bus Device Class Specification for USB Chip/Smart Card Interface Devices version 1.0, March 2001. More Information Available via http://www.usb.org/developers/devclassdocs/ccidclassspec100a.pdf, Cited 8 Oct 2007.

27. Uwe Hansmann, Martin S. Nicklous, Thomas Schck, and Frank Seliger. *Smart Card Application Development Using Java*. Springer, 2000.

28. Vesna Hassler, Martin Manninger, Mikhail Gordeev, and Christoph Mller. *Java Card for E-Payment Applications*. Artech House Publishers, 2001.

29. WHQL Testing - overview. More Information Available via http://www.microsoft.com/whdc/whql/, Cited 8 Oct 2007.

Chapter 13
RFID and Contactless Technology

Gerhard P. Hancke

Abstract An increasing number of 'contactless' systems are based on passive Radio Frequency Identification (RFID) technology. A passive RFID token is powered by a transmitted RF carrier, which is also used for bi-directional communication. RFID technology comprises of several standards, which are suitable for different applications. Electronic Product Code (EPC) tags, contactless credit cards, e-passports and access control are just a few examples of systems that use a subset of this technology. This chapter contains a brief explanation of RFID operating principles along with an overview of prominent implementations and industry standards.

Key words: RFID, Contactless Technology, Near Field Communication (NFC)

13.1 Introduction

RFID is a technology that increases productivity and convenience and is currently being integrated into many areas of society. RFID is flexible and the variety of standards and tokens available allows it to be tailored to any application. The technology also offers additional benefits such as reduced maintenance cost and extended product lifetime. The uses of Radio Frequency Identification have therefore grown remarkably and it is believed that 1.3 billion tokens were sold in 2006. The total RFID market, including systems and services, is valued at £1.4 billion and expected to increase to £13 billion by 2016 [2].

Despite its recent popularity, RFID technology has been around for more than half a century. It is commonly believed that the concept of radio identification started in the early 1940s with the advent of radar when IFF transponders actively modu-

Gerhard P. Hancke, Research Assistant
Information Security Group Smart card Centre,
Royal Holloway University of London,
e-mail: ghancke@ieee.org

lated the radiated ground radar signals to identify airplanes. Despite early work on RFID, such as Stockman's *"Communication by Means of Reflected Power"* in 1948 [29], recognizing the potential of RFID, it took several more years, and additional advances in electronics, before the technology was implemented in further applications. During the 1960s, stores and libraries used electronic article surveillance, an early 1-bit form of RFID, for theft control. Meanwhile private and government research on the subject continued and in 1973 the first patents were filed that resembled modern systems: a token with rewritable memory by M.W. Cardullo and a passive token used to unlock doors by C. Walton. Scientists from the Los Alamos National Laboratory, who were asked by the U.S. Energy Department to develop a tracking system for nuclear materials, also demonstrated the concept of modulated backscatter with 12-bit tokens operating at 915 MHz in the same year. The basic communication principle of this system is still used today by the majority of Ultra-High Frequency (UHF) RFID tags. In the late 1980s, RFID gained widespread acceptance in automated toll collection and access control systems, which was followed by implementation in public transport payment systems and the first serious attempts at standardization in the 1990s. In 1999 it was proposed that low-cost UHF RFID 'tags' could be used to track items in supply chains. Currently the use of Electronic Product Code (EPC) tags for tracking at the pallet, case and item level is probably the most prominent RFID application, driven by government agencies, such as the US Department of Defense, and various large retailers such as Tesco and Wal-Mart. RFID technology is, however, also used on a large scale in other applications such as machine readable travel documents (e.g. e-passports) and credit cards [9, 17, 26].

This chapter is intended as an introduction to RFID and summarizes the aspects most relevant to contactless smart card systems. Section 13.2 gives a brief overview of existing systems, describing the general operating principles and available technology and discusses a number of high-profile implementations. The RF interface and communication theory are discussed in Section 13.3 and the current HF RFID standards are summarized in Section 13.4.

13.2 Contactless Technology

Even though RFID is a collective term for a number of technologies it is often used primarily to describe applications using low-resource devices, such as EPC tags. Devices used in identity and payment systems, like the cards shown in Fig. 13.1, are instead regularly referred to as "contactless" or "proximity" tokens. These devices operate in the High Frequency (HF) radio band, contain more resources and have a much shorter operating range than their UHF counterparts.

Examples of contactless tokens are shown in Fig. 13.1(a). Each token, or Proximity Integrated Circuit Card (PICC), contains an antenna and an integrated circuit (IC) as shown in Fig. 13.1(b). The IC performs modulation and demodulation of the RF channel and is also responsible for data storage and processing. The passive

(a) Example Tokens

(b) Example of an Inlay,
Showing RFID IC and Antenna

Fig. 13.1 'Contactless' Tokens

token derives its power from the RF carrier transmitted by the reader, or 'Proximity Coupling Device' (PCD). The bi-directional communication between the token and reader is also modulated onto this carrier.

The main benefit of contactless technology is its ease of use. The user does not have to physically insert his token into the reader, or orientate the token in a specific way. In most cases the token can be kept in a wallet or a purse, providing some measure of personal security. All these factors combine to provide fast transactions and ensure high throughput. Furthermore, readers and tokens have no external mechanical parts that can wear out. This makes systems more durable and reliable, especially in exposed or dirty environments, and reduces maintenance costs when compared to contact or magnetic stripe systems. The fact that the token does not need to contain a power supply adds to the lifetime of the token as well. Contactless tokens can provide the same amount of security mechanisms than contact smart cards, although sometimes cost pressures limit this. There are also several established international standards available to aid interoperability [28].

Contactless systems differ from each other in a number of ways. It is therefore important to note the alternatives offered by the available standards and products in order to decide on the best system components for a specific application. For example, the three HF standards ISO 14443 [12], ISO 15693 [13] and ISO 18092 [15] allow for different data rates and operational ranges. The growth in the contactless market has also resulted in a variety of readers and tokens. In most cases the reader's only purpose is to act as a RF transceiver between the back-end system, which performs all the processing and security functions, and the token. In general the only difference between readers are the standards that they support. Readers are also more expensive and are often installed as a long-term infrastructure investment. It is therefore common to find readers supporting multiple standards so that the same hardware can be used in several applications, possibly allowing for future changes and extra functionality.

In contrast there are quite a few tokens available that can by classified in terms of resources, security and interfaces [28]. In terms of resources tokens can be divided into three different types:

- **Memory:** These tokens only have the ability to store information. They can perform no processing in addition to read and write functions.
- **Logic:** In addition to memory, these tokens also include some fixed processing routines that can be invoked by the reader, e.g. authenticate, increment value, decrement value, etc.
- **μ-Controller (MCU):** The token can run custom processing routines and might contain card operating systems such as JCOP or MULTOS.

Tokens can implement a number of security mechanisms. Security increases the token's required resources resulting in a higher system cost, so it is important that the token used, provides a level of security sufficient for the application, without incurring unnecessary expense. These levels can roughly be defined as follows:

- **Minimal:** Anyone can read information stored on the token. Memory can be locked so no unauthorised writing of data occurs.
- **Low:** The token implements some form of authentication mechanism. Memory is password protected or mutual authentication must be completed before data is released.
- **Medium:** The token implements a single encryption algorithm used to provide authentication and encryption of data. The algorithm could be proprietary, e.g. NXP Crypto1, or an industry standard, e.g. DES.
- **High:** The token can implement a number of symmetric and asymmetric industry standard algorithms for authentication, encryption, digital signatures, etc.

It may be required that a token supports several technologies. This allows for an environment where the user can carry a single token to access multiple systems. Alternatively it provides a way to migrate to, or add, a new system while still maintaining backward compatibility with existing systems. The following tokens are available that have the ability to interact with more than one system:

- **Multiple-Technology:** The token implements multiple technologies. A good example, albeit not contactless, of this is Chip & Pin cards in the United Kingdom that contain both magnetic stripe and contact smart card technologies.
- **Dual-Interface:** The token contains one integrated circuit that has more than one interface. An example would be a token containing an IC with both a contactless and a contact interface, such as the Barclays OnePulse card.
- **Hybrid:** A token with two or more integrated circuits, with their own interfaces, functioning independently. This term can be used to describe HF contactless tokens that also contain additional circuitry to support older Low Frequency (LF) systems.

13.2.1 Applications

Contactless tokens act as an electronic credential, interacting with the rest of the system on behalf of the entity it is associated with. Initially these tokens allowed for new applications such as contactless access control and automatic toll collection. In recent years, however, these tokens have started to replace, or supplement, established technologies such as paper tickets for travel or events, barcodes in item tracking and magnetic stripes in credit cards. This section gives an overview of prominent applications in which contactless tokens are used. Table 13.1 summarizes some of these applications.

Table 13.1 Summary of HF RFID Applications

Application	Standard	Token Resources	Security
Item Tracking	ISO 15693	Memory	Minimal/Low
Ticketing	ISO 15693 ISO 14443	Memory/Logic	Low/Medium
Closed Payment	ISO 14443	Logic	Low/Medium
Open Payment	ISO 14443	μ-Controller	High
Access Control	ISO 14443	μ-Controller	High
Identity	ISO 14443	μ-Controller	High

13.2.1.1 Identification

The basic function of RFID, as the name already suggests, is to assist a system in uniquely identifying an item or a person. The simplest example of this is tracking systems where a token, storing a Unique Identifier (UID), is attached to an item. The system can then track this item by scanning the token every time it passes a reader. Systems using HF tokens have a shorter operational range than their UHF equivalents although they provide more reliable reader coverage. NXP I-CODE and the Texas Instruments Tag-It products, are examples of HF tokens used in tracking applications. In ticketing systems, tokens facilitate access to services for a limited time before being disposed of. A "ticket" can take many forms, such as a key card to a hotel room or a day pass at the local gym. Paper tickets, containing NXP Mifare UltraLight tokens, received extensive publicity during the FIFA World Cup in 2006 and were used to gain fast access to stadiums, seating areas and refreshment kiosks [25].

Contactless *access control* is popular for securing physical locations. Charles Walton first invented an RFID-based access control system in 1973. The system involved an electronic lock that opened with an RFID key card, which he sold to Schlage [9]. Since then, contactless access control systems have become widespread not only in the private sector but also with government agencies. An application closely linked to access control is that of *identity*. A token used for proof of identity must contain enough information to allow the system to verify that the person presenting it is the legitimate owner. Identity tokens therefore contain additional personal information, such as biometric data.

The latest US initiative is the Federal Information Processing Standard Publication 201 (FIPS 201) detailing Personal Identity Verification (PIV) of federal employees and contractors [6]. FIPS 201, published by the US National Institute for Standards and Technology (NIST), provides specifications for a standard Federal smart ID card that is to be used for access control. The cards are a requirement for all federal employees and contractors under the Homeland Security Presidential Directive 12 (HSPD-12). Other large government initiatives in the US include:

- The Department of Defense's Common Access Card with Contactless (CAC-C) being used as identification for on duty military personnel, reserve personnel and civilian employees
- The Transportation Worker Identification Credential (TWIC) being issued by the Transportation Security Administration
- The First Responder Authentication Card (FRAC) being issued in the Department of Homeland Security (DHS) pilots [27]

Contactless tokens are also used for national identity cards and several countries are planning to use contactless ID cards for their citizens, with China [18] recently becoming the largest implementer. The most prominent application of contactless identity is however machine readable travel documents (MRTD). By the 26th of October 2006, the USA required that 27 countries issue their citizens with e-passports in order to still qualify under the Visa Waiver Program. E-passports adhere to operational specifications as defined by the International Civil Aviation Organisation (ICAO) [11], with additional guidelines for MRTD specified in ISO 7501 [16]. By 2015, ICAO wishes to have replaced all current passports with a digital version that stores encrypted biometric data on a RFID chip. The Department of Homeland Security also wants to use passive RFID to record who is entering or leaving the US across land routes, using a People Access Security Service (PASS) card. ICAO allows for optional security protocols that provides both authentication and encryption services. E-passports have the interesting security requirement that anyone who is presented with the passport should be able to read and verify the contents, but at the same time the user's personal details should be afforded some measure of privacy. For this reason most e-passports implement the Basic Access Control (BAC) scheme. BAC derives a key from the passport number, expiry date and the user's birthday, read off the OCR strip inside the passport. The idea is that anyone legitimately presented with the passport can read the OCR data, derive the key and retrieve the data off the token inside. The European Union countries are planning to implement Extended Access Control (EAC), involving a public key infrastructure for participating parties, for future passports including additional biometric data [1].

13.2.1.2 Payment

RFID has been used in payment systems since the 1980s, when it was first used for automatic toll collection. Since then contactless tokens were implemented in several cashless payment systems. In closed systems one organization is in control of the entire payment process. In other words, customers will pay for the organization's services with payment tokens issued by the same organization. These systems often function on a 'prepaid' principle where the customer pays for credit in advance and are ideal for public transport payments. A good example of such a system is the Oystercard scheme implemented by Transport for London (TFL) using NXP Mifare Classic tokens. Closed payment systems can also be used in other environments such as service stations, e.g. the SpeedPass system implemented by ExxonMobil, or in some cafeterias and fast food outlets.

In open systems an organization issues customers with payment tokens that will be used to purchase services from other organizations. Some of these systems still operate using prepaid credit like Hong Kong's Octopus system, implemented with Sony Felica tokens. The Octopus card is used mainly for transport payments, but can also be used to pay at convenience stores, restaurants and other local services. The most prominent open payment system is however contactless credit cards. RFID credit cards have been widely deployed in the US [8] with American Express (ExpressPay), MasterCard (PayPass), and Visa (payWave) all supporting contactless credit and debit cards.

In the United Kingdom the Royal Bank of Scotland, working with Mastercard, and Barclays recently launched contactless debit cards. The Barclays' OnePulse card, developed with Visa, is intended to function as a chip-and-pin contact card, contactless debit card and an Oyster card. The lower level communication of these cards, as specified in the EMV Contactless specification [4], adheres to ISO 14443 while the application layer communication adheres to the same Europay, Master-Card, and Visa (EMV) framework and specifications as contact payment cards and transaction terminals [5].

13.3 Radio Frequency Interface

The operation of contactless systems is based on the principle of inductive coupling. The token and the reader both contain antenna coils that are coupled and interact via a magnetic field. The token receives both data and power from the carrier transmitted by the reader. The token can also send data to the reader by influencing this carrier. Collectively, these methods are referred to as near-field communication since the range between the token is much smaller than one wavelength of the carrier. This section provides an overview of communication theory and physics relevant to contactless systems. The information in this section has been adapted from [7, 21, 22].

13.3.1 Communication Theory

In order to transmit information over an RF channel the relevant data must first be encoded and then modulated onto a suitable RF carrier. Line, or data, coding changes the binary data into a signal sequence that is best suited to the transmission channel and aids the receiver in recovering the data. Modulation is the process whereby the parameters of an RF carrier is altered in relation to the resultant baseband signal. Modulation, and to a lesser extend coding, techniques can be used to shape the frequency spectrum of the communication channel. In contactless systems coding and modulation methods have two main prerequisites : to separate the 'weak' backward channel communication from the strong forward channel carrier and to allow for data transfer from the reader to the token while ensuring that the token still receives adequate power from the HF carrier.

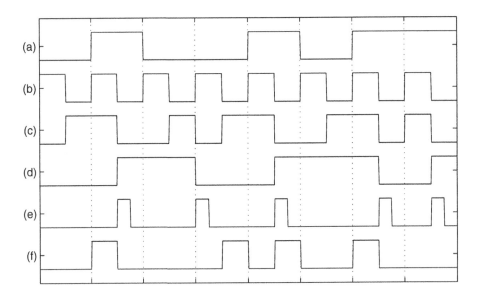

Fig. 13.2 Data coding examples: (a) Non-Return-to-Zero (NRZ), (b) data clock, (c) Manchester, (d) Miller, (e) Modified Miller, (f) Pulse Position

A line code's properties will typically be chosen to allow for the physical requirements of the transmission channel. Line codes are most often used to eliminate the DC component of the data and help the receiver with synchronization, although some codes also provide redundancy to prevent errors. HF RFID tokens use the schemes shown in Fig. 13.2.

Non-Return-to-Zero (NRZ) coding is the most used of basic coding techniques. A '1' is represented by a logical high for one clock period and a '0' is represented by a logical low for one clock period. NRZ encoding is not ideal when used to transmit data without a maximum runlength constraint, or in other words data that contains long sequences of ones or zeros. In this case there will be no signal transitions between high and low for a period of time, which can prevent the recovery of an accurate data clock. This also has other consequences, e.g. if a long sequence of zeros is transmitted using 100 % amplitude modulation it could disrupt the token's power supply.

Manchester coded sequences have at least one transition during each bit period. This periodic transition, which occurs in the middle of the bit period, can therefore be used to recover the data clock regardless of the data values. A '0' is expressed by a low-to-high transition and a '1' by a high-to-low transition. Although Manchester encoded sequences contain no DC component it requires approximately twice the channel bandwidth of NRZ.

Modified Miller coding is often used for data transmission from the reader to token. The data is encoded using Miller coding after which each transition, high-to-low and low-to-high, is replaced by a single pulse. In Miller encoding a '1' is represented by a bit period with a transition at the midpoint. A '0', if preceded by a '1', is represented by a bit period with no transition while a '0', preceded by another '0', is represented by a bit period with a transition at the start of the bit period. The advantage of Modified Miller coding is that the carrier is not interrupted for more than the duration of the coding pulse, even if a bit period is very long. This ensures a continuous power supply to the token from the reader's carrier during data transfer. The bandwidth of Modified Miller coding depends on the duration of the coding pulse.

Pulse-Position coding, which is also sometimes referred to as Pulse-Position Modulation (PPM), represents x data bits with a single pulse in one of 2^x possible time slots. In Fig. 13.2 an example of '1 in 4' PPM is given. In this case two bit periods are divided into four time slots. The data bits are then encoded as follows: '00' is represented with a pulse in the last slot, '01' with a pulse in slot three, '10' with a pulse in slot 2 and '11' with a pulse in the first slot. PPM is also suitable for reader to token communication since the carrier is not interrupted for more than the duration of the coding pulse. As with Modified Miller coding the required bandwidth is determined by the time width of the coding pulse.

Modulation is the process whereby a RF carrier's parameters are changed to represent a baseband data sequence. A sinusoidal carrier can be characterized by

$$x(t) = a \cdot \sin\left(2\pi f_c t + \phi\right) \qquad (13.1)$$

From the equation it is clear that the amplitude a, frequency f_c and phase ϕ can be varied to create distinctive carriers that are suitable to represent different data symbols. The amount that the chosen variable changes in relation to the data is referred to as the modulation index m_i. For example, m_i for amplitude modulation can be represented as

$$\frac{a_{max} - a_{min}}{a_{max} + a_{min}} \qquad (13.2)$$

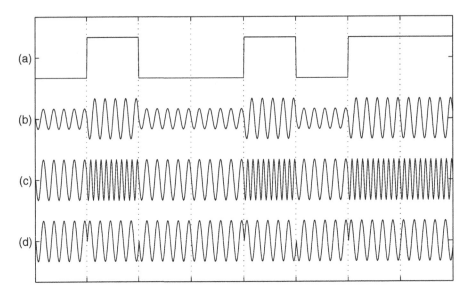

Fig. 13.3 Examples of RF modulation: (a) NRZ encoded data, (b) Amplitude-Shift Keying (ASK), (c) Frequency-Shift Keying (FSK), (d) Phase-Shift Keying (PSK)

When modulating digital data the chosen variable will only change between a set number of discrete values, e.g. high signal represented by $f = 10$ Hz, low signal represented by $f = 20$ Hz. As a result modulation is often referred to as 'shift-keying' in digital systems. Examples of the modulation schemes used in HF RFID are shown in Fig. 13.3.

Amplitude-Shift keying (ASK) changes the amplitude of the carrier to a level chosen to represent a specific data symbol. In the example shown a '1' is represented by a carrier with amplitude A and a '0' is represented by a carrier with amplitude $0.5A$. In this case the modulation index would be $0.33 \approx 33\%$. On-Off Keying (OOK) is a special case of ASK where the modulation index is equal to 100%.

Frequency-Shift Keying (FSK) changes the frequency of the carrier to represent a specific data symbol. In the example shown a '0' is represented by a carrier with $f_c = f_1$ and a '1' is represented by a carrier with $f_c = 2 \cdot f_1$.

Phase-Shift Keying (PSK) represents each specific data symbol by a shift in the carrier's phase. In the example shown a '0' is represented by a carrier with phase equal to $0°$ and a '1' is represented by a carrier with phase equal to $180°$.

The modulation process also changes the frequency domain representation of the data. ASK and PSK causes the power spectrum of the data to move from the baseband to f_c, while the spectrum power components for FSK data, as per our example, will be at f_1 and $2 \cdot f_1$.

The modulation process can be represented mathematically as follows:

$$x(t) = d(t) \cdot \sin(2\pi \cdot f_c t)$$
$$X(f) = D(f) * (\delta(-f_c) + \delta(f_c))$$
$$X(f) = D(f + f_c) + D(f - f_c)$$

where $d(t)$ is the baseband data sequence with frequency spectrum $D(f)$.

This is useful in RFID systems where both the forward and backward channel data are transmitted using the same carrier. The signal power of the backward channel can be up to 80 dB smaller than that of the carrier, which means that the reader would find it difficult to distinguish this 'weak' data from the 'strong' carrier if it cannot effectively isolate the data of interest and attenuate the carrier. Separating the two channels in the frequency domain simplifies the recovery of the backward channel data. In HF RFID the forward channel data is modulated directly onto the main carrier. The backward channel, however, is first modulated onto a sub-carrier before being modulated onto the main carrier. Modulating with a sub-carrier creates two data sidebands separated by f_{sc} from the operational frequency f_c. The backward channel's modulation process can be represented mathematically as follows:

$$x(t) = (d_B(t) \cdot \sin(2\pi \cdot f_{sc} t)) \cdot \sin(2\pi \cdot f_c t)$$
$$X(f) = (D_B(f) * (\delta(-f_{sc}) + \delta(f_{sc}))) * (\delta(-f_c) + \delta(f_c))$$
$$X(f) = D_B(f + f_c + f_{sc}) + D_B(f + f_c - f_{sc}) + D_B(f - f_c + f_{sc}) + D_B(f - f_c + f_{sc})$$

where $d_B(t)$ is the backward channel data with frequency spectrum $D_B(f)$. The resultant positive frequency spectrum of the forward and backward channels is shown in Fig. 13.4. The data at $f_c + f_{sc}$ is referred to as the upper-sideband while the data at $f_c - f_{sc}$ is referred to as the lower-sideband. The backward channel data can now be recovered, despite the presence of a strong operational carrier, by bandpass filtering one of the sidebands.

13.3.2 Inductive Coupling

HF RFID systems work on the principle of inductive coupling, where one device transfers energy to another by means of a shared magnetic field (H). This operational model is true as long as the token is placed in the near field of the reader, since the high frequency electromagnetic field (E) generated by the reader acts primarily as a magnetic field if the distance between the reader and token is less than $\lambda_{f_c} \cdot \frac{1}{2\pi}$. In simple terms an RFID system acts in a similar same way to a transformer, with the primary coil contained in the reader and the secondary coil contained in the token. Current flowing through the reader's coil generates a magnetic field, which in turn induces a proportional current flow in the coil of the token. The high frequency carrier can therefore be used for both data and power transfer between the reader and the token.

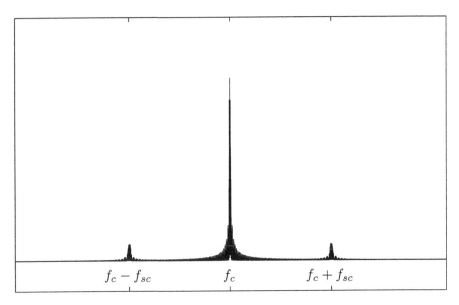

$$f_c - f_{sc} \qquad\qquad f_c \qquad\qquad f_c + f_{sc}$$

Fig. 13.4 The theoretical positive frequency spectrum of the forward and backward channel modulated using a carrier with frequency f_c and a sub-carrier with frequency f_{sc}.

13.3.2.1 Power Transfer

Moving charge, such as the flow of current in a conductor, generates a magnetic field. The magnitude of this field at a specific point is described by the magnetic field strength H. In HF RFID systems, the reader uses conductor loops to generate a magnetic field. The magnitude of the magnetic field generated by these loop antennas depends on the current I, number of loops N, the radius of the loops R and the distance from the loop antenna d. The following equation can be used to calculate the field strength along the axis of the loop antenna:

$$H = \frac{I \cdot N \cdot R^2}{2\sqrt{(R^2 + d^2)^3}} \tag{13.3}$$

In this case d is the distance from the center of the coil along the coil's axis. In general, the field strength is almost uniform at short distances (d < R) where smaller loop antennas also have a higher field strength. The larger antennas, however, have higher field strength at greater distances. A token will specify the minimum field strength it needs to function. Designing the antenna is then a trade-off between making the antenna small enough to generate a strong enough magnetic field and also making it large enough to achieve the system's required operational range.

In an HF RFID system both the reader and the token contain loop antennas in close proximity, as shown in Fig. 13.5. If a second loop antenna, with area A_2, is located close to another loop antenna, with area A_1, then the second antenna will

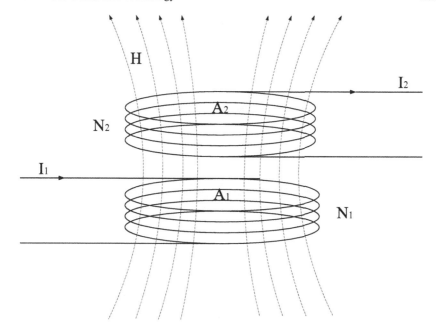

Fig. 13.5 Inductive Coupling

be affected by a proportion of the total magnetic flux Ψ flowing through the first antenna. The two circuits are connected together by this partial transfer of flux and are therefore said to be coupled. The magnitude of the coupled flux Ψ_{21} depends on the characteristics of the loop antennas, the position of the antennas in relation to each other and the magnetic conductivity, or permeability, of the medium between the antennas.

The ratio of the total flux that is generated in an area, to the current in the conductor that encloses that area, is described by inductance L:

$$L = \frac{\Psi}{I} = \frac{N \cdot \mu \cdot H \cdot A}{I} \tag{13.4}$$

The constant μ is equal to $\mu_0 \cdot \mu_r$, where μ_0 is the magnetic field constant ($4\pi \times 10^{-6}$) and describes the permeability of a vacuum, while μ_r is the relative permeability, indicating the ratio of the permeability of a material relative to μ_0.

The concept of mutual inductance is used to describe the coupling of two antennas by means of a magnetic field. The mutual inductance M_{21} is defined as the ratio of coupled flux Ψ_{21} enclosed by a second loop antenna to the current I_1 in the first loop:

$$M_{21} = \frac{\Psi_{21}(I_1)}{I_1} \tag{13.5}$$

Similarly there is also a mutual inductance M_{12} although $M_{21} = M_{12} = M$. The mutual inductance between two loop antennas can be calculated using Equations 13.4 and 13.5 and can be approximated as follows:

$$M_{12} = \frac{\mu_0 \cdot H(I_1) \cdot N_2 \cdot A_2}{I_1} \tag{13.6}$$

Replacing $H(I_1)$ with Equation 13.3 and substituting $R^2\pi$ for A the final result is:

$$M_{12} = \frac{\mu_0 \cdot N_1 \cdot R_1^2 \cdot N_2 \cdot R_2^2 \cdot \pi}{2\sqrt{(R_1^2 + d^2)^3}} \tag{13.7}$$

In practice the HF carrier transmitted by the reader is a sinusoidal alternating current. A time variant current $I_1(t)$ flowing in a loop antenna generates a time variant magnetic flux $d\Psi(I_1)/dt$. According to Faraday's law a voltage will be induced in the loop antenna that encloses some of this changing flux. Fig. 13.6 shows a simplified circuit diagram for a coupled RFID system, where L_1 is the antenna of the reader, L_2 is the antenna of the token, R_{L_2} is the resistance of the token's antenna and R_{LOAD} represents the load. C_{RES} is ignored for now and is equal to 0.

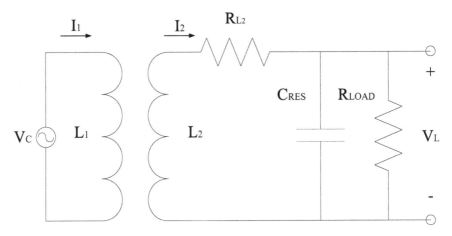

Fig. 13.6 Simplified Circuit Diagram of Coupled Token

The total time variant flux in L_1 induces a voltage V_{L1} in L_2 due to the mutual inductance M. There is a voltage drop across R_{L_2} and I_2 also induces magnetic flux in L_2, which opposes $\Psi(I_1)$, so the voltage across the load can be approximated by:

$$V_L = \frac{d\Psi_2}{dt} = M\frac{dI_1}{dt} - L_2\frac{dI_2}{dt} - I_2 R_{L_2} \tag{13.8}$$

V_L can now be rectified and used as a power supply for the token. In order to improve the efficiency of the coupling an additional capacitor C_{RES} can be added in parallel with the antenna L_2 to form a parallel resonant circuit with a resonant frequency corresponding to the operating frequency of the RFID system. The resonant frequency can be calculated as follows:

$$f = \frac{1}{2\pi\sqrt{L_2 \cdot C_{RES}}}$$ (13.9)

When operating at the resonant frequency the voltage V_L induced in a system with a resonant circuit increases by more than a factor of ten compared to a system using the antenna by itself. The influence of the resonant circuit's R_{L_2} and R_{LOAD} on voltage V_L can be characterized by the Q, or quality, factor. The Q-factor is discussed in more detail later with regards to data transfer.

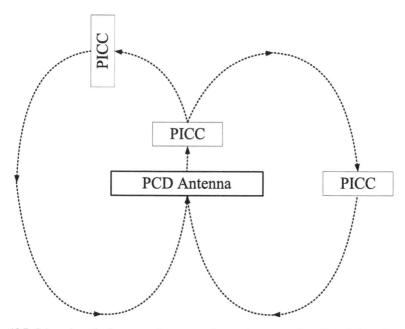

Fig. 13.7 Orientation of token to reader antenna for maximum coupling. Dotted lines show the direction of magnetic field lines.

A further practical constraint that effects the coupling efficiency is the orientation of the token in relation to the reader. In the equations above it was assumed that the antenna in the reader and the antenna in the token have a common axis. Although this is often the case the token can also be displaced or tilted in such a way that the magnetic flux enclosed by its antenna is decreased. As a rule of thumb maximum voltage is induced in the token's antenna when it is perpendicular to the magnetic field lines, while no voltage is induced if it is parallel. This results in a specific interrogation zone around the reader's antenna, as illustrated by an example in Fig. 13.7. Following the expected path of the field lines in this case it can be seen that a token parallel to the reader's antenna would be read if directly in front, or to the side, of the antenna, while a token that is perpendicular to the antenna could be read on the diagonal corners.

13.3.2.2 Data Transfer

The reader and token use different techniques to transmit data. As a result reader-to-token communication is referred to as the forward channel, while token-to-reader communication is referred to as the backward channel. The forward channel is relatively simple as the reader can directly modulate the data onto the carrier it transmits. The backward channel, however, requires that the token send data even though it is a passive device. The token must therefore modulate the reader's carrier, which in most cases is done using load modulation.

Load modulation works on the principle that the token's impedance Z_T can be altered by changing the parameters of the resonant circuit. Changing the impedance not only influences the voltage induced in the token's antenna L_2 but also the magnitude of the voltage across the reader's antenna L_1. The token can therefore amplitude modulate the voltage on the reader's antenna. It is only possible for the token to alter the load resistance R_{LOAD} or the parallel capacitor C_{RES} of the resonant circuit. Load modulation is therefore either resistive or capacitive. In resistive load modulation a resistor R_{MOD} is added in parallel to R_{LOAD}, so the impedance is switched between $Z_T(R_{LOAD})$ and $Z_T(R_{LOAD}||R_{MOD})$ during the modulation process. In capacitive load modulation an additional capacitor C_{MOD} is added, which changes the resonant frequency when switched into the circuit. Detuning the resonant circuit greatly influences the token's impedance, which causes the desired modulation effect.

As mentioned before the Q-factor is a measure of the voltage in the token when operating at the resonant frequency. It can be approximated as follows:

$$Q = \left(\frac{R_{L_2}}{2\pi f_c L_2} + \frac{2\pi f_c L_2}{R_{LOAD}} \right)^{-1} \tag{13.10}$$

Generally the value of Q should be maximised to allow for the maximum power transfer and operational range. It should be kept in mind that Q also influences the bandwidth of the communication channel. The frequency response of Q peaks around the resonant frequency and rolls off to either side, as shown by the examples in Fig. 13.8. This indicates that the resonant circuit acts as a crude bandpass filter centered around f_c with bandwidth $BW = f_c/Q$. The value of Q must therefore be chosen in such a way that it allows sufficient power transfer, while still allowing for the backward channel's modulation sidebands. In Fig. 13.8 the value of Q_1 is too high since it excludes the modulation side bands, whereas the value of Q_3 is too low since it decreases the centre frequency needed for power transfer.

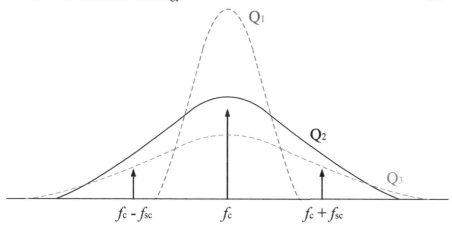

Fig. 13.8 The Effect of the Q-factor

13.4 Standards

RFID technology encompasses a range of systems from multiple vendors. To ensure interoperability between different RFID systems several standards have been defined to which these systems must adhere. In the HF band there are three main standards acknowledged by ISO/IEC (International Organization for Standardization / International Electrotechnical Commission) that deal with HF RFID technology operating at 13.56 MHz. These are ISO/IEC 14443 [12], ISO/IEC 15693 [13] and finally ISO/IEC 18092 [15]. Another standard that should be mentioned is ISO/IEC 18000, which defines RFID communication interfaces for several operating frequencies, including 13.56 MHz. The standards define, amongst other things, the RF interface, the initialization sequence and the data format. It is not feasible to describe each standard in its entirety within this chapter, so only a summary of the key technical aspects of the interaction between the reader and the token is presented. ISO 14443 and ISO 15693 are discussed in more detail since they are the most relevant to the applications described in Section 13.2.1, with ISO 18000 and ISO 18092 discussed only briefly. The information in this section have been adapted from [7, 12–15] and the reader should consult these sources for a more complete description.

13.4.1 ISO 14443

ISO 14443, titled *Identification Cards – Proximity Integrated Circuit Cards*, is commonly used in systems using logic and μ-controller tokens. This means that it is the standard of choice for e-passports, credit cards and most access control systems.

The popular Mifare range of products by NXP also adhere to Part 1–3 of ISO 14443 Type A.

13.4.1.1 Part 1 – Physical Characteristics

The first part of the standard states that the token shall have physical characteristics according to the requirements for the card type ID-1 specified in ISO/IEC 7810, i.e. 85.72 mm × 54.03 mm × 0.76 mm. It also specifies tolerance levels for the token with regard to ultra-violet light, X-rays, dynamic bending stress, dynamic torsional stress, alternating magnetic fields, alternating electric fields, static electricity, static magnetic fields and operating temperature.

13.4.1.2 Part 2 – Radio Frequency Power and Signal Interface

The second part of the standard describes the signal characteristics of two types of radio interfaces between the token and the reader. These interfaces allow for both power transfer and bi-directional communication. The token's power is provided by an alternating magnetic field at a frequency of 13.56 MHz and the reader must ensure that the magnetic field is within the range 1.5 A/m $\leq H \leq 7.5$ A/m. The operational range for systems using ISO 14443 usually extends up to 10 cm.

ISO 14443 defines two different methods for data transfer. In *Type A* the forward channel data uses Modified Miller coding with a coding pulse of 2–3 μs modulated onto the 13.56 MHz carrier with 100 % ASK. The backward channel uses Manchester encoding, which is 100% ASK modulated onto a 847 kHZ sub-carrier before being load modulated onto the 13.56 MHz carrier. In *Type B* the forward channel uses NRZ encoding modulated onto the 13.56 MHz carrier with 10 % ASK. The backward channel uses NRZ encoding, which is first modulated onto a 847 kHZ sub-carrier using PSK (0°, 180°) before being load modulated onto the 13.56 MHz carrier. The basic data rate for both the forward and backward channels in Type A and Type B is 106 kbps. Some ISO 14443 tokens and readers support higher data rates, 212/424/848 kbps, which can be selected after the anti-collision process has finished.

13.4.1.3 Part 3 – Initialization and Anti-Collision

This part of the standard describes byte and data frame formats and the initial commands used to detect and initialise communication with the token. This includes the ability to poll for new tokens in the interrogation field and choosing a token, even if multiple tokens are present, through an anti-collision process.

Type A: A data frame is identified by Start-of-Frame (SoF) and End-of-Frame (EoF) symbols and may contain multiple bytes. Each byte of data is followed by an odd-parity bit. Each frame also contains a 2-byte Cyclic Redundancy Check (CRC) that is appended at the end of the data. During the initialization phase the token acts like a state machine. The reader then issues commands to change the state of the token as required. A simplified Type A state machine is shown in Fig. 13.9. The reader uses the following commands:

- *REQA/WUPA*: The Type A Request (*REQA*) and the Type A Wake-Up (*WUPA*) commands are periodically sent by the reader to poll its interrogation field for tokens. The *WUPA* command can also be used to put tokens that have entered the HALT state into the READY state.
- *SELECT (NVB < 40)*: If the Number of Valid Bits (NVB) is less than the number of bits in the Unique Identifier (UID) then the *SELECT* command is used for anti-collision, thus it is also referred to as the *ANTICOLLISION* command.
- *SELECT (NVB = 40)*: When the reader has determined the unique identifier of the token it wishes to communicate with it uses the *SELECT* command to place that token in the ACTIVE state.
- *HLTA*: The Type A Halt (*HLTA*) puts the token into the HALT state.

When the token enters the interrogation zone of the reader it powers up and enters the IDLE state. In this state the token will not respond to any commands from the reader except *REQA* and *WUPA*, which will put it into the READY state. Readers will periodically transmit a *REQA* command to see if there are tokens within its interrogation zone. If it receives a Type A Answer to Request (*ATQA*) response it knows that a token is present and will proceed to the next step of initialisation. It is often the case that multiple tokens will be presented to the reader at once, e.g. travel and credit cards in the same wallet, so the standard must allow the reader to select a specific token. This process of selection is known as anti-collision, which in Type A is implemented using a binary search tree algorithm. The *SELECT* command is a bit-oriented frame containing the length of the current search (NVB) and a search pattern. If the least significant bits of a token's unique identifier matches the search pattern for the specified search length, that token will respond with the rest of its unique identifier. An example of the anti-collision process is shown in Fig. 13.10. In the first step the reader sets the search length to 0, which results in both tokens transmitting their whole 4-byte unique identifier and a checksum (BCC). The first collision that the reader detects is in the fifth bit. The reader therefore sets the search length to 5 and transmits a search pattern that indicates to the token whether the fifth bit should be a '1' or a '0'. Only the first token's unique identifier matches the search string, so it alone responds with the rest of its identifier. Since the reader detects no collisions it knows that it has identified a single token. Finally the reader sends the same *SELECT* command with maximum search length and full unique identifier to which the tokens responds with a Select AcKnowledge (SAK). This also results in the token being put in the ACTIVE state.

For the anti-collision to work, the token's responses must be closely synchronized with the reader's commands. Type A expects the token to behave in a synchronous manner, so it prescribes a fixed bit grid which defines when a response must be sent. This grid is defined by specifying a Frame Delay Time (FDT) as follows: $t_{\text{FDT}} = (n \cdot 128 + 84)/f_c$ if the last bit sent by the reader is a '1' and $t_{\text{FDT}} = (n \cdot 128 + 20)/f_c$

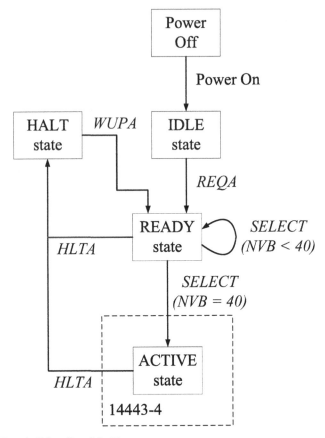

Fig. 13.9 Type A: Token State Machine

if the last bit sent by the reader is '0'. n is equal to 9 for *REQA*, *WUPA* and *SELECT* commands, while $n \geq 9$ for all other commands.

Type B: A data frame, marked with start-of-frame and end-of-frame symbols, contains multiple characters. Each character consists of a start bit, eight data bits and a stop bit, which must be followed by a set Extra Guard Time (EGT) before the next character starts. Each frame also contains a 2-byte cyclic redundancy check that is appended at the end of the data.

As with Type A the token acts like a state machine during initialization. A simplified Type B state machine is shown in Fig. 13.11. The reader uses the following commands:

- *REQB/WUPB*: The Type B Request (*REQB*) and the Type B Wake-Up (*WUPB*) commands are periodically sent by the reader to poll its interrogation field for tokens and initiates the anti-collision procedure. The *WUPB* command can also be used to put tokens that have entered the HALT state into the IDLE state. *REQB* and *WUPB* commands contain an Application Family Identifier (AFI) that indi-

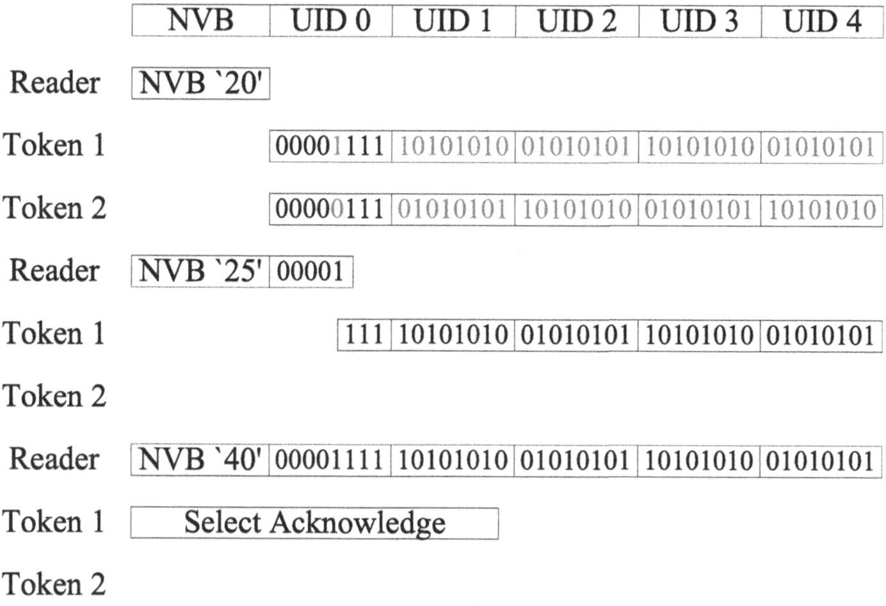

NVB	UID 0	UID 1	UID 2	UID 3	UID 4

Reader   NVB `20'

Token 1   00001111 | 10101010 | 01010101 | 10101010 | 01010101

Token 2   00000111 | 01010101 | 10101010 | 01010101 | 10101010

Reader   NVB `25' | 00001

Token 1   111 | 10101010 | 01010101 | 10101010 | 01010101

Token 2

Reader   NVB `40' | 00001111 | 10101010 | 01010101 | 10101010 | 01010101

Token 1   Select Acknowledge

Token 2

Fig. 13.10 Type A: Example of Anti-Collision Sequence

cates the type of application targeted by the reader. This field is used to preselect tokens participating in the anti-collision since only tokens with an application of the type indicated by the AFI may answer with a Type B Answer To Request (*ATQB*).

- *SLOT-MARKER*: During anti-collision the reader may send up to $N - 1$ *SLOT-MARKER* commands to indicate each time slot available for the tokens' *ATQB* responses. The commands can be sent after the end of a received *ATQB* message to mark the start of the next slot or earlier if no *ATQB* is received and it is known that the slot will be empty.
- *ATTRIB*: The *ATTRIB* command is used by the reader to select a single token. Upon receiving an *ATTRIB*s command containing its identifier, a token enter the ACTIVE state where it only responds to commands defined in ISO/IEC 14443-4 that include the Card Identifier (CID) assigned to it in the *ATTRIB* command parameters.
- *HLTB*: The Type B Halt (*HLTB*) puts the token into the HALT state.

When the token enters the interrogation zone of the reader it powers up and enters the IDLE state. The anti-collision procedure, based on a dynamic slotted ALOHA algorithm, is started when the *REQB* command is transmitted. The token checks to see if it has an application that matches the received AFI parameter and if this is the case it calculates the number of anti-collision slots N from the parameters in the *REQB* command. If $N = 1$ the token responds immediately with its *ATQB* response. Alternatively the token is put in the READY REQUESTED state and randomly calculates a slot in which to send its response. In a probabilistic system, which does

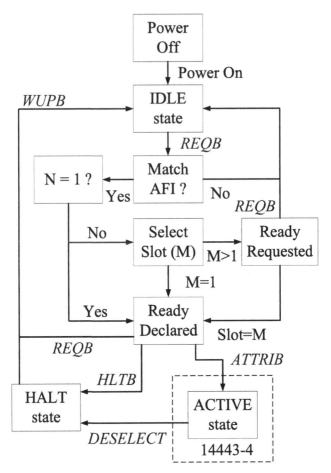

Fig. 13.11 Type B: Token State Machine

not use time slots, a token responds only if its randomly chosen slot is equal to 1. If it chooses any other slot it returns to the IDLE state and waits for the anti-collision procedure to start again. In a pseudo-deterministic system that uses multiple slots, the tokens responds within the time slot corresponding to its randomly chosen slot. Once a token has responded with an *ATQB* it is in the READY DECLARED state. The *ATQB* response contains information that the reader can use to identify and select the token. Once the reader has received a collision-free *ATQB* from the card it wants to select, it uses the *ATTRIB* command to place the chosen token into the ACTIVE state.

13.4.1.4 Part 4 – Transmission Protocol

The final part of the standard specifies a half-duplex block transmission protocol for communication between the reader and the token. In Type A tokens, additional setup parameters need to be exchanged between the token and the reader to configure the protocol, such as frame size, card identifier, etc. In Type B tokens this is not necessary as these parameters have already been exchanged in the *ATQB* response and the *ATTRIB* command. When the Type A token is selected, the select acknowledgment will contain information about whether the token implements a proprietary protocol, or whether it supports ISO 14443-4. If a protocol adhering to ISO 14443-4 is available, the reader will transmit a Request for Answer To Select (*RATS*) command to which the token replies with an Answer To Select (*ATS*). This is followed by Protocol and Parameter Selection (*PPS*), if supported, that allows for the change of data rate between the token and the reader. The transmission protocol itself allows for the transmission of an Application Data Unit (APDU) that can contain any required data. The structure of the protocol is based on the $T = 1$ protocol specified in ISO 7816-3 for contact cards, and is therefore often referred to as $T = CL$. This simplifies integration of contactless applications into smart card operating systems that are already available, especially in dual interface tokens.

13.4.2 ISO 15693

ISO 15693, titled *Identification Cards – Contactless Integrated Circuit Cards – Vicinity Cards*, is most often implemented in systems using memory tokens for tracking or simple identification. Part 1 of the standard is very similar to the corresponding part in ISO 14443, so this section only discusses Parts 2 and 3.

13.4.2.1 Part 2 – Air Interface and Initialisation

This part of the standard describes the signal characteristics of the radio interface between the token and the reader, which allows for both power transfer and bidirectional communication. The token's power is provided by an alternating magnetic field at a frequency of 13.56 MHz and the reader must ensure that the magnetic field is within the range 115 mA/m $\leq H \leq$ 7.5 A/m. The operational range for systems using ISO 15693 can extend up to 1 m.

   ISO 15693-2 defines both 'long distance' and 'fast' communication modes. In the 'fast' mode the forward channel uses 1 of 4 pulse-position coding that is modulated onto the 13.56 MHz carrier with 100 % ASK. One symbol comprises 8 time slots each of duration 9.44 μs and the modulation pulse can only be transmitted at an uneven time slot. The value n of the symbol can be determined by pulse slot = $((2 \cdot n) + 1)$ and can be 0, 1, 2 or 3. One symbol takes 75.53 μs = 8×9.44 μs to transmit, but each symbol can convey two bits of data, so the data rate is 26.48 kbps.

For the 'long distance' forward channel data, 1 of 256 pulse position coding is used, which is then 10% ASK modulated onto the 13.56 MHz carrier. One symbol now comprises of 512 time slots and takes 4.833 ms to transmit. Since the symbol can have any value between 0 and 255 it can represent 8 bits of data so the effective data rate is 1.65 kbps. The backward channel uses Manchester coding, which can either be ASK modulated onto a 423 kHz sub-carrier or FSK modulated with a 423/485 kHz sub-carrier before being load modulated onto the 13.56 MHz carrier. For the 'long distance' mode the data rate is 6.62 kbps and for the 'fast' mode the data rate is 26.48 kbps. Data are transmitted in frames marked by a start-of-frame and end-of-frame symbol.

13.4.2.2 Part 3 – Anti-Collision and Transmission Protocol

The final part of the standard provides details on the anti-collision procedure, token initialisation and possible commands. It should be noted that a large section of the guidelines given in this part is optional. As in ISO 14443 the token acts like a state machine during initialisation. A possible state machine diagram, given as an example in the standard, is shown in Fig. 13.12. The standard's transmission protocol specifies the format for command requests and responses, including a format for a number of optional commands such as *SELECT*, *RESET*, *READ* and *WRITE*. The standard only specifies two mandatory commands:

- *INVENTORY*: The token shall perform anti-collision when receiving the *INVENTORY* request.
- *STAY-QUIET*: If the token receives the *STAY-QUIET* request it shall enter the QUIET state.

When the token enters the interrogation zone of the reader it enters into the READY state. The reader will poll for tokens by transmitting an *INVENTORY* request. If a token is present it will participate in the anti-collision procedure. The token compares the mask value from the *INVENTORY* request, varying in length from 0 to 8 bytes, with the corresponding least significant bits in its 64-bit unique identifier. If it is a match, the token will reply with its identifier during one of sixteen slots marked by the reader. It is assumed that the token does not have the necessary resources to randomly choose a slot. It therefore uses the four least significant bits, not compared with the mask, to determine the slot number. For example if the 2 least significant bytes of the tokens UID is *4FAC* and the mask was *FAC* then the token will respond in slot number 4. Once the reader has the token's unique ID it can put the token in the QUIET state, or in the SELECTED state, if supported, where further commands can be issued.

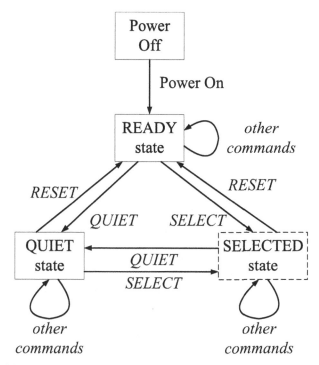

Fig. 13.12 ISO 15693: Possible Token State Machine

13.4.3 ISO 18000

ISO 18000, titled *Information Technology AIDC Techniques – RFID for Item Management – Air Interface*, defines a generic structure for use in item management applications (Part 1), along with air interfaces for operation at 135 kHz (Part 2), 13.56 MHz (Part 3), 2.45 GHz (Part 4), 5.8 GHz (Part 5), 860–930 MHz (Part 6) and 433 MHz (Part 7). It is expected that all the parts of ISO 18000 will still be revised to include fixes and allow for the extra capabilities, such as active tokens and sensors [10]. This section only gives a brief overview of the standard in comparison to Part-2 of the ISO 14443 and ISO 15693 standards.

13.4.3.1 Part 3 – Parameters for Air Interface Communications at 13.56 MHz

ISO 18000-3 defines a physical layer, collision management system and protocol values, in accordance with ISO 18000-1, for RFID systems operating at 13.56 MHz. It specifies two modes of operation intended for use with different applications. Mode 1 is based on ISO 15693 with additional specifications to allows for item management applications and improved vendor compatibility. The reader to token data rate is 1.65 kbps, or 26.48 kbps. The token to reader data rate is 26.48 kbps. A protocol extension allows for data rates of 53 and 106 kbps. Mode 2 specifies a high speed interface where the reader to tag data rate is 423.75 kbps.

13.4.4 ISO 18092/NFC

ISO 18092, which is also referred to as NFCIP-1 (Near Field Communication Interface and Protocol) or ECMA 340, specifies an RF interface and transmission protocol for communication between two inductively coupled devices operating at a frequency of 13.56 MHz. This standard allows for an active device, such as a mobile phone or PDA, to access RFID applications by acting as a reader, or a passive token, and it can also be used for short range peer-to-peer communication. Although relatively new, NFCIP has strong support from industry. A NFCIP device can operate in three different ways and it has more resources than a passive token, thereby allowing it to interface with its environment in a number of ways. The standard itself and the additional specifications for data exchange formats, record types and compatible tokens is therefore quite comprehensive. This section only briefly discusses the different modes of operation and the sections of the standard corresponding to Part-2 of the ISO 14443 and ISO 15693 standards. The reader is encouraged to read the ECMA 340 documentation [3] or visit the NFC Forum [19] for more details .

This standard defines 'active' and 'passive' communication modes between two entities, referred to as the target and the initiator. In active mode both the initiator and the target generate a RF field. The initiator will start communication and transmit data by modulating its own carrier. Once it has finished transmitting it will switch off the carrier and wait for a response. This is similar to two readers transmitting data to one another. The target then switches on its carrier and transmits a response. In the passive communication mode only the initiator generates an RF field and starts the communication by modulating data on its own carrier. The target then responds to the initiator using a load modulation scheme. In this mode one device acts like a reader while the other device emulates a passive token. Each device must ensure that it generates a magnetic field, at a frequency of 13.56 MHz, that is within the range $1.5 \text{ A/m} \leq H \leq 7.5 \text{ A/m}$. The operational range for NFCIP systems is in the order of a few centimeters.

Both active and passive modes are defined for communication rates of 106, 212, 424 kbps. The method for transmitting data at 106 kbps in passive mode is the same as for 14443A. 106 kbps data transmission in active mode uses the same modulation scheme as the forward channel in 14443A. For 212 and 424 kbps 'passive' and 'active' modes both the forward and backward channel uses Manchester code that is ASK modulated onto the 13.56 MHz carrier with a modulation index of 8% to 30% [15]. It should be noted that the backward channel does not use sub-carrier modulation. NFCIP technology was initially developed by Nokia, NXP (previously Philips Semiconductors) and Sony, which is probably the reason why the lower layer communication is compatible with Mifare (106 kbps) and FeliCa (212/424 kbps) products.

13.5 Conclusion

Contactless tokens act as an electronic credential, interacting with the rest of the system on behalf of their owner. Contactless operation can increase productivity and convenience, while it offers additional benefits such as reduced maintenance cost and extended product lifetime. A choice of industry standards and tokens also allows this technology to be tailored to many applications. As a result applications, for contactless tokens have extended beyond access control and fare collection, with contactless tokens starting to replace, or supplement, established technologies such as paper tickets, barcodes and magnetic stripe cards. This trend is expected to continue, especially in the identification and payment sectors, and with the introduction of NFC-enabled devices the immediate future of contactless technology looks promising.

It is recommended that anybody wishing to learn more about contactless technology should consult literature by the Smart Card Alliance [27] and the *"RFID Handbook"* by Klaus Finkenzeller [7]. A number of open source RFID projects also provides hardware and software that can facilitate better understanding by means of practical experimentation [20, 23, 24].

References

1. Bundesamt für Sicherheit in der Informationstechnik. *Advanced Security Mechanisms for Machine Readable Travel Documents Extended Access Control (EAC)*. Technical Guideline TR-03110, September, 2007.
2. R. Das. *RFID Forecasts 2006 to 2016*. IDTechEx, January 2006.
3. ECMA-340 *Near Field Communication Interface and Protocol (NFCIP-1)* 2nd Edition, December, 2004. http://www.ecma-international.org/publications/standards/Ecma-340.htm, Cited 8 Oct 2007.
4. EMVCo. *EMV Contactless Communication Protocol Specification v2.0*. August, 2007.
5. EMV Integrated Circuit Card Specifications for Payment Systems. v4.1, June, 2007. http://www.emvco.com/, Cited 8 Oct 2007.
6. Federal Information Processing Standards. *Publication 201-1: Personal Identity Verification (PIV) of Federal Employees and Contractors*. March, 2006.
7. K. Finkenzeller, *RFID Handbook: Radio-frequency identification fundamentals and applications*, Wiley, 1999.
8. T.S. Heydt-Benjamin, D.V. Bailey, K. Fu, A. Juels and T. O'Hare. *Vulnerabilities in first-generation RFID-enabled credit cards*. Technical report, University of Massachusetts Amherst, October 2006.
9. *The History of RFID Technology*. RFID Journal, December, 2006. http://www.rfidjournal.com/article/articleview/1338/1/129/, Cited 8 Oct 2007.
10. Institute for Prospective Technological Studies. *RFID Technologies: Emerging Issues, Challenges and Policy Options*, Technical Report EUR 22770 EN, 2007.
11. International Civil Aviation Organization (ICAO). *Document 9303 Machine Readable Travel Documents (MRTD). Part I: Machine Readable Passports*. 2005.
12. ISO/IEC 14443. *Identification cards – Contactless integrated circuit cards – Proximity cards*.
13. ISO/IEC 15693. *Identification cards – Contactless integrated circuit cards – Vicinity cards*.
14. ISO/IEC 18000. *ISO/IEC 18000 Information Technology AIDC Techniques-RFID for Item Management – Air Interface*

15. ISO/IEC 18092 (ECMA-340). *Information technology – Telecommunications and information exchange between systems – Near Field Communication – Interface and Protocol (NFCIP-1)*.
16. ISO/IEC 7501 *Identification cards – Machine readable travel documents*. October, 2005.
17. J. Landt and B. Catlin. *Shrouds of Time: The history of RFID*. AIM White Paper, October, 2001. http://www.aimglobal.org/technologies/rfid/resources/shrouds_of_time.pdf, Cited 8 Oct 2007.
18. National ID Project Moves China To Head Of The Pack In Radio Frequency Technology. February, 2007. http://www.cardtechnology.com/article.html?id=20070221PGYABPF5, Cited 8 Oct 2007.
19. NFC Forum. http://www.nfc-forum.org/, Cited 8 Oct 2007.
20. OpenPCD Project. http://www.openpcd.org, Cited 8 Oct 2007.
21. J.G. Proakis. *Digital Communications*, 3rd Edition, McGraw-Hill, 1995.
22. J.G. Proakis and M. Salehi. *Communication Systems Engineering*, Prentice-Hall, 1994.
23. rfdump Project. http://www.rfdump.org/, Cited 8 Oct 2007.
24. rfidiot Project. http://www.rfidiot.org/, Cited 8 Oct 2007.
25. RFID Technology to Debut at 2006 World Cup Soccer. February, 2006. http://www.rfidgazette.org/2006/02/rfid_technology.html, Cited 8 Oct 2007.
26. M.R. Rieback, B. Crispo and A.S. Tanenbaum. *The Evolution of RFID Security*. IEEE Pervasive Computing, Vol. 5, Issue 1, pp 62–69, January 2006.
27. Smart Card Alliance. http://www.smartcardalliance.org/, Cited 8 Oct 2007.
28. Smart Card Alliance. *Contactless Technology for Secure Physical Access: Technology and Standards Choices*. Publication No. ID-02002, October, 2001.
29. H. Stockman. *Communication by Means of Reflected Power*. Proceedings of the IRE, pp 1196-1204, October, 1948.

Chapter 14
ID CARDS AND PASSPORTS

Ingo Liersch

Abstract In this chapter we discuss eID cards and e-Passports. A number of countries have introduced eID cards and some other countries are planning the introduction. The reasons generally, are requirements for a more secure identification and additional functions like eGovernment. The US requirements for the VISA Waiver countries to issue biometric enabled Passports by October 2006. The European Commission set the implementation time-frame so that all Member States had to implement the facial image requirements by 2006. This requirements led to worldwide introductions of e-Passports.

Key words: ID Cards, eID, e-Passport, Chip, ICAO, Security, Basic Access Control (BAC), Extended Access Control (EAC)

14.1 Introduction

Security is a top priority in an age in which people fear terrorism and crime, fraud threatens national economies, while data and intellectual theft endanger the success of companies.

Subsequently, governments are driven by their citizens' security demands. The increase of daily air traffic and the technological armament of impostors, lead to new secure means of identification: eID smart cards and e-Passports.

The introduction of eIDs and e-Passports is discussed not only in Europe but also worldwide.

Personal identity documents confirm the identity of individual citizens, thus proving their legitimate residency within their homeland. Government offices, credit institutes and businesses ask for ID cards or Passports as a means of unequivocally

Ingo Liersch, Giesecke & Devrient GmbH, Government Solutions.
e-mail: Ingo.Liersch@gi-de.com

identifying the holder. Identification on the internet, e.g. for business and government transactions, requires a valid means of identification which can be provided by e-ID documents. In addition, opening a bank account, conducting valid business transactions and drawing government benefits can become impossible without a trusted means of identification. Therefore, it is in the best interests of any government for its citizens' personal identification documents to be made as difficult as possible to counterfeit or misuse.

Modern national ID cards comply with the ISO/IEC 7816 - series standards and other international norms for signatures and certificates.

14.2 ID Cards

In this chapter we only discuss cards which serve optically and digitally as an ID card. What all these cards have in common is that they are issued by a governmental institution or agency for citizens of their country. In some countries this institution is the Ministry of Interior, in other countries the police or local government offices.

National ID cards, eID, or Smart ID: Every country has it's own term for this kind of smart card.

14.2.1 Requirements and Constituents of Modern National ID Cards

Unlike SIM cards and banking cards, where the relevance of the digital function is dominant, all the features of the whole ID document are important as these documents also serve as visual identification. An accepted expression is that an ID document must be designed in a way that a policeman on a foggy night is able to recognise a person via the document and easily verify the genuineness of the document.

14.2.1.1 Card Body Material and Design

ID cards and Passports can be subjected to many kinds of stress, which is why they need to be as durable as possible in order to resist tampering, chemicals, varying temperatures, environmental conditions, and UV radiation. In addition, the images and text must not fade with age (required lifespan is up to 10 years). As a result, card manufacturers had to develop materials for the card body, ensuring the highest level of counterfeit resistance and durability. Specially developed foils for ID card production are only available for accredited security printers and card manufacturers (ID cards are almost invariably laminated multilayer cards).

Conventional materials like PVC (Polyvinyl chloride) used for credit cards, do not meet the requirements for ID cards. A market proven material is polycarbonate (PC) which is used in most ID card projects with card life cycles between 5 and 10 years. A card made out of polycarbonate consists of 4-8 foils laminated together by high temperature and pressure. Polycarbonate cards are supposed to be very stable in terms of bending, torsion, UV light and temperature. Polycarbonate is also seen as the best material for laser personalisation. However, the polished surfaces of ID cards or data pages made of PC tend to become dull within a short time, due to the sensitivity of the material to scratching. Fig. 14.1 shows a sample polycarbonate ID card.

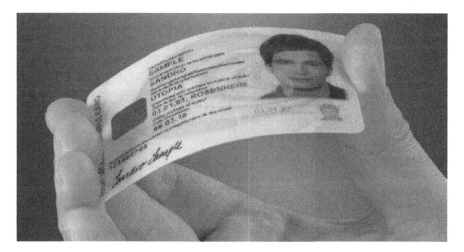

Fig. 14.1 Sample Polycarbonate ID Card

A second material used for long life cards is polyester, which is cheaper, more flexible and less scratch sensitive than polycarbonate. So polyester cards could be even more stable in terms of bending and torsion. A polyester material used for cards is PETG (Polyethylene terephthalate glycol).

A recent trend is to combine polyester and polycarbonate in compound structures or even produce single foils out of both materials in a coextrusion process. This allows the best features of both materials to be combined.

National ID cards are tailored to the individual country's history, culture and country specific preferences for colours and patterns. A number of classical or unique security features are always combined in the design.

In Fig. 14.2 the design of the Egypt ID is shown. The background security printing shows the culturally very important pyramids of Egypt. The lettering is only in Arabic because it is only an ID document within Egypt or for travelling to friendly Arabian countries.

In Fig. 14.3 the Macao ID card is shown. A lotus is integrated is the background design. The lettering is in Chinese and in English because both languages are used in the Special Administrative Regions (SAR) Hong Kong and Macao.

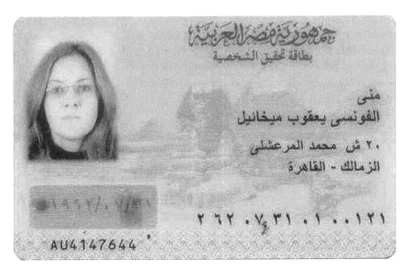

Fig. 14.2 Sample Polycarbonate ID Card: Egypt ID

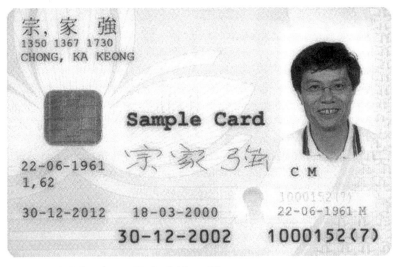

Fig. 14.3 Sample Polycarbonate ID Card: Macao ID

14.2.1.2 Card Body Security Features

Security features can be divided into three verification levels (Industry Standard):

Verification level 1:   Features recognisable using human senses without the aid of tools

Verification level 2:   Features recognisable with the aid of simple tools (usually UV lamp and magnifying glass)

Verification level 3:   Features recognisable in a forensic laboratory or machine readable elements. This includes microprocessors.

A reasonable selection of security features covers all levels of verification. Therefore security is not based purely on the number of features, but on the intelligent combination of highly secure features, which are easy to verify and cover several verification levels.

The following list shows generic security features for ID cards:

1. Verification level 1:

• Security background printing: This process allows relief structures to be worked with traditional guilloches resulting in a customer-specific design. The pallet of inks range from rainbow colours to those with fluorescent properties. This kind of design structure can be seen in principle on every banknote in every currency. Fig. 14.4 shows security background printing.

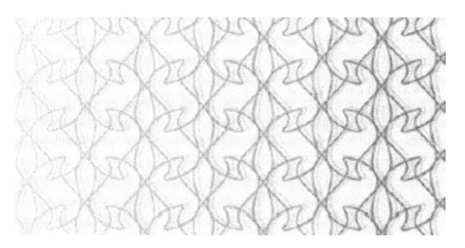

Fig. 14.4   Security Background Printing

• OVI (Optically Variable Inks): A very high level of protection, particularly against colour-copied counterfeits, can be achieved using optically variable inks. Depending on the angle from which the feature is viewed, the ink appears to change colour, normally from green to blue to violet.

• MLI (Multiple Laser Image): Is one of the most effective anti-counterfeiting measurements as it protects the personal data of the ID document holder; data which counterfeiters find most attractive to attack. It consists of numerous, tiny horizontal lenses, incorporated into the surface of the card with special laminating plates. Depending on the angle from which they are viewed, even in poor lighting conditions, the holder sees different bits of information, e.g. date of birth or a micro photo. Due to the different pieces of information revealed at various angles, this feature is virtually impossible to copy or manipulate. The following figure (Fig. 14.5) give an example of the multiple laser image.

Fig. 14.5   MLI (Multiple Laser Image)

2. Verification level 2:

• Microlettering: This feature, for example in the form of plain text, can only be seen through a magnifying glass. Attempts to copy microlettering usually fail to reproduce the feature faithfully. Fig. 14.6 shows an example of microlettering.

Fig. 14.6   Microlettering

• UV printing: Here, fluorescent inks are used, which are invisible under normal light and only reveal the hidden design under ultraviolet light. The challenge in creating these features is integrating them intelligently into the overall design. UV inks can be used for patterns, text or logos. Fig. 14.7 shows an example of UV printing.

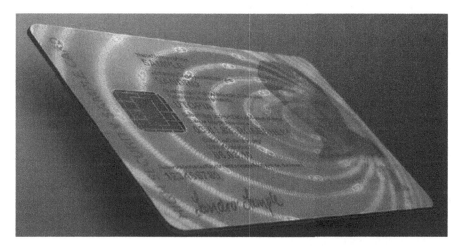

Fig. 14.7 UV Printing

• IR (infrared) printing: Inks or ink components that are only visible under infrared lighting can also help protect cards against counterfeiting. Since modern optical readers at border crossings already make use of infrared light, no additional equipment for verification is required.

3. Verification level 3:
Microprocessors offer numerous options for card administration, authentication, data access control, as well as storage and verification of biometric features. This level can also comprise secret features known only to the manufacturer and the card issuer.

14.2.1.3 Chip Hardware for ID Cards

All big chip manufacturers differentiate between platforms for credit cards, telecommunication and identification cards. Platforms for credit cards are focused on VISA and MASTERCARD certifications, platforms for telecommunication are optimised for memory an performance. Platforms for ID cards are optimised for security. General precondition for usage in ID projects is security certification according to Common Criteria or FIPS standards. For security reasons almost all platforms for the segment identification are still based on EEPROM (no FLASH).

There is no typical chip size for eID platforms. Currently the EEPROM sizes vary between 8 kilobytes and 144 kilobytes. The required memory completely depends on the country's individual profile for card applications. There is a definite trend towards bigger platforms in European countries.

14.2.1.4 Card Operating Systems for ID Cards

The market is mainly split between native (proprietary) ISO card operating systems (e.g. compliant to ISO 7816 part 1-4, 8,9) and Java Cards (e.g. compliant to ISO 7816 part 1-3 and corresponding Java Card and Global Platform specifications).

Both card types have their specific advantages, both are secure and flexible. Additionally, almost every kind of application can be realised on either platform.

14.2.1.5 ID Card Applications

Card applications are always country specific. A clear trend is the implementation of the ICAO [3] travel application. As a result, ID cards can be used as an e-Passport for travelling. Generally, the following functionalities are realised in ID cards:

- mutual authentication functions
- digital signatures
- storage of biometric information or on-card matching
- storage of personal information
- e-voting

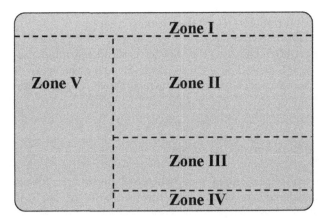

Fig. 14.8 General Layout of the TD-1 MRTD According to ICAO

14.2.2 International Standards for ID Cards

The Following standards are applied for national ID cards:

ISO/IEC 7816	ISO 7816 is an international standard related to electronic identification cards, especially smart cards
ISO/ IEC 7810	Physical characteristics of ID cards
ISO/ IEC 10373-3	Test methods of ID cards
ISO/ IEC 18013 part 1-3	Drivers License
Java Card Specifications	if applicable
Global Platform Specifications	if applicable
ICAO* Doc9303 part 3 (and technical reports)	ICAO - International Civil Aviation Organization - sets standards for Machine Readable Travel Documents like Passports and ID cards.
EU Directive CEN TC 224 WG 15	Specification issued by CEN (European Committee for Standardization) as a recommendation for eID cards in Europe
Minimum security standards for ID cards in EU	Issued by Council of European Union

* ICAO - International Civil Aviation Organization

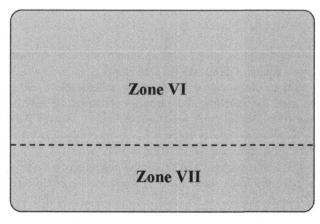

Fig. 14.9   General Layout of the TD-1 MRTD According to ICAO (rear side)

14.2.2.1 ICAO Requirements for ID cards

In the ICAO specification, the layout of **M**achine **R**eadable **T**ravel **D**ocuments (MRTD) in ID-1 format is defined. Fig. 14.8 and Fig. 14.9 show the general layout of both sides of the TD-1 MRTD according to ICAO;

Zone I: Header
Zone II: Personal data elements
Zone III: Document data elements
Zone IV :Holder's Signature
Zone V: Identification feature
Zone VI: Optional data elements
Zone VII: MRZ

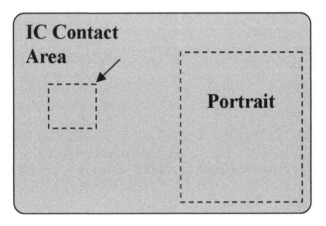

Fig. 14.10   General Layout of TD-1 MRTD with Chip

For ID cards containing a chip following layout has to be applied: Fig. 14.10 shows the General layout of TD-1 MRTD with chip.

ICAO also defines the so-called MRZ (Machine Readable Zone) for ID cards when they are used for travelling. In European countries, citizens can generally travel with their ID cards and don't need to carry their Passports. Although in the Schengen area there are no border controls any longer, these cards must feature a MRZ. Fig. 14.11 shows the structure of MRZ for ID Cards.

Please note that Passports have a MRZ comprising only two lines.

Besides the possibility to read the traveller's personal data in a fast and accurate way, the MRZ is used for BAC (Basic Access Control), as described in section 1.3.4 on security protocols.

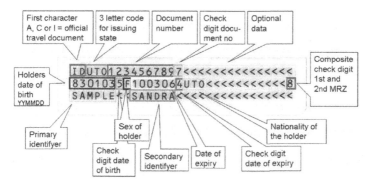

Fig. 14.11 Structure of MRZ for ID cards

14.2.3 Optical Personalisation of ID Cards

Introduction to available technologies for optical personalization of plastic cards:

14.2.3.1 Thermo Transfer Printing

By heating up individual elements within a print head, the so called dyes evaporate from the donor ribbon. The dyes are transferred onto the card surface. The temperature of every single element defines the amount of colour to be transferred and also controls the brightness of the pixels. Fig. 14.12 shows the thermo transfer printing process.

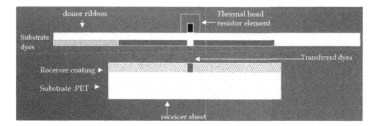

Fig. 14.12 Thermo Transfer Printing Process

The parameters to be adjusted are the temperature of the print head's elements and the combination of donor ribbon and card body. Slight changes of temperature can lead to a pale or blurred print image.

Features:

- resolution up to 300 dpi
- consumables are the donor ribbons
- thermal heads have a restricted life time (temperature stress)
- colour photos possible
- PVC and Polyester cards can be personalised

Positive Features of Thermo Transfer Printing:

- small cheap printers
- colour photograph can be realized

Negative Features:

- no polycarbonate material can be personalised
- irregular printing around security features like relief structures on the card surface
- irregular printing around a chip module
- no protection against abrasion and UV light
- blank cards must be absolutely clean
- no protection against fraud: data and pictures can easily be removed or changed (see example below)
- for the use of secure ID cards an additional protective lamination foil on the surface is necessary
- high costs due to consumables: cleaning cards, cleaning rolls, colour ribbons, lamination foils, thermal heads, drive rolls etc.

The following figure (Fig. 14.13) demonstrates the ease with which we can manipulate colour images. The image could be erased manually with no traces left. A different photograph can be added afterwards by a counterfeiter.

Fig. 14.13   Manipulation of a Colour Photo Personalised with Thermo Transfer Printing

Summary:
Thermo transfer is a technology only suitable for small numbers of cards (e.g. access cards for a company) with little need for protection, and short to medium lifetime. Thus, this technology cannot be recommended for national ID cards.

14.2.3.2 Thermo Sublimation Printing

Thermo sublimation printing is similar to the thermo transfer process described above. In this process, special coloured wax is applied on the card surface. When exposed to very high temperatures (300-400°C), the wax is sublimated (converts to a gaseous status) and then coated on the card. Due to the high temperature, the colour penetrates the material slightly and gives some protection against abrasion and UV light. In addition very high print quality can be achieved. Nevertheless, a protecting foil is necessary for high security cards.

Positive Features of Thermo Sublimation Printing:

- high printing quality
- higher protection against abrasion than thermo transfer technique
- limited protection against fraud in combination with a protection foil
- colour photograph can be realized

Negative Features:

- expensive printer
- expensive consumables (even higher costs than with thermo transfer)
- protection against fraud only together with additional foil

Summary:
In terms of quality, it provides a better choice than thermo transfer. Limited security is possible in combination with a protection layer.

14.2.3.3 Thermo Retransfer Printing

Thermo transfer printing has been further developed to thermo retransfer printing. By heating up the print head, the colour will be transferred mirror-inverted by thermal transfer printing from a ribbon to a special retransfer film. The image is then transferred onto the card by heat roller. This is a lamination process under pressure and heat. The laminated film is about 30μm thick. By using this retransfer process a high resolution is possible.

Positive Features of Thermo Retransfer Printing:

- independent from card surface (relief structures) or contact chip modules
- over the edge printing
- polycarbonate cards can be personalized

Negative Features:

- expensive printers
- high costs for consumables (additional retransfer film necessary, for one card one whole set of colour segments (CMYK) is consumed)

Summary:
Security is comparable to thermo sublimation with protection foil. As longlife cards made of Polycarbonate can be personalized, cards with a requirement for a long lifetime and medium to high security can be realized.

14.2.3.4 Laser Engraving

When using a laser engraving technique, a Laser beam penetrates through the transparent cover foils through to the opaque inner foil. As a result, the information is engraved into every layer of this side of the card. As a prerequisite, the card body material must be designed for laser engraving. Fig. 14.14 shows the laser engraving process.

Engraved images are extremely durable and they resist chemicals and withstand physical contact easily. Alteration is nearly impossible without destroying the card.

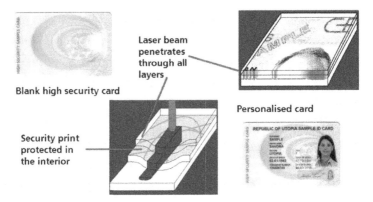

Fig. 14.14 Laser Engraving Process

Positive Features of Laser Engraving:

- most secure personalisation technology
- no consumables
- no abrasion by card usage
- no change by UV light
- higher resolution than with colour printing
- lower total costs (no consumables)

Negative Features:

- higher costs for the machinery
- black and white photo

Summary:

Laser engraving systems allow card Issuers to permanently engrave photos and other personal data on their cards. When comparing laser engraved black-and-white images with colour images, it is widely accepted that laser engraving enhances the overall card security substantially.

14.2.4 Countries and Their ID Cards

A number of countries have introduced eID cards and some other countries are planning the introduction.

14.2.4.1 Finnish Electronic Identification (FINEID)

Fig. 14.15 FINEID

The FINEID (showed in Fig. 14.15) was the first worldwide example of the combination of an ID card with an electronic signature card. The pilot phase started in 1998.

Features:

- issuance of cards since 2001
- electronic signature card
- not mandatory for citizens
- includes no biometrics
- available for foreigners after 6 months residence
- plan to include biometric information in future
- contact interface
- optical personalisation technology: laser engraving

14.2.4.2 Estonia ID

In Estonia ID cards (showed in Fig.14.16) are issued to every citizen over the age of 16. This is mandatory. An interesting feature is the authentication certificate containing the citizen's email address which can be used by government institutions or private persons.

Fig. 14.16   Estland ID

Features:

- since 2002
- signature card
- mandatory for all citizens (from 16)
- no biometrics
- official email address assigned by government
- contact interface
- optical personalisation technology: laser engraving

14.2.4.3 German ID Card ePA (= elektronischer Personalausweis)

Germany is planning to introduce a new electronic ID card in 2009. The card will feature the following applications:

- ICAO travel application, including facial image and two fingerprints
- online authentication application
- optional: qualified digital signature

The card will have a contactless interface (RFID chip). As a result this card may be read by all border control terminals equipped to read an electronic Passport.

14.2.4.4 Macao Electronic ID Card (MEID)

Macao Special Administrative Region (SAR) is an administrative division of the People's Republic of China (PRC). Hong Kong is China's second SAR. Both SARs issue their own ID cards.

Features:

- since 2002
- Java Card
- digital signature application
- "ID" application
- main use-case is border crossing between Macao and China or Hong Kong
- e-Government functions
- optical personalisation technology: laser engraving
- Multi-application card for third parties

14.3 E-Passports

14.3.1 Introduction

The traditional international travel document, the Passport, allows identification of travelers by visual verification: a photo printed into the Passport is compared to the actual appearance of the person claiming to be the correct Passport holder. A border control officer can search databases, such as international black lists, for any entries related to the person presenting the document.

The effectiveness of such border control procedures depends essentially on the identification security provided by the ID document and the verification process. It is limited by two issues: the genuineness of the ID document itself and the data contained in it, and the reliability of the visual verification process performed by the officer.

Over time, sophisticated security features have been developed and implemented in travel documents to increase the technical difficulty for counterfeiters. This has reduced the risk of unauthorised persons creating counterfeit documents. The identification security itself is, however, still limited by the verification skills of a human officer and the imagination and energy of criminals to change their identity and/or adapt themselves to the appearance of other individuals to perform an impersonation attack.

Growing international terrorism, organised crime and increasing illegal migration, have driven international efforts to implement processes, technologies and systems for improved secure identification. These efforts are based on essential progress in the fields of biometrics, microprocessor technology and cryptography. Biometric data of the Passport holder, like facial images and fingerprint data, are stored in machine readable form in a contactless microprocessor chip, integrated into the Passport document. Access to these data, along with assurance of their integrity and authenticity, are ensured by advanced Public Key Infrastructures (PKI). Thus, the travel document itself, as well as the verification techniques and processes, have been enhanced to ensure secure identification of travellers. The traditional Passport, allowing visual identification has been upgraded to a platform for electronic identification based on unique biometric features of the Passport holder. This upgraded document is the electronic Passport (e Passport) or Electronic Machine Readable Travel Document (e-MRTD).

Fig. 14.17 Example for a Mould-made Watermark and Country Code Security Threads

14.3.2 Constituents of Passports

A modern Passport mainly consists of the booklet (cover and inner visa pages), the data page and the microprocessor chip with antenna.

14.3.2.1 Passport Booklet

Due to the sophisticated production technique and integrated security features, paper used for Passports differs from all commercially available paper. The substrate consists of a mixture of cotton and cellulose, without use of optical brighteners. A grammage of 90 g/m^2 for the inner pages is chosen in most cases.

The security paper used for Passports contains a watermark, incorporated using the cylinder mould technique during the production process. Mould-made watermarks present an insurmountable obstacle to counterfeiting methods relying on scanners and colour copiers. Unlike the two-dimensional watermarks produced on fourdrinier (conventional paper-making) machines, a mould-made watermark is characterised by finely modulated transitions that create a plastic, three-dimensional effect. Either in one precisely registered position or distributed over the full area of the paper, this distinctive feature quickly becomes familiar to users and is easily recognised. Mould-made watermarks have proved virtually indispensable for effective document authentication. Therefore, their use is recommended by Interpol. Fig. 14.17 shows an example of a mould-made watermark and country code security threads.

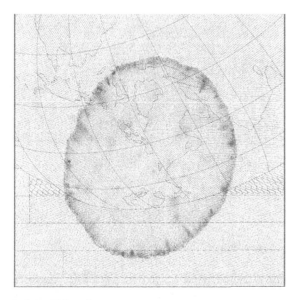

Fig. 14.18 Chemical sensitising of paper

Inner pages sometimes contain additional security features like country specific security threads, chemical sensitizing or fibres:

Chemical sensitizing:

Using chemicals such as alkalis, bleaching agents and organic solvents in an attempt to remove entries from documents, activates an invisible colourant in the paper. The result is a discoloration of the paper that makes the alteration attempt obvious. Fig. 14.18 shows an example of a chemical sensitising of paper.

Fibres:

A wide variety of fibres - monochrome or multi-coloured, visibly or invisibly fluorescent - can be added to the security paper. In particular, fibres that are invisible in normal light but fluorescent under ultraviolet light have performed well in the field. Fig. 14.19 shows an example of UV-visible and multi-coloured fibres.

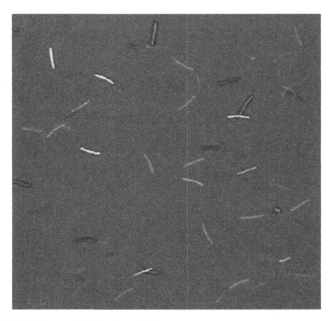

Fig. 14.19   UV-visible and Multi-coloured Fibres

14.3.2.2 Passport Data Pages

Most Passports still contain a paper-based data page. These pages are usually laminated with an overlay foil to protect the personalised information and to prevent forgery.

Increasingly, more and more countries are moving to plastic data pages made of polycarbonate or PECSEC (Brand name for a new PET-G/PC combination with better flexibility than PC) compound materials which are supposed to be more stable and secure. The chip and the antenna could be located in such a plastic data page which offers both maximum protection.

The foremost target for forgery or alteration attacks on travel documents is the data page. This is why the printing methods used for the blank data page and for personalisation are configured to form an integrated security design comprising features which are effective at all authentication levels.

Examples for security features on paper based data pages are intaglio printing, optical variable inks or protection foils with diffractive optically variable image devices (DOVID).

Plastic data pages can be equipped with security features similar to those available for polycarbonate ID cards.

14.3.2.3 Microprocessor Chips for Passports

E-Passports feature microprocessors with EEPROM between 32 and 80 kilobytes. According ICAO specify that 32 kilobytes memory is the minimum storage requirement. The precise size depends on the country specific requirements. For some non EU countries it is enough to store the minimum ICAO requirements for e-Passports and the US requirements for VISA Waiver countries.

Please note that a chip is recommended by ICAO, but is not mandatory for Passports.

The so called LDS (logical data structure) is defined by ICAO and contains a number of mandatory and optional Data Groups (DG):

DG1:   Contains the details recorded in the MRZ (mandatory)
DG2:   Encoded Face (mandatory)
DG3:   Encoded Fingers (optional)
DG3:   Encoded Eyes (optional)
DG4-7:   Displayed Identification Feature(s) (optional)
...
DG15:   Active Authentication Public Key Info (optional)

14.3.3 EU and ICAO Requirements

ICAO Specification ICAO DOC 9303 part 1[3] defines Passport requirements to ensure international interoperability and in particular sets standards for security.

By Article 6 of EU Council Regulation (EC) 2252/2004 of December 2004 (and additionally adopted technical specifications), standards for travel documents are defined: the member states decided about security features and biometrics in e-Passports.

The European Commission set the implementation time-frame so that all Member States had to implement the facial image requirements by 28th August 2006 (as a consequence all Member States also fulfilled the US requirements for the VISA Waiver countries to issue biometric enabled Passports by October 2006). Even though not all EU member states met the deadline, the vast majority did so within 2007.

The protection of the facial image is ensured by "Basic Access Control". This requires the reading of the MRZ in the Passport to gain access to the data on the chip.

As a next step in the EU, the additional storage of two fingerprints on the Passport chip will be required. The EU Commission considered this data as more sensitive and decided to protect the fingerprint data using "Extended Access Control", a system which works with a PKI (Public Key Infrastructure). Currently only the EU Member States will have access to the fingerprint data. Whether access to other countries will be granted has to be decided by the EU Committee at a later stage.

14.3.4 Security Protocols

E-Passports are equipped with a contactless RF-chip containing the digitised biometrics of the holder. The authenticity, integrity and privacy of the data stored in the e-Passport chip must be ensured. Therefore, ICAO has specified three security mechanisms:

- Passive Authentication (Digital Signature to provide Authenticity)
- Active Authentication (Challenge-Response to provide Integrity)
- Access Control (Authentication and Secure Channels to provide Privacy)

Passive Authentication (PA), provides proof of the authenticity of the e Passport by verifying a Document Signer Certificate and the electronic signature on the stored data. Currently, Passive Authentication is the only security mechanism mandated by ICAO. In an e-Passport equipped with this feature the data can be validated to verify its authenticity, but chip cloning (i.e. copying the complete data stored on one MRTD chip to another chip) or eavesdropping cannot be prevented.

Basic Access Control (BAC) should ensure that data can be accessed only with the consent of the e Passport holder to prevent skimming. Access to the data is only enabled after successfully reading of the printed Machine Readable Zone (MRZ) with an Inspection System, to generate a document-specific access key. Using this access key the Inspection System and the e Passport set up a secure communication channel.

Extended Access Control (EAC) [4] ensures that access to particularly sensitive data groups in the LDS, such as fingerprint data, is restricted to authorised parties only. Accessing and using such data is only possible when the potential user, such as an inspection system at a border control station, has a valid digital certificate and associated private key at its disposal. Such certificate(s) are generated and administrated by the country issuing the e-Passports.

Moreover, using EAC provides extremely secure data communication by the secure authentication of the Inspection System and by the means of strong (asymmetric) encryption. Implicitly the EAC protocol also prevents "chip cloning". EAC is going to be introduced in EU Member states.

Active Authentication (AA) ensures the uniqueness and authenticity of the microprocessor chip within the e Passport. This effectively prevents "chip cloning".

14.4 Conclusion

The security mechanisms and features described above constitute the state of the art of ID document security. Given the growing importance of secure identification in daily life, in the real world as well as on the internet, new technologies will be developed and incorporated into ID documents in order to stay ahead of the counterfeiters and to make identifying an individual more easy and secure.

References

1. The Silicon Trust Report, Issues 1/06 and 1/07, www.silicon-trust.com, Cited 03 Oct 2007.
2. Eurosmart White Paper on security into Smart Cards and ePassports www.eurosmart.com, Cited 03 Oct 2007.
3. International Civil Aviation Organization (ICAO). *Document 9303 Machine Readable Travel Documents (MRTD). Part I: Machine Readable Passports.* 2005.
4. Technical Guideline TR-03110, version 1.01; Advanced Security Mechanisms for Machine Readable Travel Documents - Extended Access Control (EAC)

Chapter 15
Smart Card Technology Trends
A review of the variety of applications and the market drivers

Chris Shire

Abstract This chapter examines the historical use of technology in smart cards and the trends in the future. It considers the options that are available and the choices which must be made with a smart card scheme and the issues which affect the design of the card and its applications. The influence of consumer demand is discussed and the drivers that will define the use smart card technology in the future.

Key words: Silicon, Technology, Trends, Memory, Microcontroller

15.1 Trends In Smart Card Technology – Today And The Future

Today the most common token of a person's digital identity is a smart card. In fact, smart cards and their inbuilt silicon security chip technologies are used across a whole range of applications from personal use including bank cards and mobile phones, to computer systems, and building security. They are used in diverse security processes which are likely to be even more sophisticated in the future with the increase demand for remote authentication of the user and their terminals via portals on the internet. Inside Personal Computers (PC) both desk based and portable, secure silicon based on chipcard IC technology is already authenticating the access to IT networks as well the services of mobile networks. In such open networks every device (client) as well as the server has to be secured at different levels for different tasks. In many information dependent markets the focus is now end-to-end security which involves a variety of secure devices. Existing products are evolving such consumer appliances like TV set top boxes which can now be configured to support 3rd party services, such as payment cards. Integrated circuits for smart cards generically "chipcard ICs" assembled in various formats can be the core of trust for physical or

Chris Shire, Infineon Technologies UK - AIM CC
e-mail: Chris.Shire@infineon.com

logical access, content control or as an embedded solution to ensure device to device authentication in a system.

To understand how the smart card of the future could develop, the history of smart card development must be considered, and how it has been influenced by technology, and the services it supports. In some cases the services have driven the demand for more advanced technology, in others only the availability of technology has enabled the service to be rolled out. On the other hand there are underused technologies in place today, some which have yet to fulfill the demands of the users, e.g. convenient secure biometrics, and others services such as copyright protection where security technology has yet to be accepted by consumers.

15.1.1 History

Smart card concepts were invented and patented in the early '70's. The earliest services were based around replacing cash in remote payment applications such as pay phones and vending machines; this reduced the cost of cash handling, and theft from unattended sometimes remote locations. The first mass use of the cards was for payment in French public pay phones. The French government was, and still is, an enthusiastic supporter of the technology. French companies have led the way in developing designs from the original simple memory cards to the more complex microcontroller cards with read/writeable memory and data processing capabilities. With the advent of the PC and data networks, a secure token in the form of a smart card for authentication became a useful tool in many applications from health insurance cards in Germany, to loyalty cards across Europe.

The advent of Pay TV in the early 90's demanded more sophisticated designs, as did banking cards in France which were a major driver for this infant industry and lead to the dominance of that country's industry in the global market. Innovations at the time included electronic purse systems, in which monetary value is stored on the chip, so that point of sale terminals accepting the card did not need network connectivity. These were tried throughout Europe from the mid-90s most notably in Germany (Geldkarte^{TM}), Belgium (Proton^{TM}), the Netherlands (Chipknip^{TM} and Chipper^{TM}), Finland (Avant^{TM}), and Denmark (Danmønt^{TM}) But the advent of low cost online payment processes and high cost of dedicated e-purse infrastructure and services charges restricted the take up of them in most countries.

Chipcard IC design has been has been driven by demand for Subscriber Information Modules (SIMs) for GSM mobile phones since their inception in the late 1990's. Cloning of phones had been a problem with analogue mobile phones in the 80s and various proprietary security protocols were tried, but were handset and network specific. The standardization by European Telecommunications Systems Institute (ETSI) [19] of a security element of the SIM was a huge step forward. The take up of GSM was relatively slow to begin with. Sales were focused on contract phones to business users restricted market growth. The introduction of pre-paid services controlled with the SIM, led to an explosion in consumer demand, far beyond the early estimates. In the UK alone in the past ten years the number of subscribers has grown from under 6 million [17] to over 65 million. Many people have more than one handset and the use of data telemetry systems has lead to handset penetration greater than 100% of the per capita population figure. The demand for SIMs will continue for the foreseeable future, as even with saturation of the established markets. It is predicted that the current estimated 2 billion customers worldwide will grow to over 3 billion in the next few years. The usage of SIMs is even higher due to a relatively high rate of churn. Users often change their networks and phone contracts which increases demand for SIMs, which was already approaching 2 billion cards per year in 2006. One major reason for this is the business model in countries like China, one of the largest markets, where many people buy several pre-paid SIM cards per year. The number of fixed long term contracts in China are increasing, the percentage is small, in what is a heavily cash based economy, and where only a small percentage of the population has a bank account.

The historical business of pre-paid public phone card chips is slowly fading as mobile technology has become the communications system of choice, even in the developing world. With the growing deployment of the mobile phone with SIMs comes an increasing demand for more sophisticated features. The earliest SIM designs needed no more than 8 kilobytes of EEPROM, but this has increased many times over with more sophisticated software such as SIM Toolkit. This platform supports control of services and features like over the air downloads, and content such as audio tracks, video updates, e-mail and basic internet access memory demand has grown. Given the rapid return of investment on mobile services, this has lead to the need of the largest memory on a SIM available being used as soon as possible. Historically the SIM memory size has doubled every two years, but as bandwidth increases using technologies such as Edge [1] in 2G and HSDPA [15] in 3G services this trend may grow geometrically. In other smart card industry sectors there are different trends as the service deliverables have other use cases. Volume demand in the finance sector is increasing as card fraud is a present and growing threat. But payment systems although in principle dominated by the Europay, Mastercard, Visa (EMV) specifications [5], developed since the early 90s have a very diverse range of implementations for credit and debit card, with several national and region variations. This specification defines the interaction at the physical, electrical, data and application levels between chipcard IC cards and card processing devices for financial transactions. Large portions of the specification are based on the chipcard IC interface defined in ISO/IEC 7810 and 7816. The first version of the system was released in 1994, and several upgrades have followed as the services and technology required. But since the banking services market is essentially an online business, the security element required for EMV transactions requires limited memory and security features. The typical EMV card has perhaps 4 kilobytes of EEPROM and simple symmetric cryptographic functions. It is only when additional services or multi-application cards have been required has the chip size and functionality expanded. The result is that EMV banking cards have seen a price decrease year on year since their introduction, such that chipped cards now cost little more than their un-chipped predecessors of 10 years ago.

Smart cards with contactless interfaces are becoming increasingly popular for low value payment and ticketing applications such as mass transit. Visa and Master-Card have designed a simple contactless protocol based on a magnetic stripe image data set and cipher engine. This is currently being rolled out in the USA and some other countries. Across the globe, contactless fare collection systems are being implemented to drive efficiencies in public transit. Japan, as ever the most technophilic society, has taken to contactless products in many aspects of everyday life. In London over 10 million public transport "Oystercards^{TM}" have been issued. This is likely to increase as more transport networks connecting to London start to use the technology. Across the world various contactless ticketing specifications that have emerged are often local in use and function, for example the various "Calypso^{TM}" transport ticketing schemes issued in various cities in France, were not compatible between the different city schemes. This will change with time as new regional standards are developed, so one day in the future it could be possible to buy a ticket in the suburbs of London and travel to suburb of Paris through automatic gate systems, but it is unlikely that there is an economic justification to extend it to Tokyo.

The diversity of services leads to a wide variety of designs and range of capabilities, the result is a plethora of chip designs with memory demands from 200 bits to over 2 megabytes of EEPROM, although the vast majority use of cards issued today are use under 8 kilobytes and have simple data processing. The other driver is the storage of credentials which enables the identity of the card holder to be authenticated. This leads to two factor authentication process where the presence user can be verified by the credentials authentication in conjunction with a password. Third factor authentication with the use of biometrics can lead to even more secure transactions, subject to issues of human factors of convenience and system reliability. There is a wide demand for identity management in many closed user groups, from libraries to health insurance cards, but the issues of identity theft, and remote data access is driving the fastest growing sector of used for national systems, driving licenses, ID cards and electronic passport solutions. In the future the smart secure silicon will be embedded in non-card formats to support user and device authentication for online systems such as games, content rights, and telemetry. This sector of the market may end up even larger in volume than the SIM business. One example is tagging of items. Although not traditionally part of the smart card market there is a huge rise in Radio Frequency Identity (RFID) tags used for asset tagging in logistics. With the agreement of the Electronic Product Code (EPC) Global specification [9], which has grown out of barcode standards, RFID will impact in time, other security markets as the remote electronic identification of goods, assets and perhaps even people will enable new services as yet uneconomic or perhaps even invented. But most RFID tags are by their very nature not secure but merely data carriers, and the data handling used is similar in function to that of a basic memory smart card.

15.1.2 Technology Choices

The choice of chip in card is sometimes ignored; there have even been cases where the colour or shape of the plastic card has been seen as the key feature. But there are characteristics of the chip which matter. In some cases features are promoted in terms of size of memory or speed of communication. In one European country the amount of EEPROM in your SIM has been promoted in the same way the size of engine in a sports car. However it is more important how a particular chip hardware and software perform together. Several key questions need to be considered; such as the security protection profile of the chip, the performance of the device, and the chip compatibility at the physical interface level.

The security of chip can be independently assessed according to Common Criteria [20] which has been used for all types of information security. For chipcard ICs there has been developed a protection profile PP0002 [3] , Devices have been developed which have been successfully evaluated to the level of 5+ based on this profile. These devices include numerous security features to reduce vulnerability from attack, including non-standard CPU designs, sensors to protect the silicon from various energies directed at the device and using hardware and software encryption throughout the design. Software to run on these chip can be security certified up to EAL6.

In the past "security by obscurity" was common, each design was in theory bespoke, but this in turn limited migration of design, so compromises were made. Finding such a compromise on a new chip, whose design was based on a previously "cracked" chip, made hacking almost a sport. The risk of attack versus the cost of the solution needs to be carefully considered and will impact the choice of technology. In the case of many commercial applications simple security techniques such as limiting system access to only those users holding a card with a recognized unique ID number is considered sufficient. Since most chipcard ICs come with this feature as standard, the security is not a defense against spoofing by a basic card emulator, but with the addition of a PIN, held off card, seen as acceptable. Further tactics such as traffic analysis on the usage of the card, i.e. a card cannot be in two places at the same time or the use of a timestamp in the memory can reduce spoofing in a networked environment. But for offline use cryptographic techniques maybe needed to ensure data integrity and for more high profile or high risk environments a formal security analysis maybe required. A professional risk assessment and security audit according to BS7799 and ISO/IEC 17799 should identify the issues, from which the type and features of the security required on the card can be developed. For certain government applications more formal security certification is mandated. The EU directive on digital signatures [10] has led to Common Criteria certification to EAL4 or above being demanded for the chip, the operating system, and the application. The cost, in terms of time and money, can impact a single project, but benefit can gained if the protection profile used allows for reusability of existing elements for other developments. In the USA the government has mandated that their own Federal Information Processing Standards (FIPS 140) [21] is used for cards it issues, and this standard has been taken up by private enterprises

Performance criteria are sometime assumed, but often system level issues will be affected by the chip, e.g. ensuring the software protocol is optimised for the readers it will be used with. This has come to light with transport operators of train stations and buses requiring gate interaction time requirement of 200ms or less. If a passenger is held back any longer their reaction maybe to believe the system has a fault, and to try again, this can cause disruption in flows of people at gates and even impact the reputation of the operator. The physical limitations are in some cases self imposed, to maintain some kind of interoperability the electrical and physical format of the card as specified by ISO/IEC 7810 and ISO/IEC 7816 to ensure ease of use. In the past the low level of interoperability limited usage in many instances; commands for one card could not be understood by another as the Application Program Interface (API) was specific to the chip firmware or the operating system of the card designer. This has become less of an issue as API's have become standard, such as the Java Card specification [26].

The choice of chips for smart cards has been limited by various factors. The cost of the card has been seen as a key factor, often because of its visibility to the user of the service. But the cost of cards maybe reduced into insignificance by the costs of the deployment, infrastructure and managed services. For example over 5 million employee cards have been deployed by the US Dept of Defense, the so called Common Access Card (CAC) [4], they are estimated to have cost under 10 USD each, i.e. a total of around $50 million. The system costs however are estimated to have cost over $1 billion so far. The CAC enables encrypting and cryptographic signing email, facilitating the use of authentication tools, and establishes an authoritative process for the use of identity credentials. In some cases further costs maybe incurred if a card scheme operator wants to introduce a range of cards over a period of time. This requires sophisticated card management. From an information technology network system perspective cards are essentially offline remote thin client nodes. As such these nodes are only in the network infrequently, and often randomly. However the users require instant service when online and may not be conducive to any system updates which change their interaction with the service or card. If a change to a card is proposed, or even the card is to be replaced and upgraded, the return on investment can be difficult to calculate. It be not just a simple cost versus revenue calculation, but may involve improved efficiency in data bandwidth management, reduced transaction times, faster backend processing. Another example of card scheme costs is the 100 million plus Chip and PIN [11] EMV banking cards issued in the past few years in the UK, the cost per card including issuance is around £1 each. The cost of setting up the whole system of readers and infrastructure has been reported to be over £1 billon. However the eventual fraud reduction from lost, stolen and counterfeit credit cards saved per year could reach over £250 million [29] each year.

If the choice of chipcard IC is currently acceptable, another issue is the lifetime of the product. There have been instances when a card has been deployed for a project, only to find soon afterwards the chip it was based on was at the end of its production and no further directly compatible cards could be produced. Some so called existing "standard" cards will not operate with newly introduced "standard" readers; this is especially true of contactless products where ISO operational and testing standards are still under review. If any bespoke solution is chosen, the issuer's problem is to manage the long term support and migration for the software, and any other IP used in the design. Even with testing against all known environments, a change to the host middleware quite remote from the card may leave the system inoperable if software drivers are not maintained. To mitigate this risk one option is to ensure the supply of cards and chip and supporting technology can be supported for the duration of the lifetime of the whole system. An alternative is to choose a design which can be upgraded in future, by using an open system specification. The first option can be expensive, not just for the up front investment in product and storage, but to manage the infrastructure around the card. There maybe the issue of software driver compatibility in the host. Operating systems on PCs are upgraded every few years, the software driver needs at least at the reader interface to present the same API, both logically and dynamically. Forecasting long term requirements is often an educated guess, and there several instances of simple "upgrades" which has been very costly to recover from. The option of working to a defined open specification can be costly in the short term and time consuming if several parties are involved. But the benefits from long term open interoperability have proved to be enormous.

The most successful example of an open interoperability is the ETSI GSM SIM card specification "GSM11.11" for testing of compliance of cards and mobile handsets, so that the operating system and the underlying chip hardware have be rendered academic, at least at the logical level. The specification has required several updates over the years. In some cases it has been seen as a hindrance to new developments, but with over several billion compatible SIMs issued it is unbeaten. Another example, where a single authority has successfully defined an open interface is the US government General Service Card (GSC) specification. Generated by its standards bureau NIST the NISTIR 6887 specification has sought to generate and mandate for all major federal programmes the smart card interface both physical and electrical, a so called "card edge specification". It has been developed further as the Personal Identity Verification (PIV) specification [2]. It has also lead to the ISO/IEC 24727 smart interoperability framework standard developed by ISO/IEC JTC1/SC17 WG4/TF9 working group [16]. In this way future generations of cards should be compatible with the existing terminal infrastructure and vice-versa. Such specifications have the added benefit that multiple suppliers can design compatible products, and given some sort of compliance testing resulting in economies of scale and improved commercial terms for the card scheme operators.

In Europe there exist several such "open" specifications in different sectors, one of the most active being the transport industry. The "Digital Tachograph" project, which took over 10 years to develop and is being deployed across the EU [13]. The key gain was the testing for compatibility of the readers and cards. This was set ensured by a single test house in Italy to ensure there could no question of misinterpretation of the requirements. Further examples are the new transport ticketing standard IOPTA [?]. which will form the basis of a European wide accepted travel system; in the UK this is being implemented by the ITSO group [27]. Here again testing for compliance has been a key objective of the design, and ensuring that the security of transactions can be managed across distributed and remote networks.

Across the world there are few smart card schemes which are truly interoperable. One of the few is the EMV banking card specifications. EMV financial transactions are more secure against fraud than traditional credit card payments which use the data encoded in a magnetic on the back of the card. This is due to the use of encryption algorithms to provide authentication of the card to the processing terminal and the transaction processing centre. However, processing can be slower than an equivalent magnetic stripe transaction, due to the cryptography overhead. Although not the only possible method, the majority of implementations of EMV cards and terminals confirm the identity of the cardholder by requiring the entry of a PIN (Personal Identification Number). In the future, systems may be upgraded to use other authentication systems, such as biometrics. Some local schemes using fingerprint verification of pre-authorized debit or credit card account details via an online terminal. This technique has been successfully piloted by a few retailers. One of the most successful being "Pay by Touch[TM]" which has become an accepted alternative to carrying a card in an online retail environment for some people. However there are many obstacles to taking a proprietary biometrics scheme and scaling it up to a global system.

At the global level, the only scheme using chipcard IC technology and biometrics is the ICAO ePassport. The International Civil Aviation Organization (ICAO) generated a specification [25] for electronic passports which may eventually apply to all 188 countries of the United Nations. The specification is based upon a series of ISO standard such as ISO/IEC 7501 for the format and ISO/IEC 14443 for the contactless communication, and ISO/IEC 10373 for testing protocols. A series of interoperability test sessions, financed by various governments, have been set up. The requirement derives from mandates of the US Government with its Patriot Act [28] and the EU directives [6]. They are applied to travelers from their own countries or foreigners that are from countries which are acceptable politically and have a suitable passport vetting process. Such travelers will not require a visa, only a biometric e-passport based on the ICAO specification. Travelers from non-compliant and unacceptable countries will still require a visa. Following the US mandate 27 visa waiver countries had to have their first e-passports ready by October 2006; in fact around 30 countries were ready. To ensure compliance a combination of government funded and several independent test houses have been set up. The governing model here is different from previous examples; although ICAO can make recommendations it has not power to enforce compliance. The only influence is a combination of peer pressure and rule of law in some countries to have a compatible system. The effect of these mandates has been both huge political and commercial pressure to ensure the technology was ready to meet the deadline.

The ICAO specification has three major influences on smart card technology; it has helped to standardize contactless technology; in chips, software designs, and readers to become completely interoperable. The chip was specified to have at least 32 kilobytes NVM and typically greater than 64 kilobytes. Many countries chose larger memory sizes to allow for fingerprint biometric images to be added on later issued books. In the past many contactless systems have been closed local systems. For the first time the ability to take the same smart token from place to place across the world and the data to be read and verifiable will have impact on systems integration and identity management. There are now over 50 countries introducing such passports, whose citizens represent 90% of the world's travelers. It has been suggested that the chip in an ePassport could be used to contain other information such as travel visa's or even air tickets. However according to the ICAO specification and the security profile they will be limited a single function with a locked dataset, which is government issued, with vendor non-specific biometric data included, i.e. raw images not biometric template extractions. In future even visas may have references to the identity credential stored in an ePassport, but these references are more likely to be stored on line by the visa issuing authority.

Electronic passports will become the basis of the world's largest use of biometrics systems, based initially on photographs, but later fingerprints and possibly iris scans. For the first time globally verifiable electronic files of people's identity will be produced. It is envisaged that as the US is now taking ten fingerprints from every traveller arriving by air into the country, in future such data maybe stored on the chip. This would require larger memory in excess of 100 kilobytes to store all the data. But this is not expected for some years at this time.

Passport systems will, in time, become the basis for a global public key infrastructure, allowing books and systems to authenticate each other and the data transfer between them. Once a government issued certificate becomes verifiable by third parties the opportunity it presents as a root of trust for other activities such as e-commerce is enormous.

The features of ePassports will lead to the basis for many systems. It will influence the design and demand for contactless reader and card technology for the foreseeable future. As an open standard identification design it will influence other national identity cards schemes and even may replace proprietary designs used for local and even commercial identity management and access control systems.

15.1.3 Technology Drivers

The technology used of smart cards is determined by the physical interfaces to the chip and the type pf technology used therein. There are two basic chip types used in smart cards used to keep data secure:

- Memory; which can be compared to a storage disk in a personal computer, but of course lower capacity due to smaller lower complexity chips. Secure memory cards use either non-volatile memory (NVM) such as EEPROM or Flash technology to store data. The data is secured by the use of a simple access code which controls access and in some cases by a cipher stream engine which verifies against a secured key. There are of course high density Flash memory products in a variety of form factors such as SD, MMC and others, but data is not held securely and so these are not considered smart card products.
- Microcontroller; which might be compared to tiny computer with storage, processing unit and temporary memory. Although such a chip needs extra silicon

compared with a basic memory chip, the flexibility of such a design offers higher performance which can outweigh any cost differences. Furthermore with today's dense designs, smaller chip geometries, and low gate count dedicated smart card controllers, the overhead can be measured in terms of a very few square millimeters. Microcontroller cards typically have ROM or Flash for long term program storage e.g. the operating system, RAM for temporary data processing and either EEPROM or Flash for extra program storage, e.g. applications, card specific elements such as card user details, issuer credentials. In some designs chip may have only RAM and Flash. This type of design allows the operating system itself to be programmed at the point of issuance or even updated in the field, for example over the air in a mobile phone. At present smart card designs combining two chips, a mass storage Flash memory chip and a secure microcontroller, are under development. There have been security issues in the past over the use of Flash technology, because chip designs based around standard chip design have been successfully attacked using probing and eavesdropping methods. With modern chip design security features have been incorporated which can defeat such attacks [7].

Chip types, memory and microcontroller, use technology which has been optimised to work in the conditions demanded by smart card market, with low power consumption and a variety of dedicated features to add security. These two fundamental varieties are unlikely to change in the future. The earliest memory cards capacities were measured in term of a few hundreds of bits. The largest secure memory cards today have capacities in excess of 256,000 bits. What is may not be obvious is that until 2001 the volume of memory chips sold world wide was higher than microcontrollers, as shown in Fig. 15.1. But by 2007 of the 3.5 billion chips predicted to be sold; only around 25% are simple memory and of just a few types, for microcontrollers there are dozens of types, but they are based on a handful of logical architectures developed by the world's leading semiconductor companies.

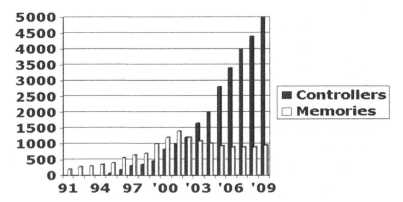

Fig. 15.1 Demand Over Time for Smart Card IC Types – Millions of Pieces

There are two types of interface; contact based, taking in over 90% of today's market using a serial protocol similar to that on a computer RS232 and contactless, using wireless, most commonly with a RF carrier of 13.56 MHz. The price of a chip depends on the complexity of the chip performance, security, and features and therefore size of chip. The underlying silicon technology has changed considerably over time. But the original ISO standard have dictated the physical dimensions and as such the processing capability. The module size defined by ISO/IEC 7810 allowed for devices not much greater than 25 mm^2, this is to allow space for the bonding wires in the module as shown in Fig. 15.2, and because larger chips might crack during normal use. In addition power consumption has been required to be less than 10mA at 5 volts for many applications. Based on silicon geometries greater than 1 micron, this inevitably limited the early designs to small memory and basic CPU functions. The speed of the serial interface limited the data bandwidth. Typical values were 19,200 bits/sec, and this remains common today for many simple cards.

15.1.3.1 Memory Card

A typical card might have 256 bytes of memory space, and unique chip number as part of the ATR and PIN based protection for a non-volatile memory to store relatively static set of data. The most common function is a simple one way counter which decrements when instructed by a host terminal. This card can be a simple electronic money counter and used in a wide variety of systems where cash handling can be difficult, such as pay phones. At one time over 100 countries issued such cards, as they offered a cheap e-purse type function which saved on cash management costs and reduced fraud. Several million a year were issued by British

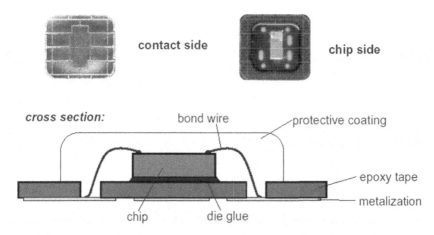

Fig. 15.2 Smart Card Module Construction – Courtesy of Infineon Technologies AG

Telecom alone in the late 1990's until their popularity diminished with the up take of mobile phones and payment by use of banking card. Still to this day high volumes are issued by some major telecommunication operators, such as in France and Mexico where banking cards less popular or not accepted. Phone cards in fact have become collector's items, like stamps, in some cases with extraordinary prices attached.

Contact cards are rarely used in mass-transit applications because of the wear and tear on the readers, although contact cards and readers are cheaper, maintenance costs can be prohibitive. For casual use e.g. loyalty cards, the contact card has proved a useful low cost authenticator of a user's privilege, although there are few national smart card loyalty schemes. However one of the most success loyalty card schemes in the UK with around 15 million issued is based on simple memory card. There are many memory cards used by small closed user groups across the world for access to clubs, work and school canteens, vending machines and other token based systems. Contact memory card costs are still a key driver for many issuers; with basic cards costing little more than a simple plastic card with a magnetic stripe, but with the added features read-write capability, simple counter options and basic security. The future of such cards although growing smaller as a percentage of smart cards worldwide can expect to be popular for the foreseeable future.

15.1.3.2 Microcontroller Card

With the introduction of small 8-bit microcontrollers in the late 70s it was inevitable that they would find their way into smart cards. Contact based microcontrollers have found their way into applications where perhaps originally a memory card may have been used. But as services became more complex, extra memory capacity has been required, enhanced security, and on card processing for application selection or data processing, microcontrollers have dominated. There are two dominant CPU designs in smart cards, one based around the Motorola designs of the 6805 and the other Intel 8051 core, though later enhanced versions are based on the Intel. Recently bespoke RISC designs have become popular. In all cases the designs have been heavily modified to ensure the data is held securely. This is crucial requirement for a smart card, if the core used in a chipcard is a standard microcontroller design chip emulation tools are relatively easily developed. In the more secure designs instruction sets have been altered to ensure data cannot be extracted or deciphered easily. Devices originally developed for simple control applications are of course cheaper to modify to offer chipcard IC functionality and so offer a fast return on investment. The card issuer may find themselves compromised and left unable to protect revenues. In addition standard designs although cheaper, may not offer the sophisticated functions required to reduce any transaction speeds.

"Unfortunately, the use of standard CPUs, descended from processors used in washing machines, telephones and toys, are still common for many types of smart cards [8]"

Only secure designs with features like cryptographic co-processors to accelerate encryption algorithms can offer the performance needed. Security sensors are built into the chips to thwart attacks. The physical design is designed so that chips cannot be probed, or the eavesdropped electronically. Today contact based microcontroller cards make up around 75% of the annual world wide issuance with of course SIM the dominate usage. The other key markets sectors are finance and identity.

Typical SIM EEPROM size in 2007 in Europe is 128 kilobytes, but each SIM design has an issuance lifecycle of 3 years or less, and the memory requirement doubles each cycle, as more services are required. In China 16 kilobytes is still the most common. As mentioned earlier the combination of a microcontroller and large Flash memory into one SIM card has been under development for several years. The trials of SIM cards with many megabytes and even a gigabyte of memory have been announced in Europe in the past year. Mass deployment is dependant several issues. Operators have to develop attractive and easy to use services. For example with a so called High Memory SIM (HMSIM), mobile operators could push content to subscribers to be paid for on "as used" basis. Alternatively subscribers could transfer entire e-mail address books or store Web pages with multimedia content on the cards, which the could be update periodically or again act as dedicated embedded Web server on the HMSIM. Another drive for HMSIM is from operators is to reduce churn of subscribers. By allowing the subscribers to store multimedia content and picture phonebooks on the SIM, subscribers will want to keep the card when they change handsets, so will be more likely to remain with the existing operator. For all these processes to be accepted both handsets and SIMs need to be developed with faster internal communications to handle the higher data demands. The most likely method is for the recently ETSI agreed USB port function to be added to both devices. However there is a restraining factor in the demand for more memory. Due to the consumer demand for mass storage Flash cards and tokens increasing rapidly, the cost per bit of standard Flash memory technology has been falling by over 30% per annum for the past few years, and is likely to continue. This means an HMSIM with 256 megabytes of Flash would lose considerable value from when it is procured by the MNO to when it was delivered to the user. To offset this decrease would require the operator to regain this value from new services based on the use of the HMSIM. How this will resolve itself is not clearly defined as yet.

Other key market sectors have their technology drivers based on their usage model. Finance cards tend to need a relatively small memory to store a banks issuing certificate, for limited lifetime of three years. The specification for most banking cards can be satisfied by a chip with 4 kilobyte EEPROM for basic EMV SDA (Static Digital Authentication) designs, and even with EMV DDA (Dynamic Digital Authentication) 8 kilobytes should be enough, plus the prerequisite support for cryptographic processing. Some multifunctional banking cards have used 16 kilobytes, where EMV is combined with internet ID or loyalty functions. The driver from the finance market has been like that of the low end SIM to reduce costs, whilst maintaining interoperability. This is in unlikely to change. Identity smart cards designs on the other hand have be very fragmented, with few standards applying as many have been used for closed user groups. Many early ID cards used little more than the ATR of the chip as an identifier, keeping the users data within the local network. This is now changing with the introduction of the PIV and the ICAO specifications. The driver for identity is not memory but the need to increase security, through enhanced chip design, and convenience in use of the card, with the introduction of contactless interoperable designs.

15.1.3.3 Contactless

As outlined one technology driver in smart cards is the physical interface to the chip. The original designs were contact chip based, but this limited the form factor of the card and readers, and reduced user convenience and resulted in contactless interface development. Originally developed from work around battery powered telemetry tokens since the early 1990's contactless battery-less, so called passive, cards have been developed. The consist of a chip, mounted in a module, which is attached to a metal or wire antenna mounted in a plastic inlay, as shown in Fig. 15.3. The whole assembly is then covered on either side by extrusion or moulding with layers of standard smart card plastic, either of a PVC or polycarbonate material.

Today they have been used in thousands of applications by millions of people, from very high volume applications such as pre-paid phone cards in Japan to very small applications for building access control cards. In the transport industry 95% of smart ticketing products world-wide currently use low cost memory cards. The typical data transfer rates of around 100 kbps allows a small number of bytes to be read or less to be written (EEPROM write rates are much slower than reading) during a transport gate transaction. The Oystercard^{TM} in London is based on ba-

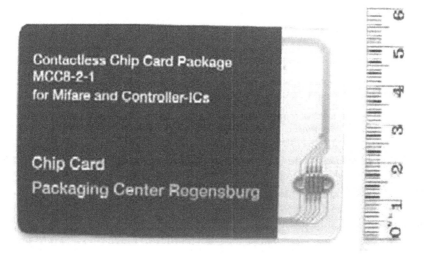

Fig. 15.3 Contactless Card – Courtesy of Infineon Technologies AG

sic 1 kilobyte Mifare^{TM} chip. Similar schemes exist in Seoul and San Paulo. In France contactless memory paper tickets have been very popular, and in the USA many major cities are or will be using the technology in the future. This trend is likely to continue. Most transport systems are closed operations, i.e. the issuance and acceptance of the cards is via a single operator. The costs of cash handling, and opportunities for fraud from paper tickets can be reduced with the use of smart card technology. Many existing transport operators have decided to maintain own contactless card schemes because of the legacy of investments in revenue collection systems, payment clearing processes. Long term contactless e-payment cards from banks such as MasterCard's "PayPass^{TM}" or Visa's "payWave^{TM}" may erode these schemes, as banks have a wider acceptance by merchants, and users. Schemes implementing contactless banking cards in transport have started across the Far East, and there are trials in the USA. Transport operators can gain from the banks efficient financial processing capabilities and, not least, the lower cost of card issuance and management.

Contactless memory cards can today have sizeable capacity over 32,000 bytes, so the content of such cards can include even biometric data, and extensive transaction records , but the lack of memory management prohibits anything more than a basic function of data fields without the use of external data verification tools. Security is limited, like contact memory card, to features such as the unique ID number of the chip, and simple pass code access management. This implies that any sensitive data must be encrypted off chip. The data transfer rates were again small due to power constraints, so typical values are 106 kbps, but there are a few options for faster communications. But the underlying driver for contactless memory card is the assumption that the terminal it is used with is online or has a Secure Access Module (SAM) to verify the UID of the device. This function implies that the chip memory can be reduced to little more than a few bytes. As a result there are contactless memories with 128 bytes or less, which have been issued in their millions for transport applications mounted in a disposable paper ticket carrier. In the contactless payment sector slightly more sophisticated memory chips with a simple cipher engine to generate a cryptogram have become popular in the US payment market. Although in principle these devices could be open to cloning, the online networks can determine if a device has been duplicated by the transaction analysis (one card cannot be in two places at the same time) and by mitigating any risk by limiting the value of any one transaction.

In the same way microcontrollers have become the technology of choice for contact cards the desire to have contactless microcontrollers has grown. However the power requirements of the chip technology have limited the functionality of the card to much lower levels up until the last few years. One of the highest volume programs in Europe has been a contactless transport micro card in France, where ASK have deployed several million using a basic 8 kilobyte card. In Japan where contactless cards are the preferred technology of choice, the New Media Development Association (NMDA) [23] program has plans to deploy several million very large memory capacity cards, in excess of 0.5 megabyte, for a citizen's records management. These NMDA cards were developed with the cooperation and support of the Japanese government and several large IT suppliers, to produce an interoperable open IT platform based around contactless cards which would offer information systems in areas such as local communities, cities, and for elderly persons. Contactless microcontrollers are available with a variety of interfaces; most have standard ISO/IEC 14443 type A or B, or like those from Infineon, who offer options for A and B. But there are several other contactless proprietary protocols which have been developed, but very few have survived in the market place. An exception is FeliCa^{TM} from Sony where over 200 million compatible devices have been issued, although this includes some memory chips. Controllers which can emulate memory cards, such as the Mifare^{TM} have been popular where systems have required an upgrade path. Some such cards can offer dual protocol options, so that either basic memory fields can be read or APDU commands and applications can be executed. Contactless high speed interfaces working at up to 848 kbps have only been in circulation since 2003. Similarly the capability of cards to perform asymmetric cryptographic algorithms whilst in contactless mode has been a recent achievement, Data memory sizes on these cards today is typically around 16 kilobytes today, for basic city cards for combined transport, payment and city services application. The introduction of ePassport has led to a demand memory space of in excess of 64 kilobytes. In addition the security functionality and certification required by governments has driven the need for higher performance with low power operation.

In the same way that specific industry sectors have pushed the contact card technology requirement, again it is being repeated for contactless. But future demand is pushing the technology in two directions, low memory options, under 1 kilobytes, and higher memory options with up to 500 kilobytes for multiple biometrics. The financial market across the world is looking to take on other services as described earlier, but with extra convenience of contactless and enhanced security. Within a few years low end contactless microcontrollers will have enhanced cryptographic functions with two factor authentications only required for high value purchases via one of two interfaces.

With contactless designs there are other alternatives with completely different form factors, e.g. the key fob, coin shaped tokens or in the cover of a mobile phone. More enhanced designs are possible with a RFID enabled mobile phone, where the data might be stored in the SIM, and transacted via a RF link, such as Near Field Communication (NFC) [14]. This concept is being promoted by a consortium lead by Sony, Philips and Nokia. NFC proximity technology is standardized in ISO/IEC 18092, ISO/IEC 21481, ECMA (340, 352 and 356), and ETSI TS 102 190. It is based around ISO/IEC 14443. It will allow two options: for the phone to act as a token, or as a reader of other compatible tokens. The advantages to the user to download, or upload over the air transaction data such as value, or even content may lead to completely applications.

15.1.3.4 Dual Interface Cards

Another driver, legacy support, has lead to the combination of contact and contact-less interfaces on a card being implemented, as shown in Fig. 15.4. This is with either a single monolithic device with a contact based module which has buried connections for an RF antenna or as a so called hybrid card with two independent devices, one contact, and the other contactless embedded in a card. The most common function is to allow some sort of logical access to a PC network and physical access to a building.

A dual interface card offers the chance for the user to identify themselves in a variety of locations and systems with one set of credentials. It can therefore become an electronic identity for all types of transactions and any audit trail and rights management can be verified wherever and when ever the card is presented.

A hybrid card can be used in a variety of combinations, with one contact chip for the logical access and one contactless chip can be proximity or vicinity for physical access. In this way the two functions can be tuned to meet the needs of the user and the operator(s) where there is no for data to be passed between them, for example a banking card and a entry card or perhaps a city services card and bus travel card, any reconciliation is done offline and infrequently.

The dual interface card with a single chip offers efficiency in issuance and card management. If there is one central authority e.g. a city council offering a concessionary travel pass combined with kiosk service access for some of its citizens, one card can offer the possibility of a variety of readers that can interface to a variety of systems. This flexibility of use in multiple interfaces can be optimised in a single

Fig. 15.4 Monolithic Dual Interface Card – Courtesy Of Infineon Technologies AG

step personalization, this offers faster issuance. The single data set on the card provides for quicker consolidation process across different services. In the back office a single middleware system can be used so reducing transaction processing. The management processes can be simplified with a single chip card, with a single security profile so reducing provisioning costs. Finally the multiple interfaces can improve user convenience and time.

Dual interface cards do have issues, if there are multiple scheme operators sharing the card, who owns the data and who has the leading relationship to the user. For example, a student card has two applications from two independent issuers, the college and a retail loyalty scheme. If the college revokes the card, when a student finishes a course, the loyalty scheme operator may have extra effort to reconcile the unused loyalty points on the card. In principle dual interface cards mean dual interface infrastructures. Somewhere in the hosting database the logical access and physical access networks have to be connected. Dual interface cards may need separate software drivers for each interface i.e. proprietary messaging protocol for each type of communications maybe considerably different. It has only been a recent innovation where the communications method has been transparent to the card or host. In many physical access control systems, control is often separate from the logical network management. For example the access card to a building may be under the control of the HR department, but the PC access is an IT management issue. The question with dual interface cards with multiple applications is often "Whose card is it?". The answer to this political question can determine the type of technology used. However existing separate physical and logical access systems may need upgrading if complete compatibility is to be achieved following the introduction of a dual interface card. In the final analysis the convenience of contactless can now be extended from simple memory card to complex crypto-controllers with readers capable of reading the all, be it with varying transaction times. With the introduction of such contactless banking cards, and e-passports, the future is contactless without doubt; dual interface is likely to be a transitional product, much like the audio cassette was between the vinyl LP and the CD.

15.1.4 Technology Trends

In the past smart card chip designs have changed as silicon technology has improved. The underlying trends seem likely to continue and in some cases accelerate. Smart chip cards have existed for around 30 years, in that time many billions of cards have been issues, in 2007 it is expected that over 3 billion cards will be produced, and based on historical figures the average number of cards issued is predicted to grow by around 15% per year. As the average chip complexity increases the actual cost per bit is falling, this may not be in direct proportion to Moore's Law [18] but certainly it is closely coupled. If the past ten years are considered some strong technology trends are seen: The line geometry, which is the smallest feature size of a chip, has been reduced by over 80% This means if chips function took 20 mm^2

in 1996, it is now more 97% smaller i.e. under 0.7 mm^2. The reduced feature size has improved speed, and reduced current consumption, new memory designs has improved the size further. A high end 128 kilobytes EEPROM SIM chip today is around 10sq mm, which if fabricated in 1996, would have taken several kilowatts of power! The speed of the processor allows fast transactions, using 1996 technology you would have had to wait several minutes to get money from an ATM. A summary of the changes in features for a typical smart cards from 1996 till 2006 have been outlined below Table 15.1. The features do not reflect any one card, but are guidelines for trends in the market:

Table 15.1 Technology Changes Comparison

	1996	2006	Comment
Geometry	700nm	120nm	90nm will be deployed in 2007
CPU	8 Bit	32 Bit	2006 uses RISC designs
ROM	20 KB	200 KB	Typ OS takes 150 KB in 2006
RAM	0.5 KB	8 KB	Up to 16 K in 2006
EEPROM	8 KB	64 KB	Max in 2006¿256KB
Voltage	5 V	1.5-5 V	Variable shunt in 2006
Speed			
Clock	3.5M Hz	30 MHz	Max 66 MHz with PLL in2006
I/O Speed	19.2 kbps	2Mb/sec	Contact: USB, 848 bbps contactless
Crypto	66 mS	4 mS	512 bit RSA (with CRT)
Security Certification	rare	CC EAL5+	Protection profile changes every 2/3 years
Cost per 8 KB	1	0.1	

The demand for greater performance for lower cost from consumer products, such as computers and mobile phones, has been the economic driver behind the improvement in silicon processing. The smart card trend has followed a different path for several reasons. Firstly the demand has been distorted by the use of the SIM. If mobile phones did not use the GSM SIM, but relied on network security, as is the case for some alternative systems, then demand for smart cards would have been driven by the payment sector, which needs only low end security tokens as most of the security is in the online network. The new electronic ID sector demand would not have justified development of large memory smart cards, and may well have taken a different path, perhaps using online verification of identity credentials from national databases.

The trends for the future however may not directly follow the same lines. Although the cost of a low end chip may have fallen as silicon costs have reduced and economies of scale have reduce card assembly costs, the demand for more features has meant that average price of a card have been maintained, whilst at the same time the demand for memory depends on the application, as shown in Fig. 15.5. In some markets the memory size is likely to remain relatively static; in others as more services are demanded the memory requirement is likely to grow geometrically.

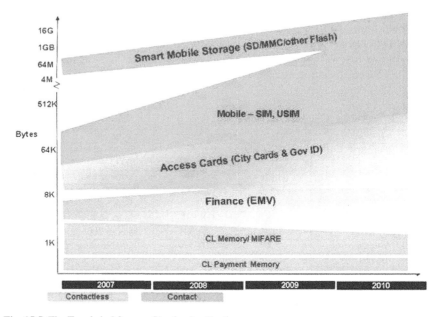

Fig. 15.5 The Trends in Memory Size by Application.

The underlying design features of chipcard ICs are not likely to change for and new applications. Considering the markets in turn, each sector is constrained by legacy issues which preclude the security functions form being changed, the emphasis will be to use the technology to improve the efficiency of the services.

The financial payment markets are in a process of consolidation. EMV cards are not ubiquitous at present, but 10 years from now may be practically universal. The interface on a banking card may change from contact to contactless but the underlying demand as a certificate carrier and digital signature device will remain relatively unchanged. The demand for higher security will increase. Therefore the demand will accelerate in the USA further towards contactless, where the pressures of its consumer convenience society are sure to have huge effect. The world wide take up of EMV will influence even the USA payment cards, which with around 1 billion magnetic stripe cards, may become the prime target for fraud when the rest of the world takes up EMV chipped cards. With the growth of contactless payment cards, EMV payments over the contactless interface will become standard. The market will fragment with dual interface cards to support legacy systems, small memory cards or tokens for low value transactions and for larger values a contactless microcontroller card with DDA functions, and authenticated with a PIN. People already have different cards for different purposes, e.g. personal, business, internet; it can be extrapolated that the number of payment tokens per person could double in the next 10 years. The underlying chipcard IC function and security which not change significantly, so pressure on cost reduction from process improvements will continue

As stated before the transport market is currently considering the move to low end contactless memory cards. This is part of the underlying drive to the cost of physical ticket out of the system; this is not only the ticket itself, but the processes of issuance, payment handling and back office infrastructure. If banks move into the transport transaction space then the transport operators may no want to issue their own cards. A few transport systems are testing the use of electronic tokens stored on mobile phones and read via NFC, again another driver away from operator specific tickets. As a result transport smart cards and even paper tickets may follow the way of pre-paid public phone cards and become a product which is used only by operators which do not have an on-line service, or cannot afford the upgrade costs.

The identification market as outlined before will be dominated by the move to electronic passports and other national programs. The technology to support the demands of governments to identify users is driven by various security threats, rather than any economic driver. Already in the USA visitors are required to register 10 fingerprints and a facial image at point of entry. For passport applications in future this will follow. It has been foreseen that identity documents might one day also carry this data and include even iris images. This would demand chips with capacity of up to 256 kilobytes or more for personal data, in a contactless format. The world wide trend of government and private requirements to identify individuals by use of smart cards is undoubtedly going to drive demand for other identity cards. Although multifunction or multi-application technologies exist, and seem convenient for the user, the simple process of a card issuing authority being able to verify user's credentials from their own data on the face of a card and in the chip is very strong. However for one authenticating authority to accept another's format and data, e.g. a library card as an alternative to a transport ticket, is legally, politically and physically a major step. It is probably cheaper to issue separate tokens by the various issuers. In the UK alone if employers, local authorities, and central government agencies plans come to fruition in the next 5 years, the average adult may have 5 or more such ID cards. What is certain in the security of elements on and in these tokens will increase, as the counterfeiting of identity document activities by criminals and terrorists will not disappear, so designs will have to become more sophisticated in the future and secure chipcard ICs will be a key differentiator.

The mobile phone market, as described, is the largest influence on the chips designed for smart cards. The basic functions have remained essentially unchanged for 10 years. The legacy of several billion phones predicates that SIMs cannot change quickly despite the predicted increase in memory, speed, to support new software and interfaces to support NFC and USB. One example is even the new SIM form factor announced in 2003 which is just the chip module embedded in a plastic housing 12 mm by 13 mm, it is delivered in a standard credit card (ID1) size format and be pressed out during a phones set up. This format reduces the space taken up in the phone allows for smaller designs, but there has been limited usage up till now.

There have been some moves in very low cost phones to remove the SIM and its socket as a discrete assembly and merely solder the module to the motherboard of the phone. This reduces cost of handling of the SIM, which is a complex logistics operation and ensures the phone can be restricted to use with the network operator offering the phone. It is only the huge legacy the SIM card issuance model by the operator, which precludes the module disappearing. If the business model changes and phones dedicated to an operator and not frequently upgraded becomes popular then the SIM may end up as a small chip in soldered into a phone. It would require the user to download their details stored in the SIM onto another phone when replacing the phone. It could reduce the churn for the operator, and reduce the grey market for subsidized phones. There have been some moves to produce a SIM-less GSM phone, where the security functions on the SIM have been integrated into the baseband chip of the phone. Although as yet not supported by ETSI, this might become attractive in some markets where cost of the whole package is more important than perhaps security or mobility of the SIM information. The very long term trend will depend on consumer acceptance as much as cost. The mobile phone is quintessentially driven by convenience. The SIM will survive as it becomes the focus of the user's rights management for content in the user's environment rather than just a security function for the operator. If a SIM does become such a repository, then leaving a phone at home will be like leaving one's door key, car key, wallet and passport behind. How then to ensure the data integrity in case of loss or theft will become a crucial service for the operator and the user.

Over the years various complex assembly smart cards with more than a basic data processing function have been developed, though until now few have made it past the prototype stage, with production volumes numbered at best in the thousands. These cards are much like concept cars, and have been designed to satisfy either a bespoke user group or to show off new technologies. The integration of display technology from LCD to OLED has been tried. The ability to display on the surface of the card details such as a value of a transaction, an authentication cryptogram or perhaps the balance of points is superficially attractive. However the mechanical stress exerted on such a display when a card is flexed, and the power requirements of the display, resulted in the cards being unable to survive for long in everyday use. Should a technology which offers very low cost assembly and ability to withstand the bending and torsion stress inside a wallet or purse become available, this might change. A more likely use case is if the card holder can read and interact with a card via NFC with their phone. This then only requires the security of any data transferred to be preserved, a simple software process rather than a complex mechanical design.

One concept which has generated attention has been the process of card holder authentication. The psychological attraction of verifying literally who has hold of a card by use of an integrated function such as a PIN pad or a fingerprint biometric sensor is very strong. Adding a PIN pad has been tried but since some users write or scratch their PIN on to the back of the card this is not considered a secure feature. The inclusion of fingerprint sensors, as shown in Fig. 15.6 has been under development for some time. There are two fundamental obstacles. The first is mechanical, to withstand the daily use a sensor much be able to withstand the card being flexed.

The most suitable current devices are so called stripe sensors; around 10 mm by 3 mm, based on silicon have been encased in a larger metal module to reduce the stress on the chip, but this adds extensive costs to the card.

Fig. 15.6 Fingercard – Courtesy of Infineon Technologies AG

The second issue is one of data handling. The standard smart card CPU does not have the processing capability to run the graphics processing algorithms required to extract a biometric template. As a result when a user inserts the card into a terminal and swipes their finger across the sensor, the data from the sensor in transmitted to the terminal and analyzed, i.e. a temporary biometric dataset is extracted. This data can then be transmitted back to the smart card for comparison to the reference data template held securely on the card. If a match is made, the transaction can proceed. To extract and manipulate this data sophisticated processing is required. At present the cost of this infrastructure has exceeded any benefit derived to the card issuer or card holder. As with the display concept, if fingerprint sensors in phones become popular for access control and as screen navigation pads, as has been already deployed in Japan, it would be easy to extend the feature to require a user to have their card/phone and their finger on the phones sensor. Other biometric recognition processes of the users' voice, facial features and even iris could also be supported in this way. It would be technically feasible today to demonstrate a card being verified by all of these functions. However the time taken to ensure the user aligned all their biometrics and was processed correctly might be unacceptable for anything but very exceptional cases.

Another function for inclusion in a complex card assembly has been the addition of power source into the card. For contactless cards the limits of physics have precluded data being processed beyond the range of the induction power of a reader. Data reading can be further, perhaps up to one or two meters, for simple memory devices. With the addition of very thin batteries a more powerful processor can be embedded, with perhaps added environmental sensors for temperature, light, or pressure. With such a construction the card or token can be set a task to monitor a process and report when required over a distance of several meters. This technology is more of a telemetry function rather than a smart card for secure applications, but there might be an overlap in the future where mobile objects need to have their integrity managed remotely such as shipping containers, cash transit boxes, or even vulnerable people.

Finally in the area of complex card assemblies there are several concepts for cards which serve a very specific need. SIM cards with other integrated wireless links such as Bluetooth™ or WiFi have been demonstrated, but the business case for such a product has yet to be developed.

Long term future developments for smart cards are dependant on the balance of commercial justification, the availability of technology and the acceptance and demand from the card user. The concept for one card to hold every application that a user might need in day to day life is technically feasible today. The commercial justification is difficult because of the diverse interests of the various application stakeholders. Some users might find the concept attractive, but others are concerned by the thought of the possible loss of all their personal data if such a card is lost. Currently many people store on their mobile phones their entire address book; if the phone is lost it can take months to recover their contacts. Mobile phone operators are offering an back up service, not out of altruism but rather than such a loss of contacts has been related to reduced number phone calls and texts and so reduced revenue. A smart card with large number of functions would require an equivalent back up process to store the personal details, content and credentials of the user. There is the alternative perspective that as the world becomes even more networked, by the use of a federated identity, a card or token could be reduced to holding a single credential, a sort of single sign-on function to the digital world. These concepts, such as Microsoft CardSpace™, are attractive for users needing to access a multitude of applications, but there is again privacy concerns that should such as system be hacked, then a user's credential could be misused and either counterfeit or cloned credentials could take a very long time to cleanse. The most commonly held view is that the number of single function cards will continue to multiply. If the UK central and local Government proposals for e-government are fulfilled then within 5 years it is likely that many adults may carry 5 or 6 smart cards for access to government services including driving licence, passport, ID card, health card, travel cards, road-charging cards and local city service cards.

15.1.5 Emerging Applications

There is a new trend for the use of chipcard IC technology which is in the development of the new form factors or equipment which is not a card. These can be grouped in two generic areas: embedded, where the security function is still a discrete device but is connected to other non-secure devices, and integrated where the security function is part of a larger device. These two approaches have similar advantages and disadvantages irrespective of the actual application. The underlying driver is the business case and is balance of the function, cost, security and data management: each of these elements have to be considered in detail before a decision is made as to what format is used.

15.1.5.1 Embedded Security ICs

Embedding of a chipcard IC normally takes the first step of repackaging the chip into a circuit board assembly. This can be done crudely by wire bonding the chip to the PCB and covering the chip in a resin to protect the device, or by first assembling the chip in a standard plastic IC housing, in the past dual-in-line, but in recent time in a surface mount package as shown in Fig. 15.7. This has the advantage of preserving the security integral to the design of the chipcard IC and of course making it easier to assemble. It can require the chip to be modified to provide an electrical interface which can be used with the other chips on the board such as the CPU or DSP. A chipcard IC normally communicates using the ISO/IEC 7816 serial protocol. Most multi-chip logic designs can provide a serial interface which can be matched to the chipcard IC, but this often requires some software overhead to match the data framing and timing requirements. Some chipcard IC designs have had standard serial interfaces added such as UART functions added or USB. In some cases where the volume justifies the cost a specific interface for the application has been developed. This is the case for the Trusted Platform Module (TPM) used in PCs as a root of trust for Trusted Computing designs [12].

Fig. 15.7 TPM – A Surface Mountable Smart Card IC

Cost is of course the main driver, any change to a chipcard chip, may require the device to be re-certified by an approved security evaluator, this can add time and further cost. Another issue is the area that the security device and its connections take up in the overall assembly. In products such as mobile phone space is at a premium. Finally the embedded device needs managed during its lifecycle: at the beginning when it is to be initialized, this maybe for the injection or generation of cryptographic key pairs and the personalization of the chip, during normal operation when updates maybe required in the field and when the product is disposed of, to ensure security data is either protected or erased. This lifecycle management is specific to the application, but if the complete product integrity is to remain unblemished, then a security profile needs to be defined at each stage to prevent attack.

There are several publicly known systems of secure embedded designs which have been successfully deployed. Probably the most popular is in the pay-TV set top box used in various broadcast systems from terrestrial, cable and satellite receivers. The copyright protection requirements of the systems has employed various digital decryption designs based around either ASIC or full custom ICs which use fast data processing to rearrange the video and audio TV signals. The decryption of the data is sometimes done inside a PCMCIA card a so called conditional access module. In many designs the key for the deciphering is kept on a smart card, this is partially to ensure that the broadcaster has some control via the user of the rights management, and partially to secure the access control from potential attacks by people wanting to steal the content. For many cable systems where the box is constantly in a two way link to the network, the security control is embedded in the box and can be verified easily. The cable box remains at all time the property of the cable operator, and with the security and the identity built into the box, can only be installed with the operators consent. With a simple unique identity for the box the integrity of the connection can be authenticated, and the content can be decrypted with keys downloaded from the host server. The keys maybe kept internally to the baseband decryption devices or on a PMCIA module. The variety of security architectures is partially a commercial issue, to ensure that systems supplied by one broadcaster cannot be used for another, or even the same broadcaster in a different country or region. New initiatives such as Open Cable Application Platform (OCAP^{TM}) are being defined in the USA, which in principle will affect not just the security but the whole network architecture, and may allow an open market for systems and content. It might be described as the GSM standard of the cable TV world. Long term the same process could be applied to Satellite and even digital terrestrial broadcasts, but the commercial pressures and political issues will deter this happening.

In the past decade embedded security in cars and other automotive vehicles has increased. The keyless entry systems used for door access and engine immobilisers have become almost ubiquitous. The RFID link between the car and key uses one of the standard 400 MHz UHF bands for telemetry. Originally the security protocol used data coding techniques which originally were based on a fixed code sequence. This was easily cloned by eavesdroppers using radio scanners, who captured the code and rebroadcast it later. Then so called "rolling codes" to stop this attack were developed and more recently codes which dynamically changed during use. The chip security has been minimal, relying on the key being kept physically secure as a sufficient deterrent. The motivation for this extra security, was driven from insurance companies to the reduce consequences of theft. Its introduction was originally discussed in the late 80's but was considered too expensive for most cars. The simple process of offering a discounted insurance premium, on vehicles with extra security, brought an almost overnight revolution, and literally drove the use of embedded security.

An interesting example of embedded security is the new digital tachograph has been introduced across Europe. This design uses a combination of security processes to ensure the data recording a driver's behaviour complies with local and European laws on time and speed, is held securely. The driver's identity and most recent driving information are held on a smart card. The data recording the behaviour of all drivers of a vehicle for the past year are held encrypted in the vehicle unit in the cabin. The data in the unit can only be read by an inspection authority, or police, who have their own smart card. Finally the vehicle data is generated from the engine of the vehicle, via a special sensor which picks up rotation information and sends it encrypted to the vehicle unit. The sensor design is a special custom design based on chipcard IC security principles but engineered to survive in the environment of a gearbox for the life of the vehicle. So there is a chain of security from the machine to the terminal to the user, and extendable to any inspection system. It has been considered to use similar technology for private vehicle applications such as road pricing, but this one of many possible solutions. Automotive security maybe further enhanced with embedded security devices in the future if demands for authentication of drivers, service technicians, or perhaps even electronic driving permits becomes imperative. It is conceivable that a vehicle could be controlled to allow only a certain performance in a specific geographic area, or period of time or for a particular user, might be managed with advanced chipcard IC technology in combination with some form of location based service. At present at least one insurance company has used GPS technology to test the concept of ensuring that a car is used only at certain times and within a known region. But it does not link directly to the driver and does not verify its installation during use. But as with immobilisers, this maybe the first step into the future.

15.1.5.2 Embedded Financial Security

Another use of embedded security is in point of sale systems where a terminals authentication keys are held on a Secure Access Module (SAM). Most commonly the SAM takes the form of a SIM shaped token, and may be a microprocessor smart card with a large EEPROM used to store the private keys of the card scheme operators or transaction acquirer; this may be a bank or similar institution in the case of transport authority. Terminals may have space for several SAM's if the unit is to be used with several schemes. There have been developed a number of very large memory SAMs with several megabytes of memory in a separate memory chip in the SAM, similar to the HMSIM mention before. In the long term these expensive designs will be replaced by HMSIMs offering lower costs to terminal manufacturers.

15.1.5.3 Infosecurity Technology

As software a commercial product in its own right, software and content suppliers have wanted to ensure some sort of rights management on the use of their IP on the hardware of their choice or use by only authorised users, in some cases software licensees. To ensure the integrity originally simple logic designs manipulated signals or data, this modified data was taken as sign of authenticity by the software on the host computer. The logic was encapsulated in a discrete module plugged into the host communications port in the form of a "dongle". When the dongle is not present, the software runs in a restricted mode or refuses to run. Dongles are used by some vendors as a form of copy prevention or digital rights management because it is much harder to copy the dongle than to copy the software. The original devices were used with minicomputers and later games machines in the 1970's, their mere presence was deterrent. With the advent of the PC software became even more transportable; the result was that dongles were worth counterfeiting. Dongles then started to incorporate increasing security features. Modern dongles use chipcard IC technology with both key material and even software applets encrypted into the device. The most common form factor is in the form of a USB key, but there are many variants. Some are simple mechanical devices which allow a SIM card to be inserted. Some designs include some form of two factor authentications, where a display on the dongle must be read every time it is used, with such a cryptogram can generated as a form of one time password. Three factor authentication is now possible; where a fingerprint sensor has been incorporated on to the device. But if the cryptographic information provided by the dongle can be cracked or hacked, then the software can be pirated. The only solution is to embed security into an otherwise open platform, and allow it to be switched on when required.

This next step is now being deployed. The PC and in future any device which uses open platform, such as a PDA, or smart phone, may have embedded a security chip, in the form of a "Trusted Computing" device. Essentially a chip card IC with a special serial interface suitable for the host architecture, it provides a root store for a set of private keys, which have been set up by a known trusted source. The result is that software rights for the platform can be determined and checked every time it is switched on. Depending on the use model these rights can be controlled by the software owner, or the user. With the addition of a smart card or secure dongle a whole software rights environment can be defined. This reduces the chances of a platform being infected by malware or being used by unauthorised users. It creates new opportunities for innovative business models such as pre-paid computing [22]. In a corporate environment it places control in the hands of the network administration, to determine what hardware and software are allowed on a network.

One of the first large commercial deployments of Trusted Computing has been with the new Microsoft Vista™ operation system. Currently the Enterprise and Ultimate variants of Vista have a utility for disk encryption called BitLocker™. It enhances data protection by bringing together two major sub-functions: drive encryption and the integrity checking of software components. Drive encryption protects data by preventing unauthorized users from breaking Windows file and system protection on lost, stolen or inappropriately decommissioned computers. This protection is achieved by encrypting the entire Windows volume; with BitLocker, all user and system files are encrypted including the swap and hibernation files. Integrity checking the software components helps to ensure that data decryption is performed only if those components appear unmolested and that the encrypted data is located in the original computer.

In the future IT systems will become more secure as trusted computing devices are embedded into computer peripherals such as keyboards, screens and other devices, as well as other systems which use IT infrastructure such as games machines, media systems and perhaps even televisions. In another decade it is foreseeable that users may have as many chipcard ICs in embedded in their environment as they have in their smart cards today.

15.1.5.4 Integrated Security IC Technology.

The underlying drivers of increased security and reducing manufacturing costs have generated a third option for the use of security IC technology, that of integration into another IC. The prime market is for consumer multimedia equipment, such as mobile phones, games systems or other devices which need to secure software content or service integrity, where content is played by the user. Certainly the security of these platforms has been an issue, and the trend to open systems allows for various cyber attacks. A solution under consideration is to incorporate security into the media functions on the platform. This has the advantage of reducing the costs and handling of a separate security device. A mobile phones media functions are generally located in a specific media processing chip, the "applications processor", but there is a tendency to integrate this device into a single chip device handling all digital functions. If such a device were compromised then the content could be manipulated. Solutions to include some form of security function are being developed; the choice is based on economic and security issues. From an economic point of view the cost of the device is only part of the equation, the cost of ownership through the entire lifecycle of the product and its content can be a dominate factor. If a product, as with many consumer designs, has a short lifetime then these costs have to be amortised quickly. In the case of games machines, this hardware cost has in the past been offset against revenue from the games software over several years. If the product is a mobile phone, which might have a life time of 18 months and where there is a necessity, because of the various models to have an open system design, costs can be significant. There is a dilemma where operators want to offer freedom of choice to their users whilst protecting IP. There are some proprietary designs being piloted, but the more accepted solution is likely to be based on DRM standards developed by Open Mobile Alliance (OMA) [24]. This is based upon a PKI process where keys are kept on the SIM or the handset in encrypted software. In future it is possible that a baseband device might incorporate the cryptographic processing. But there are issues: such a fully integrated chip cannot be designed to be 100% compliant to the protection profile of chipcard IC, not only because of cost, but the influence of data processing performance. If part of the chip is designed to be secure only some of the protecting features will be usable. So as in the past for such devices a compromise of performance and security must be reached. One solution maybe to make the whole assembly tamper resistant, but this can be an expensive process for little gain, if the algorithms and keys can be siphoned out from one unit, it maybe the content is then free to use many times over. One implication is that security functions may be kept separate and not integrated in all but the most high volume designs.

15.2 Conclusions

In summary the factors which have driven chipcard IC technology in the past thirty years are likely to be same for at least the next ten years: These trends for smart cards can be summarised in a simplified roadmap made up of four elements; technology, functionality, form factors, and not least security, as shown in Fig. 15.8.

The physical limits on the silicon used will be pushed further; the trend in average memory size is likely to accelerate rapidly as multi-megabyte SIMs are issued. These will be is based on innovative Flash memory designs using two bits/transistor concepts so making the memory even more dense and cheaper per bit. To accommodate the demand for more content, faster interfaces will become standard, for contact based designs the T=0 serial interface may become the RS232 of the smart card world, supported but only used for legacy systems, USB may become the con-

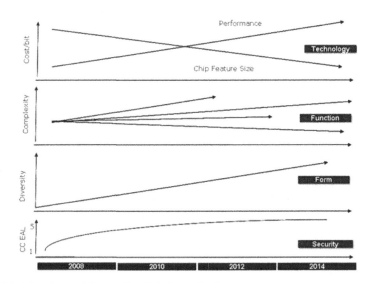

Fig. 15.8 A Roadmap of Current Trends in Smart Cards.

tact interface of choice. As logic designs use silicon geometries lower than 100nm, clock speeds could pass 100 MHz if required, and the power consumption per bit will fall proportionately. The trend to contactless designs running over fast interfaces will grow; if 848 kbps is available in 2007, then in ten years, it is feasible that a version of wireless USB measured in several Mbps may become popular. The functionality as result will be come very diverse as different applications drive smart card technology in different directions. The result will be a number of form factors from the basic card format which is likely to remain the dominant visible form for many years to come; the demands for integrated and embedded functions will dictate many other instances. The security of products has a limit in terms of the current common criteria accreditation process. The highest currently is EAL5+high, which uses some features used in the more formal EAL6 criteria. Most current smart cards do not have a high security evaluation; many applications do not need it. But more applications will require a formal security assessment. The criteria will continue evolve, but it is likely the overall the assessment demand will plateau, and the focus will move the security of the complete system. The underlying trend that drives the mass acceptance of designs and reduces costs is interoperability. It is unlikely there will be one card edge specification, more likely the plethora of anagrams such as CAC, EMV, GSM, ICAO, IOPTA etc is likely to grow, but it will be relatively few compared with the thousands of proprietary specifications which exist today. Above all the demand for increased security is certain to intensify. Government backed projects will influence many designs, and will impose security guidelines on a wide range of applications which interact with government systems. The trend for falling costs not just in silicon but for all aspects of chipcard IC design will continue. Card scheme operators will spend less on developing new bespoke designs but buy more standardised designs with the confidence that they will be fast, interoperable and secure.

^{TM}: **Trademark: all products, services and licenses marked thus are copyright of their respective owners**

References

1. A white paper from Ericsson THE EVOLUTION OF EDGE Feb 2007,via http://www.ericsson.com/technology/whitepapers/3107_The_ evolution_of_EDGE_A.pdf, Cited 03 Oct 2007.
2. A set of specifications are publicly available http://csrc.nist.gov/piv-project, Cited 03 Oct 2007.
3. Bundesamt für Sicherheit in der Informationstechnik, "Certification Report BSI-PP-0002-2001 for Smartcard IC Platform Protection Profile", and "Certificate BSI-PP-0002-2001", 11.07.2001.
4. Case study whitepaper by Smart Card Alliance 2001: http://www.smartcard.gov/information/cac_case_study_full.pdf, Cited 03 Oct 2007.
   US official information https://www.cac.mil/Home.do, Cited 03 Oct 2007.
5. Copies of the EMV specifications http://www.emvco.com/, Cited 03 Oct 2007.

6. Council Regulation (EC) No 2252/2004 of 13 December 2004
7. Dr. Peter Laackmann, Marcus Janke, Infineon Technologies AG " Integral Security from FLASH to ROM " SECURE Issue 1/2003 ; download from www.silicon-trust.com, Cited 03 Oct 2007.
8. Dr. Peter Laackmann, Marcus Janke, Infineon Technologies AG "Would you Trust your Confidential Data to a Washing Machine Processor?" SECURE Issue 1/2004 ; download from www.silicon-trust.com, Cited 03 Oct 2007.
9. EPC standards: http://www.epcglobalinc.org/standards/, Cited 03 Oct 2007.
10. European Union Directive establishing the framework for electronic signatures: " Directive 1999/93/EC of the European Parliament and of the Council of 13 December 1999 on a Community framework for electronic signatures. and "Commission Decision 2003/511/EC adopting three CEN Workshop Agreements as technical standards presumed to be in accordance with the Directive
11. Figures from Visa 2005 http://www.visaeurope.com/pressandmedia/factsheets/chipandpin.jsp, Cited 03 Oct 2007.
    more information can be found on www.chipandpin.co.uk, Cited 03 Oct 2007.
12. For information on "trusted computing".More Information Available via www.trustedcomputing.org, Cited 03 Oct 2007.
13. Further information can be found on the UK government website http://www.digitaltachograph.gov.uk including links to the 1000 page specification. Cited 03 Oct 2007.
14. Further information on NFC can be found on the NFC Forum website via www.nfc-forum.org, Cited 03 Oct 2007.
15. High speed data packets description http://hspa.gsmworld.com/, Cited 03 Oct 2007.
16. ISO/IEC 24727-1:2007 PDF version (en) can be found on the ISO website www.iso.org, Cited 03 Oct 2007.
17. Mobile Operators Association figures: http://www.mobilemastinfo.com/information/history.htm, Cited 03 Oct 2007.
18. Moore's Law is the empirical observation made in 1965 that the number of transistors on an integrated circuit for minimum component cost doubles every 18 months. It is attributed to Gordon E. Moore a co-founder of Intel.
19. Standardization process information via http://www.etsi.org/, Cited 03 Oct 2007.
20. The Common Criteria Organisation, "Common Criteria for Information Technology Security Evaluation V2.1", 1999. Source: www.commoncriteria.org/docs, Cited 03 Oct 2007.
21. National Institute of Standards and Technology http://csrc.ncsl.nist.gov/ has published FIPS 140-1 http://csrc.nist.gov/publications/fips/fips1401.htm "Security Requirements for Cryptographic Modules" concerns physical security of smart card ICs, Cited 03 Oct 2007. bibitemChapter16.18prEN 15320 Identification Card Systems - Surface Transport Applications - Interoperable Public Transport Application (IOPTA) 2/4/2006 http://www.cenorm.be/CENORM/BusinessDomains/TechnicalCommitteesWorkshops/CENTechnicalCommittees/WP.asp?param=6205&title=CEN/TC%2B224, Cited 03 Oct 2007.
22. See "Flexgo" from Microsoft as an example of payPC project. More Information Available via http://www.microsoft.com/emerging/JobsOpportunities/FlexGo.mspx, Cited 03 Oct 2007.
23. See NMDA references in Japan via http://www.nmda.or.jp/clic/index-en.html, Cited 03 Oct 2007.

24. See Open Mobile Alliance. More Information Available via
    `http://www.openmobilealliance.org/formoreinformationandspecifications`,
    Cited 03 Oct 2007.
25. The full specification can be procured from ICAO an introduction is available
    `http://www.icao.int/icao/en/atb/fal/mrtd/overview.htm`,   Cited   03
    Oct 2007.
26. The JavaCard specification can be licensed from Sun Microsystems
    `http://java.sun.com/products/javacard/specs.html`
    and its implementation is managed by Global Platform
    `http://globalplatform.org/`, Cited 03 Oct 2007.
27. The specification in ten parts is available for download from
    `www.itso.org.uk`, Cited 03 Oct 2007.
28. The Uniting and Strengthening America by Providing Appropriate Tools Required to Inter-
    cept and Obstruct Terrorism Act of 2001 " USA PATRIOT Act" See section Title IV A ,
    summary can be found here
    `http://www.cis.org/articles/2001/back1501.html`, Cited 03 Oct 2007.
29. UK banking group APACS
    `http://www.apacs.org.uk/resources_publications/card_fraud_`
    `facts_and_figures.html`, Cited 03 Oct 2007.

Appendix A
Source Code for Chapter 12

A.1 C Language

```c
#include <stdio.h>
#include <stdlib.h>
#include <time.h>
#include <unistd.h>
#include <string.h>

#include <PCSC/wintypes.h>
#include <PCSC/winscard.h>

#ifndef TRUE
#define TRUE 1
#define FALSE 0
#endif

/* PCSC error message pretty print Macro */
#define PCSC_ERROR(rv, text) \
if (rv != SCARD_S_SUCCESS) \
{ \
    printf(text ": %s (0x%lX)\n", pcsc_stringify_error(rv), rv); \
    goto end; \
} \
else \
{ \
    printf(text ": OK\n\n"); \
}

int main(int argc, char *argv[])
{
    LONG rv;
    SCARDCONTEXT hContext;
    DWORD dwReaders;
    LPSTR mszReaders = NULL;
    char *ptr, **readers = NULL;
    int nbReaders;
    SCARDHANDLE hCard;
    DWORD dwActiveProtocol, dwReaderLen, dwState, dwProt, dwAtrLen;
    BYTE pbAtr[MAX_ATR_SIZE] = "";
    char pbReader[MAX_READERNAME] = "";
    int reader_nb;
    unsigned int i;
    SCARD_IO_REQUEST *pioSendPci;
    SCARD_IO_REQUEST pioRecvPci;
```

```
BYTE pbRecvBuffer[10];
BYTE pbSendBuffer[] = { 0x00, 0xA4, 0x00, 0x00, 0x02, 0x3F, 0x00 };
DWORD dwSendLength, dwRecvLength;

printf("PC/SC sample code\n");
printf("Do NOT use it unless you really understand what you do.\n\n");

rv = SCardEstablishContext(SCARD_SCOPE_SYSTEM, NULL, NULL, &hContext);
if (rv != SCARD_S_SUCCESS)
{
    printf("SCardEstablishContext: Cannot Connect to
    Resource Manager %lX\n", rv);
    return EXIT_FAILURE;
}

/* Retrieve the available readers list.
 *
 * 1. Call with a null buffer to get the number of bytes to allocate
 * 2. malloc the necessary storage
 * 3. call with the real allocated buffer
 */
rv = SCardListReaders(hContext, NULL, NULL, &dwReaders);
PCSC_ERROR(rv, "SCardListReaders")

mszReaders = malloc(sizeof(char)*dwReaders);
if (mszReaders == NULL)
{
    printf("malloc: not enough memory\n");
    goto end;
}

rv = SCardListReaders(hContext, NULL, mszReaders, &dwReaders);
PCSC_ERROR(rv, "SCardListReaders")

/* Extract readers from the null separated string and get the total
 * number of readers */
nbReaders = 0;
ptr = mszReaders;
while (*ptr != '\0')
{
    ptr += strlen(ptr)+1;
    nbReaders++;
}

if (nbReaders == 0)
{
    printf("No reader found\n");
    goto end;
}

/* allocate the readers table */
readers = calloc(nbReaders, sizeof(char *));
if (NULL == readers)
{
    printf("Not enough memory for readers[]\n");
    goto end;
}

/* fill the readers table */
nbReaders = 0;
ptr = mszReaders;
while (*ptr != '\0')
{
    printf("%d: %s\n", nbReaders, ptr);
    readers[nbReaders] = ptr;
    ptr += strlen(ptr)+1;
    nbReaders++;
```

```
    }

    /* read the reader number given in command line */
    if (argc > 1)
    {
        reader_nb = atoi(argv[1]);
        if (reader_nb < 0 || reader_nb >= nbReaders)
        {
            printf("Wrong reader index: %d\n", reader_nb);
            goto end;
        }
    }
    else
        reader_nb = 0;

    /* connect to a card */
    dwActiveProtocol = -1;
    rv = SCardConnect(hContext, readers[reader_nb], SCARD_SHARE_SHARED,
        SCARD_PROTOCOL_T0 | SCARD_PROTOCOL_T1, &hCard, &dwActiveProtocol);
    printf(" Protocol: %ld\n", dwActiveProtocol);
    PCSC_ERROR(rv, "SCardConnect")

    /* get card status */
    dwAtrLen = sizeof(pbAtr);
    dwReaderLen = sizeof(pbReader);
    rv = SCardStatus(hCard, pbReader, &dwReaderLen, &dwState, &dwProt,
        pbAtr, &dwAtrLen);
    printf(" Reader: %s (length %ld bytes)\n", pbReader, dwReaderLen);
    printf(" State: 0x%lX\n", dwState);
    printf(" Prot: %ld\n", dwProt);
    printf(" ATR (length %ld bytes):", dwAtrLen);
    for (i=0; i<dwAtrLen; i++)
        printf(" %02X", pbAtr[i]);
    printf("\n");
    PCSC_ERROR(rv, "SCardStatus")

    switch(dwActiveProtocol)
    {
        case SCARD_PROTOCOL_T0:
            pioSendPci = SCARD_PCI_T0;
            break;
        case SCARD_PROTOCOL_T1:
            pioSendPci = SCARD_PCI_T1;
            break;
        default:
            printf("Unknown protocol\n");
            return -1;
    }

    /* exchange APDU */
    dwSendLength = sizeof(pbSendBuffer);
    dwRecvLength = sizeof(pbRecvBuffer);
    printf("Sending: ");
    for (i=0; i<dwSendLength; i++)
        printf("%02X ", pbSendBuffer[i]);
    printf("\n");
    rv = SCardTransmit(hCard, pioSendPci, pbSendBuffer, dwSendLength,
        &pioRecvPci, pbRecvBuffer, &dwRecvLength);
    printf("Received: ");
    for (i=0; i<dwRecvLength; i++)
        printf("%02X ", pbRecvBuffer[i]);
    printf("\n");
    PCSC_ERROR(rv, "SCardTransmit")

    /* card disconnect */
    rv = SCardDisconnect(hCard, SCARD_UNPOWER_CARD);
    PCSC_ERROR(rv, "SCardDisconnect")
```

```
end:
    /* We try to leave things as clean as possible */
    rv = SCardReleaseContext(hContext);
    if (rv != SCARD_S_SUCCESS)
        printf("SCardReleaseContext: %s (0x%lX)\n",
        pcsc_stringify_error(rv), rv);

    /* free allocated memory */
    if (mszReaders)
        free(mszReaders);
    if (readers)
        free(readers);

    return EXIT_SUCCESS;
}
```

A.2 Perl Language

```perl
use Chipcard::PCSC;
use Chipcard::PCSC::Card;

use warnings;
use strict;

my $hContext;
my @ReadersList;

my $hCard;
my @StatusResult;
my $tmpVal;
my $SendData;
my $RecvData;

#-----------------------------------------------------------------------------
print "Getting context:\n";
$hContext = new Chipcard::PCSC();
die ("Can't create the pcsc object: $Chipcard::PCSC::errno\n")
unless ... (defined $hContext);
print '.'x40 . " OK\n";

#-----------------------------------------------------------------------------
print "Retrieving readers'list:\n";
@ReadersList = $hContext->ListReaders ();
die ("Can't get readers' list: $Chipcard::PCSC::errno\n") unless ...
... (defined($ReadersList[0]));
$, = "\n  ";
$" = "\n  ";
print "  @ReadersList\n" . '.'x40 . " OK\n";

#-----------------------------------------------------------------------------
print "Connecting to the card:\n";
$hCard = new Chipcard::PCSC::Card ($hContext, $ReadersList[0]);
die ("Can't connect to the reader '$ReadersList[0]':
$Chipcard::PCSC::errno\n") ... ... unless (defined($hCard));
print '.'x40 . " OK\n";

#-----------------------------------------------------------------------------
if ($hCard->{dwProtocol}!=$Chipcard::PCSC::SCARD_PROTOCOL_T0 &&
    $hCard->{dwProtocol}!=$Chipcard::PCSC::SCARD_PROTOCOL_T1 &&
    $hCard->{dwProtocol}!=$Chipcard::PCSC::SCARD_PROTOCOL_RAW)
{
        print "Don't understand the active protocol, reconnecting to the card:\n";

        my $active_protocol =
        $hCard->Reconnect($Chipcard::PCSC::SCARD_SHARE_EXCLUSIVE,
                          $Chipcard::PCSC::SCARD_PROTOCOL_T1,
                          $Chipcard::PCSC::SCARD_RESET_CARD);

        die ("Failed to reconnect to '$ReadersList[0]': $Chipcard::PCSC::errno\n")
        ... unless (defined($active_protocol));

        if ($hCard->{dwProtocol}!=$Chipcard::PCSC::SCARD_PROTOCOL_T0 &&
            $hCard->{dwProtocol}!=$Chipcard::PCSC::SCARD_PROTOCOL_T1 &&
            $hCard->{dwProtocol}!=$Chipcard::PCSC::SCARD_PROTOCOL_RAW)
        {
                print "here is '$hCard->{dwProtocol}'";
                die ("Still don't understand the active current protocol:
                the card may be mute.\n");
        } else {
                print '.'x40 . " OK\n";
        }
}
```

```
\#-------------------------------------------------------------------------------
print "Getting Status:\n";
@StatusResult = $hCard->Status ();
die ("Can't get card status: $Chipcard::PCSC::errno\n")
 unless (defined ($StatusResult[0]));

printf "  ReaderName = %s\n  Status = %X\n  Protocol =  %X\n  ATR = ",
      $StatusResult[0], $StatusResult[1], $StatusResult[2];
foreach $tmpVal (@{$StatusResult[3]}) {
      printf ("%02X ", $tmpVal);
} print "\n";
print '.'x40 . " OK\n";

\#-------------------------------------------------------------------------------
print ("Exchanging data:\n");
$SendData = [0x00,0xA4,0x00,0x00, 0x02, 0x3F, 0x00];
$RecvData = $hCard->Transmit($SendData);
die ("Can't transmit data: $Chipcard::PCSC::errno")
 unless (defined ($RecvData));

print "  Send = ";
foreach $tmpVal (@{$SendData}) {
      printf ("%02X ", $tmpVal);
} print "\n";

print "  Recv = ";
foreach $tmpVal (@{$RecvData}) {
      printf ("%02X ", $tmpVal);
} print "\n";
print '.'x40 . " OK\n";

\#-------------------------------------------------------------------------------
print "Disconnecting the card:\n";
$hCard->Disconnect($Chipcard::PCSC::SCARD_LEAVE_CARD);
undef $hCard;
print '.'x40 . " OK\n";
\#-------------------------------------------------------------------------------
print "Closing context:\n";
$hContext = undef;
print '.'x40 . " OK\n";
```

Index